Mirror of My World

Reflections on an Undiagnosed Autistic Childhood in the 1980s and 90s

Copyright ©2025 Christian Karen Berman. All rights reserved.

No part of this book may be reproduced in any manner whatsoever without written permission except in the case of brief quotations embodied in critical articles and reviews.

NO AI TRAINING: Without in any way limiting the author's and Henry Gray Publishing's exclusive rights under copyright, any use of this publication to "train" generative artificial intelligence (AI) technologies to generate text or images is expressly prohibited. The author reserves all rights to license use of this work for generative AI training and development of machine learning language models.

For information, contact: henrygraypub2022@gmail.com

Publisher's Cataloging-in-Publication Data

Names: Berman, Christian Karen
Title: Mirror of My World: Reflections on an Undiagnosed Autistic Childhood / Christian Karen Berman.
Description: Granada Hills, CA : Henry Gray Publishing, 2025. | Includes 200 b&w photos.
Identifiers: LCCN 2025902570 |ISBN 9781960415400 (hardback) | ISBN 9781960415394 (pbk.) | | ISBN 9781960415417 (ebook)
Subjects: LCSH: Berman, Christian Karen | Autistic people - Biography. | Families. | Parent and child. | Grandparent and child. | Popular culture. | Upstate New York (N.Y.). | LCGFT: Autobiographies. | BISAC: BIOGRAPHY & AUTOBIOGRAPHY / Memoirs. | BIOGRAPHY & AUTOBIOGRAPHY / Women. | BIOGRAPHY & AUTOBIOGRAPHY / Disability.
Classification: LCC RC553.A88.B47 2025 | DDC 616.85882--dc23
LC record available at https://lccn.loc.gov/2025902570

Cover Photos © 2025 Christian Karen Berman. All Rights Reserved.

Made in the United States of America.

Published by Henry Gray Publishing
17020 Chatsworth Blvd. #1125, Granada Hills, California 91344

For more information or to join our mailing list,
visit HenryGrayPublishing.com

Mirror of My World

Reflections on an Undiagnosed Autistic Childhood in the 1980s and 90s

Christian Karen Berman

Granada Hills, CA
"Select books for selective readers"

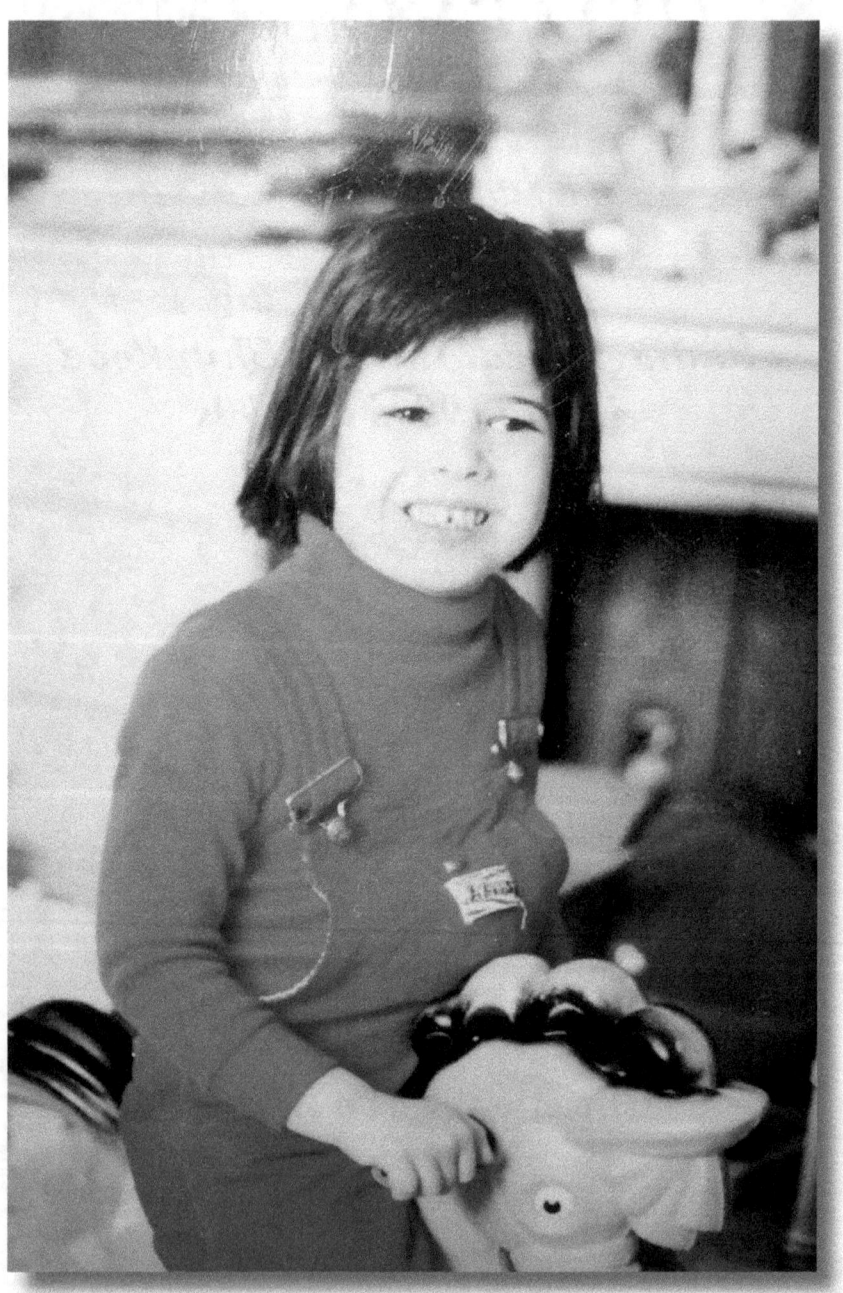

"Christian's inspirational story is a lesson in living authentically in a world that often pressures us to conform while dealing with the struggles of being on the spectrum."

> \- Bill Kirchenbauer
> Actor, *Just the 10 of Us* and *Growing Pains*

"Over the past many years, Christian Karen Berman has been one of the most interesting and complex people I've gotten to know through social media. I have witnessed her extreme highs and lows as she attempts to have a meaningful life. She is, above all else, a survivor. Her book illustrates her amazing journey."

> \- Howard Murray
> Director, *The Big Bang Theory*, *The King of Queens*, and many others

"This is a fascinating look into Christian Karen Berman's world! Family, everyday joys, sickness, and trials—it presents a unique and enlightening story through a lens of love and family."

> \- Keith Thibodeaux, actor and musician,
> TV's "Little Ricky" on *I Love Lucy*

'*Mirror of My World* is a poignant and insightful memoir, where the author reflects on her journey growing up with undiagnosed autism. Her detailed memories of childhood in the 1980s will transport readers to a world both familiar and forgotten and provide a unique insight into autism. With warmth and honesty, this book invites you to see the beauty in difference and the power of remembering."

> \- Laurie Stephens
> Ph.D., Licensed Developmental Psychologist,
> Lumina Counseling

"Many parents would love to read a book like this because they have children they want to understand better."

> \- Lynn Kirchenbauer

FROM THE PUBLISHER

When Christian Karen Berman contacted me about publishing her memoir, I was skeptical. Most memoirs are written by people who've overcome insurmountable odds or lived extraordinary lives—celebrities, politicians, history makers. But as I began reading, I found myself drawn into her story for its sincerity, and the effortless way I suddenly found myself observing the world through her eyes, the eyes of someone who, at age 25, was diagnosed with Asperger's syndrome, a form of autism.

As becomes evident in her recollections here, people with Asperger's find it challenging to interact with others, making them socially awkward. They often exhibit repetitive behaviors and have few interests, which they sometimes obsess over. And they may also be above-average in intelligence and language skills.

All of that is on view here—obsessions with dolls and food, reluctance to leave the comfort of home and family, an incredible memory, and—the clincher for me—an abiding love for a mother and father who seemed to go out of their way to create a protective bubble for their two children, Christian and her younger brother, Larry.

In addition, if you're a child of the 1980s or 90s, you'll find Christian's recollections very triggering, in a good way—her naming of specific toys and foods and TV shows will set off a flood of fond memories of a simpler time.

This memoir will also touch your heart. You'll find yourself feeling like you know her father, her mother, and her extended family, through good times and bad, through reminiscences that are often humorous, occasionally scary, but always sincere and overflowing with an aching sense of yearning.

Christian's memoir shows you don't need to have led an eventful life to write a captivating memoir, because every life, in its own way, is extraordinary.

Enjoy!

Bruce Scivally

FOREWORD

Mirror of My World: Reflections of an Undiagnosed Autistic Childhood in the 1980s and 90s gives unique insight into the world of Christian Karen Berman's autism from birth to adulthood and losing her parents. You'll get a bird's-eye view into her intelligence, as well as her childlike idiosyncrasies distinct to how she navigates the world of outside judgments, plus a variety of relationships she has both fostered, and been abandoned by.

This is an important book to better understand the brilliance and the struggle of everyday challenges autistics face by living in a society fostered for neurotypical minds.

Berman is a worthwhile person to listen to. She's not always been easy for others to understand or appreciate, yet a glimpse into her world will show you her value, as well as that of others who are sometimes cast aside in society.

Three vital things to know:

1. Autism is NOT a character defect... *yet many on the autism spectrum are treated as such.*

2. Autism is NOT a *one-size-fits-all* state...*like non-autistic people, no two are the same.*

3. Autism is NOT developed from 'mean parenting', or 'from parents doing their own research' (two of the most absurd characterizations ever stated)!

Autism is a neurodevelopmental disability a/k/a difference that mainly affects communication skills, sensory sensitivities, social interaction, and cognitive function. These are often accompanied by a variety of co-concurring additional challenges that often need additional support.

You'll note that Berman was diagnosed with Asperger's at the age of 25. Later, in 2013, Asperger's was removed from the DSM5 and is no longer a given diagnosis. It became confusing for many people who believed their Asperger's went away when it was simply the label that disappeared. This type of misunderstanding is relevant to how language, communication, comprehension, processing and more is greatly nuanced for many populations.

A common hallmark of autism presents in the form of literal thinking. Much of this can be learned information when presented with reasons why things are as they are yet rarely derived in a natural or instinctive way.

It's often assumed that a person who makes eye contact must not be autistic, which is only one symptom that does not adhere to all people on the spectrum. Similarly, other symptoms vary in each person. I like to explain autism as a main dish and things like eye contact, executive function challenges, sensory sensitivities, and other common symptoms are parts of an à la carte menu.

Rightly so, near the end of this book, Berman states, *"I have this unforgettable personality if you know me..."* That statement does apply. In her forties, Berman is 'childlike' yet also self-aware. She is a smart, wise, talented young lady who is exceptionally misunderstood as she misses social cues and embodies challenges with Executive Functioning (*organization, planning, self-regulation, etc.*). Like her, in today's society of perpetuated misinformation, the autistic population as individuals are a vulnerable community beyond their personal neurology.

There is an experience called *"Double Empathy"* where non-autistic and autistic people expect the other to grasp how each of them think. Both risk mutual frustration as they don't neurologically synchronize in receptive, or perceptive communication styles. Consider Windows vs. Mac computer differences. Or speaking two different languages with neuro mechanic differences.

Autistics generally speak and understand in very concrete and specific language. If a non-autistic person asks the other to *"save them a little ice cream,"* they may look down upon the autistic who leaves a small teaspoon of ice cream at the bottom of the carton. However, being literal should not be mistaken as inept or void of intelligence. Take note, the request was accurately followed. If explained in a literal manner, next time the same request is made 'learned behavior' is likely to prevail. Giving a reason WHY in requests to autistics can be very helpful in avoiding mix-ups.

Neurotypical nature is filled with non-verbal expression, while Neurodivergents nature isn't natural in deciphering nuances, intonations, and "beating around the bush" communication styles.

Mo' to the point: Early intervention for autistics is significant. Nomenclature such as "High/Low Functioning" is an adjective, not a diagnosis. Each autistic person is a spectrum within themselves that inhabits mostly unseen challenges along with noticeable gifts. Example: If someone's hearing is distorted, or their muscle tone is underdeveloped, or challenged with under or over-developed sensitivities, you would not easily know. However, those who inhabit these things, certainly do. Respect that versus insisting they change what they cannot. Understand that these differences are merely that, simply - differences :)

Mo Bailey, MCC, Acceptance Innovators
Autism & Advocacy Educational Consultant for
Families, Educators, NeuroDivergents, & Media

Christian Karen Berman

*This book of essays by
Christian Karen Berman
is ideal for browsing.*

*You can read it cover-to-cover,
or just flip to a random chapter
and read it like a bedtime story.*

*However you do it, we hope
you enjoy the experience.*

DEDICATION

To my hardworking Daddy, who all his life gave his all and tried his hardest, and tried to accomplish all he could. I definitely learned my work ethic from him. He was my security blanket, my whole world, and I still love him and miss him more than anybody.

To my Mommy, I love and miss you all the time. I wish we had been a little closer when I was older, but you were the sweetest Mom in the whole world.

To my Grandma Lee who loved me more than I'll ever know.

To my Grandpa Jules David Cohen; I only got to know you for six short years, but I was always so happy when you came to visit and so sad when you left to go home. I still am.

To my brother Larry, who's been like a second mother to me. He reminds me so much of our Mom. He makes sure I have a good meal every day, he takes me to all of my doctor's appointments, and when he can, he takes me for a fun outing or to buy some good snacks. He makes sure I have nice clothes to wear that I like, that are cute and comfortable. If there's a baby doll, toy, or something I really like he makes sure to buy it for me. He takes good care of me and I love him very much.

And to my good friend Bruce Gold—a world-renowned spiritual healer, professional singer, and songwriter, he's been there for me and Larry for several years by phone. He's like family to us, always loving, encouraging, and supportive. Always gives us the best advice, and his time, and he has enriched our lives so much by just calling to say hi and to see how we're doing and having a good talk when he has the time. He inspires me to try harder and do better and be the best me I can be. I couldn't have done half the good things I have with my writing and artwork without him to encourage me to go out of my shell and to try to succeed. When no one else was there for us, he gave us so much of his time and care to help us through the hard transition of losing our Dad. Larry and I are both lucky to have him in our lives and we love him very much.

To my friends Bill & Lynn Kirchenbauer, thanks for always being good friends to me and for all of your support whenever I need it.

Mo Bailey, as busy as you are, you always made it a point to write me back or call me if I needed you and help in any way you can.

Laurie Stephens, when Larry and I need you for something, you make the time to write back, call if you can. Thanks for always being a supportive friend to us.

To my parents' good and longtime friend Aunt Diane, thanks for being such a good friend to my parents, Larry, and me and helping us all out when we needed you to.

To my Uncle Henry Berman, even though I have only really known you since after my Dad died seven years ago, thanks for being on the phone when you could and for being so caring.

And last, but not least, an extra special thanks and appreciation to my friend & publisher Bruce Scivally, for without all his help, time, patience, understanding, and believing in me, this book would not have been possible.

Christian (Self-Portrait, drawn at age 7...or maybe age 8)

CONTENTS

	From the Publisher	vi
	Foreword	vii
	Dedication	xi
1	My First Year	1
2	A New Home	5
3	My Baby Doll	7
4	Son of Sam	9
5	My Documented First Years, Before I Was Diagnosed With Autism	11
6	Age 3	15
7	Starting Nursery School	19
8	My Two Boyfriends at Age 3	21
9	Who is Going to Take Me to the Doctor?	23
10	My First Chanukah	25
11	The Tarantula	27
12	Becoming a Big Sister and Other Memories	29
13	I See London, I See France, I See Karen's Underpants	31
14	Good Timing, Close Timing	37
15	The Splinter	39
16	The Pool	41

17	Cassette Tape of Four-Year-Old Me	43
18	Losing a Tooth	49
19	Pop Goes the Socket!	51
20	The Cat Came Back the Very Next Day, the Cat Came Back, She Just Couldn't Stay Away	55
21	Let's Give This Kindergarten Thing a Second Try	57
22	Age 5-6	63
23	Nap Time	65
24	A Child's Gut Instinct	69
25	Kindergarten: The Other Half of the School Year as It Happens	71
26	Flowers for My Mother	75
27	Last memories of Grade K	79
28	My Cabbage Patch Story	83
29	Age 6	87
30	Swim Class	93
31	The Neptune / Flagship Dinner	97
32	Age 7	99
33	The Stevensville Hotel in the Catskills	101
34	Day Camp	103
35	Second Grade Dilemmas	105
36	The New Plaid Tan Couch	107
37	Larry is Lost in Sears, Larry is Missing	109

38	My Brother's Convulsion	111
39	Spring	115
40	Mount Kisco Mall	117
41	Blood Poisoning and Rubber Bands	119
42	Taking Medicine and Being Sick	121
43	Going to the Beach Club	125
44	Chicken Pox	129
45	Grandma Lee's Apartment	133
46	The Cool Benefits of Being Age 7	137
47	A Day in the Life of Me as a 7-Year-Old	139
48	The Old-Fashioned Big, White Chenille Blanket on My Parents' Bed	143
49	Visiting a Relative	145
50	What 7-Year Old Me Did With Orange Juice	149
51	My Favorite Toys of the Mid- to Late-1980s Growing Up as a Little Girl	150
52	Trip to Grandma's House	153
53	An Artist in the Making: Artwork Ages 6-11	156
54	My Birthdays	165
55	Trip to Bensonhurst, Brooklyn, Avenue P	169
56	Age 8 Through Age 11 and House-Hunting	171
57	My Active Imagination and Need to Play Gets Me in Trouble	173

58	Playtime	175
59	Stuck on the School Bus	177
60	Hebrew School	181
61	My Parents Forgot to Pick Me Up After Hebrew School	183
62	Hair Pulling	185
63	Surprise	187
64	The Fourth Grade	189
65	Other Miscellaneous, Quick Memories, Ages 6-9	193
66	My Favorite Foods of the 1980s and 90s	197
67	Going to the Nevele	199
68	At the Nevele	205
69	A Poor Christmas	211
70	One of My Best Christmas Memories About My Mom	215
71	I Cut My Hair	217
72	Starting a New, Bigger School	221
73	The Girl Bully	223
74	The Bully Part 2	227
75	Male Child Psychiatrist	231
76	Christmas	233
77	Jean From the Heathcote Bootery in Scarsdale, NY	235

78	The Wedding	241
79	Snow Day	243
80	Our First Night at the Nevele	247
81	Grandma Lee Babysits	251
82	Memories and Thoughts of My Pretend Sister Jen	253
83	Sweet Sixteen Party in Manhattan	255
84	Bronchitis	259
85	Going to My Classmate's 1950s Birthday Party in the 5th Grade	263
86	Lyme Disease Testing	271
87	Memories of My Mom	273
88	Happy Halloween	277
89	Happy Halloween Memories	279
90	My Toys	281
91	Going to Mount Kisco	285
92	Snacks	287
93	Christmas, Age 12 — Early 1990s	289
94	When Bicycle Tires Meet Wet Green Grass	295
95	Crime in the Local Library	299
96	Bad Attitude	301
97	Back to School 7th Grade	303
98	End of a Good Day	305

99	Bullied	307
100	Summer	309
101	Elevators and Day Camp	313
102	First Day of 8th Grade	315
103	The Last Day of the 8th Grade Before Christmas Vacation	319
104	My Saint Patty's Day at Age 14	323
105	Taking Medicine as a Teenager	329
106	The Never-Told Story of My Grandma Lee	331
107	Hospital Stay	335
108	The Rye Town Hilton	341
109	Losing Grandma Lee	347
110	A Happy Thanksgiving	357
111	The Last Day of School Before Christmas Vacation, 10th Grade	359
112	A Baby Sister!	365
113	Connecticut	369
114	Everybody's Sick (It's About Everyone Being Sick)	373
115	My Late Teens	377
116	One of My Good Deeds	379
117	Dog Bite	385
118	The Little Fugitive	387
119	September 11, 2001	391

120	My Daddy	397
121	November 27, 2009 - My Late Grandma Lee's Birthday	403
122	Losing All My Best Friends in the World	415
123	Bronchitis, Part 2	419
124	Hurricane Sandy	427
125	My Dad's Favorite Movies	431
126	My Mom's Favorite Movies	433
127	The Night Our Car Got Stolen	435
128	Food Poisoning	439
129	Breaking Daddy Out of Greenwich Woods	441
130	Stories of My Daddy	445
131	Dr. Stephen L. Berman	455
132	Beverly Joan Cohen Berman	461
133	Before My Dad Got Sick, Our Last Saturdays Went Like This...	465
134	Back to School Memories	469
135	What I Miss Most About My Mommy	475
136	What I Miss Most About My Daddy	477
137	Memories of My Mother	479
138	Thoughts of My Mommy and Daddy	483
139	The Cat in the Mirror	487
140	About the Author — Christian Karen Berman	491

Christian Karen Berman

MY FIRST YEAR

This is the story of the day I was born! It was June 6th, and I was already three days late. I used to be late for everything; now I'm early! When I was born I didn't cry. I was too shy to cry in front of strangers. Daddy said the doctor said I will make up for it later on. Daddy always wanted to call him and tell him he was right—I more than made up for it!

Daddy—a teacher—had to leave to go to his school, Horace Mann. It was graduation day. He left his wife and newborn baby girl to rush to his students' graduation day!

On the way back to our garden complex a policeman stopped him for speeding to give him a ticket. He said his wife had just given birth to his daughter. Then the policeman asked for proof. Daddy luckily had my birth card with my name, height, and weight on it. I was 6 pounds 14 oz and 21 inches. The policeman was amazed; his wife had just given birth in the same hospital to a baby girl, too. He told Daddy this was just a warning and to be more careful and drive slower.

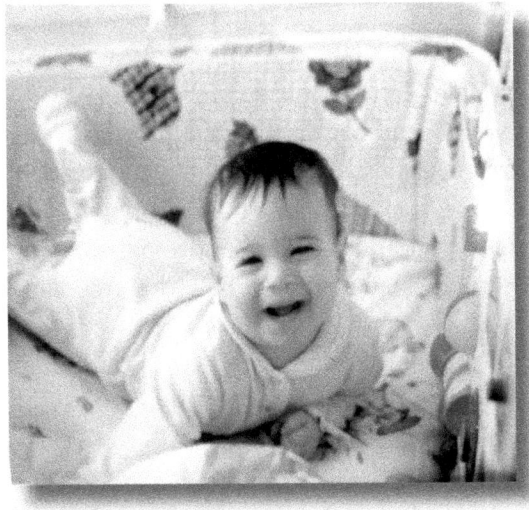

Daddy had to change into his suit and tie. They left in a hurry because my Mommy went into labor. She probably just threw on something comfortable. When he finally got to school and told everyone his wife just had a baby, they said "Why are you

MIRROR OF MY WORLD

here? Why did you come to school? Why aren't you with them?" I think he went for the cookies and cake and to brag; he did love his school!

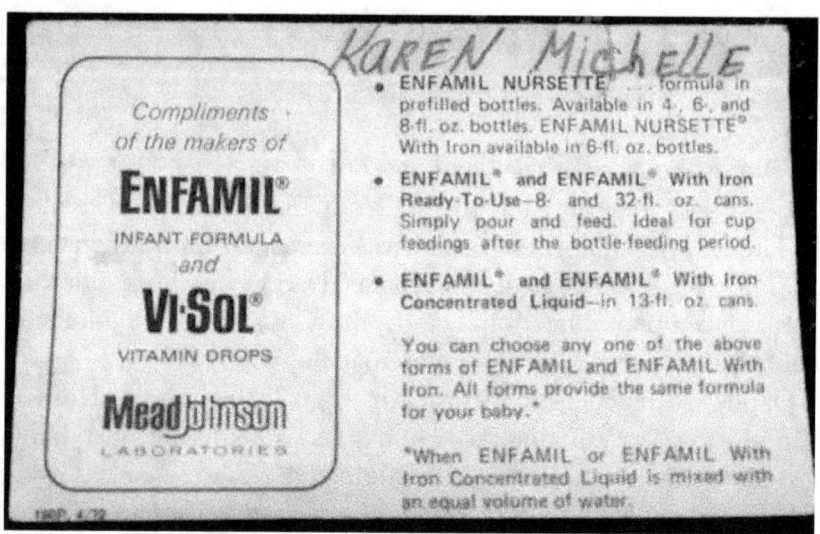

Back at the hospital, the nurse told my Mom not to get up and to stay in bed. She didn't listen. She did get up and fainted onto the floor. I think she lost a lot of blood giving birth. I was her first baby. I was born in only two hours—I was a quick delivery!

I was born in Saint Agnes Hospital. Three nuns blessed me, then they gave my parents and all the new parents a free steak dinner to celebrate! They also gave them a plaque about little girls, saying they were made of sugar and spice and everything nice. They even took my first photo!

My Mom was discharged three days later. When Daddy was carrying me up the stairs (we were on the second floor), he said he was holding me tight, so afraid he would drop me. He had a car seat for me but didn't take the baby carrier seat! He said I was all nice and clean and then I needed my diaper changed. My parents didn't know how to do it, or what to do, so they called the building super's wife! (Even at age six, I could change my Cabbage Patch Kid's diaper. I told Daddy that, too!) Well, she changed me and they watched and learned.

We only stayed there for a year after I was born, because the people on the bottom floor didn't like my crying and the 2 am feedings. They heard Daddy pacing the floor with me. I had great lungs for a little baby. I wouldn't stop crying! Back then, I couldn't say why, but I know why—I was scared, sad and lonely. I had separation anxiety. I felt unloved and rejected. I guess I felt safe, loved and secure in my parents' bed, except I told Daddy he could've crushed me, rolled over on me, I could've fallen into the middle of the bed and got hurt. He said he had no choice or no one would've gotten any sleep! I was a very clingy baby, so my parents slept with a six-pound newborn in their bed. I would cry all night if I didn't.

When I was a baby growing up, Daddy took photos of me and brought them to his class to show to his students and they "oohed" and "aahed." They loved looking at each photo, and he loved proudly showing off what a cute baby I was. I wish he had gotten me into acting.

My Dad used to go to the pharmacy and ask for a six-pack, he'd joke with them—not a six-pack of beer, but six cans of Similac formula.

One night I couldn't stop crying to go to sleep and my parents didn't know what to do (The neighbors in the apartment complex didn't really like my Dad walking the floors with a screaming, crying baby all night; they even told him so). He called the pediatrician-on-call, who figured out there was probably soap residue accidentally left on my baby bottle nipple when he was washing them and I was in pain from gas bubbles. The doctor said, you got some schnapps? My Dad had many mini-liquor bottles from friends. The doctor told my Dad to give me a shot of whiskey on a teaspoon. It did the trick; I was out like a light, and now everyone could finally get some sleep.

They bought me a big twin size bed at age one, because they thought it was just the crib. The doctor said to put a baby gate by my door so I couldn't get out.

My Dad used to look forward to coming home after work, holding me on his stomach and watching reruns of *Hogan's Heroes*, while

MIRROR OF MY WORLD

waiting for my Mom to finish cooking dinner. My Mom said the baby foods I liked best were Gerber's Beef and Apricot.

They were good parents.

A New Home

This is my Mom and I was just born here, only a few days old. I lived in the Garden Complex Apartment until I was one year old. My maternal grandparents lived there, too, but a few apartments away. Later we moved to a house. Mommy said the house was my one-year-old birthday present. I think they moved because of all of my crying in the middle of the night. We have lived here ever since. This house was built in 1954 and had a few owners before us. My parents slept with me in the double twin bed. I had my own bedroom with a very nice crib, mobile, and toys, but no one could get any sleep.

Mom's shirt had her initials, very popular in the early 1980s. This is the back of the building near the parking garage. We're on the grassy part by a tree. I remember this place from when we went to visit my Grandma Lee when I was a little bit older. They wanted a bigger house to move into, but they needed both my grandparents' help and a mortgage to move into our new home. The owner, Mrs. Malcolm, was in her mid-70s. She sold the cheap swing

MIRROR OF MY WORLD

set that she promised my Dad came with the house to a nearby neighbor with a little boy. Then at the very last minute, before my parents were to move in, she was about to change her mind and stay and not sign the papers. Then she finally decided it was best to move to Miami, Florida.

I'm glad I got to live and grow up here.

I loved my Mommy. If she was still alive and healthy, I would go on Mother/Daughter Days with her. I had a few as a young child, but not enough. I'm glad I missed many days of school, some real sick days and many hooky days, because I got to spend more time getting to know my Mom.

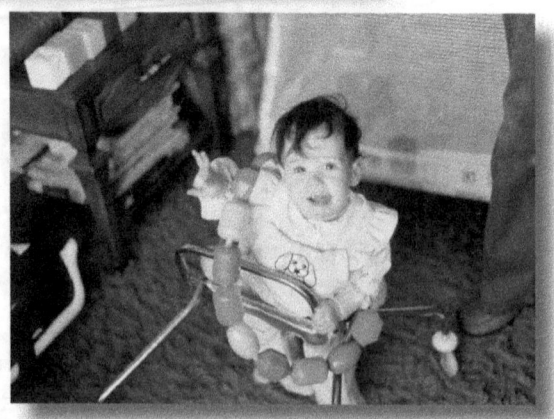

MY BabY DOLL

When I was six months old my Mom got me a hard plastic baby doll by Horsman. She gave it to me in my baby crib. She said I was afraid and jealous of it. I think she gave it to me too early and I wish it was a nicer-looking baby doll; it had a very hard body. My Grandma Lee crocheted a yellow dress for her, with one white button in the back. When I was two years old I dropped it out of my baby carriage and it's leg got run over by a car, yes, a big car and the lady got out and felt so bad and wanted to check if I was okay. She must have went over a bump. She handed me my badly injured doll. Her kneecap had a big, irreparable dent. The lady felt so bad that she hurt my baby doll. I don't remember this, but my Mom had told me the story a few times. I'm not sure if the lady wanted to buy me a new baby doll or not. I'm sure my Mom told her it was okay. Ironically, after the baby doll was run over, I now loved it even more. It became so much more special because she survived getting run over by a really big car (cars were big back in the 1980s).

MIRROR OF MY WORLD

SON OF SAM

During the late 1970s, there was a serial killer on the loose that scared everyone in New York including my parents to be. A couple years after Son of Sam, during Halloween night, a man knocked on my parents' door during Trick or Treat. They had just moved in our new and beautiful home in August, two months before. I was a one-year-old baby (I'm not sure if I was asleep in my crib or where I was). My Dad had expected a small child dressed up in a cute Halloween costume to give candy to. Seeing a grown man, he was scared. He said, "Bev, get the gun and call the police!" The man said, "Okay, I'm leaving," and thankfully did.

My two young, scared parents were shaken up, but relieved he finally left and nothing worse happened. We didn't really have even a toy gun back then, but Dad was trying to scare the guy off. I don't know if he was homeless and wanted money, or candy, but my Dad didn't want to wait and take a chance to find out. He could have robbed them, tied them up, hurt them, kidnapped me, or worse stuff like you see on the news. It was one of the scariest Halloween nights ever. I think after that my parents locked the door, turned off all the lights, and went to bed with little me.

MIRROR OF MY WORLD

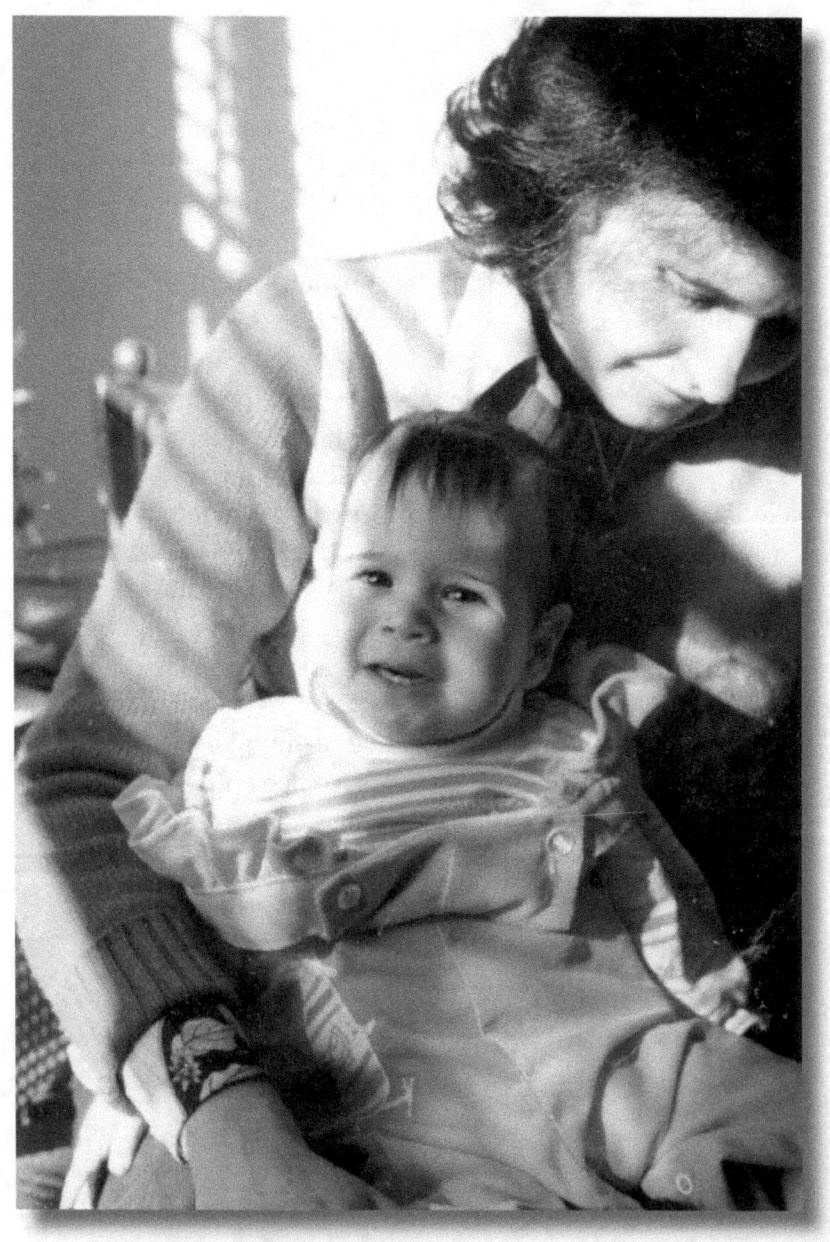

Christian Karen Berman

MY DOCUMENTED FIRST YEARS, BEFORE I WAS DIAGNOSED WITH AUTISM

I was looking in my Dad's dresser drawers where he had some VHS tapes and found a few audio cassette tapes of me and my parents from around 18 months to three years old. I want to share the love I heard.

I had a good childhood and was very smart and the center of my parents' world, their whole world. It was a loving house. Before I was age two, my Mom would say a nursery rhyme and I would finish the words. Oh, how I love to go up on a "SWING," up in the sky so "BLUE". My Dad would ask where my best friend "Ichael" was. I wouldn't say Michael, I would drop the M. They thought it was cute and called him that, too, Ichael on the bike. I had three boyfriends, two Michaels and a Jason, plus a girlfriend June and her mom, Bertha.

So many people came to my second birthday party—two neighbors, Merida and her one-year-old daughter Sonia, my maternal grandparents, and Michael's parents—that I wondered how so many people even fit in our tiny dining room. I dunno what presents they bought me, but on the tapes, my Dad asks me, "Did you get new shoes?" With such excitement and love, I say, "No." He asks, "What's on your feet?"

I had the sweetest baby voice when my Dad kept calling me "little girl." My parents' voices didn't change much over the years. I wish I knew how lucky I was to have such beautiful, sweet, loving parents. When I was older, sometimes I didn't appreciate them as much. I guess many teenagers and twenty-year-olds feel the same way. I regret having meltdowns and wishing I had better parents, not all the times, but the times I wasn't as good as I should be. No one is perfect and the teenage years were hard. I also had an eating disorder. I'm sorry Mommy and Daddy for running away from home or the times I pretended to for a few minutes, hiding in the walk-in closet, and the times I made you worry. I feel so bad about that now. I guess other teens were worse, but that is no excuse for my poor behavior. I love and miss you, Mom and Dad.

My Dad was trying to get me to talk into the tape recorder and asked me who I loved. I said Mommy and Papa. Papa was my maternal Grandpa, Jules David Cohen. He asked me many times at age two and three, and finally I said, "Mommy and Daddy." My Dad was overjoyed. He never got upset or hurt that I didn't say his name, he just kept trying. Not liking talking into the tape recorder at a young age, I would say, "no no no," so my Mom gave me the nickname, "the No No Girl." I was just asserting my independence at age 20 months. I talked well and had a great vocabulary for under two years old. At three, my Dad said I was finished talking, because when I put my thumb in my mouth that means I was finished talking. I did not know I sucked my thumb. Daddy had told me the doctor wanted to put some yucky nail polish on my thumb to get me to stop at four, because it was bad for my teeth, but I didn't remember that.

When I was age three, My Mom had told me I was potty trained at 18 months, maybe that's when she started potty training me, because on the cassette tape, my Daddy said it was a very hot day on July 24th and I was three and only wearing a diaper. That really surprised me. They did ask me at age two if I had to go pee in the potty. On the tapes, I called Milk Maid, an ice cream place we would go to often, Duke Maid. I listed the foods I ate—Cheerios and orange juice for breakfast, lunch was a hamburger and fries and Coca Cola or Pepsi. I didn't know or remember that I drank that at age 2, giving a baby caffeine. Is it odd to give your baby caffeinated soda? This was the early 1980s. We also went to McDonald's before I was age 2 and got a hamburger and fries and a Coke for me. I also ate a donut from Armonk. I sure ate a lot for a skinny little tiny baby, I guess just a few bites, I was small.

The things I did as a two and three-year-old: I went in the kiddie pool in our backyard as early as May. Rode my trike, watched my Daddy do the yard work, went to Armonk PlayLand Park (the playground with the ducks), and went on the swings and slide, McDonald's, Milk Maid, Michael's house, Armonk, the Neptune Diner, Sears…

They did live every day to the fullest back then and I did a lot more things than I thought and remembered. I don't remember much from age two and three. I guess I went to the pediatrician, too. My mommy was taking a nap and my Daddy told me to wake her, I said "Wake up, Mommy, wake up, Mommy," and then Daddy said, "Tickle her feet, go tickle her feet." Then my Mom said, "You woke me up." She had a sweet voice, too. So did my Daddy. I miss those happy days when I was their whole world and so loved. I was surprised to find these tapes, I think I had heard one many years ago as a child or young teenager. My Dad said it was hard to get me to talk and say one word. At three, I was singing "Happy Birthday" to Mommy, Daddy, to the bathroom and window, too. I was a real sweetheart. My Dad said I was such a cute, pretty baby.

Every day was heaven back then. I could feel the love.

MIRROR OF MY WORLD

AGE 3

For my third birthday, I remember age three for a few seconds. There was a party in the dining room, and we were waiting for other two- and three-year-olds to come. There were decorations, tablecloth plates, and party hats. I was probably wearing a party dress. I'm not sure what presents I got. My parents served hot dogs, potato salad, coke, apple juice, birthday cake, and ice cream. Quite a nice spread for a toddler's birthday party.

They did not say if I got any gifts or not, I don't remember. I think I got a Fisher Price crying baby doll from Grandma Gert that someone named Morgan for me (on my dad's tape recordings, I can be heard pronouncing her name "Grandma Dirt"; it took me a minute to figure how to say it correctly). I might have also got a Fisher Price mini-kitchen and a record player. I'm sure there was a nice cake, not sure what kind, probably from a local bakery.

It's weird no one took photos; my Dad told me that around that time his camera wasn't working and he couldn't afford to fix it or get a new one. They actually had camcorders in the early 1980s, but of course we couldn't afford one until the late 1980s. I dunno why, but I wish he'd taken photos. I wish I had the swing set and baby sister they kept promising me, too.

My other memory of age three—I had to go to get my 3-in-1 shot at the pediatrician. It was the first shot I remember and it hurt. I was upset by this and remember afterwards sitting in the office chair. The doctor said I don't have to get another shot till age 11. I was relieved; I knew that was a long time away.

Later that night my Dad said he found me unconscious on the floor and foaming at the mouth. So he picked me up and rushed me and my Mom to the hospital. He gave me to the staff there to work on me. I remember lying on the floor. I remember being in a silver metal baby crib in the hospital. I had a bad reaction to the measles, mumps and rubella shot. I think I was there a few hours or overnight.

MIRROR OF MY WORLD

Later my Dad said the high mercury content in the vaccine gave me my autism. It's a very argued-over, controversial theory; my Dad had bought a book about it. In many cases toddlers changed overnight, not being able to talk. I'm lucky I recovered, but it might have given me mild autism. My brother had a similar reaction, but not as bad as mine.

My parents took me to the Brickman Hotel. I looked down at my feet there and saw red bricks. I wondered, is that why they call it Brickman's? In the hotel room, I heard my Mom saying to my Dad something like, "When is the cleaning lady going to bring more toilet paper?" I was in the bathroom and said, "I only used one piece," and showed her the one little square.

I thought milk was called "Duke." "Milk" sounds like "Duke." I would say to my Daddy, "DUKE IN A PUP," which meant "milk in a cup." When I was only age three, I was curious what would happen if I stuck my finger in the dried, cracked nipple. I did, and it broke. My Mom looked in our local pharmacy and everywhere. She couldn't find Nuk nipples anywhere, only Gerber, and those tasted like rubber and you had to sterilize a needle and put it in the nipple to make the hole bigger for the milk to come out easier. I had to switch to a big cup at age three-and-a-half because of it. I remember the milk or juice gushing towards my mouth fast, not like sucking the milk out of a nipple. A sad first stage of many to come of losing a piece of my babyhood and growing up. At age three-and-a-half, I was smart enough to figure out cause and effect, all by myself, too.

That night at the hotel, my parents knew I couldn't go to sleep without my "Duke." My Dad took us to the bar (for grown-ups who drink liquor), I'm not sure of the time, but just before bedtime between 9 and 10 pm. He asked for milk for my baby bottle. The guy gave him milk in ice cubes in a large take-out cup. I remember back in the room Daddy pouring the milk and ice in my 8 oz. glass baby bottle. I was thinking, or said, I don't like ice. I drank it anyway. I couldn't sleep until I had that. I slept in the middle of the bed with my parents; my brother wasn't born until a year later. My Mom had a miscarriage when I was three.

Christian Karen Berman

I was in a babysitting group at the local temple and I was looking in closets and asking for Dr. Steve. I knew how to say *Analysis of Covariance* (the title of Daddy's book), too, Daddy taught me! He was always worried that I was a very skinny, sickly child like he was. Told my pediatrician that I don't eat anything. It's in the report. And my Mom said I only eat pizza and chocolate. He was always there for me when I was sick, which was pretty often most of my childhood. I slept in bed with my parents off and on, mostly on until my teenage years. Even as a girl in the 8th grade I missed him so much when he went to school. I remember when I didn't want him to leave me, I'd lie in bed crying, holding his red pin-striped button-down shirt. My Mom called the switchboard lady many times trying to reach him to calm me down. I think I always had separation anxiety, to him mostly. He didn't come home until 4:30 pm or later. I always was very happy when he finally came home. I'd run downstairs and yell for everyone to hear the famous words, "Daddy's home!"

My parents got me lots of toys, anything they could afford. They loved surprising me and making me happy. Cabbage Patch Kids, Care Bears, a *Sesame Street* Big Bird plastic rocking horse, one of my very favorite loved toys.

MIRROR OF MY WORLD

Christian Karen Berman

STARTING NURSERY SCHOOL

I would sit on the floor and cry. I saw the fun sand table, and the big play kitchen, but I just wanted to go home with my Mom. The teacher picked me up and put me in my Mom's arms. My Mom never picked me up, even though I was about only twenty-five pounds. She thought lifting heavy things would make her miscarry; she was trying to have another baby. I made such a strong impression on my teacher over the last week, she told my Mom that I wasn't ready for school yet and it would be best if I didn't return. I got kicked out. She didn't accept me at age four, still not ready. She had my three-year-old brother a few years later and refused to accept him, too, remembering me. What an impression sweet, cute little three-year-old me had made.

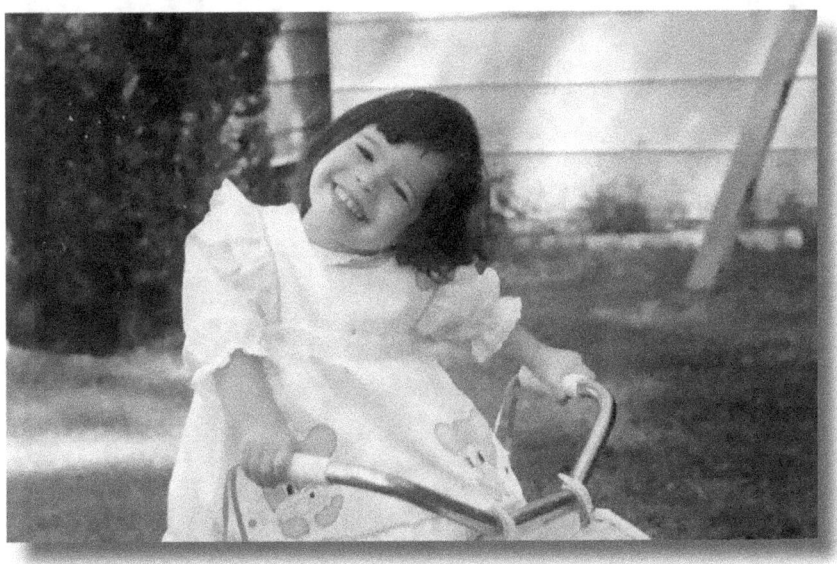

MIRROR OF MY WORLD

[Christian Karen Berman]{.underline}

MY TWO BOYFRIENDS AT AGE 3

Michael B. and Michael K. They were both three. I remember my parents taking us and one of the Michaels and his parents all out to the Neptune Diner. Michael had spaghetti and marinara sauce. I got something else I wasn't liking, probably the usual—a hamburger, fries, and ketchup. I wouldn't eat and wanted the same thing he had. I was jealous, so my parents changed my order. Then Michael said to me, "Did you do that because I'm eating this?"

I used to borrow toys from him, like foam multicolored people that fit in to place. He lived down the block. He was cute. We went to visit the other Michael at a Chinese restaurant in the winter one time. My parents stopped in just for a few minutes to say hi. I remember just enjoying munching on the crispy noodles. No, we didn't stay to eat dinner; I don't know why. But I loved those crispy noodles. Yummy!

MIRROR OF MY WORLD

Christian Karen Berman

WHO IS GOING TO TAKE ME TO THE DOCTOR?

This story I have no memory of and was told by my Mother. My Dad was at work. We only had the one car at the time, the big white Oldsmobile my Dad needed and drove to work; my Mom didn't know how to drive back then. I must have woken up sick. My Mom called the doctor to make an appointment for me. Not sure if it was a stomach bug or a sore throat.

I think I had woken up in an empty big bed after my Daddy had gone to work. My Grandpa Jules was at work, too, in the tailor shop, so he couldn't just leave work early to take me to the doctor. My Grandma Lee didn't drive either, and Grandpa Jules had the car. I really wasn't feeling good.

My Mom wouldn't take me to the doctor for no reason, especially if there was no way to get there. I musta been running a fever and she was worried—was I well enough to walk all the way half a mile down to the bus stop and take public transportation? I know my Mom could have afforded it. Being under five years old, I was free (that did work many years after that, too).

I guess she figured I was too sick to walk all the way up to the bus stop and wait, so she started calling neighbors. She called our good, older friend Mrs. Newman who lived across the block

and a few houses down, back then I'd say she was in her mid 60s. She had a short grey man's haircut and was slightly overweight. She was thrilled to take me to my pediatrician in her car. I don't think she had any kids of her own and I brightened her boring day. She thought I was a delight.

I do remember that office. They had lots of spring rocking horses and gave out lollipops after.

Why don't I remember this, when I was three years old? My thoughts are that I was there so **often being sick**, it wasn't something new and exciting to remember, though it was the only time Mrs. Newman took me.

MIRROR OF MY WORLD

<u>Christian Karen Berman</u>

MY FIRST CHANUKAH

I remember I was age three. My Mom was at a temple and I was in a babysitting service and my maternal grandparents were there, too. There was a bunch of two- and three-year-olds with me running towards a big box of Chanukah presents for them to pick one out. The toddlers ran fast and ferociously down the hall and got there fast, grabbing the biggest wrapped boxes. I wasn't like that. I was walking with my Mom behind me, wanting to stay close by my Mom, but a little worried; when I got there every other kid took a nice-sized wrapped box. My Mom was worried there was nothing left in the box for poor little me. Back then, I was shy and a Mommy's girl, not a go-getter like all the other toddlers. I looked deep in the box. There was one small, thin and flat wrapped present left in there just waiting for little me.

My Mom seemed more disappointed than me and when we were walking outside to the car, it was cold and wet. My grandparents were waiting, and my Mom was talking about my present, saying it's probably a book, or something for the floor. She wished I had been more aggressive like the other kids that ran and grabbed the biggest and best presents. My Grandpa Jules was assuring her it would be a nice present. I didn't care much about presents then, I just loved my Mommy, but back then I didn't like books and I was hoping that it wasn't a book. I got in the backseat of the car and opened it and, sure enough, what was it but a book. Oh, well. My Grandpa Jules loved to read me books. I did not like sitting still listening to someone reading a book (I was told that by my Dad). I guess I had ADHD back then. That's all I remember. The meaning of this is, it's not about the presents you get, but the family you have and love.

When I was three, my Mom thought I was too old to still be pushed in the baby stroller. I was all of about twenty-six pounds. I carried my big green plastic pail and shovel on the long walk to the park with her. It was down a long block, up a wooded trail and down the sidewalk of a busy street and local market, easily a mile each way. We shared a very fine bottle of apple juice, Cheddar or Pretzel Goldfish crackers and half of a tuna fish salad on a poppy seed roll. I would climb the saucers at the playground, while my Mom would watch or follow me. This was a baby playground, too—no swings, and it was local. Other playgrounds were much better, but my Mommy didn't drive then or maybe we only had the one car and Daddy needed it to drive to work in the Big City.

Christian Karen Berman

THE TARANTULA

I'm age four. My parents were doing some gardening outside, so I was with them. I believe my mother went to Amodio's to get marigold flowers to plant. My Dad's taking photos of me. It's a sunny, boring July day. My brother is in my Mom's big stomach, but I'm hoping it's a girl and he will be here in a few months. It will be fun to have a cute baby to play with, but I like being an only child and the center of their whole world. They treat me like a little adult more than a child, though. I'm shy, clingy, quiet, and well-behaved.

My parents wander off somewhere. I think they went inside the house and I don't feel safe alone outside by my little self. I walk to go in and see a big furry spider or crab the size of my Dad's big hand or even bigger, something on the porch steps that's so scary and shouldn't be there. I run quickly to the side of the house down the grassy side part, my heart racing with fear. I want to go inside, but I can't. I scream Mom and Steve. I'm not sure if I called him Dad, my Mom called him that so I know I called him that later, not sure what I called him at four. I scream their names again with all my might. I'm not sure if the back door is open and not sure how to get into the house. I'm about 35" and 32 pounds. I slowly and hesitantly walk back to the front door. The monster is gone and not there. I didn't know what scary creature it was, just that it would want to run after me and hurt me. I quickly and carefully go on the porch and into the house. I'm not sure if at four I had the words to tell my parents about the big spider and what happened. I don't clearly remember that part.

MIRROR OF MY WORLD

Christian Karen Berman

Becoming a Big Sister and Other Memories

It's the 1980s and I'm age four. I remember when my Mom was pregnant, first when I was three and she had a miscarriage. I always wondered if that was going to be the little sister my Grandma Lee had promised me. Why did my Mom have to lose the baby? It was a fetus, but it would have been great to have more siblings. Then one night at dinner when I was probably still age three my Dad showed me a picture of a fetus in my Mom's baby book. It was a big hardcover aqua blue book with a picture of a blue-eyed baby on the cover. My Mom said, "No, don't show her that, you'll scare her and give her nightmares." I did have a nightmare about that once—my Mom was right. When my Mom would lie in bed, I would put my head on her stomach and say, "Hi, boy girl, girl boy." I wanted a little sister. My Mom didn't have an ultrasound; in those days they only did them if they thought the baby was in trouble. They might have had one done on me—the doctor thought I was going to be breech. Luckily, I wasn't. My Mom had natural birth twice. She did say she ate a lot of mac and cheese when she was pregnant with me, so she wasn't surprised it was my favorite food as a child.

I slept in my parents' bed as a child. After my brother was born, when I fell asleep, my Dad carried me into my room and put me in bed. He said he had to carry me out and put me in my own bed in my own room or my brother would never have been born. I slept with my parents on-and-off (mostly on) until I was almost a teenager. It was called the family bed. My brother slept in his own bed.

My Mom got me a baby doll that looked and felt real to get me used to being a big sister and having a new baby. In October that day finally came. I remember being in the front seat in the middle right next to my Dad, driving to the train station to pick up his

MIRROR OF MY WORLD

Mother. It was one of the few times in my life I saw her. She lived in Brooklyn, N.Y. The first time without a car seat, my legs didn't even go off the seat, I was about only 35 inches and 35 pounds, if that much. The car seemed huge, they couldn't find anyone to give them another car seat and they couldn't afford one. Technically I should have been in a child safety seat for a few more years, but they didn't have strict laws back then so it was okay.

I remember being in the hospital. It's fuzzy in my memory; I think my Grandma gave me a baby doll named Morgan. I remember looking at my Mom from a distance in the hospital. At home she needed to sit on a plastic tube called a donut. I wanted to play with that and sit on it, too. I wasn't allowed near the baby. I was sad about that. I felt hurt and jealous. I looked from a distance—I wasn't allowed to hold him. I think one of my Grandmas or my parents had read that the first child might be Jealous and try to hurt the baby. I was feeling very left out those few days and months. I remember my Dad trying to take photos of my brother. In one you could see me looking sad. I was the little adult and used to get all the attention.

Also, even though it was pre-Covid, the hospital gave my Mother a stack of light blue hospital masks for me to wear whenever I was near my brother, because I had a cold when he was born. I think I felt inferior, like a bit of an outcast. I do remember my Grandma Lee saying, "Next time it will be a girl." They never kept their promise of giving me my baby sister. Later, when I was a young adult, my Dad said he couldn't afford another child. All of their friends had three kids. I had to carry a Kid Sister doll around as a child and pretend she was my little sister. I was good at pretending. I almost believed it myself.

I use to climb on the dresser and all of the furniture too. I remember a big yellow playpen in the living room; I wanted to go into it, too. I remember the bris, my brother screaming and crying. It was in the dining room. People came. I remember being happy when he fell asleep in the playpen so Mom could spend some time with me. I played with my Fisher Price doll house, and would sit on this foot-tall dictionary as a chair, while my Mom would cook a hot dog, cut it into little slices, and serve it with ketchup and a slice of bread. I must have drank apple juice, I can't remember. Then when my baby brother woke up, she would put him in the baby carriage and we would all walk to the park. I wished it was a double stroller. I was only a small four-year-old and the playground was a mile away, and I had been walking there since I was age three.

We didn't have a swing set. The house was supposed to come with one, but the old lady sold it before we moved in, to another neighbor with a young son. She also made my parents wait: she was thinking of backing out of the house sale at the very last minute, but luckily she decided to move to Florida.

This house had three other people living here before us. I do wish my parents had bought a bigger house, but they were poor and couldn't afford more. I remember Larry would cry and my Mom would go and bring him down. I remember the smell of his baby carrots and mixed cereal; it smelt good. My Grandma Lee fed me a soft-boiled egg. I did not like the slimy part and would have much rather had the Gerber mixed cereal. I didn't even get a sippy cup but went right to a big cup. It wasn't easy.

It's sad the passages of time like graduating to a big cup, one step closer to being a big girl. They had sippy cups back then, but my Mom shopped in a local market and pharmacy, not much of a selection there. I tried to fit in my baby brother's baby clothes. When he was a year or two older, I could just about fit into them. I did feel my Mother loved my brother more than me. It made me sad, but I was too shy or didn't know how to express my feelings at such a young age. I do remember when my Dad was changing where the furniture was placed in the room I sat in the corner and cried because I didn't like change. I think I was age five then. He tried to comfort me.

When Larry got a little older, he was fun to play with. My Mom even got me some boy clothes, because I wanted to wear my brother's clothes. I was age nine then.

I hope you enjoyed my memories. It's nice to go back. I wish I could stay there, when times were happier and the future was bright, so much to look forward to back then. I feel at a standstill now, not sure what to do next.

MIRROR OF MY WORLD

Christian Karen Berman

I See LONDON, I See FRANCE, I See KAREN'S UNDERPANTS

When I was age 4 in July of the early 1980s, my dad had to go buy or pick up something at Sears department store or Jersey Camera. It was in the mid-morning around 10 or 11 am. My Mom wasn't feeling up to going, which was rare for her. She was pregnant with my baby brother at the time. I didn't know the baby I wanted would be a boy; I was expecting and hoping for a girl. I think my Mom was having morning sickness. She had told my Dad to put on my red short shorts with a bright yellow Tweety Bird character sewn on the bottom of the right side and white or yellow rims around the red shorts. I had just turned four last month and still needed someone to help me get dressed. It was elastic waist shorts, in a size 3T or 4T. My dad was in a hurry to leave, so we left. I liked to get out early and do things with my Daddy all the time, even though I was sad to leave my Mom behind; I liked the three of us as a team. But I wasn't worried, I knew she'd be okay and we'd be home soon.

My Dad owned a 1980 White Oldsmobile Cutlass Supreme. It was a huge car, with hot, sticky light tan leather seats and hot metal seat belts with a silky smooth thick black sewn belt that clicked into place on the side. It was about 80 degrees outside and going to be a hot day. I had just stopped using my big, black, leather baby/child car seat. It held up to 42 pounds. I was about 32-35 pounds (I actually fit in this same car seat until I was 10 years old and 60 pounds, but then my dad removed it from the car. I was very sad about that, but I didn't question my dad at such a young age. I was well-behaved and even rather shy, even at home most of the time and even better behaved and quiet at school.

The seat seemed so big to me and the light tan leather had sewn-in lines in it. It was hot inside the car. My Dad had to turn on the AC. It took a while to cool down the car with the chilly air blowing out the vents. When my dad took off my seatbelt, I had just nervously realized that my Mom and Dad forgot to put my shorts on. I felt funny, embarrassed. I didn't have it quite in me to tell my dad and he didn't seem to notice. We quickly got out of the car and walked in the hot parking lot garage. Then out of the darkness of the smelly garbage lot into the bright, hot sunlight of the sidewalk. My Daddy took my hand tightly and was pulling me along. I went to my dad's thigh at my height, I think I was 37 inches tall to be exact.

I was very self-conscious for a little girl who just turned four years old, looking around the sidewalk at other little girls walking with their Daddy or Mommy and looking closely to see if the other little girls' shorts looked really short, like underpants, like mine. At least with terry cloth being a popular style right now for toddlers and short shorts, I thought maybe nobody will notice. Maybe they will think I am wearing just shorts. I felt very embarrassed that people would see that I left the house in my underwear. My Dad was in a hurry and my Mom who was sick usually dressed me. If you think of a four-year-old you think of a cute little toddler. I even felt too old to pull that off, that I'm four-years-old and cute and dunno any better. I look up at a cute girl, maybe around my age, who is riding on top of her Daddy's shoulders. Man, I wish my Daddy would do that with me. Her shorts also look like short terry cloth shorts, but my main fear and concern now is my pale yellow terry cloth underwear cannot pull off the short shorts look of the early 1980s.

I'm nervous someone will find out. My dad stops walking and looks down at me and talks to me. Oh no! My Daddy asked if I'm in my underwear. I say yes, kinda shy, and then he gets really nervous and pulls my hand back into the dark parking garage and we start walking back to his big white car. Then my dad opens my door and I crawl up on the big, oversized seat and get in the car. He's like, "We got to go home! Oh no, what is your Mom going to say about this?" (he worries). "Why did you leave the house without your shorts? Did you know that? Mommy's going to be surprised. we have to go home now." I felt relieved I was back safe in the car where no one can see my underpants now. If anything, the seat was even hotter and burning my tush and my legs and the leather seat was also so sticky, sticking to my soft skin and the seatbelt was hot metal, too. My dad strapped it around my small and thin waist. Then I'm almost thinking, Mommy is going to be so surprised at this, it's funny. I went out in my underpants in public. I know, I'm relieved, but I'm kinda still nervous, but smile excitedly, this is going to be good and funny. I wonder what my Mommy will say about this.

I was nervous some of the ride home about feeling half naked on the car's hot seat. My dad pulls in the driveway and we quickly walk into the house. My Mom notices right away, saying, "You took her out in her underpants? Well, did anybody notice or say anything? You forgot this"—holding up my red *Looney Tunes* shorts, with the little bright yellow Tweety Bird embroidered in the right bottom corner. "I noticed just after you left." I now quickly put them on myself. They were a little snug, but I felt so much better back in my shorts than being half naked.

This story had been told to me over and over through the years, many times over, so I wouldn't forget it. A family joke, if you will, until I was in my 20s or even 30s and my parents would still laugh about this among themselves. "Remember when you were four you went out in your underpants? Remember when Daddy took you out in your underpants? I see London, I see France, I see Karen's underpants."

I didn't mind, looking back. I was glad it seemed to make my parents happy reminiscing, but at the time, I was quite ashamed of walking down the sunny sidewalk by Sears in just a T-shirt and my pale yellow terry cloth underpants. I'm kinda like the "Ramona Quimby" character from Beverly Cleary's books like I used to read about, but for real, and I didn't read them until I was age eight. I'm only age four here. This was just me being me. It's a good memory to look back on, because if I had worn my shorts to Sears that day, I probably wouldn't have remembered this, because it would have just been a regular, normal day, nothing special to stand out and remember. I'm now glad they forgot to put my shorts on, because it gave my parents such joy over the years

MIRROR OF MY WORLD

looking back at this day when I went out half naked and shortless. Now, in retrospect, everyone was so busy getting on with their day, no one but my Daddy and I noticed. And even if they did, I doubt they would have said anything, because I was with my dad. Oh, dads don't notice little things like this. Kinda still funny now.

Christian Karen Berman

GOOD TIMING, CLOSE TIMING

One day mid-March, later in the afternoon around 4 pm. I was getting ready for my neighbor's niece Susan to come over and play with me. We were going to play with dolls. I had a Fisher Price Jenny doll and she had another kind, but I can't remember which one. I guess it's something little girls just did in the early 1980s, just like that old doll commercial. They were popular in the late 70s to mid-1980s. I was only four years old and she was seven years old, so she was an older friend of mine. I had seen her once before in our neighbor's house. She was eating a bag of banana chips and gave me a few chips. I don't remember her being happy to have to share with me, but her Mom suggested she should. I vaguely remember feeling funny, weird, queasy, about 10-15 minutes before she was due to arrive at my house. I wasn't the best at expressing how I was feeling at such a young age, but I told my Mom I don't feel well and my tummy hurts or feels funny.

She quickly walked me to the downstairs bathroom and I threw up right away in the toilet a few times until I felt better and got rid of the stuff in my stomach making me feel really sick. It must have been something bad I ate, but I can't remember what; my memory here is a bit fuzzy. The next thing I know there is a knock on our front door and who is it but little Susie who was supposed to come over today and play with me. My Mom frankly told the seven-year-old girl I couldn't play dolls with her today, I was sick and just threw up. I had followed my Mommy to the door and peeked out a little and heard what my Mom said. I looked on the porch. To the best of my recollection, Susie was tall, thin, had sandy blonde and light brown hair a few inches past her shoulders, parted in the middle and no bangs. Boy, that was close. If she had come a few minutes earlier I might have thrown up on her. Oh my goodness, I'm glad I threw up before she came, but I still felt a little sick. I

MIRROR OF MY WORLD

guess I was glad to get out of that playdate and have more time with my Mommy trying to get me to feel better.

I can't remember what happened after she left. My Daddy might have still been at work and not home yet, because I don't remember him here. I guess we went back into the bathroom to make sure I was done and then my Mommy put my jammies on, gave me a little Mott's apple juice and put me to bed early in my parent's big bed, but my memory of this event stops after my Mom closes the door and Susie leaves. I'm glad I had such a good Mommy to take care of me, play with me, and read to me. At that age she was my security blanket and my best friend. I loved her more than anybody, but I wish she picked me up more and put me on her lap. She was pregnant around that time so she didn't want to, but she rarely picked me up. My Daddy would pick me up in the upstairs hall to touch the smoke detector, I dunno why, because it was high on the ceiling I guess. I loved my parents so much.

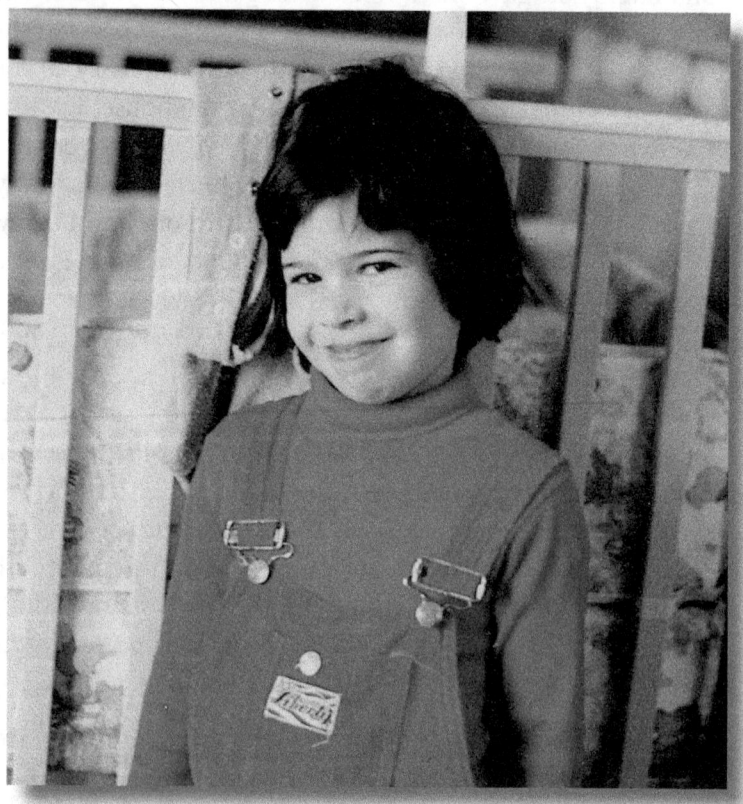

<u>Christian Karen Berman</u>

THE SPLINTER

I think I got the splinter from our wooden porch, but I just remember the part where my Dad was looking at my hand, finger, or palm, I'm not sure. I had just turned four and it was summertime. We were in the kitchen by the stove. He took out a needle from the cabinet and turned on the flame of the stove and was sterilizing the needle. I saw the red, pink glow, how terrifying. I ran into the living room to the couch by where my Mommy was sitting and was on the couch kinda hiding behind her and on her lap. Daddy came in and sat down and asked me to give him my hand. I was too scared and didn't want to. I knew he was trying to help me, but I also knew it would hurt like the shots they give you in the pediatrician's office. He took my hand and I buried my head into my Mom's chest in pain, crying "Ouch!" and I felt it hurting and him digging in my skin to get the little piece of wood out. He finally got it out and I looked. It was pretty big. The skin was a little broken, but I guess my hand/finger felt better. I think he dinged just a little more to make sure he got it all out.

Now, he wanted to put Mercurochrome disinfectant on my finger. He had a little brown bottle of it and there was a dropper. He filled up the dropper and put some interesting red paint stuff on it, but it stung, not fun or happy, but an experience. Be careful not to get any more splinters. My Dad knew just what to do without even calling my doctor or the hospital, how smart for only being a Dad for four years and a mathematics teacher. I didn't really trust him just sorta. I only remembered since I was age three, so I only really knew my parents for only one year. It was nice being age four. I wish I could go back for a long happy visit.

MIRROR OF MY WORLD

THE POOL

I was age four. It was late one hot summer's night in July or August. My Mom was very pregnant with my baby brother, Larry. My Dad took us to the Greenwich Y, an outdoor beach club and swimming pool. I was in the baby pool. It was about 8 pm. It was getting dark and only we were there. I thought that was kinda scary, maybe the air conditioning wasn't working, because we never did stuff like this.

I couldn't swim yet, not until age ten, and I was wearing a red bathing suit with a little red string at the waist with a red heart, so cute. It was worn-in and piled a lot, but I liked it. The water was cool but didn't seem that clean to me, but at age four, I was too small to go into the big pool. I was just about three feet tall, if that much. It was a nice adventure for a baby, but I didn't feel like such a baby.

MIRROR OF MY WORLD

Christian Karen Berman

CASSETTE TAPE OF FOUR-YEAR-OLD ME

This takes place in the early 1980's. It's today's equivalent of a YouTube vlog or podcast. My Daddy was asking a three-and-a-half year old me at this time what I did today. Apparently, my three-year-old friend that lived a few blocks away named June punched me but I didn't cry, I said, but punched her back softly. So interesting hearing a three-year-old me give the play-by-play. I had no idea three-year-old toddler girls duked it out in the early 1980s and I knew all about punching, too. I was the sweetest girl and only punched her back to stop her from punching me anymore. Fascinating. Boxing toddlers. Why didn't her mother Bertha intervene? Then we played ball, then I had to go.

So interesting hearing about the life I had as a three-year-old. I was a very busy, active little girl, always on the go. Also, my Grandpa Jules came over and brought me cookies, as usual—yay, the yummy green-and-pink leaf kind and pretzel-shaped cookie I liked, but he couldn't stay long, and then I said my grandparents had to leave soon, too. Daddy asked if Grandpa was in a bad mood because he said sometimes he is. I guess having diabetes, when his sugar dropped he would be grumpy, but I had no idea a three-year-old would know anything about bad moods. Most people are extra sweet to toddlers, and three-year-olds only knew love and happiness and good moods, as their life is mostly carefree and fun, no worries, and I consider anyone 4 and under a toddler. That's why baby-toddler clothes are called 4T, there's even a 5T, meaning five-year-old toddler. That's old-school guidelines; today I hear anyone over two is not a toddler anymore, maybe because I'm guessing they are more advanced today. I did sound very young for age three. I had sneezed a few times and LOUDLY my Dad exclaimed, "God bless you, my

MIRROR OF MY WORLD

baby," or "my girl." My Mommy also sneezed a few times later on in the tape recording.

Next in the cassette tape I was four and it was July 1st and 2nd. I was talking about what I was eating. Grandpa Jules took me out for pizza. Times haven't changed that much. Then my Daddy said we had just gotten back from the Nevele. I had no real memory of going to the Nevele at age four. Only age three at Brickman's, unless I thought my Brickman's memory was the Nevele. I have no parents to verify this and my baby brother wasn't even born yet, but if this is so, I might have been drinking from a baby bottle until age four. I'm not sure, though. I thought it was only three-and-a-half, but it could have been age four, which would be interesting. I did love my "duke" (milk).

I said I went to the Day Camp. I also have no memory of this. Just turning four years old is so young to be all alone in a hotel Day Camp with mostly older kids. Did my Mom come and stay with me and I just visited for a little while? Probably, or I would've cried, just like at Nursery school. I have no memory at all of this, but I heard it come out of my four-year-old mouth, so it's all true. At the Nevele in the Safari Lounge, they had hors d'oeuvres; I had little cocktail franks, meatballs and little baby knishes. It sounded yummy and an older ten-year-old me has a photo of that, so I remember that quite well, with mustard, too. I drank apple juice and ginger ale. My Dad was always afraid of breaking his camera by accident, which is probably the reason I have no photos of my three and four-year-old summer vacation in a hotel. And also at this time, I remember he had said that he couldn't afford to have his camera fixed because it broke. I guessed we used the money to vacation at the Nevele instead. I think I also heard my maternal Grandma Lee and Grandpa Jules Cohen came with us, maybe shared adjoining rooms and probably also to babysit me, so my parents could spend some time alone. It's the same place where they honeymooned. They always got the same room as they had on their honeymoon, room 612. I always wanted to go back there one last time, I long to. I left a tiny little piece of white paper rolled up in a ball in the corner of the room in between the radiator and

Christian Karen Berman

the wall. Besides wanting to see if it's still there, it was my happy place, a second home for us. My Dad always requested room 612.

I also ate Rice Krispies there and said the food was good and the pool looked dirty. Out of the mouths of babes. My Daddy said no, it didn't, and I said the water was green and the room was green (meaning the thick, plush carpeting) with white walls. Another really interesting thing I confirmed, I had vaguely thought and remembered that at age three I would change my name every week, never liking my real birth name and expressing that at an early age three. I thought I had liked and changed my name to Jennifer. Where did I hear the name Jennifer at age three and knew it was pretty? Daddy did call me Jennifer at age four on the cassette in one taping. In another taping, he called me Stephanie, which technically should have been my real name, because it's tradition in some families to name the first born daughter the girl's version of the father's name; my Daddy's name was Stephen. I still wanted to change my name to Stephanie, liking this name, but had no memory of this from age four. Where did I ever hear that name, unless I watched *Archie Bunker's Place* way back then. It's one of the reasons I still like the name Stephanie today, as in Archie Bunker's little niece who comes to live with them,

Stephanie Mills. Today I also like that name, influenced by Stephanie Tanner of *Full House*, a popular TV sitcom I grew up watching and saw many times over.

What I realized is that little three-year-old is still me, still the same old me, wanting to change my birth name. I had been born Karen Michelle and tried to accept and like my name, but never liked it. It never seemed cool or like me, such a dull, boring name. My good friend Bruce Gold recently told me, with all the "Karen" name-shaming sadly going on, that the name Karen is like the word "caring" and means caring, to help me like it better, and since my loving Grandma Lee and parents named me that out of love, he wanted me to realize that and like it, too. I went through a myriad of names over the years before deciding on the name Christian at 18, which Bruce also said is no name for a Jewish girl. I went through boy names—Marty, Douglas, Dennis—then Punky, Emily, Kay, Kay-Kay, Savannah, Mallory, Connie, Kristen, Amanda, and probably a few more, too, but I can't recall them all right now, though I wish my parents found and gave me another, better name. My Mommy wanted to name me Allison, but my Grandma Lee liked how the initial K looked and thought it would bring me better luck.

Getting back to my tape recording, my Dad introduced my "sisters" to the tape recording (I always wanted a sister; I was promised a sister by my Grandma Lee—"next time it will be a baby sister." Her name would have been Lindsey or Julie. If I was born a baby boy, my parents said my name would have been Kenneth or Kenny.) One of my sister/baby dolls was named Bernadette. How did a four-year-old me learn of such a nice name? The only Bernadette that came to mind was "Peters." I said to my Dad I didn't want to do anymore. He said, "You asked me to record you," so then I said "okay" and started to talk and take over the radio show myself, talking loud into the Mic, a four-year-old podcast host, very impressive for a toddler that was told she wasn't ready for nursery school, four years old going on forty. I have always been a leader and one-of-a-kind and my personal adult assessment of a four-year-old me only proves I am a special, unique one-of-a-kind individual. I don't know of many three and four-year-olds with their own opinion, ready to change their name and be their own person before pre-school. How interesting.

My parents never expected, thought or planned that I would find these tapes a good seven to eight years after they died and enjoy listening to every word as an adult myself, even older than they were when they made the tape recordings. Daddy did these two full cassette tapes in excellent condition, his idea. My Mom had asked when I was only age two, "What are you doing this for?" He said, "For us." I wish my Daddy had boxes of these treasures and did them every week so I could remember and learn more about me, my family, and my life before my real memory began to remember, but money was tight and my Dad was busy all school year, being a teacher, so I guess that's why. I bet they're looking down happily from Heaven and listening, too, and grateful for what my Dad did record. And you know what? It sounds just like yesterday, it's true. (Me smiling now peacefully, happy and content, they were relaxing to listen to and sounded just made.)

MIRROR OF MY WORLD

Christian Karen Berman

LOSING a TOOTH

At age four or five, maybe four-and-three-quarters, I lost my first bottom tooth too early. My Mom and grandparents were worried. My Dad was at school most of the day, so I didn't see much of him back then, unless he wanted me to eat my dinner. My parents didn't take me to the dentist until about age seven. Luckily my teeth were good, but I remember when I woke up in my parents' bed, my Mom was saying, "Let's look under the pillow and see what the tooth fairy left you." She seemed so excited—more so than me. I hoped there was money there so she wouldn't be disappointed. There was a quarter, dime and nickel. I didn't understand the tooth fairy and didn't believe in it, even at four. I wasn't even sure what good the money was for, but better than nothing. I think I accidentally found my tooth lying on the floor once; another reason not to believe.

I was kicked out of nursery school for crying too much and wasn't accepted in the preschool, because they remembered me from nursery, I made such a good impression on them with my lungs at the young age of three. If I had attended school, I might have learned more about the tooth fairy lady my Mom was talking about.

My Grandpa Jules said he hid some money under my bed for my tooth. He was a World War II hero and owned two custom tailor shops, for men's suits. I ran upstairs and pulled my parents' covers off the bed and looked under both pillows. He said it was where I sleep. I ran downstairs and frantically said I looked all over; I can't find it. He said look under the pillow in your bed. That was the last place I'd look. I never slept there. I ran back up, looked, and there was a dollar. That was nice of him. He wanted me to sleep in my own bed. He would come after school and read to me. My

MIRROR OF MY WORLD

Dad told me I hated to sit still and listen to him read. Just before he died, I wanted him to read me *Peter Pan*, but his eyes were bad from diabetes and he couldn't see good.

I'd make grass cakes and dirt in my little toy oven for him. He would play heads and tales with me with a quarter, take walks with me around the block, and tell me school was only five days a week (I thought it was an eternity).

One thing I hated—he would bring me nice toys, even a doll carriage, and then once every few weeks or months, make me pick a toy or stuffed animal cat or dog that he gave me, that I didn't want to give, and donate it to the Salvation Army. I was all of four, my parents were poor, I didn't have many toys, and he said, "If you don't pick, I will," so I was forced to pick one. I was a loving child. To a child, it's a real friend, not a toy. I know he was teaching me to be generous, but it actually made me be selfish to be forced. If it was something I didn't want or need any more it would have been a different story, but I was just a poor baby myself.

My Grandpa Jules did put me on his lap and would swing me under his legs high for fun. When he swung Larry at 18 months under his legs, I felt jealous.

Christian Karen Berman

He never told me about World War II or the old days. I think he thought I was too young and he would scare me. I remember he used to cut my fingernails. He woke me up from a sound nap for Thanksgiving dinner that my Mom and Grandma cooked, that I didn't want to eat. I was tired and would rather have slept. It took years for me to like turkey. I'm still working on that.

The first day of kindergarten and how does my Mom wake up a five-year-old who never attended school yet? She loudly comes into her room where I sleep—I was sound asleep on her side of the bed—singing, "We're in the Army now, we're in the Army now, you gotta get up, you gotta get up, you're in the Army now." She did that a lot when I was age five. I didn't know what the Army meant, but I didn't like getting up for school like that. To full-day kindergarten, no less. I got a full scholarship to Solomon Schechter Day School. When I was interviewed at age four-and-a-half on my first try, I was very bright, could even count to 5 in Spanish and to 20 in English. I knew my alphabet, I can't remember what they asked, but I vaguely remember it and my parents told me they were very impressed with me, plus I was so cute, too cute. Cute with brains, plus a Dad with a Ph.D.

MIRROR OF MY WORLD

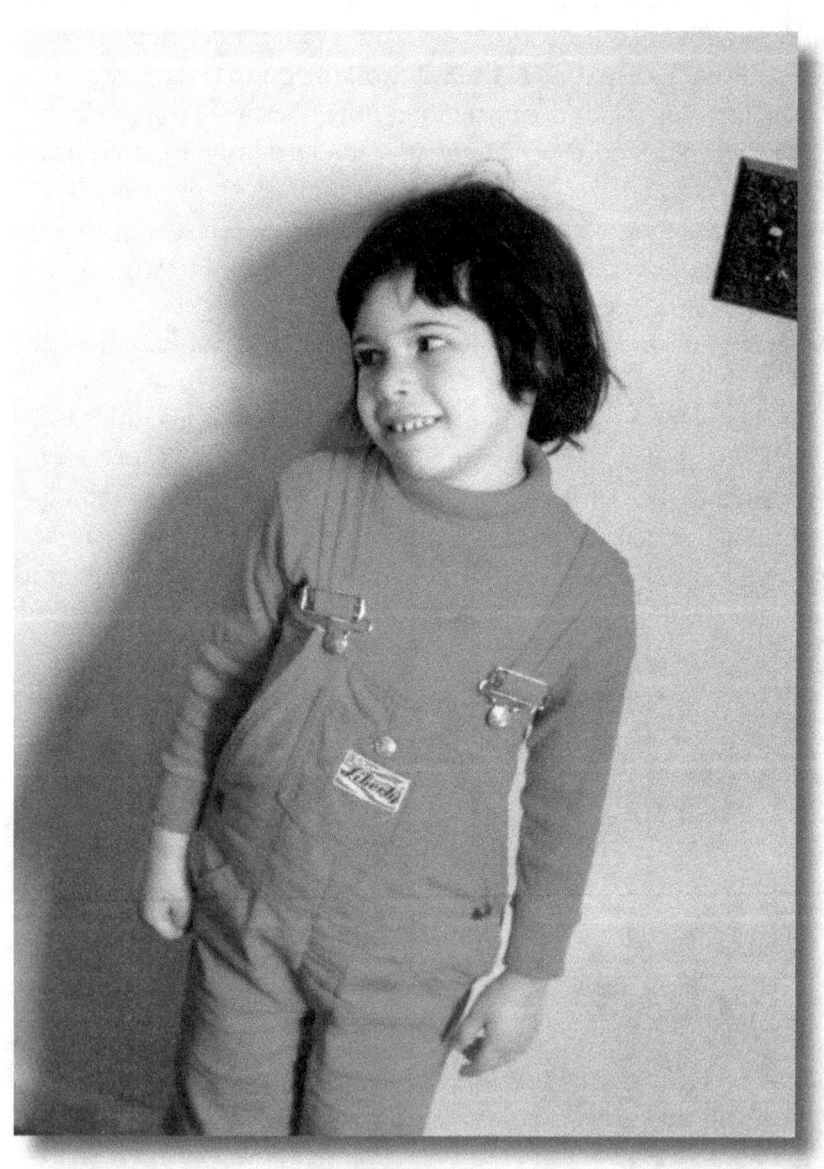

POP GOES THE SOCKET!

When my Daddy took me and my Mom to Sears one warm spring afternoon, my Mommy was looking in the women's section for clothes for herself and 4-year-old me was bored and playing and hiding under the circular women's clothing rack. My Daddy got worried when he didn't know where I was and couldn't find me, then saw me and was kinda mad at me for hiding and playing. He yanked me out so fast, up and outta there, then my arm went dead limp. He pulled it out of its socket, only I didn't know what happened; it happened so fast, I wasn't sure what had happened. My arm felt really weird though, not good at all. I knew something was wrong. My Dad rushed me and my Mom out of the store in a hurry. The next thing I know, my Daddy was being nice and let me sit next to him in the front seat, being extra nice. I knew something was wrong. Luckily my old pediatrician was like five minutes away. He rushed me in there, the office was mostly empty, it musta been after lunch. They took me right into the examining room. The doctor saw me right away and put me on the table and popped my arm right back in. It felt much better after that, so much better, like normal again. I was just bored and playing. I was only 32 pounds. I should have been in a stroller.

MIRROR OF MY WORLD

<u>Christian Karen Berman</u>

THE CAT CAME BACK THE VERY NEXT DAY, THE CAT CAME BACK, SHE JUST COULDN'T STAY AWAY

Age 4. For some reason, I still have no idea why, my Mom made a play date with two girls two blocks down. They were about the ages 9/10 and 12/13. Maybe their Mom missed having a little girl and saw us walking on the way to the playground one day and invited me to come to play anytime I wanted; my Mom was sweet and would say yes. I remember being there and I guess my Mom walked me down to their house to play. Considering my age, it sounds more like babysitting or wanting a baby sister. I remember walking in the kitchen, because I was unhappy and missing my Mom and wanted to go home. I wasn't sure why she left me here, by myself, but I never liked to be left alone or go anywhere without her. Then I noticed Pepperidge Farm Double Chocolate Chip Cookies on the kitchen table and their Dad sitting there eating some. He looked nice, slightly overweight, mid 40s to early 50s, some dark brown hair. I looked at the box. Their Mom offered me one, I accepted it and tried it. As much as I missed my Mom and wanted to go home, I couldn't turn down a delicious chocolate cookie. By the way, don't think they make these anymore. Yeah, I was a real kid, me and cookies. My Mom got the plain chocolate chip, always being conservative. I think I had asked to go home many times and if my Mom was coming to get me in-between bites and nibbles of my yummy chocolate chip cookie. I don't remember them offering me any milk to go with my cookie. I was only four so not sure how elaborate my vocabulary was at the time, but I probably said "I want to go home, when's my Mom coming to pick me up, where's my Mom?"

I don't remember much of playing with the pre-teens, maybe they showed me their dolls and toys, but clearly they were a bit old to be playing with a four-year-old. I felt outta place there and just wanted my Mommy. Finally the two girls took their 10-speed Schwinn bikes and would take me home while I walked in the middle, which turned into running fast ahead, faster than the two girls on their bikes. They said I was fast and to slow down and kinda giggled in awe of cute little charismatic me. Hey, I wasn't showing off, I missed my Mom and I had to get home and see her, I didn't like to be apart from her. I'm not sure why I was in such a hurry to get home, it's not even that I didn't feel safe with the two girls (too young to have ever heard of kidnappings on the news, yet to learn about stranger danger; though I did have my instincts, mostly I felt funny away from my Mommy). I just really missed my Mommy. They might have been 11-14 for all I know, but it's hard to judge anyone's age at age four; everyone seems so much older than you. I was also in great shape for a four year old. Must be all those long walks to the park my Mom would take me on, almost every day, a mile there and back, I'd say. It seemed to be April, kinda cool and dreary, but warm enough for the girls to wear shorts and T-shirts.

I was happy when I started to get close to the dead end and be able to see my house. I was getting excited to see my Mom. I ran ahead and quickly down our driveway and then up the one cement stair into the pathway and opened the storm porch door, the girls trailing behind me waiting outside to make sure I got home safe and sound. I climbed up on the front door step and slowly opened the big heavy white wooden front door myself and peeked in, I don't believe I knocked or that the door was locked. My Mom then got up from the couch looking tired and was surprised to see me back so soon and wondered what happened. The girls might have said hi to her and that I missed her and wanted to come home and they left. They seemed like nice girls. Maybe if I was a few years older we could have been real friends. I think my Mommy was taking a short nap while I was gone. She needed a good rest. I was just so happy to be home and back with my Mommy. I think my baby brother was napping and my Daddy was still at work. It seemed around 4 pm on a weekday.

Christian Karen Berman

Let's Give This Kindergarten Thing a Second Try...

I can remember my Mom walking me 1.4 miles away to my second Kindergarten on my first day of class in late September or early to mid-October. We walked past my friend June's house. She was a pale-skinned, pink-cheeked, very white blonde-haired girl, with thin fine shoulder-length hair and thin, my age. Then past our accountant's house at the time, past many neighborhood houses on the street that I didn't know, down and up hills to get to our final destination, my first day at my second school.

The first Kindergarten was a full day. I was so bright I earned a scholarship to private school after a long interview at age 4-3/4's. A bunch of the heads and teachers, two to three women, maybe one man, asked me a bunch of questions. I don't quite remember what, but probably how to recite the alphabet and count to 20, which I was doing verbatim since age two. By now I could count to cinco by heart in Spanish/Espanol. I was also a cutie and sweetheart and no doubt I impressed them and won them over. But a couple months in, I threw away my chance and a golden, once-in-a-lifetime opportunity to start off from the top of the ladder, but I gave it away because I missed my Mommy so much and needed to be with her and was working my way down the ladder. It was too long a day from 7:30 am to 4 pm to be away from my Mom, who I loved so much. I had just turned five and I hadn't even learned to sleep in my own bed yet. It was too much pressure to be in such a structured environment all day with a bunch of strangers I didn't know. This is where the separation anxiety and autism comes in. As smart as I was, I couldn't relate and make friends easily with the kids my age, nor did I have the interest to. It was fun stuff. I did not like nap or the homesickness I felt for my mother all day, longing and lonely for her We spent every minute together. We were very close at age five; it hurt and was hard to be apart from her and went against my grain.

When my Daddy had signed me up for this public school Kindergarten, it was because we lived closest to it and it was free. The main office there had told him that he could wait another year for me to go to Kindergarten. He could legally hold me back until I was age six, like maybe I'd be more mature, prepared and ready to start then, able to handle being a Kindergartner better and understand more, but he signed me up right away. As a Ph.D. in education and as a teacher and parent, he did not want to waste a year of my life and have me fall behind the other kids my age. When I first heard this I must have been in my early 20s. I so wished I had another year to be a toddler and stay home and go to the park and play with my Mom, little brother Larry, and my Grandpa Jules, lots of free time, no schedule, to come and go as Mommy says. Right now as I write this as a 40-something-year-old, I realize my father was correct. Life is short, don't waste it standing still, move forward, not backward, but still to have one more whole year as a baby with my Mom to play, no worries of anything, school, waking up early, going when I didn't feel well, just trouble fitting in and having to learn to be a real person, a little adult student—it's hard to pass up a free year frozen in time without a care in the world. Maybe ditching school another year sounds like a precious gift. Well, can't change my mind now. That's long over, my teachers and parents long gone, but it was sure a treasure to pass up. Maybe I woulda got sick of staying home and liked school better, or got into an unhealthy rut, but back then my parents were healthy, so how can you think like that? And I was smart and deserved another chance in Kindergarten to succeed.

The first thing I remember is when there was recess on this tremendous playground and this scary humongous metal slide where there was a large gaping space between the ladder and the slide part. I saw the other kids do this, kinda climb over or swing over it and they were my age and could do it, but I was so afraid to, but tried not to let on, worried I'd fall through and hurt myself. Well, more worried about falling. I was never seriously hurt, so I didn't put much thought into the consequences of my actions until I was in my mid-20s, which is just right about when they say your brain is fully developed. I was small and thin and made it through in one piece. If I had slipped through, only being 39 pounds and nine feet off the ground, I probably woulda been okay. I can't remember what I was wearing that day, my light blue frilly dress, my green overalls and a yellow turtleneck which I sometimes wore, or what. My Mom left me there and would walk back to pick me up in a few hours. I was in the afternoon class. I can't remember if she stayed with me that day. Maybe yes. I was sure clingy to her at that age, so much so she had to sit next to me in Sunday school at age five and they let her stay so I would stay, and I was the only five-year-old with my Mommy sitting right next to me. I guess she was my aide and my security blanket, of course.

I met Eileen in my second Kindergarten class. The first memory of her was in art class in Kindergarten. I believe we had to draw a steamboat for Ms. Pierce, my teacher. She loved me; I was one of her favorite students and this was her very last year teaching before retirement. I liked her so much, too; she was probably in her late 70s when she retired. Well, Eileen was a sweet, beautiful Asian girl and she drew as well as any adult artist, to my surprise, and me having trouble drawing and it looked like a five-year-old drew this. She tried to draw part of it for me and teach me how to draw it, coloring in the tiny little squares with different color markers. I tried to copy her lead, but it wasn't nearly as well drawn as hers. I'm not sure if the teacher noticed, but she didn't seem to mind.

One day on the school bus just before my stop, I asked Eileen to get off the school bus at my bus stop, too. I'm not sure if I asked her if she wanted to go to my house or said why don't you come to my house to play, it'll be okay with my Mom. My spur of the moment idea. I did not ask my Mother. So unlike me and out of character, so spontaneously, to think of something to do, so social myself. Not shy, very outgoing and assertive, I wanted her to come home with me. I must have liked her an awful lot. It was something I can't ever remember doing before or after on my own accord. I knew my Mommy would be surprised. I wanted to surprise my Mom. Did I wonder if Eileen's Mom would be worried or mad at

MIRROR OF MY WORLD

one of us? I kinda knew at five I probably shouldn't be doing this without permission, but I guess my desire to live it up a little and be happy came before my common sense and following the rules. It was like I hope she says yes or I'll kind of convince her to come. For some reason, I didn't want to take no for an answer. Luckily she was pretty easy to convince and was happy to follow my lead. I'm not sure who was older, but she was a little taller than me and more mature. I remember us walking home the two half-blocks alone to my house. Ha-ha, couldn't wait to see how my Mommy would react. What would she say? She met us by our driveway and said she was going to call Eileen's Mom and tell her I invited her over for a playdate. This was usually my quiet, relaxing time; I'd watch reruns of *The Magic Garden* on **PBS** or play with my Mom and toys, or go wait outside for my Grandpa Jules and Grandma Lee to come visit after work and give me cookies and candy and play with me and take me on a walk around the neighborhood, which he didn't that day.

It's so easy to make friends as a little kid. All you need to do is find a kid you like and say, "Do you want to be my friend?" and just start playing together and be instant friends and start talking about anything and everything you want. Only one rule—be nice and be a real friend, which sounds fair and easy enough, that is, if the kid is a nice kid. In the adult world, there are so many unwritten rules that you must follow, it makes it impossible for even the nicest compatible people who are not on the autistic spectrum to be real friends. Age, marital status, kids, job, income, race, house, car, appearance, weight, style, how you dress, how you act, how you treat other people, places you like to go, do you have pets, do you like animals, similar hobbies and interests? Are you selfish? Greedy? The list can go on and on to infinity, my lord. Kids, even if they're not the same race, age, interests, they are so sweet and innocent. They are honest, though, but not judgmental until their parents teach them to be so critical of others, then they are usually the not nice and accepting kids. We ruin them and their natural kind and thoughtful generous instincts, and usually at a very young age. Sometimes we don't even have to teach them rudeness and hate; they are sponges and follow our lead. That is sad to be closed-minded and where the problems of the world start—to leave people out, bully, teach them who is good and good enough and the right people. It might be too late for the adults to think differently after being set in their ways so many decades, but to put this on loving innocent beings makes it sad for them and the rest of us. Let them love fully with open hearts and leave unkind critical judgments out. Everyone should be equal, no one's better than you. That's why by the time most kids are teenagers, they got problems.

I guess we watched my favorite TV show in my parents' bedroom (we only had the one big wooden TV set from the 1970s), or I showed her all my toys, dolls, and my bedroom, maybe gave her the grand tour of the house, but my memory cuts out here and feels blank. I can't quite remember this part, but what I do remember is this must have been a bit of a special occasion, plus we needed a bigger table to eat at. We all ate in the dining room, my parents and me and Eileen; I guess my one-year-old baby brother was there, too, in his high chair. My Mom served us her famous tuna fish and egg salad with onions, celery, and mayonnaise and onion powder and paprika all mixed up together as tuna fish salad and Saltines crackers, possibly a little red potato, or veggie, don't remember this either, because I didn't eat much. Well, everyone was eating but me. I was just licking it, licking the tuna salad off the Saltines and picking at it. My Dad confided in this little five-year-old Asian girl like she was one of his teenage students or an adult, kinda whispering down to her and sharing a secret, like explaining me to her, that I don't like to eat much or I'm a picky eater. He asked why didn't I eat the crackers, too. I said, "Only lick it off the crackers, not eat it plain. I like to lick the salt off of it." That meant the food was too bland as usual. Eileen nodded her head and understood. My Dad always kinda spoke to the few friends I had like they were older than me. Well, I guess they were in many ways, plus they always seem older when they are not your own I heard that by June Cleaver, I believe, on the TV show *Leave it to Beaver*. It's true.

Soon after, my Dad called Eileen's Mom to come to pick her up. She got to stay over for dinner. I had fun breaking the rules. I

MIRROR OF MY WORLD

was kinda sad she couldn't stay longer, but by now it was after 6 pm and getting late and she had to go home to her Mommy and Daddy. I gave up my quiet alone time for this. A fun, interesting memory.

As long as we're not hurting anyone, we should all break the rules sometimes and be spontaneous and live it up a little. Life is short and these fun little things you wish to do, but usually don't, sometimes mean the most in our lives. Skip school, skip work, go on a unplanned trip, reach out to an old friend you haven't talked to in years, try a new restaurant, buy that expensive, frivolous toy you've been wanting, just to make yourself a little happy.

Silly, little fun things like that make the hard, sad days worth living. But always be kind and caring and respectful to everybody and help where you can (my good friend Bruce Gold taught me this last sentence and many other things that I am still learning and applying to my life to help me have a better life).

AGE 5-6

My Dad used to say I refused to get on the bus at full-day kindergarten at the private Jewish school Solomon Schechter. I earned a scholarship for being so bright. I don't remember that, just that if my Mom came and stayed with me all day like she did in Sunday school, I think I could have survived the 8 am-4 pm day. I couldn't even attend nursery school without having a major meltdown. I remember when I was first starting there, you had to bring a blanket to nap on. My Mom brought my yellow Winnie the Pooh baby blanket with satin trim and a plastic smock for painting, and an extra pair of underpants just in case. We kept it all in our wooden cubby. One crisp autumn day, the teacher was stirring three big pots of mashed sweet potato, mashed yams, and mashed butternut squash. It smelt good and I was looking forward to trying it. She came around and gave everyone a sample on a paper plate. I said I didn't want any, I'm not sure why, maybe I felt nervous to try it, but she gave me a cup of fruit punch. I always wished I had tried it.

Another time in school we did this art project with Honeycomb cereal. Some kids said it was edible, but never being in a real supermarket I wasn't sure, so I was just gluing it to my paper. We did a lot of art in kindergarten. We stepped in big finger-paint tins, we had to take our socks and shoes off and be in our bare feet. We put both hands in one tin, they were green, blue and red. Then we put it on a big roll of white paper. Another time we made these mobiles out of colored construction paper. The teacher put glue on them and sprinkled glitter all over it to make it magical and pretty.

MIRROR OF MY WORLD

Christian Karen Berman

Nap Time

I didn't like nap time. You had to lie on a hard floor with the rest of the class. I once actually fell asleep. I woke up feeling so groggy and disoriented. All the other kids were in different groups doing other things. I just walked up to the teacher being the last one up. Did anyone actually sleep besides me? They let me sleep. I didn't feel good after my nap; I just wanted to go home. I was told by my Dad there was a teacher I liked that left early, and I wanted to leave early and go home, too. Years later she apologized to my Mom in the Kosher store, that she had to pick up her daughter from school and she's sorry I dropped out. Yes, I was a kindergarten drop-out.

I didn't make it far in that school, it was such a long day for a five-year-old. Sadly, my arts and crafts projects, my baby blanket and other stuff was left behind in my cubby. I always felt bad about that. It was not a planned move, so maybe my parents felt bad about the whole thing; that's why they never went back to retrieve my belongings.

My Dad enrolled me in half-day afternoon kindergarten in the local public school. They had told him I could wait another year until I was ready. I had just turned five a few months before. Sometimes I wonder if I would have done better in school if I waited a year. He thought it was about time I start school. Having a Ph.D. in education, he loved school. I just loved being with my Mommy at that age. I would have loved another year just spending quality time with my Mommy, walking to the local playground and sharing a tuna salad on a poppy seed roll, pretzel or cheddar Goldfish, and a bottle of Veryfine Apple Juice.

At age five, I always use to be waiting for my Grandpa Jules to come over after kindergarten. I would sit out by the flowers, when I wasn't digging for live worms or pretending it was a sandbox. One day I was inside and lost track of time, distracted with something else. I heard my Grandpa in the driveway and ran out the door as fast as I could so he'd know I was waiting for him, I loved him so much. I pushed open our first big, thick, heavy wooden door, then ran through the walk-in porch and pushed the big glass storm door and broke it. I think I was too small to reach the door handle to open the door, so I just pushed hard on the glass. It must have been old and brittle. It had a big spiderweb crack in the middle. I was scared. My Daddy was at work; he would be mad if I broke our glass door.

I ran down the sand-colored cement pathway and my Grandpa came running to me to look and see if I was okay. He must have seen what happened. It happened so fast, he wasn't worried about the door, but he wanted to look me over and see if the glass cut me anywhere. My hands were cut and bleeding. I just about ran through a heavy glass door hands first.

I was panicked, not worried about myself, of course. I kept telling Grandpa, look what I did, I broke the glass door, my Dad will be mad at me. I was more frantic that our glass door was hurt than my cut-up bleeding palms. Some of the glass shattered instantly upon contact with a 40-pound, 40-inch, five-year-old little girl. He checked there was no glass in my hand. He took me to wash my hands in the bathroom sink under cold water, maybe put on a Band-Aid.

I was still upset, but now about my hands, it was very traumatic what happened to me. He had bought a bag of mini-chocolate and vanilla ice cream cups to surprise me. He gave me one to eat in the backyard on a lawn chair with a wooden stick. My blood sugar must have been low after all that happened. It was yummy.

He always bought me assorted green and pink leaf-shaped butter cookies from the bakery, or my Grandma Lee would bring me chocolates, like nonpareils. It must have been Friday, that's when they usually brought me sweets.

My Dad came home from work soon after. He wasn't upset at all. It was an accident; I never did anything like this before. He wasn't happy, but picked up the broken glass and took down the whole door to have it replaced. I remember he wanted me to go with him to pick up the door when it was finished. I did. The guy recommended a plastic storm door this time, because my parents had young children and he didn't want something like this to happen again. The guy there said, "Is this the one who did it?", meaning me. My Dad nodded and said yes. Oh, he's heard about me. I went everywhere with my Daddy then, even to fix my mistake. We still have the same storm door my Dad replaced. It held up well during all our hurricanes and blizzards. I think we got our money's worth.

MIRROR OF MY WORLD

Christian Karen Berman

A CHILD'S GUT INSTINCT

The bus came. I remember getting on it and being the only child on the whole school bus, which was odd and that never happened before, and it felt weird. I'm surprised my Mom trusted the male bus driver and let me get on with him. I remember sitting in one of the back rows, all alone on the big, long yellow school bus. I was only about 40 inches and 40 pounds. I felt scared being the only girl on the bus with a male driver. I'm guessing he looked 40s and I think he was Spanish. I never learned or knew about Stranger Danger yet or kidnappings, no one taught me yet, in spite of Etan Patz and Adam Walsh. But intuitively, I wondered if I would really make it safely to school and off the bus. Maybe I instinctively read his mind, that's the only way I can explain how I would know this and feel intimidated and helpless. I didn't know what would happen, but since there were no other kids on the bus, I felt very vulnerable, like a sitting duck, so to speak. I mean, just because there is only one small girl, doesn't mean he shouldn't do his job right. Did not think this way then. I felt he might not go to school, but keep driving and take me with him and didn't think there was anything I could do about it, no time to think of a plan, but I felt intimidated, but dunno why. Thankfully, whether I was right or wrong, he did the right thing and dropped me off in the circle in front of my elementary school. I felt relieved.

By the end of the day, it was over and forgotten and no need to tell my parents, because nothing happened. But I did strongly feel something was unsafe, being the only five-year-old on a big empty school bus, with only one man driver. I do still remember that feeling, like something bad could happen and something feels wrong, but I guess it was just strange to be the only child on the bus. Or maybe he thought it wasn't worth the bad consequences so he did the right thing, maybe the few (I can't remember how many) other little kids were out sick. Either way, I'm so glad nothing bad

MIRROR OF MY WORLD

happened that day, because no one ever taught me to scream, kick and resist, like if you were getting kidnapped. My Grandma Lee taught me at age seven to scream when I was out sick with chicken pox and had 102 fever, but was bored of staying in the house all day and wanted to play in the indoor porch. Luckily nothing happened and it never came to that, but she must have read the newspaper or watched the news, because she knows. I guess my parents didn't want to scare me. Feeling great empathy for all of those little kids who never go home and have a life and have the chance to grow up into their own unique person and give such happiness to their parents, because they weren't as lucky as me and never made it back home to their Mommy and Daddy... I do watch the news and feel for them and honestly dunno why I was thinking like that, that day, but being so little and loving my Mommy, you got to be extra careful, even in the 1980s. It wasn't a perfectly safe world, but I dunno how I knew that. This was just something I sensed. I could have been 100% wrong, but coming from only love, it was out of character for me to be thinking like this. Nothing at all happened, though, and it was only a few minute ride, but my young, little mind went there.

Christian Karen Berman

KINDERGARTEN: THE OTHER HALF OF THE SCHOOL YEAR AS IT HAPPENS

THANKSGIVING

I remember in Kindergarten, before or after Thanksgiving break, not sure which one exactly, the teacher saved and pulled out a wishbone from a real turkey and explained she would pick two kids out of the whole class to tug on the wishbone and the one who got the bigger piece of the bone their wish would really be granted. I so hoped she would choose me. As a kid, having not only an adult tell you this, let alone a teacher, of course no doubt you would believe it's true without question, just as the tooth fairy and Santa Claus are real. I stood out, I didn't really believe in either at a young age. I was smarter than your average five-year-old. I do feel I missed out on the magic, though, but this I one-hundred percent believed was true. I was so hurt, sad and mad I wasn't picked, so my wish wouldn't come true. For a while I was mad about this. What would I have wished for? I had most everything I needed. Maybe a new doll, or toy, a swing set, a baby sister. I don't think I thought that far ahead, just that I missed a chance for anything I wanted to come true. I'm not sure how long I felt bad about this—a few days, weeks, months, years—but enough to still remember it. When a teacher tells you something, you tend to believe it and not question her, especially at only five years old and I don't remember telling my parents about this either, but to be fair, I wasn't a very chatty chatterbox of a five-year-old.

I do remember my Grandpa Jules waking me up from a deep, sound sleep on the couch on Thanksgiving evening just before 5 pm to come eat turkey with my parents, Grandma Lee, and my baby brother who didn't eat solids yet. I was very tired, kind of annoyed and not hungry, even though my blood sugar had that low feeling I've come to know better over the years. I did not like the tasteless, bland, possibly chewy bird. Generally speaking, my family wasn't good cooks.

CHRISTMAS

Our school principal, Mr. Owen, dressed up as Santa Claus and came into our class. We were waiting for Santa and excited for him to come. I think we all knew, or maybe it was just me. Growing up as a little Jewish girl, I wasn't really taught about Santa Claus, but my parents didn't discourage me from knowing about him from TV and watching shows about him. Mr. Owen was about 5'11" and 210 pounds. He was in late 60s with short white, grey, and blonde hair. He sat on a chair in front of the class and we all got in a line, maybe shortest to tallest, like they did during fire drills, and each one of us sat on his lap to my best recollection and he gave us each a small, thin book like a little square. It was the classic, *'Twas The Night Before Christmas*. He asked us what we want for Christmas first and then gave us a candy cane, too. Christmas was always such a happy time, when everyone's a little nicer and closer and the world as a whole seems more tender and loving. It's cold outside, warm and loving inside.

DO we Have a Sickie?

One afternoon I remember waking up in my parents' big bed (which was in fact a double twin bed, just to keep it honest) after my nap. My Mom was sitting by the lamp on the night table near the window, the sun shining through the dim room's white curtains, no lights on now on my Daddy's side of the bed. I was closer to the door by the hall and the bathroom, on my Mommy's usual side of the bed. I had my afternoon Kindergarten class coming up soon at around 12:30 pm. For some reason, my Mom could tell I wasn't feeling well, maybe because I didn't take naps much anymore, or I felt warm and looked sickly. I had already missed a lot of school being sick and it was a bright sunny afternoon day. My day wasn't all that long. I told her I wanted to go. I honestly can't remember for sure if I went or not, but I think I did.

BUS STOP

I remember my Mom would walk me down the long block, up a hill and down again and we would sit at the curb by someone's driveway and she would bring along a Care Bears book with me and read me a few pages while we waited for my bus to come. She had the time then and wanted to instill the fun of reading and quality time, I guess. Well, you know what, that didn't really work. At night she was too tired and rushed after giving my baby brother Larry and then me a bath after a long, full day. So now was the perfect opportunity for a short, but sweet, story time. I think I liked it, but when she started to read, she didn't get too far, because the bus always came. Moms.

I GOT BIT HARD

I'm age five-and-a-half, running up to our neighbor Dell's medium fifty-pound black dog Pepper. He was alone, by himself, on our front lawn and it was hot. He jumped and snapped at me and bit my hand. Broke the skin, but no blood. My Grandpa Jules picked me up quick and carried me into the house to the downstairs bathroom to wash my hands quick under the cold water. It hurt a lot and was scary. I didn't know if I was hurt badly. I wasn't, just shaken up and scared. He never did that before. I was afraid of dogs for a while after this.

MIRROR OF MY WORLD

Christian Karen Berman

FLOWERS FOR MY MOTHER

The school had sent home permission slips to our parents, if they wanted to give us a few dollars to buy flowers from the nursery that would come to our school and plant themselves in the front yard of our elementary school (pun works out well here). My Mom must have given me a few dollars and I remember her telling me to buy marigolds. I saw pretty other flowers, but I listened to my Mother and bought the flowers she wanted. They were kinda yellow, orange, gold colored, like dandelions, much later in my life, like the teenage years. She liked pink and purple pansies, but for years in school, every year it was those same marigolds. Don't get me wrong, there's nothing wrong with those flowers. They now remind me of my Mother, but dunno why she chose those. Nice people do tend to like the color yellow—it's bright and happy. Well, I also loved surprising my Mommy, like the only reason I started art in school was so that I would have a tangible present to bring home to my Mom to make her happy.

I looked forward to surprising her with my little goodies from school, paintings and drawings, even school work, but not so much. If you played house with the other kids and played with the kitchen, you would have nothing to take home to your Mommy. My Dad was always busy at school and I don't remember him in the picture much, until dinner time when he wanted me to eat my dinner. Yes, I was one of those picky kids that didn't like some foods and wasn't hungry and hard to get to eat. Being so small my tummy was small and didn't get hungry as much. Plus, no offense to my parents, but they weren't the best cooks, except for my Mom's homemade cookies and muffins that only happened once in a blue moon on a snow day and my Daddy's special Psskettie, Skettie.

I saw this beautiful cherry blossom tree, but I didn't know the name back then. It was a big tree that smelt like pretty perfume and had pink and purple flowers all over it and all over the ground, too. The best, prettiest tree I ever saw since then, these trees have always been one of my favorites. I picked one of the best in one piece off the grass to give to my Mother. She would really love it, it would make her so happy. I really loved my mother. I thought it was okay, because it had already fallen off and was just sitting on the ground with hundreds of others. I brought it back to my class with me, like my friend. I didn't want to let it out of my hands to keep it safe, from being taken, or thrown out. I even took it off the table I was sitting at. I believe I was going to wash my hands at the sink. Then these two boys said that they would watch my flower for me and to please let them watch it and they would take good care of that and convinced a five-year-old me to trust them with MY FLOWER, FOR MY MOMMY. I wanted to trust them, so to be nice to them, I brought it back to the table and as fast as they both could, they ripped the most beautiful flower to my mother into shreds and killed it. Poor little flower for my Mommy...

I got mad and made a mad face at them, maybe squinted my eyes at them and shook my head no a few times, folding my arms together. But I didn't let them know how hurt I was inside. I didn't let my feelings show, not that they would care. They wanted to get a rise outta me, is why they did this. They laughed and thought it was funny, even. Can you believe how mean and cruel some little kids are? I didn't even trust the teacher to tell her about it. No one knew what had happened but us three. Is there some kind of unspoken rule—don't trust the teacher, authority figures— because I never really did. It was kids against adults, you couldn't trust anyone. No one would really hurt you back then. Kids might exclude you, say bad things about you, teachers might be mean and not let you go to the nurse, but besides being emotionally hurt, back in the 1980s, you never would really get seriously hurt at school. I was so sad. I couldn't get another flower. I couldn't give this one to my Mom. It was torn up and hurt into little pieces and I had to throw it out in the trash.

I never ever told my Mom. I wish I did. She might have known more of how much I love her. Why tell? I couldn't give her the flower. I didn't want to make my sweet mommy sad. Didn't want

her to know I had trouble at school. My teacher was nice and I really liked her; wish I told her, maybe she would have gotten me another flower to give to my Mom. Public school and bullies teach you to put on a tough front. Sad we all have to, because the world is so mean. You learn young in public school to not let the little things get to you and to have a somewhat "thick skin," but underneath, I still clearly remember all the little and big hurts done to me, what was said or stolen, so it mattered. It's hard growing up in a world where having a thick skin and tough exterior is needed to survive. I could have cried and gotten them in trouble and ran to the teacher, but I was stronger than I thought and let it slide. I wasn't a little sissy, as they would say back in the day. I was a tough kid, with a little, sad, broken heart.

   I have thought about this event often in my life—not what was done to me, that I was manipulated and tricked by kids my age, but that I never got to give my Mother that sweet little flower,

MIRROR OF MY WORLD

meant just for her. She had a garden, too. She loved roses, tulips, irises and we had this small white umbrella looking like a flower bush, with soft fur inside. I loved our yard. My Mother would've known how much I loved her and she would have felt happy. That is what bothers me the most. Why were the boys so mean? Unhappy home life, or that's how most boys are? Maybe they weren't loved enough. I don't really care. They hurt me. They wanted to, and that's what they cared about. Would it have changed anything with me and my Mother? Larry was becoming her favorite, or so I thought. I guess she knew I loved her. I hope so, but I wish this event never happened. To learn to have to wear a tough front at age five, especially if you're just a little girl... man, life is tough.

Christian Karen Berman

LaST MeMORieS OF GRaDe K

Two or three firemen dressed as firemen came and gave a talk to our Kindergarten class about fire and "Stop, Drop and Roll" and gave everyone in the whole class a little red plastic fireman's hat. I loved that. Not sure if we got a coloring book or page or not. I can't remember if we got to go outside and look at a real fire truck. Maybe, not sure. I do remember getting excited over having my own fire hat I got for free. I think I needed more toys in my life back then.

Easter. My teacher colored hard-boiled eggs for all of us kids. A black girl in my class named Asia had such short fingernails, too short, I noticed at such a young age, too. Graham crackers and apple juice for snack. Me, telling wishful thinking to my Mom that my teacher picks me up and puts me on her lap. I guess I liked her and wanted her, too, or needed more physical affection at home.

I sadly don't remember much hugging or being picked up much as a child. Me, talking with this little black boy at my table before class was dismissed about something I forget, maybe going over each other's houses and my teacher listening to us talk and smiling at us and marveling in our sweet conversation, I could just tell that at age five. The thing is, most adults, teachers, parents, think five-year-olds don't know or understand much, won't remember much, aren't real people like them, because that's how we're often treated, like babies that dunno much. Big surprise for all of you adults and parents out there, little picture has Big Eyes and Ears. Even kids that aren't as bright, we all understand so much more than you think, maybe more than adults do, so please treat even the youngers babies like real people, because we are. We're not dolls or anything, you know.

The last day of school, my Grandpa Jules went with my Mom to the Parent/Teacher meetings with Ms. Pierce. He was so proud because she only had the most glowing praise for me, more than he expected for a little girl who didn't like going to school or reading. I guess my Daddy was working and couldn't come. I'm sure my Mom was so proud to ask her Daddy and that he came and heard so many wonderful things about his granddaughter. Unfortunately, he died two months later. He lost out and I lost out and my Grandma Lee and Mom were broken-hearted for many years after that. They never quite recovered. As young as I was when he died, he spent a lot of time with me and loved me a lot and I have many memories of him, even though he did treat me as a little adult often, and gave me tough love—that I sometimes didn't like as much—but he was a soldier in the War, as Edith Bunker would say, "World War II, The Big One."

It didn't affect me as much as I would have thought. I don't think I understood what happened, but he was in a happy place like a big playground in the sky, with lots of candy and ice cream as my Grandma had implied to me. I was too young to really understand all this and know how to react and I didn't want to upset my Grandma and Mom any more than they already were. My Dad said since I didn't seem too upset, they thought getting me therapy would just upset me more. There was so much going on the summer I turned six. They wouldn't let me look inside the casket like I wanted to.

Then first grade started. Long story short, I dunno why I wasn't more upset and crying for my Grandpa. Guess I knew he wasn't coming back. I do clearly remember touching my heart often after he died, to check if it was still beating or it would stop like my Grandpa's heart and not wanting my family to cry over me at my funeral if I died. I thought that at age 8, still remember feeling someone was watching me and performing for them, showing off when no one was there. On-stage syndrome. Did I think someone from the outside was peeking in my windows? Maybe yes. I also thought that Tootie and the girls from *The Facts of Life* could see and hear me as well through the TV set in my bedroom at about age seven, so I had a big imagination and not a firm grasp on reality in a good way. I could be friends with my favorite characters—He-Man, Skeletor, the cast of *Today's Special* and *The Little Prince* cartoon, too. I tried not to lose my imagination, because in reality, you need imagination to be happy and invent things and make dreams come true.

Also, my Mom thought that losing my Grandpa is why I had such trouble in school, trouble with academics and making friends, socializing, understanding things better. I did regress and wear my size 3T toddler clothes to the first grade and my teacher said let her wear whatever she wants as long as she comes to school. I lost a few pounds too. I never really wanted to grow up, it just wasn't me. I was having too much fun just being a cute little kid.

MIRROR OF MY WORLD

Christian Karen Berman

MY Cabbage Patch STORY

To my best recollection, it was around Hanukkah time. I was too young to know much about the Cabbage Patch Kid doll craze back then. I must have been around age five or six. I didn't know parents were waiting in line and going from toy store to toy store and beating up other parents and jumping counters just to grab even a bald boy doll. I think my parents knew other kids were getting them and saw it on the news or in the Sears Wish Book (by the way, the Sears Wish Book, if you didn't know, is every kid's bible and favorite book that they look at and carry it around since it comes in September; by Christmas, it's all marked up, circled, slightly ripped or pages folded and torn out. They usually need a new one by the time Halloween comes around, especially if you have many kids. I dunno how ours lasted a year, but they had kids clothes in it, too, and there was birthdays, so it was the most used book by me in the house. I'm sure every 80s kid and every generation of the Sears Wish Book understands—it showed the newest and most popular dolls, toys, sleeping blankets, and tents, and it was a must have in childhood, where all your hopes and dreams might come true, and a time when your parents could still afford to buy your love, not that they needed to, but most could.

I think a few girls in my class might have had a Cabbage Patch Kid. I didn't ask for one, barely asked for anything back then, I was not a spoiled child whatsoever. If my parents bought me something, it was loved, played with, appreciated until it almost disintegrated, or well-loved. Not like today's kids that get bored with a toy in fifteen minutes and want a new toy to play with. I think my parents had just got me one that day and couldn't wait another minute to give it to me. They told me to sit on the couch and that they had a surprise for me and were going to give it to me now, I guess as an early Hanukkah present. I was nervous, excited. I didn't know what they got, I think I knew it was a doll. My

MIRROR OF MY WORLD

Mom was sitting on the right side of me on the old tan orangey couch and my Daddy brought over a bag and a box. I took the box and looked at it. I looked at it a little closer and closer. I think they wanted to open it or help me open it and I gave them a sad, disappointed look, "It looks weird, it looks different. This doesn't look like a Cabbage Patch Kid." I think some of the more affluent, richer kids in my class like Vicki already had one so I knew what they looked like and showed my Mom. She said, it looks like you got a copy, not the real thing, a cheap copy. It was in a small square box I remember. I felt something was wrong with it. I didn't even want to touch it, let alone take it out and play with it and I was not that kind of kid, I never rejected even a 5&10 cheap plastic doll. My Dad said something like, but I paid $24.95 for this. I was surprised they didn't know. My Dad or Mom both said they couldn't find a real Cabbage Patch Kid, it was sold out and hard to find. I'm not sure if it was cute or ugly, but if you were a kid in the 80s, you just had to have a few. It was the rule of the 80s. Even grandmas got them for themselves, most never opened them; I see a whole slew of them on eBay from 1983, 1984, 1985, brand new, still Mint in Box. Did they just collect them and store them in their attic?

I guess I thought they were special. Not sure if my Dad returned this to the local cheap store or I kept it. I think they returned it and needed the money back to keep looking and find me a real one. This one just looked weird to me, it was "Flower Kids," like a real cheap imitation. I'm pretty sure she went back. That year for Hanukkah, I got a small baby that walked in a walker with batteries. I guess I liked that better, but it was nothing to write home about and the only gift I remember. My Mom being a retired medical assistant to a cardiologist and my Daddy being a teacher, we didn't have much money to go around, so we had to watch all the budgets, the food budget, too. A little later my Mom got me an official real Cabbage Patch Kid doll, she had long dark brown yarn hair that she wore in the back in a ponytail, olive skin, just a smile, not teeth and wore a checkered yellow dress. It's not the one I would have picked, but I loved her just the same, especially because my Mommy bought her for me special and brought her to the 1st grade with me one time. I think my Mom surprised me with her after a long day of school. She paid $32.99 to my best memory. Soon after they must have been easier to get, because I also got a CPK with tan hair and skin and big green eyes and a mullet wearing maroon overalls and a white blouse underneath. No matter how she looked, I loved her and played with her, because my Mommy bought her for me with love and she was mine, all mine. I would diaper her, with her diaper. I just knew how, maybe from watching my Mom diaper my baby brother. Then she got me my very favorite Cabbage Patch Kid, with lemon yellow yarn hair, blue eyes and one little white tooth sticking out. She looked a bit like Gargamel, the scary, bad older guy on the *Smurfs* cartoon with that one tooth sticking out. She had a yellow and blue striped workout outfit and she was so cute. I did wish I had blonde or red hair as a kid, so I liked dolls with that color hair.

MIRROR OF MY WORLD

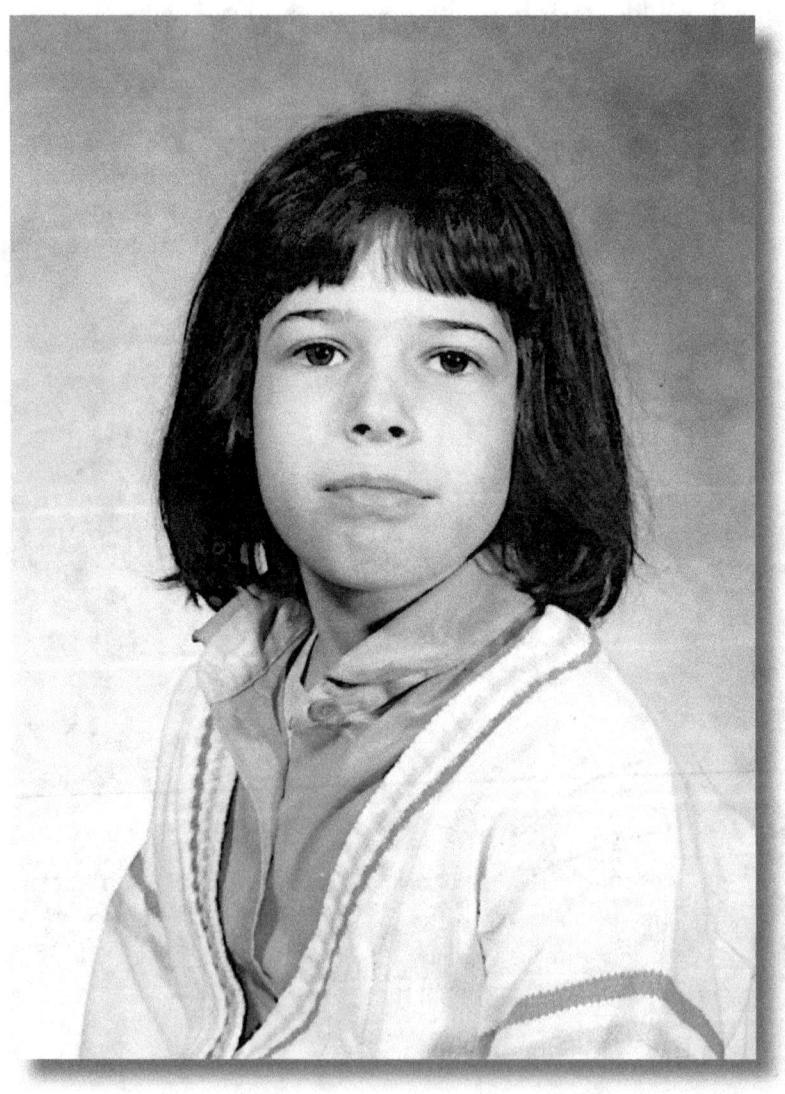

AGe 6

At age six, I was like a baby, my Mom said I still insisted on wearing my size 3T toddler clothes or I wouldn't go to school, the first grade. I don't remember that well. I'm surprised I could fit in a size 3T at age six, but my pediatric records said I was only 38 pounds. I was small, a picky eater. I did have swimming class in the winter, though. At age seven, I was 45 pounds, so I must have been eating better.

I'm age six, I'm about 41" inches in this photo. We were visiting my parents' friend; this is their backyard. My Grandma Lee cut my hair until I was age ten.

My Grandpa Jules got me a cheap baby doll from the 5&10. He had got me one like that before and my Mom and Grandma Lee said he shouldn't have, he REALLY shouldn't have, so it made me protective of it and love it even more, because my Grandpa got it for me and because they hurt her feelings and didn't like her. I was a good kid. It was the last birthday he would share with me, sadly; he died of an accidental insulin overdose and induced heart attack two months later.

When I was age six, my parents invited one of my best friends in the first grade over, Vicki. She had beautiful red, silky hair, bangs and a long ponytail. I wish my parents let me grow my hair that long. My grandma wouldn't let it get more than an inch past my shoulders. I wished it, but didn't talk much at age six to voice my opinions. I don't know if I could or just wanted to listen to my Mom, so it never got long, until I was age 12.

Vicki came over after school for a playdate, I was so happy to have her at my house. My Mom put on my favorite after school TV show to watch with her. I couldn't watch it. I'd rather play with my friend.

We played with my Fisher Price doll house, but got bored quickly, so we went up to my bedroom. I showed her how I climbed behind my bed by the wall. She followed me and accidentally knocked my night lamp on my night table over and it broke into pieces. My Dad came up and picked up the pieces, but my parents felt very sad about this. So did I, and guilty. It was an accident, and my idea. We were both only small, 30-something pound six-year-olds.

Then Vicki came up with an idea—we would have a coloring book contest, the winner gets a prize, who stays in the lines and colors better. We sat at my child-size table and colored, not sure whose was really best. I think hers was best, she won. I told my Mom she has to get a prize; she knew the deal.

My Mom got a Sears bag from the broom closet and I looked through my old baby clothes in my dresser drawers. I was a very generous, giving child. I was thinking if I won, I'd want something nice and special like that. It was for her Cabbage Patch dolls. We both had a few of them.

I asked my Mom which baby outfit I should pick and give to Vicki. My Mom looked sad when I picked something the cardiologist she worked for had given me when I was born; it was a pink and white Terrycloth onesie, with a big yellow duck sewn on the side, that snapped up in front. I was sensitive to my Mom's feelings, I loved her so much (my generosity and thinking more of others has tapered over the years, from other people, so called friends not being as kind back to me, starting as early as elementary school; how mean kids and people and a hard life ruin the kind, giving, sweet, innocent souls).

    I then chose something else. I picked a sage green or light blue dress and panties set. It was sweet and cute. My Mom agreed and put it in the bag and gave it to her. I even wanted to give her two of my baby outfits, not sure if Mom talked me out of it or not, I was such a generous child, because I was brought up with such sweetness and love. I knew the Golden Rule before it was even taught to me it in fourth grade. I liked to make others happy.

    I always felt bad and regretted giving Vicki the precious dress my parents gave me as a baby and wished my Mom had told me no, we are not allowed to give away your baby clothes and said let's choose something else, like a box of crayons or one dollar. My Mom was a sweetheart, too, and didn't want to squelch and discourage my generous nature. A year later when we weren't friends, she said she would give it back to me if I wanted, but I knew about being an Indian giver and I didn't want to be one. It didn't feel right to me as much as I did really want it back. Why do kids act like this? My heart was too giving if that's possible.

    I would sit with Vicki at lunch. One day a friend gave us her hot lunch tray. I'm not sure if the girl ate any; it was pizza and salad drowned in Italian dressing. It was so delicious! Vicki said don't use the fork, she might have used it, so we picked at it together with our fingers. We knew nothing about gross germs yet.

    I always got PB&J, every day, didn't eat it. Oh, the money my Mom could've saved! if I took a few bites that was a lot. The teacher once had to check if I was eating. I barely drank or ate at age six; I did not like my Mom's food and cooking at all. Vicki and I got this oatmeal or Girl Scout cookie. She said to be careful and eat it slowly, take little bits, it might have needles in it. It must have been near Halloween, the story of needles in Girl Scout cookies and candy by evil, sick adults. We also shared homemade Chex Mix someone's Mom packed them in a plastic bag, so yummy. I would have

MIRROR OF MY WORLD

finished the whole bag myself; it was one of the best things I ever ate as a six-year-old. I didn't have time to finish the yummy Chex. Another girl said lunch was over, took the bag from me, and threw it out in the trash. I'm not sure this all happened in the same day, though. Vicki was very creative. She would make small animals out of leftover tin foil. I tried to copy her and do the same.

Another day in the 1st grade, my Grandma got a prize in her Raisin Bran cereal, Alphabet stickers (that's the kind of educational prize you would get in that cereal, if any at all). She gave it to me special; she thought it would make me happy. I made a big mistake and took it to school to show the other kids. You don't save anything for later at age six, you live in the right now. Then I couldn't find it at the lunch table, and then I saw this other girl in my class stole it, had what my grandma had given me with love, then she said it was hers, not mine, and wouldn't give it back. I felt bad, sad, and I wouldn't go to the teachers—I didn't trust them.

Another time at the lunch table, some of the other 1st grade girls, not Vicki, were egging me on to say the F-word, which at age six, I knew nothing of. They said, "Let's see if you can spell." They spelt it out. I couldn't understand, so clever them said, "What sounds like duck and starts with F?" I finally got it that time. Then some said "ohhh" and "oooh" and then they laughed at me and I kind of knew it was a bad word I shouldn't say.

At recess I had brought my mini 3" plastic Cabbage Patch Kid with red yarn hair and my friend Vicki said to the girl who stole the Alphabet stickers to give her the letters to put on my tiny doll's back. I said it's not for me, but for my doll; it's not her fault she's my doll. I had the lowest self-esteem for a six-year-old. The girl gave me the letters.

I think I spelt it right. I could copy sentences off the blackboard at age six, not sure if I could read or not then. Once I got bored copying the sentences off the green board and I told my teacher my throat hurt and it was red and she asked me to open my mouth wide and looked. I don't know how I accomplished this—I wasn't really sick or was I? (it was because I would rather be at home watching TV)—but I got myself sent home.

Mrs. Roberts was our teacher, going around after lunch saying, "Who wants to try a big green pimento olive?" She had a big jar and gave us all square little napkins. She came around and gave us each one olive. I was looking so forward to trying it, but the cool girls were saying it's gross and yucky. I wanted to be cool, too, so I said I didn't want one. The teacher said, "Shame on you, if you never tried it and didn't want to. If you already tried it and didn't like it, that's another story." I tried one in my teens, love them still. Kids.

On a field trip we went to a museum. Everyone had to carry off the school bus a box of these big, thick crayons and a pad to draw a picture of what we saw. I was the only one in the whole class who kept dropping the box of crayons and the teacher had to help me put them back. After the third or fourth time, she gave up and carried them for me. This would only happen to me.

There was this assignment in the 1st grade, to keep a secret from your parents, then at the end tell them. The reward would be a big beautiful Olympic red, white, and blue ribbon and gold medal you wear around your neck. Either I didn't understand or missed a few days of school being out sick, but long story short, the secret—I really do love my brother—I didn't tell or told too late. My Dad had to write my teacher a letter. Still, I didn't get the medal. Only a few didn't in a class of over 20 kids. I had trouble understanding and following directions early on. It was mean not to give all the six-year-olds a medal. I thought I did it right; I was a small six-year-old.

MIRROR OF MY WORLD

<u>Christian Karen Berman</u>

SWIM CLASS

Age six—Dad's taking me today to Swimming Class. It was a Saturday, sometime in the winter months. Maybe my other friends in the first grade were enrolled in swim class at the Y, so my Mom enrolled me, too. I couldn't swim at all. I was a small and skinny six-year-old, 41" tall and 38 pounds. It was around lunchtime at home in the kitchen. My Mom was sick with a mild case of the flu and always took me to all my swim classes, but today she told my Dad she couldn't take me, she wasn't feeling up to it. She was taking care of my baby brother, feeding him some baby food. He was about two years old. I'm not sure what I ate, but I bet they didn't get me to eat much. It was a struggle to get me to eat most anything (I liked the wing dings and mashed potatoes and gravy at Sears or grilled cheese with Italian dressing on top or veggie lasagna. You should see my pediatric records—won't eat anything but pizza and chocolate, refuses to eat, not eating, Dad says she won't eat—stuff like that all throughout age four months until age nine.)

My Mom didn't want me to miss a swim class, it was probably expensive and she wanted me to get her money's worth. Grandma Lee was at her apartment I think, maybe so not to get sick. I don't remember her here this day, just our family. My Mom gave my Dad instructions, where to go, what to do, what does six-year-old me know. I felt nervous but did as I was told. I probably wore my swimsuit under my clothes. I even had a navy swim cap, just nylon. My Dad didn't want me to miss swim class, either I guess. He somehow made it to the right swimming pool at the Y. It's like January or February out there, cold.

He starts to bring me into the women's locker room with all the mothers and their daughters. They ask where my Mother was and tell my Dad to get out. They seem upset, angry, and embarrassed there is a Daddy in here. He can leave me here alone or take me into the men's locker room, which he does so I can take my clothes off. He somehow finds the men's locker room and walks in with little me. My Dad is 6' and in his early 40s and I barely go to his waist. There is a bunch of men in the men's locker room, looking surprised at the sight of little me. They looked shocked and cover up their privates sitting at the wooden or metal benches. I'm not understanding why everyone looks upset to me. At that age, I have no idea what I did wrong and the looks I got, but I know something's up and seems wrong. The Men seemed older to me, I guess from 30s to 60s. My Dad found an empty spot to help me take my clothes off and put them in an empty locker. I had a swimsuit underneath, so no big deal for me. I feel awkward, but don't know why. I don't know much about girls' and boys' privates at this age, never even owned a Ken doll and I'm that not modest as of yet, just feel strange and weird by the reactions of both the women and especially the men. My Dad hurries and takes my socks off and gets the hell outta there and to the big swimming pool.

In swim class, my young class goes to the back of the big pool. The kids in my class are in the lowest swim group—ages three to eight, or age five and six, I'm guessing. They have us walk slowly down the diving board or plank. You can either jump in all by yourself and the swim teacher will catch you in her arms (hopefully) or be let down slowly by holding on index finger to index finger by the swim instructor. This seems scary and dangerous to 41-inch me. The pool must be eight feet deep, and I can't swim. I hold on to both the lady's fingers for dear life and I'm carried by the other swim teacher to the side of the pool. I'm too frightened to be having much fun, scared of the water, but like being carried. It's so deep and I'm so little.

Then class is over. I'm happy to see my Dad, but now we have to go back into the men's locker room and my Dad has to help me take off my wet bathing suit and help dry my hair, which got wet under the swimming cap. It's freezing cold outside (there's even some snow on the ground) and you know what they say about going out in the cold with wet hair—you'll catch your death of cold. We walk in, all the men freeze up again and quickly and nervously cover up. My Dad walks to the middle of the locker room to our locker. I'm still not sure why they're reacting like that, but I think

I'm starting to understand now. I did ask my Dad why are they acting funny and looking at me like that, what's wrong, haven't they ever seen a six-year-old girl in the first grade? He said something like not many Dads bring their little girls in here, but your Mom is sick, and I can't leave you alone in the women's room. My Dad helps me discreetly lower my one-piece swimsuit and with a towel around my waist, covering me up, put back on my underwear and clothes. My socks are thin nylon boys socks, navy blue. I have no idea why. Then I put on my royal blue winter coat with white sheepskin underneath, red knitted hat by grandma with ears and a chin strap and mittens of course, held on to my coat with metal clips so I don't lose them. I'm sure my Daddy was thrilled to do this, as a teacher, day and sleepaway camp counselor. I'm sure he was terribly embarrassed. Shunned by both mothers and men. He was just doing the job of a single Dad today. I'm glad he went or I might not remember swim lessons at age six.

MIRROR OF MY WORLD

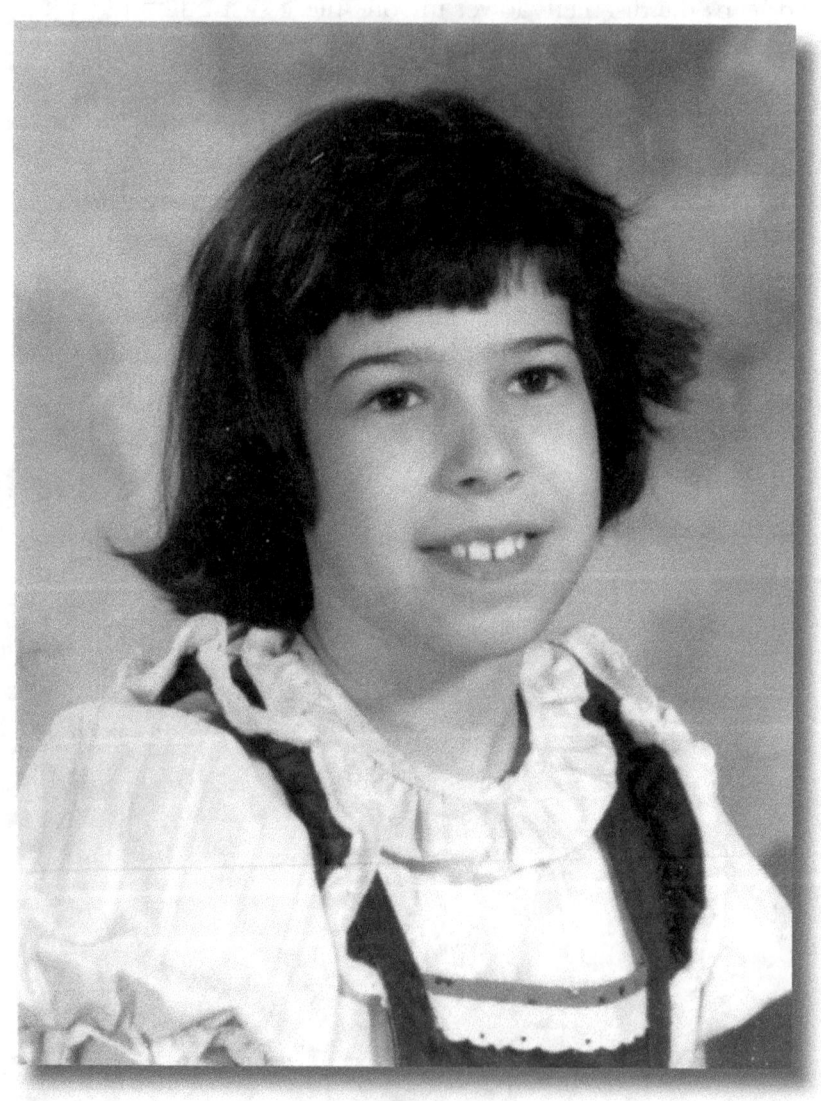

<u>Christian Karen Berman</u>

THE NEPTUNE / FLAGSHIP DINER

They changed their name sometime in the late 1980s. My family used to go there when I was a kid. When you first walked in, you'd see a big lobster tank and I would always gravitate to that. Then you would see the cakes, pastries, and cookies behind a glass window. I would then stare at that. Then the big pastel assorted mints—don't touch until after dinner. There usually wasn't a line.

One time we went there and the glass door slammed on my middle finger. I was about seven or eight years old. When we were sitting down and the waitress asked what I wanted for dinner, my Dad told her what happened and said I was more concerned about my finger. I was holding it. I should have dipped it in the ice water.

Another time when I was six, Larry would get a highchair or a clip-on toddler seat. I asked my Dad to ask for a booster seat for me. I felt left out. I was all of 38 pounds as a six-year-old. Once I brought my cabbage patch doll and I think she got a clip-on seat. When you first got there, they'd pour you ice water and give you fresh popovers. You'd open it up and put a pat of butter on it and it would melt. I was a picky eater. I liked the Yankee bean soup and the tuna fish salad plate. Sometimes I'd only ask for a side of mashed potatoes and rice. Other times Daddy would just order me a pizza burger and fries. He'd get a Cherry Coke, he'd say with extra syrup. It must have been the old-time way they made it? We all got Cherry Cokes over ice. My Mom would always ask the waitress for lobster bibs for us kids, so we wouldn't get food and ketchup on our shirts. She would put them on us. I'd have griddle cakes with lots of maple syrup, or fried chicken. Thanksgiving was the best; they had chestnut stuffing and creamed spinach, and my parents would get two plates and share with us kids. Dessert was chocolate layer cake. I don't believe back then we ordered from the kid's menu, they musta had one. Maybe my parents didn't know. When I was older, we ordered from it in other places.

There was a smoking section back then, lots of smoke. We sat in non-smoking, but it came over sometimes. We usually only ate there on weekends. We were too busy and tired on most school nights. Maybe once in a while, though. Once this little girl with long blonde hair sitting in the booth in front of us had two daddies or uncles bring her a big white teddy bear. I think I was 11 or 12, she looked like six or seven, but seemed happy. I wanna go back to the good old days, but can't. I wish I still had a loving family to dote on me.

AGE 7

When I was seven, my three-year-old brother was in pre-K. When he was being interviewed, I was playing in the other empty pre-K class happily with a Fisher Price toy cash register. My same nursery schoolteacher scolded me, saying I was too old at age seven and I would break it. My Mother kindly, without asking her, bought me the same cash register shortly after to play with for my own to keep.

I was in first grade on a field trip. It was raining. I'm not sure where we went, maybe the playground or the Bronx Zoo. My friend Vicki was sitting next to me on the bus and unkindly said it was raining because it was MY BIRTHDAY. That made me feel bad and I tried not to believe her. Then our first-grade teacher Ms. Roberts put a construction paper crown on my head and everyone sang "Happy Birthday" to me and I said I was six instead of seven. My mistake. She corrected me. My Mom brought the boring

MIRROR OF MY WORLD

undipped Ring Dings, like circular Devil Dogs with cream in the middle. I can't remember any presents. There might have been, but honestly, not much of a party, and no big party at home. I didn't have many friends and my parents didn't have much money. I did get a Cabbage Patch Doll and a My Child Doll and a Care Bear, but not sure if that was my birthday present.

Christian Karen Berman

THE STEVENSVILLE HOTEL IN THE CATSKILL MOUNTAINS

We went there in July for our summer vacation. I had just turned age seven. I wish I remembered more about this hotel. I remember having a sliding open glass door to the outside of the hotel room. In the early morning around 7:30 am, me and my Dad would walk out and the green grass and dandelions and flowers by the swimming pool would be covered in dew, a wet mist on everything. It was cool weather, in the low 70s. My parents kept wanting me to go to Day Camp. I was small, thin, shy and quiet. I didn't want to leave them. Larry was age two-and-three-quarters and still in the Prego baby stroller.

I remember they had some outdoor games. I was bored and with my Dad who had just golfed a tennis ball into a large plastic cup. I think he got it in and I was trying to pull the golf club out of his hands wanting to try it myself. My Dad said I was too young. Then the older guy who was working the game said, "Hey, let her try." He hands me the golf club and I gently, but strongly aim for the cup and it stops right in front of the cup. He smiles and walks up to me and says, "Good job." He gives me a prize, a yellow plastic thing that says Stevensville. I can't remember what it was, but I thought I won; maybe that's where you're supposed to hit it to. Then my Dad said it was because I was so young and came so close to getting it in the cup, that's why he gave me the prize.

Dinnertime I remember. I really should have been in the Day Camp, because my parents didn't know what to do with me and I wouldn't eat much at all. At dinner almost every night I would only eat seeded Rye bread drenched in pink Russian Dressing with pickles in it. It was very good. To me, the other food wasn't edible. I would eat two of them. I can't remember the other food, but maybe I wasn't hungry. It was adult food, maybe a relish tray,

MIRROR OF MY WORLD

steak, turkey. My Dad was happy I would eat that. It was always a little battle to get me to eat. I was little, picky, not hungry. One night they came around and took our photo and put it in a rectangular key chain you look through. They did that in the mid 1980s. I still have it somewhere. I'm not sure if my Daddy went to the nightclub. Larry and I were so young. Grandma Lee stayed home. I'm not sure they would trust a hotel babysitter. At six or seven I barely talked much, quiet and shy even to my parents.

Christian Karen Berman

Day Camp

I remember my Dad said I could get a soda from a vending machine. One of my happiest memories there. I was running ahead of my parents, down the red and orange carpet, the twisting halls of the hotel. I thought I had seen a soda machine around here and I was thirsty. I stopped in the middle of the hall—I'd found the vending machine! Yay! It must have cost 50 cents back then. I looked at all the soda flavors—Pepsi, Coke, 7-Up, Sprite, RC Cola, Orange Slice and then my favorite, Welch's Grape Soda. Cool! I'm getting that one. First time I ever tried it, too. My Mom put the change in and I pressed the grape soda and it luckily came right out. My Dad helped me open the tab on the pop top and I had a big sip. Yummy, yummy good. I think my Dad had a big sip, too.

Then my parents walked me into the Day Camp cafeteria. There was a pretty seven-year-old girl sitting there. I was in the camp a few minutes before, but not wanting to stay. Our parents ordered us a snack dessert of sprinkle cookies. We sat and shared them with ice cold milk. Then I said she sounded just like my other friend Vicki and she started to change her voice and said she didn't want to sound like anyone else, so I didn't want to mess her up, so I said now she sounded exactly like her and she started talking in her regular voice again.

At night at Day Camp in the main lobby, this was after dinner, a bunch of padded grey metal chairs were set up for the kids. The music playing loud was "Jump for my Love" by The Pointer Sisters. While it played a bunch of little kids, including me, were jumping up and down to the song. The counselors told us to jump to the song. This was our after-dinner activity. My parents were there with me and I still remember this.

I remember we came home with a couple of little white ping pong balls from one hotel and a yellow golf ball from another hotel. Not sure if it was this hotel though; it might have been the Nevele.

MIRROR OF MY WORLD

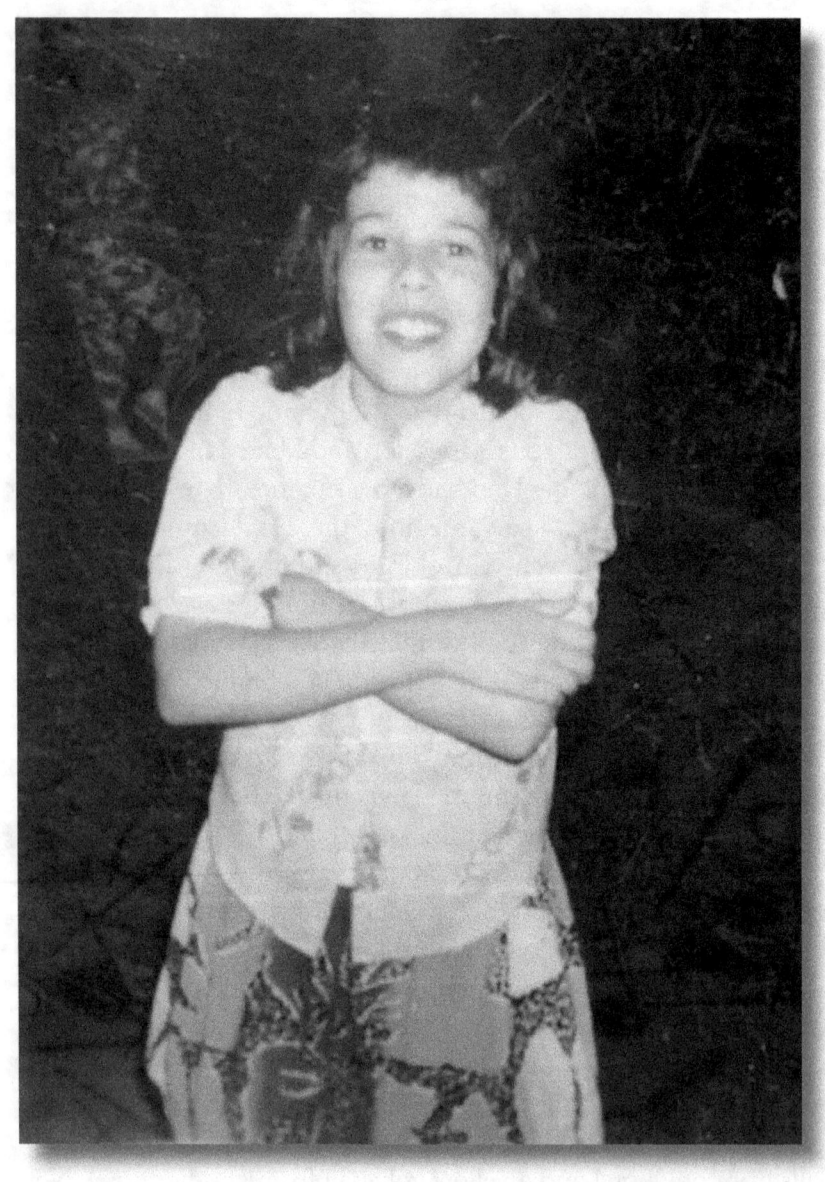

Christian Karen Berman

Second Grade Dilemmas

I used to take little toys to the bus stop with me and wait with my Mom and some other kids on the next block under the porch roof. The toys were my little friends. My Mom used to read to me when I was younger while we waited for the bus, a Care Bear book or a Cabbage Patch book. I always wanted to give the toy back to my Mom before I got on the bus, so they wouldn't get lost or hurt. I always forgot. I would then wave at my Mom on the bus showing the toy so she would know I had it with me, twice with two different Mini Cabbage Patch Kid dolls. Another time I took my light blue My Little Pony, with hot pink hair. I would hide the pony under my shirt and in my desk from the teacher in fear she would confiscate it and lock it in her desk until the end of the year. That scared me so much, I loved my pony and I would have been so sad and missed my pony terribly all year.

Math class. I was 7. I was in Mrs. Major's class. I was in her husband Mr. Major's class in the 6th grade middle school in the 1990s. I was wearing my grey Care Bear rainbow sweatshirt inside out. They sold similar styles and I wanted a cool shirt like that. My teacher noticed I was wearing my shirt inside out. She made me take off my shirt in class and put it on the correct way. I was wearing a floral printed undershirt underneath. Another time I got in trouble, she thought I was copying someone's answers. We weren't taking a test or talking, can't remember, but I wasn't. She said she was going to send me to the principal's office. I walked over as she sternly picked up the phone and dialed. I said in a sweet, scared voice, "Can I please have one more chance?" She said yes and hung up and I went back to my seat quietly. I honestly wasn't sure what I did that was so wrong. They sure kept the kids in line in the 1980s and this was public school.

They had given us kids some kind of yummy taffy in class. I was between seven to nine years old. I had it in my pocket and I was

MIRROR OF MY WORLD

walking down the hall. It was probably after lunch, because I was free to walk in the hall. I'm like, "I always save everything for later, why don't I enjoy this right now?" I slowly open it, wax paper and a small cylinder shape, and put the light green candy in my mouth. It's a good flavor of sour apple, chewy, I love it, enjoying it. Two girls walk over to me and say I'm chewing gum and you're not allowed to chew gum in school and they're going to tell on me and get me in trouble. I tell them it's candy and not gum. They don't believe me, then one of the nicer girls says, "Is it paper? I chew on paper." So I say yes, it's paper. The mean girl says something like, "Don't lie, I know you're lying." The nice girl says, "it does look like paper." The other girl says if you throw it in the trash now I won't tell. So I take a few more chews, keep my word and walk down the hall, throw it in the trash. I turn around they don't even care to look at if I did. The one time I try to do something different, a little fun and spontaneous, I get caught and almost in trouble. Is this only me?

Christian Karen Berman

THE NEW PLAID TAN COUCH

When I was about seven years old, my parents bought a new tan couch with a few stripes on it, a better place for my Grandma Lee to sleep than the old orange floral couch, now that she was staying here almost full-time and not at her old apartment alone. The couch was big and wide and when I sat at the end, my feet didn't even go past the seat, that's how big it was. I was 45 inches and pounds at age seven. As soon as it was delivered, I think I started jumping up and down on it like it was my parents' big bed, even before the delivery men had left. I did happen to be a bit of a show off back then at times, more often than not, plus we didn't own a trampoline. So for fun sometimes I did jump on it like when my parents and Grandma weren't looking, sneaky me. It didn't have the biggest bounce, but I made do. Three-year-old Larry started copying me. My parents did not like that at all and said I would break it and to stop. I didn't think I weighed enough to break it, though. I tried to listen, but sometimes jumped on it.

The couch came with many extra pillows. I would take them off the couch and put them on the carpet and tried my best to build a pillow fort. My parents did not like this either, and said I would break the couch and get the pillows dirty. Larry sometimes tried to help me and play at my request. I got bored easily and was a very active, thin child. My parents did not seem to want me to enjoy our new couch, just sit on it and be quiet. My Grandma did tell me once why don't I just sit and rest, why I wasn't tired. I always liked to be busy with something during the day and got bored easy. Grandma Lee did rest a lot though, with her eyes closed.

We had no TV downstairs at the time and nothing much to do than play with Fisher Price Toys, like The Garage, Mainstreet, The Doll House and Farm. We had this big, round, dark brown leather hassock I loved and it had wheels on the bottom of it. You

MIRROR OF MY WORLD

could sit down on it and roll around the living room carpet or turn it on its side and roll around. I would lie over it and go down head first. My Grandma Lee told me not to do it after lunch, that I would throw up. I didn't eat much, so I knew I wouldn't, it would stay down. I would sit on top of it, too, and slowly roll down. It didn't occur to me that I could get hurt and I never did get hurt on this. My parents did not want me playing with this toy, either. They sure made it hard to have fun around here sometimes.

Everything in the house was my playground, you could hide in the cabinet under the kitchen sink or the broom closet. You could have a band with the spaghetti pot and boiling pot and play the drums with the utensils. Who needed toys when you were so little with a big imagination? I would climb up and sit on the counter top. My Mom would give Larry a bowl and some dry spaghetti sticks and sometimes some water. The spaghetti strainer was a weird alien hat. Upstairs, the baby dressers you would climb on and sit on top. The stairs was a mountain and you'd tie a tie to the banister and hold on and climb up. Who needs Fisher Price when you have a built-in play center? I'd climb and hold onto the side of my parents' gigantic armoire, too, so to stay on.

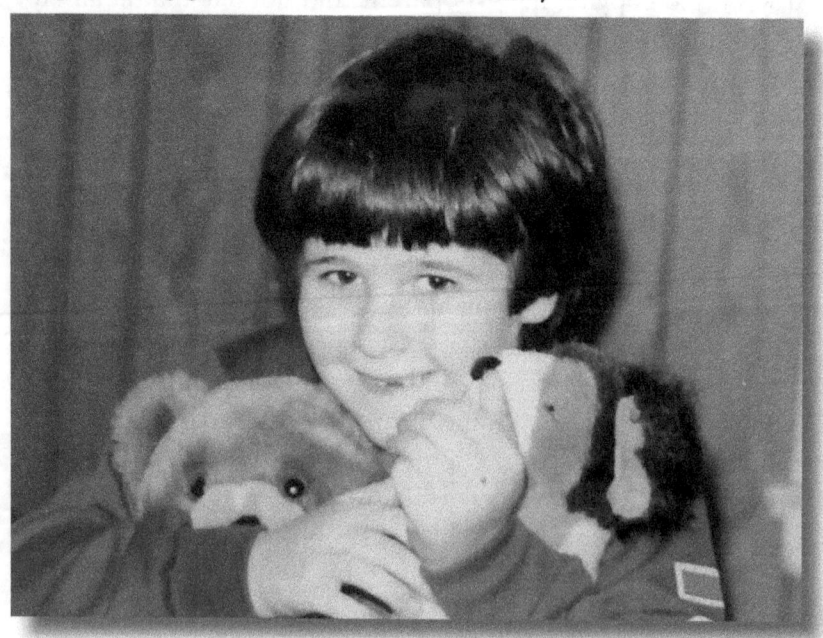

Christian Karen Berman

LARRY IS LOST IN SEARS, LARRY IS MISSING

I'm age seven-and-a-half. My parents leave me to babysit my three-year-old brother Larry alone in the Shoe Department at Sears Department Store, so we can rest and they go off shopping in different directions. I never was told to watch him before, less alone in a big store. It was kinda empty, though. They just assumed I knew how, being four years older than him and in the 2nd grade. I think this was around March or April. They should have still had him in a big baby stroller, if you ask me. He was small then. My brother Larry says, "I'm going to go look for Mom," I say okay and stay put. I was tired, I guess. We were like the same age, so I think nothing of it when he asks that. A few minutes later or sooner my Dad comes back and asks where is Larry. I say he went to go look for Mom. My Mom comes back alone and uh-toh, I'm in major, big trouble now. This is not good. Then my parents look for someone to help them fast, mad at me, really mad at me.

    The manager pages Larry on the loudspeaker and asks that all the customers in the store go look for a three-year-old little boy, with brown hair and eyes. Every customer in the store starts looking for a three-year-old toddler boy, because they're told he's lost. I dunno what jail is at seven, but I knew I'm in super, major, big trouble and even though I never went off on my own before, since I'm already in such big trouble, I start to wander off and look for him myself, feeling really bad about myself and guilty, not caring if I get lost or taken. I feel so bad, I dunno if I know about kidnappers yet, I don't think I do, I just worry my parents will be mad at me and hate me and never forgive me and not love me anymore. I miss Larry, too. I'm worried about him, getting taken, I guess, or never finding him again, or what will happen, fear and panic is heavily in the air, a thick, scary fear. I should not be going off on

MIRROR OF MY WORLD

my own. The store is huge and I'm still pretty little myself, maybe only 48 pounds. There is a big escalator. I can get really badly lost myself. I dunno what I'm doing, but I'm trying to get out of being in trouble by finding my baby brother.

Luckily someone finds him and walks him back across the white, glossy big, thin, tile aisle across from the escalator to the shoe department to bring him to his Mommy and Daddy. I'm off the hook now, I think, I hope. I honestly didn't understand what watching him meant, keeping him in one stop and holding him hostage and captive until one of my parents came back. I wasn't taught yet and nobody told me. My Dad just assumed I understood the task at hand. We'll, I didn't. Adam Walsh was kidnapped in a Sears just a few years before in 1981 at age six. I heard this a good 15-20 years later, so that was why it's such a big deal. Now that I'm an adult, I know it was my parents' fault for feeling this was safe, being so trusting and naive, not thinking something bad could happen. I was only a seven-and-a-half year old child myself and could have been taken, too. Larry wasn't taken, but wandered off across to the women's section. He was looking for my Mom. She should have taken him with her. Being relatively the same age, I was just cool with him looking for our Mom, didn't give it another thought, not like I was his parent. I never babysat before, I didn't know. I'm glad he was found just a few minutes later and nothing worse happened. Before, I might have got lost and wandered off on purpose, too. I had felt so bad, so guilty. I was forgiven, but still I didn't know this wasn't my fault back then, In the mid-1980s, it just wasn't safe to have a seven-year-old 45-pound girl babysit a three-year-old in the Sears Shoe department. It was kinda empty, too.

Christian Karen Berman

MY BROTHER'S CONVULSION

When my brother was three, he had a convulsion. He was sick with a fever all day. It was just after his three-in-one shot. I just happened to be at school. Many days I was home sick or just didn't feel like going; this day I think I actually went to school. I was seven and in the second grade. It was quite a year between the chickenpox and being home for a week, plus trying to get out early by going to the school nurse, pretending to be sick. Sometimes after I was faking sick for my parents, I actually got sick for real soon after, so maybe I felt it coming on or I pretended so good, I really made myself sick somehow, with a fever and everything. Then my parents were like, "I didn't know you were really sick." I didn't, either. "So that's why she was acting like that and didn't want to go to school," my Mom said. But I also didn't like to miss my TV shows and my Mom.

I remember when my Dad got home, we had to all drive to the pharmacy to pick up some medicine for my brother. When we got into the pharmacy waiting to pick up my brother's pink liquid amoxicillin medicine, that's when he dropped down right next to me. My parents, in shock, tried to grab him.

I was so scared I just ran out and couldn't stay in there. I was on the sidewalk. It was very scary and traumatic. Thinking back that probably only made things harder on my parents, having to worry about your little seven-year-old girl getting lost, running away or getting kidnapped. I didn't feel that little sometimes, even when I was seven. Then they came out carrying my brother. We all rushed back to the car. It was in a big open parking lot. I quickly followed my very worried, frazzled, panicked parents. My Mom said to my Dad to hold his tongue so he didn't swallow it. My Dad sat in the back seat holding him on his lap. I sat in the front with my Mom. She drove quickly to the pediatrician's office, only a few miles down. We might have just come from there, the doctor might have seen him first, I think so, but my memory is a bit foggy on this point. Not sure.

My Dad must have carried him into the pediatrician's office. It was close to 5 pm and they were empty, just closing up. The doctor was there and my Dad rushed my brother, who was kinda unconscious, into the office. There were a few nurses there. I was in the waiting room. My Dad came out while my Mom was in with my brother.

My Dad said that my brother would have to be admitted to the hospital. To seven-year-old me, rarely ever going to the hospital, I thought that was the absolute worst thing in the world and I started crying real tears and sobbing. A person who I thought was a nurse but found out later she wasn't and was just applying for that job, put me on her lap, talked to me, asked why I was crying, and said it wouldn't be that bad and they would help him get better. My Dad just watched her, thinking it was so sweet what she was doing.

It was after hours and only my brother was there. She calmed me down and I finally stopped sobbing hysterically. I rarely cried much, never in public, but I thought hospitals were really terrible, the worst thing that could happen to you. Later my Dad told me it was because of how she put me on her lap and calmed me down that got her the job as a nurse. I did that. If it wasn't for me, she might not have got hired. My Dad was also surprised I was so upset about my little brother. He didn't know I cared so much.

My Dad drove right to the hospital. At the hospital the pediatrician called ahead and got my brother a private room. My Mom was going to sleep over and stay with him. We were all in the room, I was climbing up on the rails of the large baby crib. The nurse told me—quieter rudely, I remember—to get off, that I would break it or something. That made me feel sad. I think I was just looking into the crib at my brother. I was only 45 inches and 45 pounds. It was getting late. My Dad and I had to say goodbye and leave. I was pretty attached to my Mom at age seven, so this was hard for me. I was sad to leave half my family behind in a small room. My brother had an IV drip attached to him, a small bathroom too. He was wearing a baby hospital gown that was like yellow with little teddy bears or bunnies on it, so cute, I wanted one. Then we had to walk out. My Dad left first. I was walking slowly behind in the large hallway. I remember clearly asking if I could sleep in the big bed with him. He said yes. I don't remember if I ate dinner or what I ate, but knowing me, my Dad had trouble getting me to eat on a good night, so I'm not sure I ate at all. He would complain to my pediatrician that I did not eat at all, would only eat pizza and chocolate. It was in my doctor's report.

I remember the next day when Mom and my brother came home, my Dad or I asked what they ate. My Mom said they had Cheerios for breakfast and a cheeseburger for lunch. My Mom and Larry bonded more there. She said she had to walk his IV drip to the bathroom with him. Larry was feeling better so they let him come home, but I think they gave him an EEG, a test for seizures, and took many blood tests just to make sure he was okay. Then they just thought it was the high fever that caused the convulsions. I didn't go to school the next day, but I can't remember if it was because my Mom was in the hospital or if it was a Saturday.

MIRROR OF MY WORLD

SPRING

I was age seven, it was March. It was the first time I had been able to go out wearing my winter vest and not my winter coat, the first real sign of spring. It had warmed up. I had been allowed to zip the pink and grey arms off my coat, pretty cool. There was still a little snow on the ground, but it was nice to be able to wear my coat vest. I had been wanting to do this for a while, I pictured doing it. It was a beautiful, sunny, warm summer day. My Dad had the patio chairs outside in the backyard. I somehow managed to convince my Mom to get Dole Pineapple Fresh Fruit Ice Pops. I was sitting outside enjoying one. Maybe my brother or Dad was, too. I was just looking at the clouds and living in the moment. That alone made it a good day.

MIRROR OF MY WORLD

Christian Karen Berman

MOUNT KISCO MALL

Age seven, at the Mount Kisco Mall, we went to this place that had a gigantic Raggedy Ann and Andy rag doll sitting on a big wooden swing hanging in the middle of the room from the ceiling. Thank God I didn't know about the story of Annabelle the killer, evil doll or I would have been so scared and had nightmares for a long time. As it was, I would look and stare at them and think, I never saw ones like that, so big. They scared me as it was. My Dad was ordering pizza bagels for all of us, that's what they served. I wish I knew the name of that place. it was made of all oak-type wood. The food was so yummy, and I didn't like many foods back then so that's saying a lot coming from me. I guess we had Coke, Pepsi, or RC soda. I didn't have much say in the food or drinks we got as a child. After that we looked around the really nice wooden mall, 80s-style. There was this cool store with big cowboy hats. I wanted one, but they were expensive and probably wouldn't fit 45-pound little me. There was a big water fountain in the middle of the mall.

Then I saw this store, maybe a toy store or the Hallmark store. My Grandma Lee came with us. I saw through the glass store window a little stuffed Yorkie puppy, so cute, probably by Russ. I saw it driving home with me, as I looked in the back window with him, that thought flashed in my young mind. I knew I had to have him and couldn't leave without him. I asked my parents for him. "Can I have him, can you buy him? I want him, *pllllease*." They said no. I stayed and looked at him sadly, kinda whining, like I'm not leaving here without him, I don't want to go. I believe he was all of $10 in the mid-80s (I Googled $10 from the mid-80s and it's $28.95, so yeah, so much more expensive than now). I think they said they can't afford him and I have enough stuffed animals. I think I might have been in tears by then, crying for wanting him and saying, "No, I'm not leaving and I don't want to go home."

MIRROR OF MY WORLD

Then my sweet Grandma Lee that always did everything she could to make me happy said she would buy him for me. I felt happy and smiled and got all peppy again and thanked her so much. My Dad walked in with me and I picked him out and he paid for him with the $10 my Grandma gave him. Then, just as I pictured, in the brown Ford car, I was in the back with my doggy, happily smiling and we watched in the back window for a while.

  Once home, this is what I did with all or most of my new stuffed animals or dolls as in my mind, they were real—I gave them a grand tour of my whole house, showing him the downstairs bathroom, dining room, living room and finally the upstairs bedrooms and bathroom to make him feel at home.

Christian Karen Berman

BLOOD POISONING AND RUBBER BANDS

For some reason I remember almost every day of being age seven, more than any other year of my life. I wonder why.

I'm seven, it's nighttime just after dinner. My Dad is probably busy grading papers. I'm bored. My Grandma Lee knows I always wanted freckles. I find one of my Dad's red Flair markers that he uses to grade papers with, B, C, D, D-, whatever the case may be.

I go into the downstairs bathroom and can barely see in the mirror. I have to stand on my tippy-toes or stand on the toilet seat to see my face. I'm a girl and do what girls do, like what I see my Grandma do (my Mom never wore makeup or lipstick), I draw red on my lips like lipstick. I'm looking really pretty. Let's put some freckles on now. This is fun! Dot, dot, dot on my face. I'm looking really pretty now, like Raggedy Ann or Punky Brewster. I need a few more, to make sure you really can see them good.

No one knows I'm doing this. I walk into the living room, show my Grandma Lee and then I find a huge rubber band and put it around my neck, it's a beautiful necklace. I'm playing dress up with what I got. Before I can even get the rubber band around my head, my Dad sees and gets mad, runs over to me, Papa Bear protecting its baby cub, and quickly yanks it off around my hair, harshly. I'm not sure what's happening, it happens so fast, or why what I'm doing is wrong. Then he sees my red lips and pulls me or carries me to the kitchen sink. He picks me up and holds my face near the running water in the sink and scrubs my lips with Brillo hard, to get off the poisonous ink. I'm not liking this and trying to pull away and kinda crying. He's done and tells me to never to do this ever again, that I'll get sick and die of blood poisoning or something like that. It really scared me. I was kinda shaken up. I was just playing, I didn't know it was bad, what I did.

I go upstairs to my bathroom now and wash the stupid freckles sadly off my face. I don't want to get blood poisoning. I'm sorry.

MIRROR OF MY WORLD

My Dad really loved me and cared about me and was just making sure I wouldn't get sick. This is why young kids need supervision—they don't know what they're doing is wrong. Sometimes even teenagers don't know what they're doing is wrong.

It's hard being a good parent.

Christian Karen Berman

Taking Medicine and Being Sick

The first time I remember taking medicine was in the late 1980s. It was St. Joseph baby aspirin. They were orange and looked and tasted like a little tube of candies. It kind of made me shutter and feel sick when I took them. I remember one time when I was seven, my Dad and brother were home sick. I didn't want to go to school if they got to stay home. So, my parents let me, but weren't happy with me. I was jealous they got to stay home and I wanted to stay home and be with the rest of the family.

I was hungry, my Mom was out shopping. I looked in the refrigerator and found some shrimp salad. My Mom loved that. My grandma was probably downstairs, too. I had that with Wise potato chips and to drink, water, Ssips, or Hi-C Fruit Punch juice box. then I started to feel sick and run a fever. Was I sick before or made myself sick, because I felt guilty everyone was mad at me for playing hooky? Either way, I told my Dad I felt sick. I think I had a little fever. He made me take a few of those icky candies. I went to lie down after.

Another time, it was the last day of school before Christmas vacation. I didn't want to go to the second-grade Christmas party, just didn't like leaving the comfort of my parents' bed, TV, toys and stuffed animals. Well, my Mom took me to school with my brother and stayed with me. It wasn't so bad. I was making a Christmas card with green construction paper, differen tcolored magic markets, and adding stickers. I think there was candy canes, candy, and maybe cupcakes. The teachers were lenient since it was the last day. I went out in the hall a few times. They didn't seem to mind. I still wanted to go home, even though it was fun and my Mom was there.

When we finally got home I still said I wasn't feeling well. My Dad had me take my temp. It was high, 102-104. Was I sick all along and no one knew it or took my temp, or did I make myself sick by not wanting to go to school? We were all surprised. My parents said, "She really was sick all along, maybe she was coming down with something." I didn't know that. I thought I was faking, too, and just didn't feel like going to school.

Then my parents made me get up out of a sound sick-sleep the next morning. I'd slept in their bed, my Dad had trouble moving me out; I slept there most of my childhood. A few times, when I was seven, I actually slept in my own bed, which was a great accomplishment for me. But mostly even as a seven-year-old I cried. I was scared of ghosts and monsters and I felt unloved (in the daytime I rarely cried; I didn't like to show my emotions then). Daddy tried to put me in the hall next to his room on a blanket. It was hard to sleep in my own bed! I once said I'll do it when I'm 11, because it felt like 11 was so far off it would never come. I wish it never came! I liked being a cute, happy little kid!

We went to the pediatrician. I was there often. I could barely get up and didn't want to go. I was too tired to move. I somehow make it to the car and lie down in the back seat like it's a bed (there was no baby car seat rule until the year 2000). I was 45 pounds.

I remember the waiting room. It had many spring horses to ride on in different sizes, from toddler to my age. One time even my Grandma went with us. Well, they got your weight, once my pediatrician asked me my phone number, he was impressed I knew it. They stick a long white stick down your throat that hurts your tonsils even more. After, the lollipops that taste like banana or my medicine, yuck. They had some little toys, but at seven they must have thought I was too old. I just got yucky lollipops. I'm not sure if I had strep throat or tonsillitis or what, but at home my parents said if I take this pink medicine that taste like bubble gum, they'll give me a present. I wanted what they bought for me. In the bathroom, my Dad poured the pink stuff on a teaspoon and I took it, but when I leaned down in the sink to get a sip of water to wash it down, I always spit half of it out. Why? Why did I? It didn't taste that bad. I think I was allergic to amoxicillin because I remember being afraid of feeling like I was swallowing my tonsils. My Dad said I would be okay.

My Dad gave me my gift anyway, a child's hairbrush, comb and mirror set he picked up at the pharmacy with my medicine. One time he got me a big panda bear and the pharmacist told me to take good care of him. My Dad did call the doctor, because I guess he saw me spitting out my medicine all the time. The doctor said to put it on ice cream and sprinkles. The same doctor who said if I didn't go to school don't give me any dinner. My Dad had a hard enough time getting me to eat dinner. It needed lots of ketchup, but my Mom gave up trying to feed me and gave me Swanson TV dinners or Kraft Mac and Cheese. I did like her tuna salad; always ate that. We were so poor; it was two cans of tuna mixed with two eggs, onion, celery, and mayo for three adults (parents and Grandma) and two kids.

I'm age seven. My Dad and I were leaving the local market. He just bought the basics for lunch like roast beef, rolls, potato chips, potato salad and coleslaw. He finished up paying and last time we were there he surprised me by buying me a bag of peanut M&Ms. I waited for the very end thinking he would do the same this time. We didn't have much money. After we walked out to the white sidewalk by the car, I told him I thought he was going to buy me a bag of peanut M&Ms like last time. He walked right back in and I followed. He bought me that bag of M&Ms. It was sweet of him. Maybe he just forgot or was short on money, but it made me happy enough to remember this little detail of my life. I can't even remember the month for sure, fall or spring.

Another time I went with my Dad to Big Top (the toy store) in April. I'm not sure why we had to go, but I always liked to tag along with my Dad and make the most of each day. I knew we couldn't afford much, so I always picked something inexpensive to play with and enjoy. This time I picked a pack of play money and coins. It was educational for me to learn how to count my money, plus fun to play with.

Another time when I was seven, we went to Finest, which used to be the Big A&P. It was dark, grey, and cloudy out there. It was starting to rain and downpour. My whole family ran in to do our real grocery shopping. Larry was age three. I used to try to climb up in the shopping cart all by myself and sit in the small, hard, metal baby seat in the front and barely fit in comfortably, just for a few minutes though, until I was eight, and around 4 feet tall and 50 lbs. I would also climb in the cart with the food.

MIRROR OF MY WORLD

My Dad got frozen cylinders of Tropicana OJ he would make, Red Gatorade, Skippy Creamy Peanut Butter, Welsh's Grape Jelly, and Quaker Minute Oats. My Dad liked this Hungry Man dinner they don't make any more—breaded veal cutlet with marinara, Fettuccine Alfredo, green beans and apple cobbler. It was so good that my Dad didn't want to share it with me. Mom got me the turkey and stuffing and fried chicken ones. She couldn't get me to eat much of her cooking. My Mom liked Pepperidge Farm cinnamon raisin bread they would toast with cream cheese. Chips Ahoy cookies (didn't like these much), mixed berry fruit on the bottom yogurt, and Ellio's frozen pizza. She would buy Hi-C and Ssips fruit punch and Mott's Apple Juice boxes for school lunch. I liked a mini box of double chocolate chips and any rainbow cereal, chewy fruit bars, and Quaker Chew granola bars. I always wanted a toy from the toy machine, like green slime. Of course, I rarely got that. Luckily, they had prizes in the cereal then.

When we were leaving it was a major downpour, torrential rains, coming down in buckets, so much so that my Dad had to make a run for the car, despite thunder, lightning, and big puddles, and drive to the entrance to pick us up so we could all get in without getting wet. That was fun. Back then, I loved adventures like that—the rare hospital or doctor trip, plumbers coming over, hurricanes, blizzards… I thought it was so exciting. My life was boring, so I always loved some adventure that my parents' thought was a bother and inconvenience.

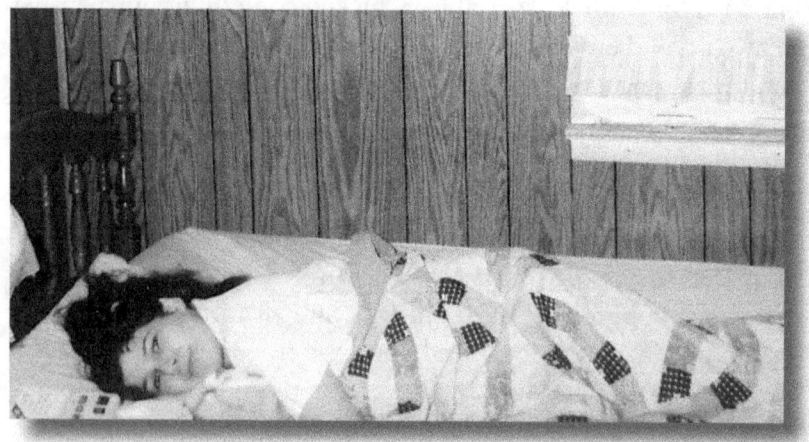

Christian Karen Berman

GOING TO THE BEACH CLUB

My parents called it that. I was between ages three and 12 when we would go there many times during the summer months. It was two outdoor swimming pools in Greenwich, Connecticut. It was only about 15 minutes from our house. It had one big swimming pool with a diving board, the other a kiddie pool. It had outdoor BBQ pits to make charcoal-grilled hamburgers and hot dogs. It smelt great—the smoky, burning smell. It had a run-down old playground, metal swings and maybe a slide and grassy areas. They used it for a day camp, too, in the summer. It had a place to shower with checkered tiles, but it smelt bad in there, like sweaty body odor. I noticed that even as a child, we never showered there; we bathed at home.

The day before, we would go to the supermarket, maybe the A&P or Gristedes, to get supplies for our picnic lunch that we would pack in a white Styrofoam picnic basket. My Mom would get Wonder Bread, two cans of Chicken of the Sea or Star-Kist tuna fish, and a peach, nectarine and plum, but just one or two per person. My Dad would get the important, good stuff that made the trip. He'd get the Little Dutch Boy Chocolate Biscuit cookies or chocolate-layered wafer cookies. We'd eat those going up a very steep hill, in the car in a woodsy area on the way to the Beach Club. That made it so special. He couldn't wait until after lunch, he couldn't wait until we got there, we had to eat it on the drive up, passing around the cookie box for everyone to take one or two cookies. My Daddy, the fun one, like a big kid. I always saw other parents there giving their kids Ritz Crackers. I wanted that. I don't think my Mom bought that, but maybe I didn't ask her for them.

The morning we are getting ready to leave, I put my swimsuit on under my clothes and make sure I use the bathroom before we leave. I would not want to use a strange bathroom. I'm very excited and can't wait to leave. My Mom is packing up the picnic basket, the cheap kind. I left two bites I bit out of the Styrofoam from last year and since it was in the basement, they might have thought a rat did it. I told them I did it. I just liked the feel of the texture. I spit it out and didn't swallow it. Seven-year-olds. They needed to buy a new basket. Hmm, what did it cost? Five bucks?

Then on the road, going up the woodsy trail, eating the chocolatey cookies, mmmm. Once we arrive there, my Dad pulls his car to the side to show a guy his beach club membership card I.D. to let him in and then he goes to park in the parking lot. It's kind of grey and a bumpy ride in the gravelly, rocky parking lot. We get out and walk to the metal gates and enter.

I want to run around first and go on the swings. I want to play. My parents want to eat first. My Grandma Lee made us the tuna fish sandwiches, with mayo, cut in half for everyone. She didn't want to come with us. It's hot and sunny, about 75-80 degrees. My Mom and me have to enter through the women's locker room. My Dad and brother went through the men's locker room. Ours was pink checkered, theirs was blue checkered, just so you didn't get confused. I brought wings, floaties; I didn't know how to swim until age 10.

Once through the metal gate my parents would find an empty grass spot to spread out our beach towel and set up the picnic. There were napkins, too, and the sandwiches wrapped in tin foil. I wanted to swim first. No, you had to eat first; guess they were hungry or didn't want the mayo to spoil. I didn't like to eat. It didn't interest me much ever. (If we went to Sears we'd havta eat first; I was just excited to go look at toys. The food was okay, but I wasn't that hungry, wanted to look around at toys and get an inexpensive one. That made me so happy.) There were lots of parents and kids sitting down on beach towels eating or swimming, having snacks. I eat maybe half a sandwich, maybe half a fruit. I don't remember if we had potato chips or not. To drink, either juice boxes, Coke, Pepsi, Gristedes, Mott's Apple Juice, orange juice, lemonade; I can't remember what I drank. I must of not drank much, glad I didn't need to use the bathroom. I did not like the sitting and "waiting an hour after we eat rule" enforced. I said to let us go swimming first. I had to watch everyone else and keep asking if it's time yet. At age seven, I had to go in the kiddie pool anyway and I couldn't swim, and I was too small to go in the big pool, it started at three feet, I had to have my Dad come and watch me. I was 45" and the water went up to my neck, the wings were cheap and wouldn't even hold me and make me float. I had to stand on my tippy toes, so it didn't matter if I went in the kiddie pool, it only went to two feet or so anyway.

I went in and sat in the baby pool with a few other toddlers, laid on my tummy, tried to swim, splashed, then asked my Dad if I could go in the big pool. He went in with me. I think I tried to hang on to him at first and then hold on to the side of the pool and kicked, then tried to swim. (I had indoor swimming lessons at the Y at age six in the winter months, but I didn't learn to swim.) I put my head under the water to get my hair wet. It was pulled back into a ponytail. It only went a bit past my shoulders, though. Grandma Lee probably did my hair with a rubber band. My Dad made me get out, then I had to wait to go back in again.

One time there was a teenage girl and her parents sitting next to us on a blanket. I was age seven or eight. She must have fainted; she was lying down unconscious, and her parents were trying to put a wet washcloth in her mouth or wake her up. They were worried about her, but not panicked. They did not ask for help or call an ambulance. I don't think I even saw a payphone. How would they call, in the

MIRROR OF MY WORLD

1980s? They were just kind of waiting for her to wake up. Did she have an eating disorder or just dehydrated? I was closely watching this, not much else to do while just waiting to go back into the pool anyway. I wondered why no one came over and tried to help. While this was happening seven-year-old me kept asking my Dad when I can go back into the big pool. He said when my hair dries. So, I take my hands and wring out my ponytail so it was dry and then said a minute later, "My hair's dry, can I go back in the pool now?"

I think my Dad noticed the fainted girl. She had to be over 12 to early 20s, so I'm thinking teenager. Not sure why no one did nothing; she was just lying there. Maybe it happened before, maybe one person came over or if that was just her family, did everyone just mind their own business back then? I was too young to know. My Dad noticed it too, maybe that's why he didn't want me to go back in, but I asked him so much, he just said yes and happily I went back into the big pool. There weren't any kids my age that was playing with me; every family kept to themselves. It was the late 1980s.

After they said "last swim," I went back in the pool one more time. We had been there two or three hours and Mom was packing up the picnic basket. It was sad to leave, but I loved the water. After we left the swimming pool part, my Dad let us go to the old playground. It was a walk over past the BBQ pit and picnic table part down a grassy field. The playground was hot metal and we went on the swings with a black rubber bottom to sit on, maybe a slide. I said they need to fix up the playground. After that we walked back out to the parking lot and left. Years ago, when I was much younger looking at the woody part as you enter where we lived I said, "Look at all the scenery." My parents didn't know where I heard and got that big word from. Neither did I; I was age four to six. I'd like to drive past there again, even my old Grandma's Garden Complex. I miss the good old days so much.

Christian Karen Berman

CHiCKeN POX

Now the first time I heard about this I was seven. It was February, my family was sitting in Epstein's, the local Jewish Delicatessen. I was eating a hot dog, because I was only seven. My brother was sitting next to me, and across the table was my Dad and Mom. I think my Grandma was at home. My Mom was talking about chickenpox. I wasn't sure what she was talking about and I thought for sure she was talking about Chicken Pops. In my seven-year-old mind I pictured a big frozen chocolate pop with chicken flavored Ice cream, Chicken Pops.

That night I got bad food poisoning from the frankfurters, as they were called there. It was the worst I ever felt. They never took me to the hospital because back in the mid-80s, you only went there if you were dying. I had thrown up too much. I was lying in the middle of my parents' twin beds, my head in the middle of the beds, pressure, tightness in my head, threw up too many times. I had a big rectangle ice pack and washcloth for my headache. I was lying next to my Jenny doll who was wearing the white hospital sweater my parents brought me home from St. Agnus in as a newborn. I felt like I would die. I never felt more miserable in my life. The slight good note in all of this—no school tomorrow. I would have rather went to school than be this sick. I'm not sure if my Dad called the deli to complain or not or called my Doctor.

I was at choir practice with the cantor from our temple. I was at his house with the other kids from my Hebrew school class. We were practicing singing. Then he broke this delicious orange chocolate bar into little squares and gave us each one to try. It was one of the best things I ever tasted. That night I was scratching the side of my elbow a lot. It must be a mosquito bite, I thought. I finally showed my Mom. Chickenpox. So that's what she was talking about. No school for me again. I don't remember being that sick, just having itchies pop up all over. I was told not to scratch or pick them, there would be scarring. I probably had a low-grade fever, tiredness and sore throat. I don't remember feeling that bad, just surprised that I wouldn't be able to go back to school for a week or two. It was probably to protect the other students from my terrible disease. Back then, I just didn't think about that. It was another vacation for me. My Grandma knew I liked freckles and said I'd be getting many more of them. I just watched Nickelodeon, *Pinwheel*, *Today's Special*, *The Little Prince*, *Belle and Sebastian*, The Disney Channel, *You and Me Kid*, *Pooh Corner* and my afternoon cartoons, *Inspector Gadget* (I liked Penny) *He-Man and She-Ra*.

During that time my parents were taking my old baby crib out, the one I screamed, cried and refused to sleep in during my first year. Larry was three and outgrew it and getting his own bed. I now loved the baby crib, would lay down in it after second grade, relaxing, looking up at the ceiling and room from a weird angle, playing with the mobile and crib toys, maybe daydreaming, when I wasn't climbing around all of the dressing tables and furniture in the room, pretending it was mountains and I was friends with She-Ra. It was devastating to see it go. It was a fun toy and comfort. I was 45 pounds at seven, very skinny and I still fit in the baby crib. I'm not sure I related my feelings about this to my Dad. I had a hard time expressing my thoughts and feelings, like I wanted my hair to grow long like my friend Vickie's and my Grandma kept it shoulder length. I knew how I felt in my head but was either too shy to say it or didn't have the words for it, not sure. Even at age 9 or 10 and my Dad was removing the car seat I still loved and sat in and fit in. Maybe I was very well-behaved or thought my opinion wouldn't matter.

Two men came to bring in my brother's new twin bed and assemble it. Larry wasn't kept away from me. My Mom wanted him to catch chickenpox and get it over with. One of the men overheard me or my Mom saying I'm not in school because I have the chickenpox. He said, "You have the chickenpox?" He ran out of there real fast. The other guy stayed and said he never had the chickenpox before. They looked in their 30s. I felt insulted he ran out because of little me.

I said hi to my younger neighbor and school friend, Sonia, from my bedroom window and showed her my tiger that played music. She had the same one. I was also playing with my Funshine Care Bear, many toys in the middle of my room. When my Mom finally took me back to second grade a week later, Mrs. C.C. didn't want me at first. "She still doesn't look too good. Are you sure she's ready to go back to school? It's not too soon? Is she all better? Did the doctor say it's okay, is she having any symptoms?" I was all for that, I would have loved to go home and play for another week. And this was coming from the teacher who wouldn't let me go to the nurse's office anymore because I played sick one too many times.

MIRROR OF MY WORLD

Christian Karen Berman

GRANDMA LEE'S APARTMENT

After my Grandpa Jules Cohen died, my Grandma still kept her Garden Complex apartment. She gave me the cute little piggy bank, cream-colored with bumps and pink and green colors on top, looking like it was from the old days. Grandpa would put all his lose change in it and say, "This is for Christian, I'm saving it for Christian." Thinking of little me. On the same note, on my sixth birthday, two months before he died, he gave me a cheap $5 doll he got at the 5&10 and he had got me something similar on my fifth birthday and my Mom and Grandma wasn't happy and was like why did you buy her that, but I loved it, because it was from him and I didn't want him to feel bad, especially because no one else seemed to like her. I didn't want to hurt the sweet doll's feelings, too; my Mom taught me that. After he died my Grandma put that little plastic doll, with long, golden blonde pigtails and wearing a red plaid dress, away in the closest to save it. It was the last thing he bought me. Till this day I still have her in the same closet in the same house. My Grandpa went to the last meeting with my kindergarten teacher, Mrs. Pierce, with my Mom. He came back proud of me. Mommy, too. My Dad must have been at his school, teaching other people's kids.

My Grandma Lee would stay in her apartment for a few days, maybe a week now and then, to keep her independence after my Grandpa died. Maybe to look at her old things or do some knitting. But it wasn't often, though. It was hard for her to live alone, being in her in 70s and needing our help, love, and support. When we visited, she would make me the same dish—chopped egg salad and Franco-American Spaghetti on a plate next to it. She had a special, brown wooden two-step chair for me. I was small. I looked around her apartment by the big front window, where there were seashells she collected by the beach and saved (you could hear the sea in them), and a Starfish, too.

MIRROR OF MY WORLD

When you would walk up the stairs, it had a bit of an old smell to it, the apartment. In the coat closest was two old light blue boxes of big, hard, shiny pretzels. In the kitchen there was a few jars of different old pickles, *The Flintstones* glass cups they collected from McDonald's, or Welch's jelly. There was a breakfront with dining ware in the living room and comfy old chairs, in a green floral print. There was another room with a brown wooden hope chest and old National Geographic magazines from as old as 1976, plus old Sears catalogs. Those I enjoyed looking at when I was a little older.

One day, we visited after a birthday party I went to for a classmate. I was seven, they probably served pizza and cake. I got a cool goodie bag. Oh, how I loved those cheap treasures. It was a green and pink plastic thing with a string and you would try to get the ball in the top cup, a plastic maze, a thing you blew out and made noise, bubble gum, a lollipop, a metal noise thing you would swing with your hand, a plastic whistle, a bouncy ball, plastic jelly bracelet, some things like that. Can you tell I didn't get many presents as a kid? loved even cereal prizes, like the slimy spider that you would throw on the wall and it would slowly crawl down. It didn't take much to make me happy back then. I was showing my parents and Grandma my little gifts and felt kinda sick. It was late afternoon, 4 pm. I told my Dad I wasn't feeling good, maybe a sore throat and tummy ache. He gave me a Hall's honey lemon cough drop and said it would make me feel better. Then I started to feel worse and went to the bathroom and threw up. Then I felt better.

Afterwards, Grandma took me into her bedroom with my Mom, opened one of her dresser drawers and gave me tan and red knitted moccasin sock slippers to put on my feet to keep them warm. A friend gave them to her and they fit me. She said to rest in her bed a while until I felt a little better. Her drawers had treasures, different embroidered handkerchiefs, pretty ones, all kinds of different colorful yarns and beautiful assorted buttons of all kinds, sizes, styles and colors. I loved to look through them. Her dresser was hand carved wood with designs and beautiful, with so many thin layers of drawers in a dark cherry wood, not like the cheap kind they make today, this had to be from the 1940s. She had a white layered jewelry box, filled with some old pins, buttons, pennies and a little jewelry. My Grandma used to donate money to Israel or a Jewish fund and would get in return this most delicious, fine, milk, gourmet, Israel Chocolate and give me a big piece to taste. Best thing I ever tasted. Kept it in her fridge.

After my bath at home, she would comb out my hair and sometimes braid it. She taught me how to braid it myself at age seven (my Mom couldn't do hair at all). She also played cat's cradle with me whenever we got that red candy-striped string from a bakery box. She told me stories, too, like she had to give her beautiful dress to this anorexic 14-year-old friend/girl because her Mom told her to. When I was older (age ten), I felt bad she was never in the newspaper, so I wrote a newspaper article about her, and also one about the earth being invaded by UFOs, flying saucers, and aliens. She always told me, I love you more than you'll ever know.

It was so nice to be loved by her.

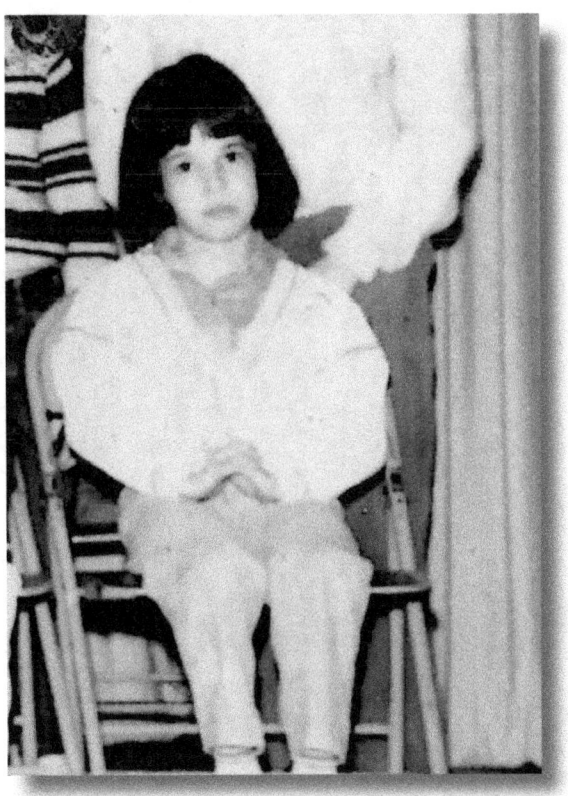

MIRROR OF MY WORLD

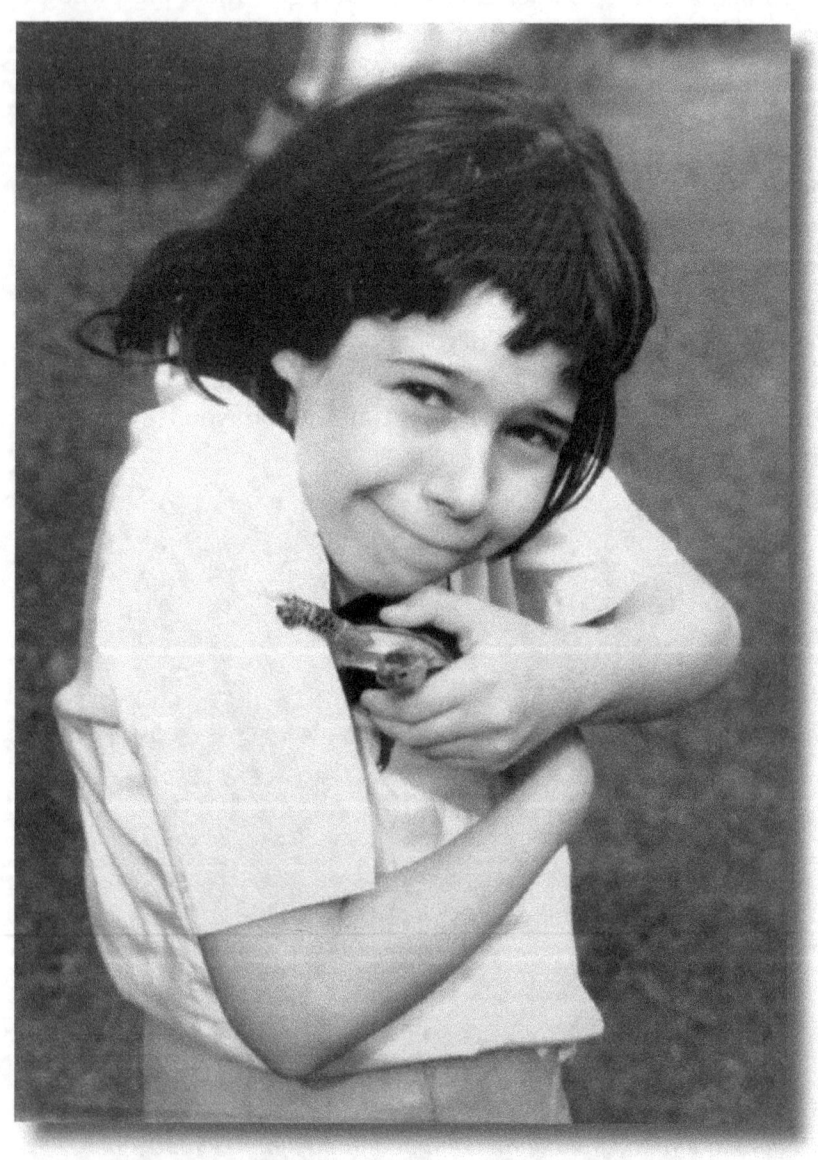

Christian Karen Berman

THE COOL BENEFITS OF BEING AGE 7

I got to share Chiclets gum with my friend. I got my first pack of Skittles candies and tried purple cotton candy at my friend's birthday party. My Mom got me *Garbage Pail Kids* cards and a small plastic *Thunderbirds* sword, a Trapper Keeper, I got two Cabbage Patch Kids, Stride Rite Velcro sneakers with rainbow sides (the girls in class had to take off their sneakers and two of them had the same ones, they weren't sure whose was whose and went to get mine, too, and got them all mixed up; I was only age six here, never sure if I actually got my own sneakers back… six-year-olds), Hi-C and Ssips juice boxes instead of just Mott's Apple Juice box. I joined the Brownie's and got a uniform. I tried to write cursive before it was taught, copied my friend. I got to eat Swanson frozen dinners and drink red Gatorade. I got a He-Man action figure and PJs. I learned to braid my own hair from my Grandma Lee, learned to play cat's cradle with her. Tried candy buttons for the first time and molasses chocolate candy, Oreo ice cream, Watermelon Ring Pops, Fruit Rollups. I got my first plastic charms necklace with lots of charms (that was for getting stung by a bee and having to take Benadryl for the first time; I fell right asleep on our couch). My Dad and Grandma surprised me with this—a black plastic jelly bracelet. Tried Red Hots little cinnamons for Valentine's Day. Got aqua My Little Ponys and Funshine Care Bears. Got a slimy jelly spider you got in kid's cereals, you threw on the wall and watched it crawl down.

MIRROR OF MY WORLD

[Christian Karen Berman](#)

A Day in the Life of Me as a 7-Year-Old

I'm sound asleep at the end of my parents' double twin bed on my Mom's side. The old night light is turned on. My Mom walks in and throws a Quaker Chewy Chocolate Chip granola bar on my bed, that means it's time to wake up and open my granola bar. My hands are still tired and numb from sleep so it's hard to take the wrapper off. It's about 6:50 am. I get up to go to the bathroom, come back and open my granola bar and eat it, then have a drink of water from the faucet in the sink. It's cold and good. If it was the weekend it would be Cheerios. Once we were outta milk and creative me used orange juice. Then my Mom lays out my clothes to wear, something comfortable like pink jogging pants and a sweatshirt.

Once I wore my brother's Winnie the Pooh PJs under my shirt. I just really liked it. That day I was bribed by both parents to go to a half day. it was a full day, though, and I didn't want to go all at. I asked if they would buy me a Hello Kitty that you wound up and it played a lullaby, if I went. I negotiated well for a seven-year-old and they agreed. I went to school with my Care Bear sweatshirt rolled up to show off my brother's Winnie the Pooh PJs that day. I was pretending to be a bit sick, because my Mom said that was why she was taking me home early and I got my Hello Kitty as promised.

Another time I accidentally forgot to give my Bluebell (*My Little Pony*) to my Mom at the bus stop, so I was carrying her around most of the day so my teacher, Mrs. C.C., wouldn't find her and confiscate her from me the rest of the year. That would have really hurt me; she was almost real to me. I would hold her under my shirt, hide her in the bottom of my shirt, or put her in my desk. She made it through the whole day with me in one piece.

One day my Mom bought me a pack of *Garbage Pail Kids* cards when I was age seven, when I skipped school that morning with

MIRROR OF MY WORLD

a small Thunder Cats plastic sword. I felt like the coolest second grader ever. Those cards are for big kids and teenagers. My Mom tried to have my principal, Mrs. Manning, call the truant officer on me like back in my Grandma's day. Mrs. Manning said there was a flu going around and it was probably better I stay home. I was going to hide behind my bed. The secretary gave my Mom my homework and a bunch of cute little sheets of bear stickers. Better than my pediatrician; he only gave yucky tasting lollipops. They had a treasure chest I wanted toys from, but they never offered it to me when I was actually sick; they thought at age seven, I was too old for cheap plastic gadgets like jelly bracelets, plastic whistles, too much cool stuff.

I'm waiting at the school bus stop with the other kids, going out in the rain, hoping if I got wet enough I wouldn't have to go to school and just having fun being a kid. When I got there I was wet enough to be sent down to the office. The principal gave me a paper towel and said, "You can dry it yourself, can't you?" I'm a big girl of seven.

It's reading comprehension and I can't comprehend it. The teachers asked another seven-year-old to explain it to me. I'm not sure what she's saying, but oh well. I tried other times to fake being sick to go home to my Mom and watch Nickelodeon. I go to the nurse holding my head and saying I have a headache. I had faked sick so many times now she refuses to send me to the nurse's office. It's lunch time now. I get the same as usual every day **PB&J**. I hate it, the jelly especially. My Mom told the teacher I'm not eating my lunch and once she even brought the nurse into the library with me and sat at a table with some saltines to try to get me to eat. I took a few bites. I hate the food, not hungry, would rather have school pizza for lunch. She still goes by my table to check on me and I take two bites to show I'm eating so as not to get in trouble. The other kids get Doritos, Chex mix, Gummy bears. I got Wise potato chips and Chips Ahoy cookies to go with it every day and a Hi-C fruit punch drink in my lunch box.

It's a long bus ride home. Even though I'm only a mile away, I'm the last to be dropped off. It seems like an hour on the bus. I get home about 4 pm just in time to have my Hershey's chocolate bar and watch cartoons. Luckily, I don't even finish my juice box. I never go to the bathroom at school and at seven, I didn't figure out drinking more makes you go more.

I'm sucking my chocolate bar to make it last longer and enjoying some *He-Man and She-Ra* cartoons. I'm tired and lying on my parents' bed resting. Then I go into my room and lay in my baby crib to relax and look at the ceiling in different ways. It's almost 5 pm. My parents are making me dinner. I go back into my room to watch the Cartoon Network and my Mom makes me a Swanson fried chicken or turkey and stuffing. I don't like my Mom's cooking very much. She makes a good tuna fish salad though. I'm going into my walk-in closet to play after dinner, swinging on the coat racks. There's a white wooden plank to sit at the end of the walk-in closet, my parents' old clothes and some of my younger clothes. I use it as my hide out and club house. I love the built-in monkey bars to swing on—how fun! Luckily, I'm only 45 pounds or they might break off. I have a baby blanket and a few toys in the back with me. I try on my Mom's old fur coat. Then my Mom comes looking for me and say's The Cosby Show is on. That gets me out fast. I love Rudy, she's about my age and cute. I come out, a little dusty and worse for wear to watch one of my favorite TV shows.

It's bedtime now. I'm a little hungry, sleeping in my bed, My Mom brings me a Kraft cheese and white bread sandwich. I call it cat nip. I'm pretending I'm a cat and eat it in pieces. I think I just drank water from the faucet, not sure if she brought me a Mott's Apple Juice box. I sleep with my Glow Worm to protect me from monsters and ghosts in my dark room. I have a Care Bear Funshine Bear, too. Larry's in the other bed going to sleep. I don't think I was your normal seven-year-old.

What do you think?

MIRROR OF MY WORLD

Christian Karen Berman

THE OLD-FASHIONED BIG, WHITE CHENILLE BLANKET ON MY PARENTS' BED

I used to sleep in my parents' bed when I was a kid, sometimes even as a teenager. There were many blankets and old quilts, they didn't have weighted blankets back then and my Dad liked it warm. This particular blanket would let you pull white strings out. Whenever I would need a string, I would pull one out. Not sure how old this blanket was, but I was about seven. I needed a swing for my Mini Cabbage Patch dolls that I would tie to the metal part on my desk drawer and put around the 3" Cabbage Patch's waist and swing her as a swing and then maybe my Strawberry Shortcake or Heart Family doll would try to save her. I enjoyed doing this so. I would even put my little dolls in the bathroom sink and fill it to the top with water so they could go swimming. My Mom told my Grandma. She didn't understand how I liked playing in the water so much.

I would tie some of the string to the wooden side part of my parents' bed, so my little dolls could play there, too. I'm not sure they noticed some strings missing, but it was old and the strings were coming undone anyway.

Kids.

MIRROR OF MY WORLD

<u>Christian Karen Berman</u>

VISITING A RELATIVE

My memory on this trip is a little fuzzy, trying my best. I was seven years old; my parents were driving with my brother to New Jersey to visit Aunt Florence, I only saw her this one time and she had to be in her 70s then. My Grandma Lee stayed home. It was a long trip on the road, three hours. My Dad was driving; he always drove for long trips. We were in the big, white 1978 Oldsmobile, tan leather seats inside. It was a big car. It was August in the mid-1980s. There was a black leather baby car seat in the car, all hot leather and some metal, not sure if anyone was sitting in it, though. I sat in it off-and-on until almost age 10. I looked out on the highway and cars, wondering when we would get there.

We finally arrived—yay! There was green grass, a large yard in front. I ran out of the car and we all walked in the back way to greet her. I didn't even have to go to the bathroom. I looked around. We were hungry, at least I was. She offered us sharp cheddar cheese. She was slicing the brick of cheese into many slices for us all to eat. I don't think I ate yet that day; I don't remember my Dad stopping off on the highway for lunch, maybe a diner. Well, we all ate some cheese slices. I ate at least three. I kept coming back for her to slice another piece of cheese, which made me think I was hungry and didn't eat yet and it had to be around 2 pm by then. For many reasons, you don't want to force a seven-year-old to eat before a long road trip. My Mom might have packed some Hi-C juice boxes and chocolate chip cookies or some snacks and sandwiches, in the car for the trip. Then she served chocolate cake, I loved this, ate mostly the chocolate frosting and even asked for seconds and thirds. She was serving a chocolate ice cream on a cone too. By then I was full.

I remember after, going to the Holiday Inn to sleep over, it was too long a trip for my Dad to drive back that night. I remember

MIRROR OF MY WORLD

starting to feel really sick and headachy, not good at all, yucky. My Mom wheeled my brother in the stroller to the hotel room and I went back to the parking lot with my Dad to help carry in the overnight bag and some other things. I carried the navy stroller bag. I was feeling sick and headachy walking. I was happy to be going with my Dad, though, and helping him.

We walked into the motel, up a carpeted ramp and found our motel room. I was happy to be there and told my Dad I didn't feel good and had a headache. I laid flat on the bed. It was such a nice, thick, plush tan, rich velvet blanket, cozy. The radio was on, playing some nice soft background music 80s soft rock. I felt icky, funny. I got up and ran to the bathroom and threw up in the toilet. Now my parents believed me and knew I was really very sick. I was in the bathroom a while, trying to throw up more and get it all out, while having a splitting, sick headache. This part I remember well. Then after, I felt a little better and went to lie back down on top of the velvet blanket with my Mom right next to me. I still had the yucky headache, though. I don't think they called my Grandma Lee or the pediatrician.

I was listening to the soft, relaxing music, happily starting to fall asleep. My Dad and Mom were talking about ordering dinner, room service. They couldn't take sick little me down to the restaurant. My Dad ordered two grilled cheese sandwiches, fries, ketchup and two large Cokes with ice. That's what they ate back then. My Dad asked me if I wanted anything. I said no (he used to put Italian dressing on my half-sandwich to make me eat it).

The next morning, I felt all better and cured. So much better, sick headache and sick stomach all gone. We drove to another old relative in their late 70s, a couple's house and they had no kids. They cooked for us in their kitchen eggs, home fries, bacon and ketchup. I was hungry, I ate some, with O.J. I remember the man took my Dad in the closet/bathroom and took out his eyeball. He had an eye missing and it was replaced with a glass eye that looked real. Not sure if he let me see or my Dad hold it. That sounds cool, don't think I saw, just heard about it from my Dad. I don't know how he lost it—the war, sick, cancer.

Then they drove us to the lake. We parked in the parking lot and got out. There was docks, grass, and adults and kids swimming in the lake. I took my and Larry's two Fisher Price Little People with me. I went to the dock. I just took off my shoes, maybe got my feet wet. Wanted to put the plastic little people in the water to see if they would float or sink, play with them. I wasn't allowed in the water, didn't even have a swimsuit. I couldn't do it, though—I was afraid they would sink and I would lose them. That's the last thing I remember. My memory always went black after this, can't remember what else happened. Maybe I feel asleep in the back of the car, can't remember anymore.

MIRROR OF MY WORLD

Christian Karen Berman

WHAT 7-YEAR-OLD ME DID WITH ORANGE JUICE

1) I would mix half Mott's Apple Juice with Tropicana and make my own special, more interesting drink. Before age seven, I didn't even get Hi-C fruit punch or Gatorade, I got water, had to jazz up the juice.

2) I would freeze it in my Mom's ceramic cups and put in a spoon or hold it with a paper towel and try to break the No-Popsicle Rule, at least no Red Dye # 40.

3) We ran out of milk one early morning; I figured out what to do—put O.J. in my Cheerios. It tasted like fruity Cheerio's, not bad for a seven-year-old mind.

MIRROR OF MY WORLD

MY FAVORITE TOYS OF THE MID- TO LATE-1980S GROWING UP AS A LITTLE GIRL

1) Age seven, He-Man. I watched the cartoon every day, had the PJs, had He-Man and Teela action figures, but wish I had the whole set. For a little girl, I sure loved He-Man. Skeletor scared me, but I loved him, too.

2) My Fisher Price Record player. I would play my parents old records on it and some of mine. Carpenter's, Annie, and Happy Feet.

3) Glow Worm. My parents thought if I had this at age seven, I would finally sleep in my own room and not be afraid of the dark. It worked sometimes.

4) Strawberry Shortcake doll. I loved the strawberry scent and her red hair and cute kitty.

5) Slinky, Silly Putty, Koosh Ball, plastic snakes and Water Snake, Slap Bracelets, the first fidget toys.

6) The sticky spider you got in sugary kid's cereals in 1986, that you threw on the wall and would slowly walk down.

7) Popples.

8) Wuzzles.

9) Freaky Freezie gloves my Mom bought me at age seven. I had the glittery, light blue one with rainbows and hearts. I know they have them now, but they made them better back then. Everything they made better back then.

10) Pogo ball.

11) Minnie Mouse Velcro Roller Skates.

12) Hasbro Softies, My Little Pony, it was white with rainbow hair you can brush.

Christian Karen Berman

13) Fisher Price Little People Main Street.

14) Fisher Price Coin Jammers, red and yellow. My Mom put $2 in it every day for school lunch in the 4th grade.

15) Mini Plastic Cabbage Patch Girl with red yarn hair. Carried that out to dinner and wet her hair in the bathroom, took her too school, too, and My Little Pony, the blue and hot pink hair one.

16) Rainbow Brite. I would cry to her sometimes and tell her all my problems. I loved her hair and dress, too.

17) My Buddy, Big Doll, Brotherly Love, Not Scary. Kid Sister, too.

18) *Garbage Pail Kids* Cards. My Mom bought me a pack at age seven, when I skipped school with a small Thunder Cats Plastic Sword.

19) Transformers or GoBots. I had one, thought it was so cool.

20) Heart to Heart Bear.

21) Skip It, hot pink color.

22) Hula hoop. I was great at this.

23) The red wand from the Tag reading system. I liked hearing it beep. It was to help you learn to read hard words. Larry and I played with that.

24) The Cookie Counter Yellow game. Larry and I had one. Cookie Monster would juggle cookies and you try to hit the button so he wouldn't drop them. Speak and Read and a reverse calculator toy called Little Professor. I liked Cookie Counter best, played it until I was 13.

25) My Soft Little Tiger that played a lullaby when you turned the metal key. I had a soft white and yellow lamb I liked, too.

26) This big 24" baby doll from the Sears Christmas Wish Book. It was bald, made well, and would wear my brother's old baby and toddler clothes.

MIRROR OF MY WORLD

Christian Karen Berman

TRIP TO GRANDMA'S HOUSE

I was seven or eight years old. My Dad was talking to Grandma Gert the night before in his bedroom on his tan Princess phone from the 1970s. It was all worked out—we were going to Brooklyn that next morning. At this age, I never spoke to anyone on the phone, so I told my Dad I didn't want to go. I was scared to go into New York City and Brooklyn. I just knew it was dangerous and with the crime, maybe we would get hurt or killed in a car accident. It was also about two hours away, because of all the traffic and jam-ups. I started to sob and cry real tears too, because I was afraid. My Dad hugged me and reassured me it was safe and we would be fine. I was still scared. I think he sensed I was, too, but he didn't let on. He rarely ever went into the city.

After out short talk, I went right to bed with my parents. My brother slept in his own bed in my room or the hall floor on a Winnie the Pooh quilt by choice, I can't remember, he was transitioning from the crib and I would cry in my room and not sleep, I had to sleep with my parents. There were a few nights I did sleep in my own bed, but it was hard for me. Some nights I did it and was brave. I thought when I'm 11 I will have to sleep in my own bed, but it was so long away, I didn't worry to bother thinking about it. It was more like age 15 when I slept in my own bed regularly.

That next morning, Grandma Lee, the only Grandma that lived with us, did not want to come and would be fine staying home by herself. My Mom was worried about my brother and being on the highway for a few hours and not being able to pull off, so she brought a big empty bottle, maybe Mott's Apple Juice or a Pepsi bottle, just in case he had to use the bathroom. His pediatrician had said that to my Mom. Luckily he didn't have to use it. I packed a diaper bag with Hi-C fruit punch, some kind of snack, cookies, maybe a coloring book or little toy. I can't remember, but at that time for even a 15-minute trip, I would get excited and pack the diaper bag. I loved going anywhere and would pretend it was a vacation. My Grandma never let me bring my stuffed dog or stuffed animals or dolls in fear I would lose it and cry.

On the road I looked out on the highway and saw lots of cars and road. My Dad was listening to 1980s soft rock on the radio. I don't even think my brother was in a baby car seat and he was only three-and-a-half years old; the car seat was in our other car. I can't remember seeing it on this trip. On the way there we got lost or stopped off somewhere, by houses next to one another and concrete sidewalks with a square with a tree and a little patch of grass. My Daddy told me that Grandma Gert lived in the city and there was no grass there. I took that literally and was so excited I saw a patch of green grass. I picked a few pieces of grass to show the Grandma I never saw before what grass looks like. I think my Dad thought I was being silly. I thought it was an amazing thing I was doing. Eight-year-olds, you gotta love them, big hearts.

When we got there, it was an apartment complex. I got out of the car and we all went into the apartment where my Dad grew up. We were all glad we made it here alive. No one was mugged or hijacked or anything, it was a miracle. Their place smelt a little like old and dirty laundry, especially the closet Grandma Gert showed me. It had some bags of old stuff. While I was there, I played with the piano my Dad learned to play on and had lessons from age 8-11 years old. I couldn't play, but that was the only fun thing to do there; my Grandma Gert had nothing to entertain us. She was 74 years old. I didn't think to go exploring and inspect the closet she showed us. I believe Larry took a nap in my Dad's old bedroom. Daddy played the song "What the World Needs Now is Love Sweet Love." He had the music notes and lyrics by the piano and I sung the songs typed on the paper. Daddy played by ear. It was the most beautiful and memorable moment; my Dad played well. That song and me singing I remember most. He might have played "Do You Know the Way to San Jose" and "I Just Called to Say I Love You." He loved those songs, but I can't remember for sure, maybe something else from an old musical, like *Kiss Me Kate* or *Oklahoma*. I couldn't play at all. I remember telling my new Grandma I was bored about four times in the three or more hours we were there. It was rude, but kids speak the truth.

No one had eaten all day, so while Mama Gert was preparing lunch, she made Daddy and me a snack. Us poor folks had white bread and mayo for a snack. Her bread was in the fridge and she was going to toast it to warm it up for us. I said I don't like it toasted. She said it was cold and she had to warm up the bread. I didn't like that. I can't remember what I had to drink, milk maybe. For lunch she made seasoned chicken, with potato and RiceARoni, something like that, and my Grandpa Joe with a big, sweet heart who had bad Alzheimer's, asked if she gave Larry a present. She said she gave him a toy truck, a little Fisher Price one. My Grandpa Joe sadly died a few months or a year later. I don't believe she gave me anything. One time I got a pink sweater from her, not sure what time. She rarely gave me anything. Once she bought Larry and me Fisher Price Time Jammers watches, because my Mom said she couldn't afford them and asked her if she could please buy them for her grandchildren.

Also, when I was 12, we visited her again and that time we all walked to the local playground. It wasn't much—metal playground and blacktop, old, empty and kinda run down, I recollect. I met an old lady friend of hers who guessed my age and thought I was age eight. When it was time to leave, I was kinda happy to go home. I thought it was pretty boring there. As an adult, I would have asked my grandparents a million questions and took notes, looked at old photos (why didn't my Dad bring the camera?), and with permission explored the house and looked through my Dad's old things and drawers and closets. I was seven or eight then and my thinking was too young to be so deep. Toys and playing and kid shows were my life. My Dad said a few years before he died he had a cousin Laurel that lived in California. I couldn't find her, but I wanted to. She'd probably be in her mid-80s if she was still alive.

MIRROR OF MY WORLD

AN ARTIST IN THE MAKING
ARTWORK AGES 6 – 11

Mural of Bert & Ernie from *Sesame Street*

My earliest surviving artwork, a gift for my Dad.

MIRROR OF MY WORLD

Drawing I did in 6th grade of actress Rachel Jacobs, who played Alice, Arnold's girlfriend, on *Diff'rent Strokes*

She-Ra and Swift Wind drawing, age 8

Bird from *The Little Prince*, drawn when I was 8 or 9.

MIRROR OF MY WORLD

This turned out looking like Elyssa, my classmate from the second grade. It was done about a dozen years ago and was recently honored in an art show.

Christian Karen Berman

MIRROR OF MY WORLD

For this one, titled *Pretty Bird*, I won the Catholic Youth Organization contest for 2nd place at my school, Our Lady of Good Counsel Academy. I was in the 5th grade and 11 years old.

"A Little Touch of Heaven" (2004)

Illustration for an original teleplay I wrote for a *Mary Tyler Moore Show* spin-off, showing Mary Tyler Moore and Ed Asner as "Mary" and "Lou" with two orphans.

MIRROR OF MY WORLD

Christian Karen Berman

MY BIRTHDAYS

I saw this stuffed dog at Raiders Pharmacy around age seven. It was by Russ and was white with floppy brown ears and had two or three little, cute baby puppies. I wanted it more than anything in the world and waited for it. I was not a spoiled girl at all. It was about $20 in the mid 1980s and that's all little eight-year-old me got, but I was happy. I wanted to take her places with me, but my Grandma, who paid for her, said I would lose her and be sad and cry.

I went to other big birthday parties, like pizza parties, with lots of big presents, and I was jealous. They got so many big and cool toys I really wanted, but my parents could not afford much. Those parties had to cost $100-150 in the mid-1980s. Also, since I didn't have many friends, I was the quiet, shy girl in the class that was like the youngest and smallest. My parents were afraid not many friends would come and inviting the whole class would be expensive. I did get really cool goodie bags I loved. I think it had lollipops inside, bouncy balls, things you blow and it made a party noise, jelly bracelets, a little ball with a string attached you get in the cup, mini pinball games, party favors like that.

I was age eight and my brother was age four. We were invited to my Dad's estranged brother's second wedding in a temple in Brooklyn, New York. I remember having the diaper bag in the back seat of my Dad's car and our estranged Grandma Gert was sitting in the back with us and I did like her and the company and seeing her. It was probably the third time I could remember. I think she saw me as a baby, not sure though. She saw Larry when he was born and brought me a baby doll she named Morgen, but I don't remember that part. I remember picking her up from the train station. My Dad drove his car and it was the first time in my life I was sitting in the middle of the front seat and not in the back in the baby car seat. My feet didn't even go over the edge of the seat and the car felt so big. I was four and only 35 pounds and

MIRROR OF MY WORLD

still should have been in a baby seat, but my parents couldn't afford to buy another car seat. They were promised a used one, but their friends let them down. I was age four and it was legal back then, but a small four. This time, at age eight, my feet still didn't touch the floor of the backseat and barely went over the seat. I was about 4 feet and 50 pounds. Larry wasn't in a car seat either, but he was four.

It was dark outside, about 5-6 pm, and it was in the winter months, I believe, and got dark early. It was a fun adventure. I love exciting, fun adventures. In Larry's old diaper bag, I probably brought loose paper, pens, Hi-C fruit punch and maybe a My Little Pony, I used it to pack little things for road trips and still used this bag, but not for baby bottles and diapers. We got our money's worth on things back then, not just buying a new backpack to carry things. People were not wasteful in the late 1980s.

I vaguely remember my Dad's brother breaking the glass at the wedding, not much else. No one went over to say hi or introduce themselves to Larry and me. I do remember at the reception, the restaurant, we all sat at a big table and ordered food, and I ordered off the adult menu, friend chicken. My Dad's Mom told me that she would take home my leftovers and everyone else's. So, when the food came, I didn't save the best part for her, I ate all my favorite parts, the fried crispy outside part of the chicken. I never liked the chicken part as much. She shouldn't have told me that; I might have saved some crispy for her. Eight-year-old me, I'm sure you would do the same. Then when I was eating my fried chicken she turned and smiled at me, to be saying, she will be enjoying the same yummy fried chicken, too, probably to make leftover chicken salad with. She was going to have a lot of peoples' germy leftovers. Maybe it would be good, but she should have asked, "May I please take home your leftovers?" Instead, she just told me she was going to be taking them. Maybe I wanted to finish my own leftovers tomorrow and have something to look forward to, also. They probably came with mash potatoes or French fries; I can't remember if they did or not. I'm not sure if it was that good, but I didn't like my Mom's cooking much either. TV dinners were better sometimes. Maybe I was just hungry. I think my Uncle Henry paid.

Christian Karen Berman

MIRROR OF MY WORLD

Christian Karen Berman

TRiP TO BeNSONHURST, BROOKLYN, AVeNUe P

The Grandma I only met a few times in my life, Grandma Gert, Mama Gert. When I was about age seven my Dad's side of the family was coming over for a visit. This was a very big deal, for this might have been one of the first times I could remember them coming over and they only visited a few times in my life. I was so nervous and excited that morning. My Mom opened the closet in her bedroom and was putting on the very nice new comforter and bedspread and sham she only used for company (we rarely ever had company come over). It looked beautiful, expensive and well made. I slept in bed with my parents, so it would have been nice to use this more often. I think I got to sleep with it that night. My Mom also put out new towels on the rod in the bathroom. I was looking out the window many times that morning to see if my Dad's relatives had arrived yet. I told him, "I don't think they're coming, they're late." My Dad was finishing cleaning the downstairs, vacuuming, and moving the car down closer to the garage, so there would be room for their car. I just remember waiting and feeling so excited.

They finally came. My Grandma Gertrude, Grandpa Joe or Papa Joe, Aunt Florence, Uncle Abe and Uncle Morris. They were all very old, in their mid to late 70s. I was small, skinny, and cute and so was Larry. The main part I remember is just being happy and excited like it was going to be a great day and best day in the world.

I think we all went out for deli at Epstein's. They ordered tongue and didn't like it, so the waitress gave it to us. Mom thankfully sent back their rejects; it had white spots on it and they touched it. My Grandma Lee who lived with us also came. There was also Coke, pickles, mustard, sauerkraut, knishes, kasha varnishkes and maybe we got fresh tongue or pastrami or frankfurters. I think they brought Larry a little stuffed bear, not sure if I got anything or that was another visit.

Christian Karen Berman

AGE 8 THROUGH AGE 11 AND HOUSE-HUNTING

At age eight, I wrote my first book report by myself, on *Ramona Quimby, Age 8*. Got Superman PJs, orange bubble gum, learned to play Chess at age 9 by watching the other 4th graders, memorized *My Fair Lady* songs on my parents' record player, by writing them down; I had to stop the record many, many times. I would sing them to my 4th grade teacher Mrs. Brisson. Would climb the tree high in our backyard even at night. My Mom took me and Larry to Buster Brown to get new sneakers. I was age 9. They had those cute little Velcro character sneakers. They had girls' pink *My Little Pony, Purple Care Bears, Cabbage Patch Kids, Barbie*... and what did my Mom's cute, sweet little daughter get? Pink, purple, maybe aqua? NOOO! BLACK, GREY AND RED, BOYS' TRANSFORMERS VELCRO SNEAKERS, LOL. My Dad was at work, this was after school, the lady and my Mom looked at each other confused and speechless, then smiled, and the sales lady said something like, "It must be a stage. Well, if it makes her happy..." Mom said, "Wait till your Dad sees what you chose," smiling. The box had a cool cut-out thing.

I got a helium balloon, too. Maybe I was trying to be like my brother. Can't remember what sneakers he got, though.

It was to wear to my Dad's end-of-the-school-year math faculty party at Mrs. Bowen's house. I fell asleep sitting in the baby car seat on the long ride over. I was about 60 pounds and yes, even the bar still fit over my head. it was hot, sticky leather, too. Marion Lindon made the best lasagna and they had fried chicken. A three-year-old fell down the stairs one time and had to go to the hospital. I didn't see it happen but found it scary and upsetting. I use to sing and dance at the party for all my Dad's teacher

MIRROR OF MY WORLD

friends. They loved that. They had great pretzels. Age 11—yogurt drinks, Pudding Pops, pogo ball, Skip-It and Minnie Mouse Velcro Roller Skates.

My Mom always talked about moving to a bigger house in Scarsdale and we had a real estate agent when I was ages 11 to 14. We looked at many houses in Westchester, even a cool one that was time-stuck in the 1960s; everything in the house was frozen in time. I didn't know what the 1960s looked like back then, but it was weird, scary, and cool. They had strange-looking orange chairs and weird furniture. It was like going back in a time machine.

Another house had this big German Shepherd I was playing with; maybe it was the same house. We looked in Mamaroneck, too. This was all my Mom's idea. We never moved, but I think it was my Mom's dream, though. She always talked about going to Cape Cod and other places like that, but we never did. She would change the lighting fixtures, change the sliding glass doors in the shower, took off the indoor shutters and put in blinds and curtains, changed the chandelier in the dining room.

She would look at places with us to find these new things. I thought the trips were boring and liked things the way they were before she changed them. They didn't need to be changed. I never liked change. For me, back then all I wanted was a new doll, stuffed animal, or toy.

Christian Karen Berman

MY ACTIVE IMAGINATION AND NEED TO PLAY GETS ME IN TROUBLE

Remember those kiddie tunnels they had folded up and you could climb in and out,? Well, we didn't have one. So I improvised. I used our Winnie the Pooh or Care Bears sleeping bag to crawl in and out of. Why? Was it fun? I was a kid and wanted to do kid things. I was about eight years old. The big sleeping bag got twisted up as I was crawling in and out of it. I was stuck inside and couldn't find my way out. I was only about 50 pounds, too. I tried to get out, I couldn't find an exit. This was a full twin 6-foot sleeping bag. I got scared fast, panicked, and couldn't escape, so I screamed as loud as I could many times at the top of my lungs for HELP, hoping my parents or someone could hear me. Luckily, they were downstairs and it wasn't just Grandma Lee.

I kept screaming as loud and hard as I could in hopes someone could hear me. I never screamed so loud that I could remember. Thank God, my Dad and Mom came in, saw, and helped me get out. I never did that again. If it wasn't for them I might have suffocated. They weren't mad at me and I was only tangled up for a minute or two. I was okay, but really scared and shaken up. I'm glad they knew it was a real scream for help and I was not just playing, as a little kid. I did scream sometimes when I played outside, but just to show everyone I was a kid having a good time, like when I went down the driveway in the Little Tykes little plastic red wagon, when I was supposed to be in school that afternoon. Whoops! It is scary to think back on, but that's why kids shouldn't be left alone under 13, they dunno some things they do might be stupid and dangerous. They're just little kids wanting to play and have fun.

MIRROR OF MY WORLD

Christian Karen Berman

Playtime

One day I was bored and playing outside. We only had a Little Tikes plastic baby slide to play on back then. We had bought these large plastic garbage barrels. Before, we just had the waist size tin can ones like Oscar the Grouch from *Sesame Street* used. This looked like it would be fun. I was outside alone. I believe it might have been a school day and I was playing hooky. Don't worry, I got more schooling than most kids need and I didn't have enough free play time. So, I was outside on my own, in my driveway, no adults or parents around and eight years old. I started climbing in and out of the new garbage barrel. I thought this would be a good idea, fun. It was tall and went to about my shoulders, climbing in and out again, It might have come close to tipping over once, but it had wheels on one side, heavy plastic on the other side and it was a dark grey, with a little black trim in plastic. It was kinda dangerous now that I think about it, but childhood knows no fear. Well, maybe just a little fear, until **AHHH, OOH**, ohhhh that hurt so bad. I slipped climbing out of it and fell down hard by accident in my middle on the hard plastic edge of the barrel and my crotch got really badly hurt. I was in bad pain. I couldn't move for a few seconds and then tried to pull myself up and out of there quickly and climbed out and went back in the house. I don't think I told my Mom or Grandma or anyone, but I learned my lesson the hard way and never did that again. It was fun until it wasn't actually, it wasn't that fun after all.

My parents really needed to put in a jungle gym, monkey bars, a swing set and trampoline, but they never did. I asked a few times when I was older. I did get a plastic tire swing my Dad tied on a tree branch and a real tire swing from an old rubber tire, and my Dad bought some silky rope he tied on another big tree branch in the back of our back yard. That got many years of use by me. I would swing high, but it would have been nice to have a play-

MIRROR OF MY WORLD

ground or at least a swing set, like some of the other neighbors had. We did go to the playground, but it seems like only a few times a year, not as much as I needed. We did have bikes to ride and a plastic baseball bat and ball, but still not the same as a playground. We had a badminton net, but it was more for my Dad. He loved tennis. We played badminton, but I never liked tennis much. They even had us all join the local tennis club, but I barely remember even playing there once. We needed to go to Sesame Place and Hershey Park, but we never made it there or to Disney World. But the sprinklers were fun and we had a big kiddie pool for a few summers and joined a beach club with two pools, one kiddie and one adult.

All in all, I still had a great childhood, because I made the best of what I had and enjoyed what I had and made each day as happy as I could and lived each day to the fullest. Most kids back then did. Today, I just don't think kids have as much fun as we did. Maybe they don't have enough free time or get out as much. I think there are too many devices, actually. We had Apple computers when I was in the third grade, which was more like a word

processor than a computer, but magic rainbow markers and blank paper and toys that are not battery operated are the best for kids with active imaginations and want to create. That is how inventors invented things. Imagination knows no bounds and has no borders, it's as amazing as you can wish it and want it to be. Kids are happier when they create and it builds confidence and imagination. Just wanted to share that with parents that might not know this fact.

Christian Karen Berman

STUCK ON THE SCHOOL BUS

It was around springtime, in March or April, and it was a nice, warm and sunny spring day. I was age eight and in the third grade, sitting in the big yellow school bus, next to my friend and our neighbor, Sonia, who was a year younger than me. The school bus was just full of kids from Kindergarten to the 4th grade who went to our school and lived near each other. The bus driver was driving down his usual route. There was a road that went down by houses then up a steep hill and just then it stopped. All us kids were startled and didn't understand what happened. We had had bus drills in the beginning of each school year in elementary school about what to do if there was an accident, the bus driver would open the back door and either carry us each safely to the ground one at a time or we could hold his hand and jump. I always found it fun, when the bus driver would carry me down and kinda swing me from three-feet-above bus onto the pavement. I didn't get picked up often by my parents as a child and enjoyed this, to me that was fun. This is not what happened this time.

  The smoky school bus smell would usually give me a sick headache. I had had so many of those last year in the second grade. It might have also been considered a migraine brought on by the fumes and the school bus smell, because I believe I threw up a few times from it and other times came close to throwing up. My Grandma Lee would give me a wet, cold washcloth to put on my forehead and I'd go lie down on my Dad's comfy side of the big bed under the comforter to rest in the dark, until I felt better. From age seven to nine this happened often, a few times a week to a few times a month, also probably from having to wake up so early and I didn't eat or drink much at that age at all; there was no time and I didn't really like any of the food my Mom was serving for me, except the tuna fish salad and the fresh corn on the cob which she made sometimes for dinner. In retrospect, why didn't my Mom tell my pediatrician or run tests on me or even just give me Children's Tylenol to relieve my headache? It was pretty often and it felt bad. Well, it was the mid-1980s—the less medicine, the better. It was probably from dehydration, but at seven, I don't understand any of this, I'm not even sure I knew the word headache.

Back to the bus… The bus driver said we should all stay in our seats and not to worry. The bus wouldn't start and turn over, so he radioed down to the bus station to send us a new school bus that works and it should take about a half hour to get here. Then the old lady that lived in the house with all the prison black metal bars on the windows saw what happened and walked out of her house and asked if he needed her to call someone or if there was anything she could do to help. One little boy walked to the door asking for a glass of water, said he was thirsty. She said she would get him a glass of water and be right back, but quickly the bus driver declaimed and said he was okay and didn't need a glass of water (stranger danger, you can't trust anyone, it might have been poisoned—my guess why he didn't want the eight-year-old to have a sip of water). She had gray hair, looked like up in a bun in the back, in her early 70s, short and slightly heavyset. She came back out with a glass of water. The bus driver had said no thank you again and the boy was being melodramatic, saying how he was dying of thirst and that he was okay. She hesitantly walked back in the house with the water. The driver told him to go back to his seat and sit down and that they were sending another school bus right over. He did.

Then Sonia and I were talking about how we were going to miss our favorite shows on TV I was telling her about the Nickelodeon cartoon, *The Little Prince, Today's Special,* and *Belle and Sebastian,* my favorite afternoon kids shows (she knew the last show), besides *He-Man and She-Ra*. They were on between 4-5 pm and if the new bus got here in a hurry, we just might make it home in time so as not to miss it, even though I usually got home at about 3:50-4:10 pm on a good day. Then she was showing me how she was growing one thumb nail as long as she could grow it, (her other fingernails were all rather short) one inch, two inches, three inches, four inches, and that her mother, Merida, was letting her. I thought that was cool, neat. So far it was two centimeters.

I also was wondering if our parents noticed we were late, would my Mom be worried? My Dad usually came home late from work, but not THAT late, 4:30 pm maybe. Did the bus driver inform the school to call our parents? I highly doubt it. Back then, everything was more relaxed. I hoped it wouldn't be that much longer. As a kid, I had no real concept of time, no watch. The kids were pretty quiet, just sitting and waiting, the bus driver talking over the radio to the station, a few neighbors got out to watch. Luckily no kids had to go to the bathroom. Back in the day, not having to carry water bottles and Stanley cups, us kids didn't drink much, except the occasional few sips from the school water fountain, lunch box thermos, and the juice boxes our moms packed. I got one Hi-C Fruit Punch, or Ssips if they were out of Hi-C, and I usually could barely drink half of it.

Flashback—once the kids at the lunch table were prodding me to drink the whole juice box at once. I couldn't, just got a few sips in. Sometimes I would squirt some out on my shirt for attention and ask to go to the school nurse. She would give me a dry sweatshirt she had on hand and my Mom would wash it and give it to me to give back to her the next day. My shirt would go in an extra bag. I can't believe I would do that now, because of germs. Old, used, lost-and-found shirts, that was too big on me... I, like a lot of kids my age, liked to be a little show off and get attention. That's what we do, me especially. As for drinking from the water hose, as I hear, maybe just a few times. Maybe. Maybe it was more of a 70s kids thing.

The school bus has just arrived and us kids are so happy and hurrying out and we all get on the new school bus they sent with a few neighbors watching, including the old lady. We pile in the new bus and we are so happy to be moving again and leaving the old school bus behind. This one is working well and my bus stop is the one on the next block only about a mile-and-a-half down. Maybe I could have walked it; I knew where I was. Nah.

Finally, we stop at my bus stop, two blocks by my house, and I rush home. My Mom was looking for me and wondered where

MIRROR OF MY WORLD

I was and what happened. I told her we got stuck and the bus wouldn't move and stopped working. My Dad wasn't home yet, but my little brother Larry and my Grandma Lee were. I run upstairs to use the bathroom, then hurry out to see what time it says. It was almost 4:30 pm. I caught the end theme song to *He-Man* and waited for my show *She-Ra* to start, sitting at the end of my parents' bed. I was sad I missed He-Man, though. It was a big deal to me. It was a long day and I loved that show and the characters were almost like my friends. Man at Arms, Battle Cat, Orko, Skeletor, and the Sorcerer.

It was a very memorable day, something someday I might even mention in my memoirs. Luckily it turned out well, no accident, no one was injured, no one wet themselves. Maybe the bus just overheated. The rest of the day was my usual night—dinner, maybe bath night, maybe math homework, which I knew so well, I asked my mother to do for me. At that age, addition and subtraction is easy work, not even worth wasting my valuable eight-year-old time with. I don't remember the rest of the day or night, honestly. The main thing I remember that day is worrying about missing my favorite after school TV shows, not if we'd be there all night or go hungry, have no bathroom, be kidnapped, or something bad or scary would happen, like someone would break in and steal a few helpless little kids. At age eight in the late 1980s, my only real worry on that day was missing my favorite TV program, *He-Man*.

[Christian Karen Berman](#)

HEBREW SCHOOL

A short interesting story. I remember when I was age nine in Hebrew school, I really didn't like to go to Hebrew school twice a week and then I had tap dance and ballet another once or twice a week, too, for maybe six months or so, not sure. I had to change into my pink leotard after a full day at the 4th grade. The bus came around 7:45 am and I got home around 4 pm. I had to bring my pink ballet and black patent leather tap shoes. Tap was so much more fun than ballet, though it was an hour-and-a-half, 4:30-6 pm. I think Hebrew school was about two hours. So sometimes my Dad had to push me to go to these afterschool activities. I'd much rather be home relaxing, eating a chocolate bar, watching my cartoons after a full day of school. Some days I was tired and had a bad headache and didn't feel like going. My Grandma Lee, who lived with us, paid for this, because she thought it would be good for me. At tap dance the old lady cool teacher would play the theme song from *Fame*, the movie, as we danced, and there was a girl in class who liked me, with a cute little mop head haircut and light brown hair. We'd talk about what our hair color would be when we got older, because children's hair changes when you grow up and we'd look at our hair in the big glass mirror by the ballet bar, before we'd have to run across the room doing flying leaps. I liked this class better than Hebrew school.

So one day at Hebrew school, I was really bored, of course. I didn't really understand anything. This year it was a male teacher, too, which I didn't really like and thought was odd. All I knew was memorizing some famous Jewish songs. If I said a Jewish prayer it was memory, even if I

looked at the Jewish bible and was pretending I was reading it, all memory. I could not read Jewish words, nor did I have the desire or inclination to. Boring, boring, boring, no offense to the sweet Jewish people. I had French in the 4th grade, too, and in the 9th and in the 10th grade my parents tried me at Spanish. I felt the same way about that language, too. I'm surprised I ever learned English. I have no idea how I learned to read and write by age six.

Okay, in class I probably tuned out my teacher, who was talking as my Dad would say "gooblety gook," or in *Peanuts* terms, blah, blah, blah, blah. I was in my own world and started playing the desk as a drum, beating a tune with both hands. I guess it got pretty loud, not that I have noticed being in my own world and all. I might have also been hitting the top of my desk and the metal part underneath. I was really into it, it had a nice beat and tune. Then the male teacher who was probably in his mid 40s or so stopped talking, walked over to my desk and called me by name. Not sure if it was my real name; my Hebrew name was Hava Mulka. I went by just Hava. He said loudly, "Stop! Do you know what you are doing?" I looked around. Some kids and the teacher was looking at me, too. I felt embarrassed and stopped and then was quiet and didn't talk, not sure if I even said sorry. In retrospect, I was adding some life to the class by working my desk, playing on my desk, banging on some muzak, a D.J. Rocker.

It's pretty funny thinking back about the quiet, shy little me, beating on the desk to add some much needed life to that dull, boring class. It was the late 1980s, you know. I was a pretty cool little nine-year-old kid, all of 52" and 55 pounds. Soon, I was in Catholic School and didn't need to worry about going back to Hebrew school. My parents thought it would confuse me and make me feel different. I have to say, I didn't really miss it.

Christian Karen Berman

MY PARENTS FORGOT TO PICK ME UP AFTER HEBREW SCHOOL

My parents were late in picking me up from Hebrew School. It was from 4-6 pm. I think it was a Thursday. I was the last one there, all the other nine-year-olds had their Mom and Dads come pick them up from the parking lot on time. I was standing alone for what seemed to be 15 minutes or more, worried that my parents had forgotten me. I don't think I thought something bad happened to them. I didn't think things like that then. I thought everything would always turn out okay eventually then. I thought positively. Luckily, my parents didn't have me watch the news or read the newspaper back then, or I may have thought otherwise. It was cold, dark, scary, getting towards 6:30 or later on a frigid, windy September /October/ November night. Worse, there were no adults in sight, no cars in sight. The building might have been locked. I didn't know how to call anyone. I didn't talk on the phone to anyone back then, but I memorized my number since age seven, not sure if I knew my address yet. I didn't know what to do, just alone, cold, scared, waiting, waiting for what seemed like forever.

The building was lit up inside, so I walked over and peeked in, before everyone had left. Some adult man who worked there and was leaving might have asked me if someone was coming for me, if I needed to call someone or something, I vaguely remember. But for sure they would be coming soon and show up any minute. They never didn't not show up before. I started to seriously think they'd never come and get more anxious and nervous, like what would I do? The building door was locked and I couldn't see anyone in there. Will I get kidnapped? Even though my house was technically about a mile away, I didn't know how to walk so far by myself in the dark and if I left, then they wouldn't know where to find me. I'd be too scared to leave alone. I'm not even sure I thought of that back then. It was getting colder and darker. I was just standing there looking for a car to arrive or any person to come out of the building and help me. I was frozen in temperature and fear and didn't know what to do next if they really didn't show up soon, which was looking like a real possibility.

Both my parents and brother Larry finally came and were late. Not sure if they forgot me or were making dinner or running late. I was so glad to see the car and them and get in the car quickly to go home and to be warm and eat a good warm nutritious dinner. I was kinda mad at them, though, for leaving me to wait and wonder for almost 20 to 45 minutes (having no watch then, you're not too sure on time.) Possibly becoming chilled with mild hypothermia. They forgot about me or were too busy to come get me right away, didn't call or send anyone else to come and pick me up. I might have climbed up high on our backyard tree when I first got home. I used to do that sometimes at age nine and ten, when I needed to think and I was kinda mad at my parents for forgetting me, no one was around, no plan on what to do. I was a young nine-year-old, too. I was so scared.

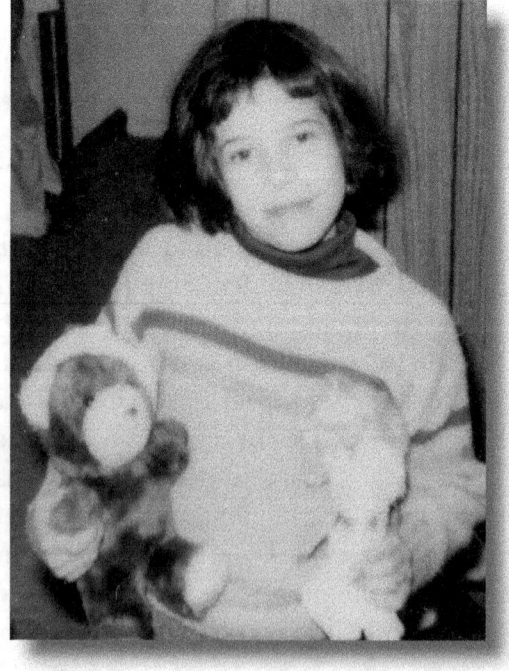

I was also so glad to be back home safe with my loving family. I think the time got away from them and slipped their mind, my Dad probably grading papers and my mom cooking our good dinner. It was all okay in the end, but a scary memory. I'm glad I didn't get kidnapped by anyone or need to use the bathroom, but as a young child I was usually good at holding it all day.

Christian Karen Berman

HAIR PULLING

I'm age 9, on the school bus on my way home. I'm sitting next to my neighbor Sonia, she was a year younger and had white blonde hair. We would talk about the shows we watch on Nickelodeon. I would go to her house, swing on her tire swing. Her mom, Merida, gave us a snack of chocolate milk and Planters Mixed Nuts, it was yummy. I know Sonia didn't like me much, though. She would say she's 40 pounds and I'm 60 pounds and I might break her tire swing or the tree branch, because I weigh too much. She also showed me her thumbnail. All her nails were short, but she said she was growing just that nail long, how interesting.

This girl in front of us, Carolyn, she was age 8, another beautiful girl with beautiful, blonde hair I liked, out of the blue, for no reason, she grabs ahold of my shoulder length brown hair and pulls it hard. It hurts. I tell her to let go. She keeps pulling harder and won't let go. She is pulling out my hair and it hurts. I told her to stop it. No one's helping me, a few kids just watching. All I can think to do is to start pulling her blonde hair as hard as she's pulling mine. She tells me to stop. I said I will stop once she stops pulling my hair. I might have said on the count of 3, not sure. Then she finally lets go, so do I. It was scary. I lost a lot of hair. I thought she pulled all of it out. She attacked me like a rabid raccoon for no reason, crazy kid. Walking home from the school bus with Sonia, she said no, she didn't pull out too much hair. That made me feel better.

MIRROR OF MY WORLD

Christian Karen Berman

SURPRISE

Age nine. My Dad was at school late with my Mom, at Parent/Teacher conferences. Grandma Lee was babysitting four-year-old Larry and eight-year-old me. It was getting so late, maybe 9:30-10:30 pm. My Grandma was getting worried, wondering where they were. You could not call them; no iPhones back them. I was just sitting on the couch, tired, waiting for them to pop in the door. Then they did. They said they had a big surprise for me in the car and brought in my new 20" black, hot pink, and purple bike. It was so cool—I loved it! It seemed so big and I sat on the seat and my Dad tried to adjust it, said I would grow into it. I was so happy, I named it Swift Wind. Best birthday gift I got up until now, it must have cost a lot. I used it until 12-14 years old. It was a wonderful bike and a real nice surprise. My Grandma was surprised, too. My brother was probably asleep.

I actually told my teacher and Dad I didn't want a birthday party in school, I didn't have many friends or feel liked and didn't want the extra attention on me. I was shy. I didn't like the round Devil Dogs my Mom would buy. She couldn't bake homemade cupcakes like the other kids' Mom's did. They were good. But my Mom didn't have the time or know-how. My Dad wrote my teacher a note and told her I didn't want to celebrate my birthday at school. She read it and said that's okay. Sad at age eight, my self-esteem was so low I didn't want to have a big birthday celebration.

MIRROR OF MY WORLD

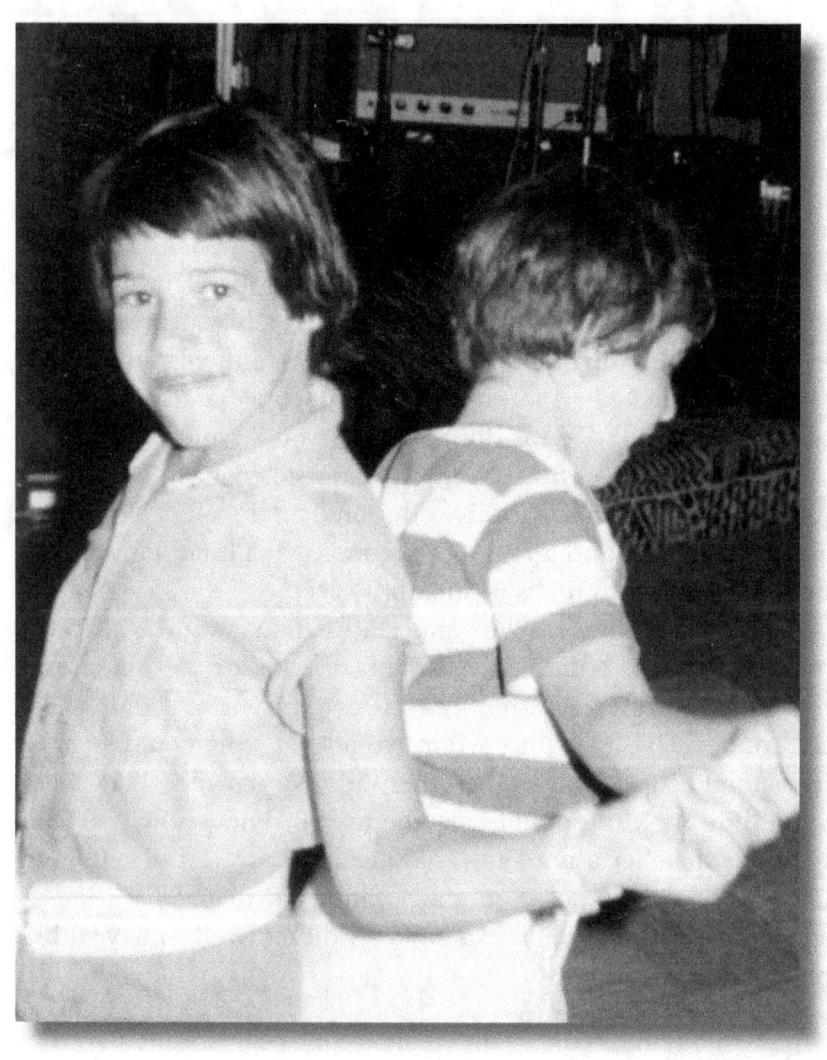

[Christian Karen Berman]{.underline}

THE FOURTH GRADE

My teacher's name was Miss Brisson. She was my favorite teacher. Now that I look back, she looks like Gena Rowlands in the movie *Gloria*, with a short haircut. I remember what I wore the first day of school at age nine—a white sweatshirt with pastel satin bows all around. The reason she was my favorite teacher was because she would tell us real-life stories from her memories, and that UFOs are real and she and her friends saw one, one night. She also told us about when she was a little girl they had a big blizzard and she was able to build a snow house with her friends, even make shelfs in the snow house there was so much snow. I tried to make an igloo myself so many times because of her story. Not many teachers I had ever shared their own experiences with the class. She told us that the real classroom was not the one we were in, but the real big world out there was our classroom, where we would be taught the most. At nine, being bored in school, the outside classroom seemed more tempting. I wish I could go back to those fun-filled days. Many years ago, I had a dream about being back in her classroom. I really wish I was still there. She sadly died many years ago.

She read us *Blubber Out Loud*, by Judy Blume. I loved it.

I was not the best student and didn't like reading as much as I should, but I really enjoyed every word she was reading. I would beautifully sing *My Fair Lady* songs from the movie with Audrey Hepburn. My parents had the record from the Broadway play with Julie Andrews and cleverly I would play the song, stop it, and write down the words to memorize them, all on my own accord. It took a while, probably hurting the record, but I still remember all the songs from that stellar movie until this day.

When they gave those tests where you fill in the dots, even as young as seven, I didn't want to be stressed, maybe it was smart of me or not, but I just filled in any dot as I went, sometimes the

MIRROR OF MY WORLD

first, middle or last. Smart that I didn't want to be bothered or aggravated, not smart, because I don't think I read the question or tried to answer the right answer. Maybe I did at first, but it was too hard for me, so I just thought I'd gamble and take my chances, yes, from seven to nine. Maybe I was too young to understand the importance of this test.

Once during quiet reading, I kept going back to find a better book to read. I never liked to read. I finally decided on *Little Bear*. I guess I wasn't in the highest level reading class, or didn't want to read an older book, but she lost patience and sent me down to the office. When I got there, and they asked why I was there, they didn't think that was a good reason to send me down, that I didn't want to read.

Mrs. Roberts was my first grade teacher. She made me carry my own big crayon box on a field trip to a museum. I must have dropped the big box six times and all the big crayons fell out. No one else, just me. It wasn't on purpose either; I was only 38 pounds and carrying paper, too, until she finally gave up and carried them for me.

I also told her my Mom was pregnant when she wasn't, and she told my Mom not to lift heavy things during a visit to her class. I got in trouble for that, too. I so wished for a baby sister for a good 18 years, the one everyone promised me after my brother was born. I finally gave up and started carrying a Kid Sister doll around and dressed her as a baby in real baby clothes to be my real little sister.

They used to show this cool, old film strip every year about two little Indian boys, brothers, getting tied up by a big, bad Indian or cowboy dude to a wooden stake in the rising ocean water on the beach. It tugged at my six-year-old heartstrings. All I used to watch was baby shows, this was teaching brotherly love. I was sad that after first grade, I never got to see it again, though I have looked for it on YouTube with no luck.

Also in the first grade, I said my throat was hurt and was red, so I got sent home. I was bored copying sentences off the green board and would rather be at home, that's why.

I had Mrs. CC for second grade, she was interesting. I once borrowed 25 cents from her to buy a big soft pretzel. She first said do you mean the long hard pretzel stick for 10 cents? I said nooo, the big soft pretzel, always trying to be a cutie and a little show off. She wrote on the blackboard for me to copy that I owe her 25 cents and to give that to my Mom. Well, anything to get me to eat. I also had forgotten to give my Mom my spelling test to sign, so I forged my Mom's name in class and my Mom had to come in and I got in trouble for that, but after a bunch of prodding from my teachers, I finally admitted it was me who signed. I honestly just forgot to ask my Mom to sign. I was a little character and loved attention.

During this time, I wasn't eating my lunch. My Mom told Mrs. CC and they saw, took me into the library with the nurse and gave me saltines to have with my PBJ. I hated that my Mom always made me PBJ. I ate a few crackers. The next day when the teacher passed I took two bites of my sandwich to show her I was eating, just for show. I hated the same sandwich every day. I got turkey sandwiches sometimes. I loved school lunch years later. My Mom didn't think I could wait in a long line, pay the money, not drop my tray, plus have enough time left to eat. I was a skinny little girl. I'm still a skinny girl and a finicky eater.

I used to go to the nurse a lot in second grade. I wanted to go home to my Mom and watch Nickelodeon. I was happier home. I'd fake sickness, say I have a headache, hold my head, I did many times, but never on the days I faked it. I wanted to go home so bad one time I said I was nauseous and going to throw up. When I really did at home, I was too embarrassed and told my Mom not to say that when she called me in sick. So that meant that when I really wanted out, it came to a point where they didn't let me go to the school nurse anymore. I'm not sure I ever got sent home in second grade, maybe once.

In third grade, I had Mrs. Spinner. I started writing a story about Nickelodeon after lunch on my own. She wondered what I was doing. She let me finish. Guess what, I grew up to be a professional writer. I write two columns a month and get paid. I also drew a picture of my Mom in class for St. Patrick's Day. I drew my mom wearing a very interesting green sweater I had created myself and told my other classmates my Mom actually had this same sweater at home.

I was such an interesting child, full of life, fun, adventure, and a large touch of innocent mischief, not meaning to get in trouble, but being a free spirit and liking to do my own independent thing at age seven and onward, including exploring our unfinished basement to find long-lost treasures out of boredom on my hooky days. I found some of my Dad's old Lego's in his old dresser drawer in the unfinished part of the basement and his thesis for his Ph.D. Considering I missed a lot of school, I really did pick up a lot of education when I was there, and from being an avid TV watcher. The TV helped raise little me.

I learned to play chess in the fourth grade. I knew nothing about chess, but the other kids in my class were playing and I guess I sort of pretended to know how to play. I played with Scott. I lost most of the time, but learned how each piece moved from him and some of the other students. For a low-level class, it was pretty advanced for the most part.

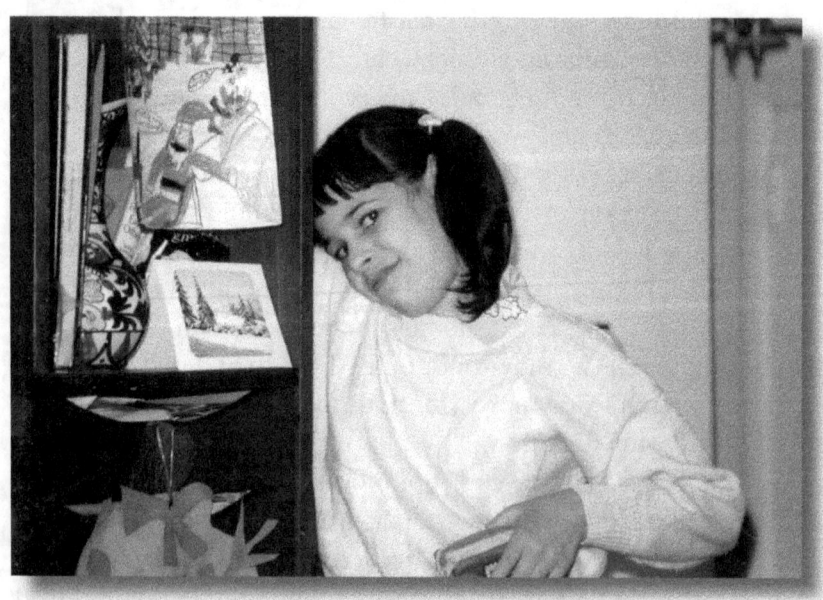

OTHER MISCELLANEOUS, QUICK MEMORIES, AGES 6-9

At age six, seven, eight, and nine, hiding under my Mom's nightgown, I was a small girl and fit. I don't remember my Mother being very affectionate with me as I wished, like hugging me often, putting me on her lap, picking me up. Maybe Grandma Lee wasn't that affectionate to her. I told my Mom my kindergarten teacher picked me up and put me on her lap. It was a lie, but more like wishful thinking. I wish more people did that with me. I wish I got more love. My Dad was the same way, but I would lie my head on his tummy to feel better when I was sick or in his armpit. He sometimes picked me up to touch the smoke detector on the top of the ceiling when I was younger, I dunno why, but I'll take it. When I was older he did pick me up more, because I jumped into his arms and he caught me but he didn't like that as much as I did. I was 13 and 14 years old and around 90 pounds.

I loved excitement when I was a child, anything out of the norm, like the car won't start on a brutally cold, borderline snow day. My parents had to wait outside for AAA to come and tow the car, so they could get to my Mom's car and my Dad was worried about being late for school and missing school completely. I could hear from outside my parents' bedroom window. I didn't wait outside, but sometimes I looked out the window or ran downstairs. It was too cold and too early, I was tired. The plumber coming to fix something. Anyone coming to fix something. I liked attention, too, and showing off for them. We didn't have company or family often and I craved that bit of attention. Having someone I didn't know come over back then was fun and exciting for me. Now, these days it's just stress and aggravation I don't want or need. I try not to feel that way, but it mostly does.

Larry had his friend Jeremy over. I was playing hooky from the second grade, not sick, but needed a mental health day. I missed

MIRROR OF MY WORLD

my Mom at school. Jeremy and Larry were ages three or four and in preschool together. Jeremy had reddish brown shaggy kind of hair, some freckles and pink cheeks, I remember from Larry's class photo. I did think he was kinda cute, but I was the older woman or girl aged seven. I was afraid to let Jeremy see me. Maybe he'd tell his Mom and get me in trouble that I wasn't in school today. I'm not sure if my Mom or Grandma had told me to stay out of the way or hide, but first I hid in the dusty walk-in closet when they were playing in our room. I was shy, but wanted to join in and play with them. Then after they came downstairs, I peeked into the kitchen when my Mom was asking them how many Ellio's pizzas they wanted for lunch. Jeremy said two slices. My Mom made him two rectangles and Larry one. I was so surprised by this; he's only three and he can eat more than me. I never had more than one piece. I'm surprised she made two. We were poor, too. He might have finished most of it. My Mom then cut the pizza up into little bite-size squares. I didn't ask to eat, just watched from the living room, peeking in. They didn't even notice me. I felt guilty for staying home from school and too old to play with them. They didn't do much of anything but eat, anyway. Maybe played cars. Then Jeremy went home. I wished I said hi and tried to play with them. They weren't having much fun anyway; I woulda made it more interesting. We coulda played He-Man or went outside.

Another day I'm home from school, it wasn't even that much in the whole year, it seems like more because I enjoyed those days so much and remember them. I think it was 27 days out, including actual real sick days in the whole year, plus I had a bad case of the Chicken Pox and food poisoning that year, besides strep throat, headache, stomach issues, so many things, so considering that, 27 days ain't bad a'tall. So it's a beautiful, sunny spring day and I'm not allowed outside, one, because I'm home from school, maybe sick, and two, I'm not allowed out by myself. So it's spring, a warm day, the front door is wide open, Larry and I are sitting on the cool tile dining room floor playing with The Little People Farm and Doll House. I'm barefoot, which I'm embarrassed for anyone to see my naked feet, even though they're small and cute my feets, I kinda feel it's dirty and wrong like seeing someone naked. I was talking to Larry about something, looking outside at the beautiful flowers. Just then I'm startled. The mailman comes in and surprises us. He's a nice mailman. He said, Hi, kids. I didn't mean to scare you. How are you guys doing?" His name was Ernie and he's known us for a few years or more. He's about in his mid-30s and African American. I was so embarrassed that he saw my feet without socks or shoes on. Maybe he didn't notice, but I felt funny about that. We were kinda waiting for him and the mail, then I forgot and he surprised us. It was around 2:00 pm.

MIRROR OF MY WORLD

Christian Karen Berman

MY FAVORITE FOODS OF THE 1980S AND 90S

1) Giggles Cookies, made by Nabisco
2) Ice Cream Cone cereal & Rocky Road cereal made by General Mills
3) Five Alive juice, by Minute Maid
4) Swanson TV Dinner, Veal Parmesan with Fettuccine Alfredo
5) Honey Nut Clusters cereal
6) BarNone candy bar
7) Rainbow Brite cereal, Ralston
8) Fruit Bars by Fruit Corners
9) Pudding Pops
10) Triples cereal
11) Crispy Critters cereal
12) Ssips Fruit Punch juice boxes
13) Product 19
14) The old school McDonalds from the 1980s, when it tasted so much better. Deep fried apple pie, the old school dark meat McNuggets, orange drink, the rich, thick ketchup...today's McD's is not as good as it used to be .The toys in the Happy Meal were also much better made in the late 80s & 90s.

MIRROR OF MY WORLD

Christian Karen Berman

GOING TO THE NEVELE

I can't remember my age for sure, but I think I just turned age 9 or 10. I had been so excited for this for weeks, my Dad had made reservations and he enrolled me in child's day camp. We were taking a walk around the block soon after and just thinking about it, the excitement soared in my little mind. My Dad had brought up the old suitcases from the basement. They were blue and from the 1970s. That "old basement" smell meant vacation to me. My Dad would bring them upstairs and my Mom would slowly wash and pack all of our clothes. I even found that exciting.

She would pack for me two swimsuits, two packs of girls printed underwear, five shirts, five shorts, two dresses, one pants, one nightgown, one PJs, socks, one Mary Jane's. She got clothes for two adults and two kids in two medium size suitcases. At age 10, I still wore a girls 6X. I was 4' 4" & 60 pounds. I was small. My brother was five-and-a-half and a few inches shorter. My own big decision—which stuffed animals to bring with me. I was only allowed two. My Grandma Lee would give me $20 to buy a souvenir sometimes, like a stuffed animal or shirt. I had Keds pink Velcro sneakers to wear. I was always so happy.

The night before, we would go out to the Neptune Diner five minutes from the house so there would be no garbage or mess left when we were gone the five days. I think my Grandma Lee came, too.

I can't remember for sure what I had, but we all started out with four ice waters and with piping hot fresh Popovers and salted butter. You'd crack open the fluffy Popover and put the butter on and it would soon melt in so good. I probably ordered the Yankee bean soup my Dad recommended and a Tuna fish salad plate; it had shredded carrot and sliced bread, too. Not sure if I got creamy Italian dressing or Russian dressing, but it was good. My Dad would get a turkey and bacon club with coleslaw and mashed potatoes or the cheeseburger deluxe or a pizza burger. My Mom like scallops, because she would bring the leftovers in a doggy bag and say it was

MIRROR OF MY WORLD

for our turtle Lucky Alexis, true. It probably came with yellow rice and creamed spinach. My brother Larry probably got grilled cheese and French fries and had it with ketchup. I think you got coleslaws all around and it came with a pickle slice on top, my Dad would ask for extra pickle slices on the side. Diners use to be good.

Mom would ask for lobster bibs for us kids so we wouldn't get our shirts all dirty. They were big, white with a giant red lobster on it. We all had Cokes. We didn't do diet back then. My Dad had a Cherry Coke, so maybe I did, too. I have no idea what my Grandma ate, maybe a BLT or fried chicken plate. No dessert, too expensive, but free mints by the handful and they gave us a free fresh mint gum pack to try. Oh, the late 1980s. Never thought I'd actually grow up, many say I still haven't.

After dinner, my grandma still kept her Garden Complex apartment to keep all her stuff & would go there sometimes to look at it or stay over alone for a few days, so my parents brought our garbage bags and threw them away in their dumpster, since we didn't want to have garbage in the garage smelling the driveway.

My Dad had cancelled the newspaper and milk for the week and told our neighbors to watch the house. If I was nine, Grandma was staying home. When I was 10, she came with us. That night in mid-July, my Dad and us kids stayed up late because My Fair Lady was on TV. I think I was only age 9, but loved it so much. I loved the singing and loved Audrey Hepburn. I knew it was so wrong to stay up late when we had to get up early and leave the next morning, but my Dad loved it, too, and we couldn't turn it off and I didn't even fall asleep watching it. We had to have been up until 11 pm or later, a long time for a nine-year-old to stay up, must have been on **PBS**. I slept in my parent's bed fine and woke up rested and so excited. Today was the day, let's start the day.

The next morning my Dad moved the car close to the garage, so no one would see us packing the car up with suitcases (you know, robbers and bad guys that want to break in and steal our TV set from the 1970s and my Care Bear and Cabbage Patch Kids). When I was nine, no VCR or camcorder, no nice camera, a Kids Kodak, we had nothing worth breaking in for, unless you wanted my Speak & Spell and Cookie Monster Counting Game.

Inside I was looking over the house at my toys, making sure I took the right ones. I had a dog that looked like Lassie and I took my blonde pigtailed My Child. I even fixed her pigtails a few days before to get her ready for the trip. I was over the moon with happiness and joy that day. My Dad had me in the kitchen before we left trying to get me to eat an Archway chocolate chip cookie. My Grandma would like those. I would suck the oil out from them, then eat them. I was too excited to even eat that morning and my Dad told me to eat a cookie and maybe drink a Ssips fruit punch juice box, then Grandma said not to force me to eat, so he didn't. I think my Mom packed the juice boxes, cookies, and fresh plums to take on the trip with us. No bottled water back then in the late 80s. We didn't have soda in the house, just kids Hi-C and maybe Mott's apple juice boxes is all I really drank, and tap water from the bathroom sink.

In the car, it was packed to the gills, maybe even a picnic basket and my backpack in there, plus a bag of snacks. As for a pad and markers, I don't think so. It was a long ride, though, two-and-a-half hours, plus we made a pit stop for lunch at the HoJo in Middletown, New York. Larry took two stuffed animals, too, maybe his backpack as well.

Larry, Mom, and I went in the house to go the bathroom again. Then to double-check that the lights were off and everything. Then finally on the road, the radio playing. Maybe we get only a mile down and then my Mom or Dad was like, we have to turn around and go back, did you turn off the stove, did you close the refrigerator, did you turn off the bathroom light? My Dad turned around to go back. We had planned to start out at 9:30 am, wanted to get on the road early and beat the mid-morning traffic rush. Now it was closer to 10:30 am. My Dad did not want to get caught in traffic. We were going over the Tappan Zee Bridge. That part scared me. What if the bridge collapsed or broke and we fell in the water? We go back home, the parents go in, we wait in the car and it's getting warm, I want to get going already. Then they come back out, everything is fine, I'm sure they used the bathroom again, just to make sure. We're finally back on the road and cruising down the highway, music blasting, sun, cars, scenery, it's

MIRROR OF MY WORLD

finally happening. Yay! We made it! We're going on vacation to the Catskills. Getting there is half the fun.

Christian Karen Berman

AT THE NEVELE

We are driving in the car, lots of traffic on the highway. If it was the time I was age nine, I remember sitting in my brother's black, hot leather car seat with the bar over my head. It used to be my car seat. He's getting too big for it at age four-and-three-quarters (it's rare even today for nine-year-olds to sit in a baby car seat, not a booster seat, but in the 1980s & 90s, it was unheard of). I stand out and had to wait until my brother outgrew it and was old enough not to need one anymore. When I gave mine up to him, I was 35 pounds and small ad still needed it, but my parents couldn't afford to buy another one for my brother. It's on the side by the window. My Dad is eating a Red Delicious apple. I wanted it, so after him eating a quarter of it, he gave it to me. That was nice of my Dad. I'm in the baby car seat because I still want to be a little kid and don't want to grow up. I'm skinny and still fit in it. I'm loving my day. I didn't know about germs then, being nine, so I happily enjoyed munching on the big apple. Honey Crisp apples are my favorite now, but back then I didn't know they existed.

The music is playing something soft rock 1980s. Then we arrive at Howard Johnson's just for lunch. We all get out. The car is my Dad's 1978 white Oldsmobile. It sounds old, but it was only 10 years old then. It's big and tan inside and the leather and metal on the seat belts is hot. The car seat is hot, too. I get out and stretch.

MIRROR OF MY WORLD

We walk in and they seat us all in a nice booth and the waitress gives us a kids menu. Daddy tells my Mom to let the kids have chocolate milk as a treat. She doesn't really like us having stuff like that. Dad orders the same for us all, the kids menu just means cheaper and smaller portions. We all get scrambled eggs, bacon, French fries and buttered toast, and us kids get chocolate milk. Daddy knows important things for a kid. He's a big kid at heart and a teacher of kids. The adults get orange juice and coffee with cream, and ketchup for everyone. We look around at the nice restaurant, then when our chocolate milk comes I mix the bottom really good with a metal spoon to make it more chocolatey. After lunch on the way out when my Dad is paying, he buys a LifeSavers green wintergreen pack and I ask for one. He gives it to me. It's really good & minty.

Now, we have to go back to the hot car, get in where everything is burning, a really hot and sunny 80 degrees. Back on the highway, I'm not sure if I went back in my baby seat or not. We see signs along the way, for Grossinger's, The Concord, The Nevele, Burger King. During the ride down the country, we pass cows and horses and a barn. It's a long ride with lots of trees and mountain greenery. It looks like we're finally arriving there. Yay! About time! We pull in and drive down the Nevele driveway. There is a gate and someone in there welcomes us. When we see the place, Larry and I start screaming and cheering, we're here, we finally made it.

We park in front by the lobby to check in. As I walk to the doors, is this a dream? I want to kiss it. This is a miracle. We waited all year to come—you know how long a whole year is to a nine-year-old little girl in the third grade—and we're finally here. We walk to the front desk and my Dad signs to check us in and gets two sets of keys for our room, 612. The bellhop helps us get our luggage from the car and packs it on the luggage rack on wheels. It's so nice, the smell of the lobby and the water fountain, postcards, it's so big and beautiful, gold banisters twisting their way upstairs, the bright red, printed carpeting, the bar and gift shop. We walk down the sidewalk to our room and the Bellhop leaves our stuff to put away.

It's about 4 pm now. We can't go to the pool, my Dad just wants us to relax and then we'll walk around to the bar to look and for early dinner appetizers at 5:30 pm. Mom helps us get dressed nicely for dinner. I'm wearing a T-shirt and shorts. It will be cold in the children's dining room, I better put on some nice pants. He takes us to the bar. There's bowls of free pretzels and I put my little hand in to grab some. The bartender looks at my Dad with two little kids in a bar.

There a large wooden dancing square, then green printed carpeting. They put out mini fried knishes, cocktail franks, and deli mustard. We all take some on a small plate and share a Coke on ice in a glass. No one drinks water in the late 1980s or 90s, unless you have no money, then you get a free glass of it, instead of soda.

My Dad brings only me into the day camp. I'm not thrilled about leaving my parents, like going to school with kids and counselors that I don't know. Larry's almost five, but he doesn't have to go, only me. There are a bunch of kids at a big rectangular table from ages three to eleven. The lady counselor who is a teen or early 20s helps me order. She picks a breaded veal cutlet, says it like a chicken cutlet. I see the other kids are better eaters and mature, eating chicken noodle soup and buttering their rye bread. They put the butter slices in a little dish of ice. When my veal comes, the counselor cuts it up for me in little pieces and pours ketchup on the side to dip. I try it and tell her I like it, it's really good. Then for dessert I order a Cherry twin pop. The power to pick my own meals at age nine.

After dinner, we go to our parents and I'm looking in the gift shop. I ask my parents to buy me a Slinky. It's only a few dollars so they do and I open it and play with it on the stairs around the lobby. It's fun watching it go down the stairs and playing with it. There's a drinking fountain there, too. I made a friend and we go in the gift shop to look again and my parents are talking with her Mom. The girl's about age seven. She buys Mini Chiclets gum and pours half the pouch in my hand for me to chew on. My Mom thought since the girl paid for it, she gave me too much. She said back to her, "They're little, you're supposed to chew on a lot." I'm living it up.

Then we go back to our hotel room to rest and go back for the nightclub. Everyone is staring at Larry and me dancing in the

MIRROR OF MY WORLD

middle of the floor. It's about 9:30 pm, everyone there is age 70s and 80s. They're ordering real adult drinks on ice. Larry and I are really putting on a show for the old folks and showing off. We are the hit of the club and the youngest ones there. I love showing off. Then we have to sit down. The show's about to start. It's dark in there. Someone comes on and tells jokes I'm too young to be hearing, but it's okay, I'm also too young to understand them. Then some famous singer comes on and sings "After the Loving." He sounds pretty good, even to me. Hard little chairs and a small table. Some waiter comes around asking if we want to buy a drink. They charge here. Daddy says no, thank you. Then after, we go to the coffee shop and Daddy and I are a bit hungry. He orders French fries, ketchup, and a Coke. We share it. I think my Mom took my little brother back to the room to get ready for bed. They were tired. Daddy and I are having a late night date. The food is good and my Dad has kid tastes. I'm just looking around, it has to be close to midnight. Then we go back to our room and I get in my nightgown and share a bed with Larry.

I'm tired and go right to sleep, then early the next morning I wear my swimsuit under my clothes so I don't have to change. You swim a lot in day camp. We walk down to the main building and my parents bring me to the children's dining room. Again, I feel abandoned. The counselor has me sit down and asks me what I want for breakfast. I miss my parents at first and I'm sad they left me here alone, but then I adjust like the other kids and order Pops cereal and milk and the camp counselor helps me make it in a bowl. I also order pancakes and lots of syrup. When it comes, a guy counselor puts two butters in the middle of them, then cuts in all up quickly into pieces and drowns it in syrup. They sure know what they're doing for being teenagers. I love it and eat most of it up. Maybe I'm not a picky eater, I just don't like the food at home. Then this three-year-old toddler boy is only eating butter from a dish and a few kids say he is going to die of high cholesterol. Then after breakfast the counselor asks us who has to go to the bathroom before we head to the camp house and then they take them there, it's right outside the dining room.

Christian Karen Berman

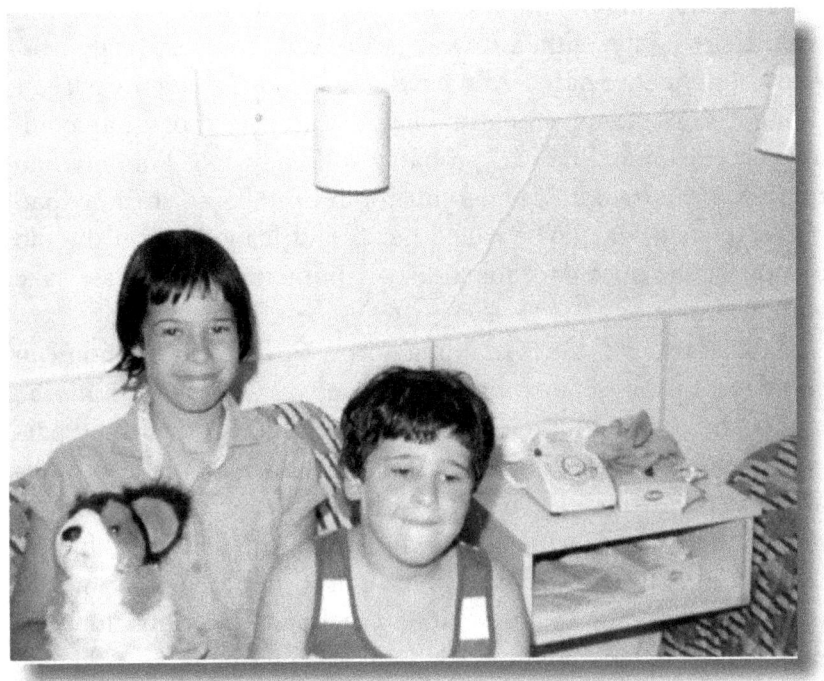

About three days later in our hotel room after the nightclub about 11:30 pm, we get a frantic and angry call from our Grandma Lee, the one who lives with us and who decided to stay home and watch the house (my parents also thought that was best). She's very hot and very upset, so much so she found us at our hotel room late at night. My parents didn't even give her the number; she was resourceful and found it herself. I was sitting at the end of my bed, Daddy by the dresser and chair by the TV. I heard an upset Grandma yelling and giving it to my Dad with both barrels, that we'd better come home right away, why did you leave me here, what are you trying to do, kill me? She can't walk upstairs and doesn't know how to turn on the A/C upstairs; anyway, she's very hot and there is no fan. She's about 80 years old and it's about 85 degrees inside the house. It kinda shook us all up. I never heard her so mad and upset in my entire life. She was miserable and holding it in to give it to my Dad—you'd better come home, when will you be home, I'm going to die here, you want me to die of a heart attack, something like that.

MIRROR OF MY WORLD

    I think after that he put my Mom on, but she wasn't too thrilled with her daughter, either. It was a scary call. We were really worried about her, we didn't even have a fan. I don't think my parents thought this one out properly. They thought she'd be more comfortable at home. She was probably so lonely, too. We only had one TV back then, in my parents room upstairs, so she only had books to read, or maybe called her friend Jeanette from the old complex (she once gave me a slice of homemade chocolate cake with no frosting).

    My Dad tried to calm Grandma down. "Ma, we will be home in two days. I promise, next time we'll take you with us." I think she had Irish blood and a temper. She was still furious with my parents, even her favorite daughter. What was the plan my Dad spoke about to my Mom—leave a day early, will she be okay tomorrow, maybe the weather will cool down, I think she had enough food in the fridge, I hope so, I would have liked her to come, it would have been fun. She did, next time (I feel bad about this now, but didn't know much about it back then; I just went with the flow of things, no one asked me what to do). We might have left a day early or she made it through. She should have called our neighbors Dell and Fred to come in and walk upstairs and turn on the A/C. She didn't. Even when I was 15, my Dad didn't let me or Mom turn it on when he wasn't home. We had to go to the local Sears to cool off when he was at school on one hot day. He thought we'd accidentally break it, it was old and sensitive and expensive to fix.

    That next summer when Grandma Lee came with us, our last day, day four, we were all sitting near the gift shop by the lobby on some couches, my Dad discussing if we had to stay another day, something I was thrilled for, because there was a terrible rain and thunder storm. He planned ahead and watched the weather every day, twice a day on the news, and somehow this caught him by surprise. He didn't know if he could afford to stay another night. We were supposed to leave in a few hours, but you could hear even inside the hotel the lightning, thunder, and heavy rain. It was too dangerous to drive two-and-a-half hours home from Ellenville, New York and the Catskills Mountains home, maybe it was a tornado or hurricane. Grandma Lee said she would pay for us all to stay over another night. I was beyond excited to get to stay another day. Why discuss it, it wasn't doable. Luckily, we could still stay in our same room, 612, and Grandma Lee had the adjoining room next door. My Dad was afraid to bring the camera when I was nine for it might get broken. At ten and on he did, so the photos here are from age , not age nine. I believe it was a Kids Kodak camera from 1987.

MIRROR OF MY WORLD

Christian Karen Berman

A POOR CHRISTMAS

I was 9 years old. It was December 9th. I had been watching as many Christmas movies on TV as I could find and trying to copy them in my own house. *One Magic Christmas* was playing often on the Disney Channel and I would try never to miss a showing. I loved the cute little girl who played Abby in it. I also watched *A Christmas Visitor* on The Disney Channel.

It had already snowed lightly here. My family being mostly Jewish (one Catholic relative) we just would celebrate Chanukah, and not in the rich way you're supposed to, with eight nights of presents. I remember at age six getting only one small little blonde doll in a baby walker, it walked with batteries. I got a plastic dreidel and gold chocolate coins. We had a Happy Chanukah sign in rainbow letters in the dining room. The next year I got a blonde doll who talked when you pulled her string. Larry and I were playing in the basement and we found it by accident and showed it to my parents, so they felt that they had to give it to me early. I enjoyed playing with it. They should have wrapped it and hid it better.

Being on the poor side, I didn't have many toys and dolls to play with so it was really special that I had a new talking doll for me and my little brother to play with and enjoy right now. I was sad and disappointed, though, that I accidentally ruined my special Chanukah surprise gift. My thinking on this was, we were too young to know any better, not having many friends and relatives and not being exposed to much TV. Just kid shows on Nick, Disney and cartoons. I guess I didn't know I was supposed to get a whole lot of cool, new exciting toys and gifts, just for me.

My parents couldn't afford much. Larry, I dunno what he got; a remote control car or truck, a stuffed dog, maybe all of the above. I just about remember what I got. I was sick at age seven during that time and lying in my parents' big bed waiting to watch *The Bear Who Slept Through Christmas*. It was dinner time to night time. I fell asleep waiting for it, sadly and ironically. I loved the Christmas cartoon *Frosty the Snowman*, too. My real name is Karen and I loved that I could identify with the character Karen in the cartoon. She was really nice like me, you don't see girls with the name Karen on TV often or hardly ever. I think it's only Karens today they sadly talk derogatorily about which is so rude and wrong; for most of the women being mean, Karen isn't even their real name. It's wrong to ruin a good baby's name forever, just because maybe one or two Karens in all the history of Karens was not nice. Look at Karen Carpenter, she was one of America's sweethearts. I dunno... maybe being as my real name is Karen and most Karens are not like this, I just felt the need to put it out there for all to read, this Karen thing needs to change. I hate for them to ruin any name by making it a bad word, but using the name Karen as a public insult is just a terrible mistake and it really needs to stop. Thank you.

After watching so many Christmas TV shows, movies and specials, and wanting to fit in and be normal and happy like everybody else, at the young age of nine I took it upon myself to go outside my front door in the foliage and find myself the best Christmas tree I could. I went to the front and backyard. I looked for the right branch, big enough to decorate. I proudly found one and brought it inside. I put it in the living room and used an old shoebox and red plaid scarf to hold up the giant 12-18 inch branch, I made it stand somehow, wrapping it in tin foil or the scarf. My Mom was not happy about this, bringing in a dirty, old branch. Well, I couldn't find a tree. I had a few ornaments we got in cereal boxes as the prize and made some out of Larry's toy cars or small toys by tying a string to them and hung them on the little Charlie Brown Christmas tree. I hadn't even seen that old cartoon yet, so I wasn't copying. It was honestly my own invention, I was pretty clever and innovative for being just age nine. I think I even put yarn around it to help it stay upright. My Parents and Grandma Lee accepted that it made me happy and let me be my creative, eccentric self. I probably made a Merry Christmas drawing and a sign, and put some Christmas cards we got on the bookshelf. I was the only one out of a family of five to be into Christmas.

As for presents, Larry found a few of his old toy cars and cool trucks to give me. We would wrap the gifts in newspaper and tin foil. Mom got me Silly Putty, a Slinky, marbles, a green and yellow plastic snake that moves when you hold it a certain way. Little toys we would wrap up and put around the tree, so I would have something to look forward to opening on Christmas day. I think she got me a truck. I was getting interested in boy toys around then.

I can't remember a big gift she got me then for Chanukah, either. She did make yummy frozen Golden's potato latkes, sweet potatoes, and chestnuts for the holiday. I got to eat a whole pint of Haagen Dazs chocolate chip ice cream one afternoon. I was playing hooky again and just finished watching *One Magic Christmas* on the Disney Channel. Ice cream was a rare treat; my Mom never bought ice cream in the winter. I even got a little tummy ache which I rarely ever got. I didn't like the food my Mom usually made and I didn't eat much.

Around that time, I went with my Hebrew school choir in the back of a van to sing Chanukah songs like "I Have a Little Dreidel" and other beautiful and fun Chanukah songs with my class at Bear

Mountain, a good 45-minute drive from home. Us kids piled in the van and off we went on a cold December adventure. I wore a white sweater, with pastel pink and purple stripes and a grey matching shirt. My Mom bought it at Sears and gave it to me to wear. I wasn't happy about this at all and didn't really want to wear it. It was a little snug and itchy, but I had nothing else dressy to wear. I thought it made me look older, like my own age. I didn't like that either.

Once the Jewish kids and moms arrived, they gave us a room with hot cocoa and sugar cookies, all you can drink and eat for free. My Mom was really proud of me. After nibbling on a few cookies and never finishing one whole cookie and doing the same with the hot cocoa (a few sips here, then a brand new Styrofoam cup there, never had I seen so many sugar cookies on giant platters and two big metal tanks of hot chocolate), I was overwhelmed with the refreshments and didn't know what to do. I was only nine. Once on stage, I was too shy and self-conscious to actually sing aloud. I just mouth the words and pretended to sing, because I truly didn't think I was as good as the other nine-year-olds in my choir. I should have sung loud, happily and clear, just for the pure enjoyment of it all, but I felt my voice wouldn't sound good and I'd mess up the song. I had low self-esteem.

A few days before Christmas I couldn't wait anymore. It turned out that looking at all my tiny awesome little gifts got my nine-year-old mind thinking, I can be happy right now if I open them. I asked my Grandma. There didn't seem to be any real rules about this and no one cared about Christmas and toys and gifts but me, so I did and opened and played with them all, happily, excitedly, kinda ruining my real Christmas. The night before, my brother Larry found a few more of his old cars to give me. He was five. I remember at age 10 and older, Christmas got better, I got more presents. As a kid, it really is about presents, celebrations, traditions, and food.

Christian Karen Berman

ONe OF MY beST CHRiSTMaS MeMORieS abOUT MY MOM

It was December 9th. I was age nine. It was a school day, but I probably was tired or just didn't feel like going to school. There was snow outside. It snowed more back in those days. It might have been a snow day for my school, but I think it was a hooky day, that made it more special. Today they call it a mental health day, back then it was a no-no, that made it extra special.

My Mom ordered garlic chicken with veggies on the Chinese lunch menu. We shared it three ways with my Grandma. It came with fried rice and egg drop soup. I was only 4' 2" and 55 pounds and a picky eater, so I didn't eat much. It wasn't something we did often or could afford back then. My Dad was at work, my brother was probably at school. Then we got bundled up in all-winter coat, hat, boots, and mittens for me. My Mom didn't like to drive much then, so we walked a half mile to the bus stop to take #63 of the Beeline bus to Macy's department store. She told the bus driver I was under seven, or under five, and I rode for free. At nine, I think I looked older than that, so I'm glad they didn't bother to question my Mom, but way back then people didn't like to make waves. This was exciting for me, a Mom and daughter day, missing school and getting to see Santa Claus for the first time ever in person.

It was quite a long walk in the slush to our local Macy's, freezing, windy, feeling a bit of freezer burn on my soft, cold face. I remember stepping on the brown shush & mushing it with my sneakers. I'd say the walk was close to a mile. Then we walked in the decorated store, saw a big Christmas tree, and took the escalator to see the big guy. He put me on his lap. I wish someone took a photo. The store was empty. He asked me what I wanted for Christmas. I was shy and didn't talk, didn't know what to say. He said a Christmas tree, so I shook my head and said yes. The best part was I got a big candy cane and a handful of mini chocolate balls. My little hand only could hold three. He looked at me like I took too many. I couldn't wait and ate one on the escalator ride down.

Then we went to Sears to pick up a Chanukah gift my Mom had ordered for me. I can't exactly remember what it was, because we did this a few times together—a baby doll, Rainbow Brite, Need-a-Littles stuffed animal. I think it was a baby doll. She ordered two because the first one never came. The hardest part was which box to pick, which baby to take home with me and love the rest of my life. It must have taken me 15 minutes to decide. I kept changing my mind. Thinking back it was one of my favorite dolls. It only cost $20. We should have taken both and saved one for later.

It was a long walk back to the bus stop, altogether I must have walked over two miles. We stopped in at Woolworths and both got a hot chocolate with whipped cream on top, an extra special treat. We rarely did something like this. I enjoyed it so much, it was so cold outside and this was nice and hot and chocolatey.

Then on the bus, a lady noticed the bag was ripping from being wet in the snow. I must have been dragging it, carrying it myself. She told my Mom. Then we got off and I carefully carried it back to our house and opened it in the hall near the living room. My Grandma Lee lived with us then and thought the doll was just beautiful and looked real. She was 24", almost as big as me. I was so happy and smiling, it was one of the best, most memorable days of my life. I really wish I had more fun, happy days like this of pure joy and happiness.

Thank you my Mommy. I love you always and forever.

<u>Christian Karen Berman</u>

I CUT MY HAIR

I decided to cut my hair, all by myself. My Grandma Lee always cut it, but she was getting older, didn't know if she would do this or would do a good job. I dunno if I asked permission, but Grandma gave me the real scissors. I wasn't even scared. I was ready to look the part of a real boy. You can't be a real boy with shoulder length hair, especially back in 1988 and you're really a girl. I did a great job, even layered my front bangs to look like a real boy. I secretly wished my Mom would take me to a barber shop to get a real boy haircut, but she wouldn't. Not sure I asked, I guess I thought it would be wrong. I was a girl, but Grandma always did it (it also might be expensive and it wasn't as common back then, but it was called a tomboy, as my Grandma said).

I didn't know this back then, but Tatum O'Neal did the same thing by herself when she was age 10, and did a great job, too. The back of my head was hard to do, it might have been cut layered in the back, crooked or uneven, but I worked on it for some time and then cried in my parents room I slept in, to my Dad, not that I was upset I cut it, but that every hair wasn't symmetrically perfect. He tried to calm me down and reassure me that I did a great job and talk to me about it for a good five, ten, fifteen minutes, too, to make me feel better so I was less upset. I then went back to the bathroom for another hour trying to make every stray hair even. Then I was finally happy with how I looked like a real boy. I hoped it wouldn't grow back for a long time, because it looked good now and I didn't want to have to do it again, but to be happy in the moment and not have to wait to be happy.

At age 10, I was about 4'5" and 65 pounds. They gave us so many textbooks in my backpack that if I didn't hold it right, I would tip over and fall backwards. It had to be 25 or 30 pounds. It also held a big blue binder, notebooks, it was packed to the gills. We did have chubbies, but to come and go from school I could barely lift the backpack.

MIRROR OF MY WORLD

I got lost in my school many times. It was scary, being alone in the basement part and not knowing which stairwell leads to your section of the building, or being on a higher floor and lost, if worse came to worst on a high floor I could have gone into a strange classroom and asked a teacher. One day in English class we got to eat a Keebler Elf chocolate cookie with vanilla frosting in the middle. When we walked in the teacher just asked, "Are you allergic to chocolate?" I said no and got a cookie, but you had to write about how it tasted and the texture and what you liked about it. That was fun, I loved it. I loved Giggles cookies, too.

Another time I was out sick and I came back and I got a pen pal, a boy one named Dennis, just like my favorite TV show. All the other girls got girl pen pals, but there weren't any girls left. Even the teacher knew I was like a boy. I felt lucky to get him, he said I hope you "fell" better.

My teacher Ms. Martin (*Timmy and Lassie* was another favorite TV show, so I just loved that her last name was Martin), she was African American. She didn't like me, neither did this girl Cathy, she would say "We-ell" (sarcastically) when I looked at her. That was a thing back then, "We-ellll." That teacher made me sit on a stool in the back of the classroom because of this girl. She said if it was the old days you'd be wearing a dunce hat. She must have gone to school way back in the 1950s or 60s. Once when I was out sick and came back, she said, "I'm sorry to say this, but it was better when you were out sick." I didn't really want to be there either and wasn't happy about it, for a 30, 40 or 50-something-year-old teacher to say that to a 10-year-old little girl is absolutely appalling and unacceptable, but as a 10-year-old child, I just felt sad and hurt, but accepted it. We respected our teachers and elders back then and rarely questioned them.

Two boys in the hall passed me and asked if I was a boy or a girl. I was being picked on because I was going through a boy stage. I was honored to be thought of as a real boy, my goal, but kinda rudely said "a girl," like, "didn't you know that?" I heard Cathy was going to beat me up after school. I think I tried to tell one of the teachers that she threatened to.

My Mom knew something was wrong and bothering me as we walked to the car. Cathy said not to tell anybody, plus I was embarrassed, I said to my Mom I would tell her if she bought me a My Buddy doll. I told her and we went straight to Big Top, happy days, to get me my own My Buddy Doll. It was October and I'd been wanting one. What a nice, sweet Mom I had. I picked out the yellow hair blond one with blinking eyes. When I got home his hair was not even or perfect like mine was. I had looked him over, gave him the once over, so guess what I did? Yes, you guessed right, how did you know, I had to go get the scissors again from my Grandma and give him a perfect haircut, too, sitting on my bedroom floor by the heating vent, no less. I was getting good at this, my parents were hoping I wasn't going to ruin him. He did cost about $30. I loved him.

In art class or my special needs class, we were tracing our hand and coloring it in to make a turkey for Thanksgiving. Even then I thought that was kinda babyish for a ten-year-old kid.

MIRROR OF MY WORLD

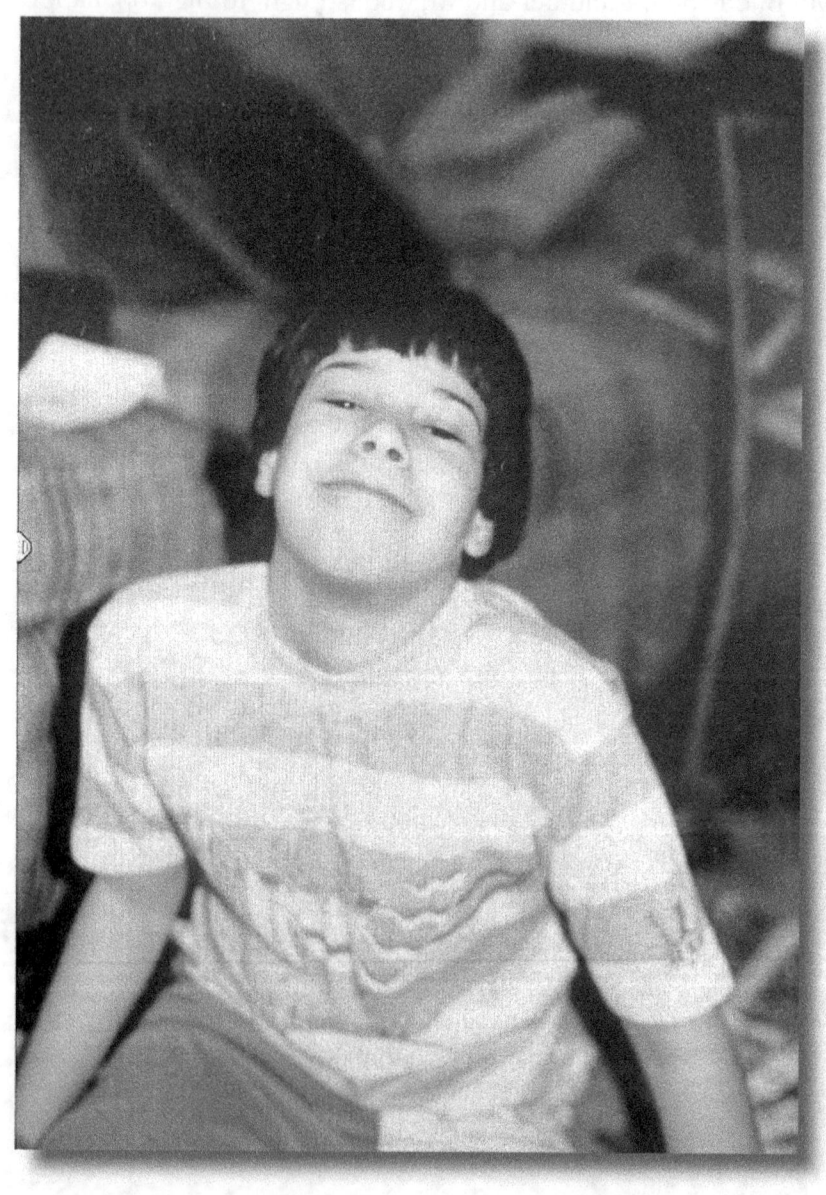

Christian Karen Berman

STARTING A NEW, BIGGER SCHOOL

I was entering the 5th grade in a ginormous, old school, but a new school for me. My Mom was starting to buy me boys clothes like I wanted, like my brother was wearing. I remember a nice white, red, green, and blue striped shirt with cuffed sleeves. I liked a lot of TV sitcoms with boys around my age—*Dennis the Menace*, *Leave It to Beaver*, a TV movie, *Dennis The Menace: Dinosaur Hunter* (1987). I was just at that age where I was happier being a boy. I was 10.

I had a short girl haircut and had been wearing boys clothes on and off for years. I remember I had these Superman pajamas I loved. I had He-Man PJs, too, and a cool He-Man action figure and Teela. I even had a dream that Skeletor got me and I said, "I'll do whatever you want, just don't hurt me." Skeletor had me lying on a bed, not sure if his gang was watching me or not but he wanted to stick a glass, mercury thermometer up my tush. I'm not sure why, but he was a bit intimidating and very real to a seven-year-old me who was sound asleep.

I watched the He-Man cartoon every day after school from ages seven to nine, most days sucking on a Hershey Bar my Mom would buy me to make it last longer through all my afternoon cartoons, including She-Ra.

Dream related, when I was around three or four I had a weird dream that I still remember to this day, where I was getting off an elevator and walking towards my parents sitting in the living room on a couch, a black & white dream, dreaming in black, brown, grey, beige white, and I sheepishly asked my parents, a little shy and scared whether they were my real parents, alluding to I have been here before in another life and doubted they were indeed my real birth parents, but I honestly couldn't remember who was, sadly. I did love both my sweet parents very much and found out they were really my best parents. They didn't even mind I slept in the middle with them most of my life, at least until the teenage years on and off, maybe if I didn't they would have accidently given me another brother or sister, except my Dad used to tell me he couldn't afford any more kids.

Once with an early dinner of potted meatballs made by my Mom with a small red potato, I mushed it all up and made little balls with ketchup, just like in one episode when Man-At-Arms made protein balls or something, I copied him that evening. There was He-Man, Man at Arms, Orko, Teela, Sorcerer, Battlecat, Skeletor…

One day waking up in my grey-and-red He-Man PJs, it was later than usual so it must have been a Saturday. I remember thinking like this is the first day of the rest of my life, like being reborn. That's a rather deep thought for a seven or eight-year-old little girl. I might have been only nine, 10 and 11, but I was happy being a boy like my brother. I liked tricking people, too. They thought I was a real boy. Even the kids in my class were confused.

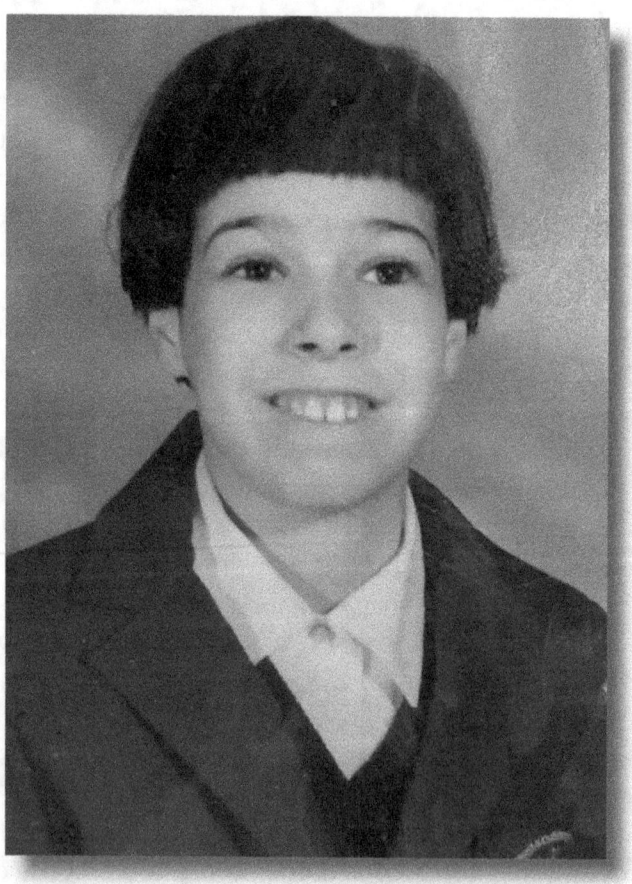

Christian Karen Berman

THE GIRL BULLY

What else was going on in my life during that time? It was early October and we would usually go to McDonald's and Sears (in the same building) on the weekends, after I watched *Dennis the Menace* reruns on Nickelodeon, and *I'm Telling* and *Ramona* on Saturday mornings on network television. I watched many cartoons and kids shows on Saturday mornings, like most kids. Or sometimes I didn't have time, depending on when my parents were ready to leave. Cartoons like *DuckTales, Chip & Dales Rescue Rangers, Gummy Bears, Punky Brewster,* and Pee-Wee Herman. I didn't eat breakfast; once in a while my blood sugar would feel really low by the time we got there. I would get a chicken McNugget Happy Meal with all the BBQ & hot mustard dipping sauces, as would my brother, Larry. It would be in a Halloween Happy Meal trick-or-treating bucket.

During the late 1980's McDonald's actually had a cool kids clothing line called McKids. It only went to a kid's size 10 and they had a shoe and sneaker line, too. I begged my Mom for these cool greyish-black overalls which had black-and-white pinstripes on some of the insides you could see, very late-80s cool kids. The overalls that went to my size in McKids, a size 10, were just my size. I loved them and loved overalls and they fit perfectly, maybe a tad bit snug is all. The ones I'm wearing in the photo, I guess I just had to copy Dennis; he was on TV a lot then.

My parents didn't know what to do about this girl bully named Cathy (most bullies were boys). She hit me, pushed me down, gave me big black and blue and deep purple marks on my hips that hurt badly. The other kids on the playground after school knew what was going on. I guess some saw, they wanted me to hit back, but I couldn't hit her or hurt her. I even tried, too. I barely gently tapped her lower shoulder and then I walked away. Even she wanted me to see if I could hit her. She wasn't scared of me. She knew I couldn't hurt her. I was too gentle and sensitive a girl who knew no violence and was just a happy-go-lucky, loved little kid, albeit a little confused about my sexual orientation, but weren't we all at that age? This girl had to have problems at home, not getting love or attention or getting hit by one or both of her parents or being bullied herself I think now, but back then I hated her. She was scaring me, making me not want to go to school and messing up my young life. But why? But I kinda wanted her to like me. In the bathroom once before she was bullying me, she wanted me to open the door for her, so I happily did. She washed her hands and didn't want her hands to get dirty and germy. I didn't know or understand germs back then, ignorance is bliss, one less problem to worry about then.

In the 5th grade school cafeteria, I craved those square pizzas they served for lunch and even bought similar frozen pizzas to compensate for missing out on them, but I wasn't allowed to buy school lunch back then. My parents always thought that I was too young, I would lose my lunch money, drop my tray, or wouldn't have enough time to eat, not that I ate much anyway. I hated the food my Mom always packed for me. I had too much going on to explain to my Mom what I wanted, yummy food like the other kids, but I didn't think she would buy me Doritos & Ring Dings. I never liked the lunches my Mom made me, I was so tired of them. Tuna was my favorite, but she couldn't make it that often, it wouldn't keep well, but I liked it better than the other lunches. I never ate the same yucky lunch she would give me almost everyday since the first grade-PB & J, plain Wise potato chips & Chips Ahoy cookies with a Hi-C fruit punch juice box or Ssips. I'd get turkey with Russian dressing once in a while, never ate more than a few bites.

There was a girl who was my best friend, she was Latino. We sat together in class and at lunch. She told me once, "Don't worry, your hair will grow back soon." My thoughts were, I hope not, I don't want it to, I'm happy with it right now, but I didn't tell her that. Inside, I was happy with my hair, smiling happy.

I had to bring my lunch in a brown paper bag, it had a picture of Garfield on it. My Mom heard from another Mom, "Fifth graders don't carry lunch boxes anymore." She didn't want me to be the only 5th grader with a lunch box, how embarrassing, she wanted me to fit in. Dressing like a boy and giving myself a haircut, I was my own person and didn't care to follow the crowd. I wanted to be who I wanted to be at the time, popular or not. It only matters what I like, I wasn't interested in being a copycat, so to speak. Besides, I loved getting a new plastic lunch box every year and looking forward to the new TV characters to choose and someone on the grapevine had to ruin it for me. It keeps your sandwich from getting smushed and is cheaper in the long run and eco-friendly, it saves trees. I would have probably chosen a *Transformers* lunch box.

MIRROR OF MY WORLD

Christian Karen Berman

THE BULLY PART 2

I heard Cathy was going to beat me up after school. I was frightened and told some classmates in health class which was the last period. Many said not to worry. I was just going to get out before she had a chance to beat me up. I had to put on that 25-pound backpack first and run down the stairwell, which was a great feat in itself. I think she was in that class with me, too. I told the health teacher, and she said she was probably just trying to scare me. Well, I saw Cathy, ran down ahead of her and got outside. I thought I was home free, then I felt a strong push and I fell straight to the ground, hard, on the rough blacktop. She got me by surprise and that hurt. Then I slowly got up.

My Mom was there and saw what happened. Cathy was going to hit me some more, but my Mom saved me and pulled her away before she could finish beating me up. I glanced at Cathy and her friends who looked surprised themselves and not happy. I then slowly pulled myself up with my heavy backpack and handed it to my Mom to carry and we both walked to the car together. I was glad to be going home. It was the last time I would be that school for two years.

At home, My Mom looked at my two big black-and-blue marks on my hip bone—blue, red, and purple—they hurt, too. Cathy was two inches shorter than me, but a good ten pounds heavier. She had no bangs, long, straight sandy brown hair, pulled back into a ponytail. My Mom called the school principal and told him what happened. He had been notified before by my Mom about this girl picking on me, pushing and hitting me once before, and he said there was nothing he could do. This time, he said that my Mom wasn't allowed on school grounds and she had no right to put her hands on the girl, which was only to pull this girl away from me before she was going to punch me while I was lying hurt on the ground. I couldn't defend myself to her, I couldn't hit back, plus she was stronger than me, and angrier.

MIRROR OF MY WORLD

    My Mom was very upset by this and just waiting for my Dad to get home from school to ask him what to do about it. The school wouldn't do anything to the girl, suspend her, or put me in a different class. They couldn't protect me and move me to another school where I would be safe. They made it seem it was my fault for not trying to get along with her, which was impossible—she hated me for some reason, probably me being like a real little boy. My Dad spoke to the school and they said the same thing. I tried to practice in our hall near my parents' bedroom that night by punching our pillows, but I did not feel comfortable fighting her. Thank goodness, this was ten years before all the school shootings or she might've really hurt me.

    My parents were at a loss. They had no idea what to do with me. They did not feel comfortable sending me back to school when the school wasn't going to help me or protect me from this girl bully who kept beating me up. Like, what was her problem? Get a life and leave me alone—how is hitting me benefiting you, and why is our school letting you attack me? In those days, calling the police for a school bully was unheard of. Even today, it's rarely done. How and why did my school back then and even schools today allow this and then viciously always someone puts the blame on the victim. The victim is not trying to become friends with the bully, ignore it, you're the one causing the problem, like why is it never the actual bully's fault? There is always an excuse to let the bully off the hook and blame the victim for causing the bully to pick on them. Should I have asked the bully to style my short hair and pick out a cute outfit for me to wear to school? She acted like an animal, just trying to get me for no good reason.

    I wasn't equipped to fight with this girl or hit her back. I was so upset by the whole thing, and confused. My Dad over the next few days frantically started calling schools. It was late October/early November. Most schools were not accepting new students once the semester had started. I wasn't missing much in school being only age 10, tracing my hand to make a Thanksgiving turkey was the last memory I had in that school. My Dad had called the school and said I had cut my hair and didn't like the haircut and wanted to wait another week before I returned to school. He told that to my teacher in the special class I had for one period. She said it didn't matter how I looked, I looked beautiful anyway, but I should come to school, but she was still understanding why I didn't want to go to school and said it was okay to stay home for a week if I wanted to. Then my Dad told the principal the real truth. Then they just didn't care, so no one called me in sick to attendance. That's the public school system for you, even back in the day, the late 1980s.

Other public schools wouldn't take me, because I didn't live in their school district. Dad tried my Jewish kindergarten elementary school, Solomon Schechter, which wouldn't accept me, either. Maybe they remembered when I was age five, I missed my Mommy and couldn't stay a full day and wanted to go home before naptime. Maybe the old principal was still there. I do tend to make a strong impression on people to remember me, not that I mean to; I hope it's more good than bad, though. My Dad was calling every elementary school in the local tri-state area. He didn't think I could handle a full day at Horace Mann Elementary. He left for school at 6:45 am for the hour commute, so I would have to wake up at 6 am, wouldn't be home until 4:30 pm, and then would have Hebrew school and homework and it would be just too much for me. Plus he would have to babysit me on the late days he had meetings & tutoring. It was a high school and not for little kids.

He finally found a school that would meet with them. Of all schools, it was Our Lady of Good Counsel Academy. My Mom & Dad went there to have a meeting with the principal, Sister Rose. She felt sorry for the poor little Jewish girl who looked like a boy that nobody wanted and took me under her wing. She told my parents at the meeting they would have to put me back in the 4th grade though, if that was okay with them, because it was a very small school and they had no room for me in the 5th grade, which was fine with them and me, an extra year old childhood with the youngsters. She said with my name I would fit in just fine, they had a Kathy, Katherine, Casey, Carry, Christina, Katie & now a Christian Karen, a lot of C & K names, like myself.

I was young for my age & small. She had them meet with me, put her arm around me and introduced me to the 4th grade class for a few minutes, but I wouldn't be able to start the next semester until after Christmas vacation, January 2nd. That would be a long, much needed school break. No school for over two months. It wasn't even Thanksgiving yet. What a nice, relaxing, fun vacation for a little 10-year-old kid—no school or school work, able to sleep late, watch any TV show I wanted to (and we had cable, too), eat anything I wanted or my Mom would give me, play with all my toys, and maybe even get a few new toys. To a 10-year-old child back then, two months was almost like a full year, you know, time went slower back in those days, especially the younger you were. Yay, for me, almost long and boring, but still what luck, no school, almost makes getting beat up worth it. But the school wasn't nice and didn't seem to want me there anyway, I dunno why not; I was a nice, sweet, skinny kid, I wasn't a bully or someone that would cause trouble. My parents had no other choice, they didn't want to home school me. Homeschooling wasn't even heard of back then unless you had to miss school for a long time because you were very sick. I would have a lot of time to play, watch TV, spend time with my Mom and Grandma Lee, and just relax. As for education, I had a Yellow Speak & Read electronic learning device to play with and the Tag system which my brother and I shared—a magic red wand pen that would beep on the letters in the book that you didn't know. It was invented in 1986, the first Leap Frog type, fun learning toy. Mostly, I would be watching Nickelodeon, Disney, and afternoon cartoons.

What did I actually do on those lazy days of no school and boredom (nice change of pace, though)?. Watched TV, played with my toys, spoke with my Grandma and Mom in the kitchen during the morning hours, and made a treehouse on the back wooden porch by bringing all the toys and junk from the garage into the porch, old toys, whatever I could find, like Larry's old baby bubble popping walker.

Christian Karen Berman

MALE CHILD PSYCHIATRIST

So my parents took me to a psychiatrist to talk to me about being bullied and whether I would protect myself or fight back. They had told my school and principal, but there was nothing the school could do. The doctor must have been expensive. He told me to take a sucking charm and if I didn't like it, just spit it out in the wastepaper basket and take another. Was he a child psychiatrist? It was coffee flavor. I sucked it a few seconds then threw it out and that was that. I thought it was for adults, gross and very possibly poisoned. I didn't want another one. Now I like coffee and coffee flavored treats, I would probably enjoy one now in my 40s. I wasn't interested in talking about the bully. There wasn't anything he could do. I wasn't that scared; I just said something like I might not be that strong or able to use my hands, but I can use my feet and kick her. I really didn't want to kick her, just show him I could take care of myself if I had to, and let me change the subject to my other problem that I was more worried about.

Of all things, when I would get my period, even though I was only a few inches over 4' & a little over 60 pounds, I was worried, looking for it in my underpants at times and waiting. I didn't want it, but wanted to see it coming. I like to control things around me. Waiting for that few red dots stains I thought I might get would probably hurt; if you're bleeding, it would have to, right?

I had very bad OCD for a 10-year-old, not just the perfection that I had with cutting my hair and my My Buddy's hair, which most 10-year-olds wouldn't even notice or could care less about. Before bed I would check all the heating vents in the whole house. I wanted to make sure nothing was near them that would catch on fire. I knew if I didn't I wouldn't feel safe and secure and I would worry that there might really be a fire, like if a paper or a box was close to one (I have been afraid of fires since I was seven or eight years old, but it used to be if a gold star sticker was on the wall near my bed I'd be safe). I felt it was my job, I called myself a steam checker. I even tried to enlist Larry's help, but it didn't work. I did all the work, even made up a theme song, "Steam checkers, steam checkers, checking the entire steam."

The doctor did not know what to say about my period problem. I must have heard about this from my Mom and Grandma, that it would be coming soon, but the scariest, most nerve-wracking part was I didn't know when. I was very nervous about it. He said something like not to worry about it, I don't think you'll get it for a while, plus there's nothing you can do about it—when it comes it comes. He was an older man in his 50s or 60s, a Jewish doctor. Probably, as Archie Bunker always says, "all of the best doctors and lawyers are Jewish men." What I know now is what the doctor should have said: you're a small, skinny ten-year-old and show no signs of prepubescent development, I think you don't even have to think about this for a good five or six years. I did get my period about a month before my 16th birthday, so all the anguish and 10-year-old worry was for nothing, I was still a little girl and should have just enjoyed my childhood more, and playing with my toys and few friends. Thinking back, my pediatrician would have been a much better choice to ask and explain my worry, and for free. He didn't know anything about kids; Asperger's wouldn't be well-known for at least another good 10 years.

CHRISTMAS

This Christmas, I decorated the tree myself. I think I did a pretty good job for a 4th grader. Larry is age seven. I look very happy in this photo. I got a Disney sleeping bag, and a Hasbro

MIRROR OF MY WORLD

Fairy Tales bird, white with a long rainbow tail you could brush & braid. I got a Disney stuffed animal from the animated movie *Oliver & Company*. I think I got a few more little things. I know I got chocolate Santas and candy canes in my stocking. Yes, we didn't have much, but I appreciated and enjoyed what I had and was given. I thought our little tree was just beautiful. I also drew a Merry Christmas sign and made homemade decorations. I fussed and made Christmas a special day. I even made a mailbox out of a cardboard box for all the Christmas Cards we received, then I decorated the house with them. I made presents for my parents, probably drawings.

Christmas means love and family. It's not really about how many presents you can buy, it's about making good memories and enjoying friend's and family's company. I think in this day, all that is long forgotten, but I hope not and I'd like to remind you, Christmas is about loving and caring for people, especially the less fortunate, and just being a good kind human being to others.

Christian Karen Berman

JeaN FROM THe HeaTHCOTe BOOTeRY iN ScaRSDale, NY

I had started going there after Buster Brown. I needed uniform penny loafers for my Catholic school, Good Counsel Academy. I was entering the 4th grade. I had transferred there in the middle of the school year to escape a bully that was beating me up after school, a girl in my class that didn't like that I dressed and looked like a real boy. Jean who worked there was nice and found me cute, comfortable Velcro kid's brown loafers. I was a child's size 3. Our older neighbor Danny, who was a retired tailor like my Grandpa Jules, measured me for my maroon plaid uniform. It really does take a village to raise a child.

Jean would always give me a friendship bracelet after and puffy queen stickers, or whatever she had in her drawer. Buster Brown gave me a balloon and maybe a lollipop. They had great shoes. I still shopped there until I was age 17. This was until the late 1990s. I got suede sneaker boots the last time I was there.

At age 11, she found me white Velcro Stride Rite's. I was a kid size 3½ then. For my 12th birthday, I got $20 from my friend at my small birthday party and I wanted the same moccasins that our neighbor Emily had. She was a few years younger than me, but they were pink and white swirl ones, like tie-dye. I went there with my Mom. She told me I could spend my birthday money and pay for it myself. I'd rather have bought a toy, but maybe we didn't have much money. Jean looked in the back and couldn't find any, just plain white or pink. I was so disappointed and she could tell and went to the back again to check. She came out with even better ones than Emily had—red, white, and blue tie-dye, like rainbow ices with cream mixed in it. I was so happy, loved them so much. They might of cost $30, I don't remember, but

MIRROR OF MY WORLD

I paid for most of it. It was the early 1990s. Then stickers and a friendship bracelet. She let me pick the color bracelet, too. I wore them on my wrist.

Another time, I wanted Keds like Emily had. I copied Emily sometimes. Jean looked hard in the back and found me Keds with a lace design. It wasn't the same, but still nice and cute. Jean always went out of her way to help me find shoes I loved. Jean had yellowish, gold hair, tan skin and was so nice to me always.

At 11½, I was watching reruns of *Punky Brewster* after school. I wanted to look and dress like her. This was in the early 1990s. I went to the shoe store needing new sneakers, wanting ones like Punky had. She was my role model at the time and she made me feel better about myself. I'd sadly rather be her than myself, though now I wish that wasn't the case and I could have loved being me; maybe it was the actress inside me, always wanting to be someone else since age six, be a friend or another actress. I wish I could've loved and valued me more, but I had such a low self-esteem, so quiet and shy, barely spoke much to anyone including my parents then.

I looked at all the sneakers available and found a multicolored hot pink, purple and aqua Reebok in a girl's size 4. The bigger my feet got, the harder it was to find cute child sneakers back in the 1990s. Now the cute sneakers go to a kid's size 7 and I can still fit. In 1998, I saw the remake of the movie *Gloria*. I loved the cute Jordan's the little boy in the movie was wearing, a black-and-white leather high-top. I don't know what kind they were, but I found a Rebook kind similar. I loved them and thought they were so cool. They were cut very small and I had to go back for a size 8½. Jean apologized for not believing me when I said they felt tight on me. They cost like $80 then. More expensive than the sneakers I buy now.

She would have sales on old sneakers from the early 1990s, like old Nikes, for like $20. I'd look for sales on baby shoes, too, for my baby dolls and ask Jean if they had any baby shoes on sale. The nicest thing Jean would do for me is give me free baby shoes for my baby dolls. I would ask to see shoes for them, tell her about them. She liked hearing about my babies and indulged me in my interest. She said to go home, try them on, and if they don't fit to bring them back and she'd give me another baby sneaker to try on toy babies. Sometimes she would look and give me two shoes for my kids. I guess older sneakers and crib shoes that never sold. They still looked new, though, some just tried on, some looked not even tried on. That made me so happy and warmed my heart, going out of her way just to make me happy and encourage my imaginative play. She remembered she had dolls she loved when she was young, too.

I also would get ballet and tap shoes from her, one for Day Camp and when I was older in my 20s, tap shoes to dance like Gene Kelly and Dick Van Dyke. I wanted these boy's black oxfords I tried on and one day my parents picked them up and surprised me with them. She knew the ones I tried on and was wanting. I was a boy's size 6½, it was $50. I would still get boy's cute Stride Rites sneakers from her up until 2009. She would look hard to find the cute ones in the biggest size for me. Also give me sticker sheets to enjoy with it. After then, the store closed.

She relocated to another shoe store somewhere else where I didn't shop or buy shoes. I just remember her always going out of her way to make me happy. After they closed, I would buy kid's shoes and Mary Jane's from Lands' End Kids online. It was hard to find a place to buy sneakers. I didn't wear out my shoes and my feet didn't grow anymore, so they lasted a long time.

I started thinking about her the other day and I don't know what happened to her, if she's even still alive. She would be in her late 70s or early 80s. Back ten years ago when I had parents, you don't think like that, but there are so few people I knew as a child who remember me. I don't have relatives. My pediatrician being the only one and yes, I stopped by a few months ago to say hi when I was at my gastro doctor, he's in the same building. He said it was good to see me and Larry and to stop by anytime. He's only in his 60s, so still young.

In the late 1990s, when my brother was 14 and I was 18, we would go to Yonkers, New York after my Dad was finished from

MIRROR OF MY WORLD

school. Dr. Iandoli was a holistic doctor who took a lot of blood test for chronic fatigue, bilirubin, Lyme disease. My brother was being tested for that. Me, too. For me it was just a fun trip. During the day my Mom would buy me a glass bottle of Diet Birch Root Beer and I would sip that. I thought it was cool, like real beer. It was expensive, too, like $2.00. I was kind of on a diet and took this diet pill. I was 103-108 pounds, so I was having a little eating disorder.

When Daddy got home from work, we'd get in the car and sometimes I would have my Dad play "Brother for Sale" and "I Am the Cute One" from Mary-Kate and Ashley Olsen, even sing along sometimes. By then I memorized some of the words. I don't think my Dad minded, but he liked the radio better. The radio had great songs too, "All I Need is a Miracle," "Roseanna," "Oh, Sherry." It took a good 50 minutes or so to get there, too. We did this once or twice a week. Larry might have been getting special injections, I don't remember. To me it was a fun trip, listening to good music. Once our Shih Tzu Ritchie came with us and I carried him in a blue snuggle to my chest. He was a puppy then; it was for real babies. I had just turned 18, my first puppy. I would play with him and he'd pull out the ponytail holder and then shake it off.

There was a pediatric dentist next door, they had video games. At that time, I rarely saw the dentist. I did see one that year and my teeth looked so good he didn't even take X-rays. He showed the nurse how well I brush; I didn't need a cleaning. After that we went to Uno's and we all got something, deep-dish Chicago pizza, the sampler, nacho's, fish and veggies. I got a giant Diet Sprite with ice. They gave free refills, then I took something to go. They had Diet Coke and a cheeseburger, fries and veggie pizza.

During that time, one early morning around 9 am, we packed up on a trip to visit a new pediatrician in Katonah, New York. I packed a bag of snacks we had picked up at CVS including Fig Newtons (before I found out they were made with wasps, yes, revolting), snack crackers, even Pedialyte (it's gross, but then it came in cute little Kool Aid-type plastic bottles). Well, in my *Healthy Kids* magazine, it looked like it tasted good. I was having tummy troubles at the time. Even the doctor said Gatorade was better.

It took about an hour to get there. We almost got lost, but then my Dad found the right exit to turn off. In the waiting room, there was a few little kids. I got to talking with one, age five or six. He was going to take an airplane trip, to visit his Grandma, I believe. I even offered him a cookie. He was waiting for the cheeseburger and water they served on the plane and saving his appetite for that meal. He broke his seven-year-old sister's wrist and they had to stop here on the way to have her wrist examined. Her Dad was with her and he was alone. I'm guessing it was by rough-housing and it was an accident. He was a cute little boy. Another little boy about six had an upset stomach and he was going to the bathroom a lot.

When the doctor saw me, he wanted me to take off my socks and see my feet. That was weird, not sure why. He got my weight, took blood from me and Larry. I brought one of my baby dolls with me dressed in real baby clothes and she sat in the office waiting for me. It was an adventure for me. I guess my parents were following up on some blood tests that our own pediatrician didn't do. Maybe he was a holistic pediatrician. I don't remember the medical reason, to me it was a fun adventure. I did have a little eating disorder, that's all.

After, we all went to McDonald's in Mount Kisco, where we would often go in the summer, but this was still the winter, cold with snow on the ground. I shared or took out a Big Mac, fries and shake. At home I wasn't feeling great, had some powdered chicken broth and water, heated. It helped, and maybe a fat-free vanilla yogurt. I was tired, then maybe watched TV and then went to sleep.

MIRROR OF MY WORLD

Christian Karen Berman

THE WEDDING

My 5th grade teacher, Miss Keller, was getting married on Valentine's Day and invited her whole Catholic school class to the church. She would soon be Mrs. Belger. It was kind of exciting, getting dressed up to go to your teacher's wedding. She was pretty, blonde hair and thin. I think her first name was Linda, which in Spanish means beautiful. I'm not sure how old she was, but late 20s maybe.

I remember that early morning being a little sick with a cold. My parents and I didn't want me to miss out on a wedding. I wore my light blue frilly dress in a girls size medium 10-12. My Mom went with me and we sat next to my best friend Andrea's mother, Regina. We couldn't see good sitting in the back rows, so Regina put Andrea on her lap and my Mom never does this, but happily put me on her lap, so I could see better, too. I was 11½, 4'7" and about 76 pounds. My best friend Andrea was 10½, 4'6" and 93 pounds. She had told my mother this once and she told me.

We watched the beautiful ceremony. Luckily it wasn't too long. Then after, my beautiful teacher, dressed in a white ruffly, frilly wedding dress with short sleeves, wanted to give a big hug to all her students who came and watched her get married. She hugged Andrea first, but when she went to hug me, I shied and pulled away. The teacher smiled and went to give me a big hug anyway. I was afraid I would give her my cold and make her sick on her wedding night. I hoped she wouldn't catch my germs. Then we all got little packages of white dry rice to throw at her car as they drove off. I think they could have been tied to the bottom of the back of the car, too. My first sweet wedding.

MIRROR OF MY WORLD

Christian Karen Berman

SNOW DAY

It was like Christmas morning or my birthday, worth getting up early to feel the happiness and joy on an official snow day. My Dad luckily got a call from his school, too; he taught at an elite private school, the Horace Mann School, in New York City, so his school rarely closed, but they did have more snow in the 1990s. A snow day meant time for cold cereal, not just a Quaker Chewy Granola Bar. It meant playing in the snow, making snow castles, snow forts, snow men, snow angels, and color-changing winter gloves, while your dad was shoveling the driveway, staying outside until you were cold and wet, then coming in and putting on dry clothes, sometimes warming up your feet in a warm water bowl, Dad cooking Thomas' English Muffin pizzas, with Hines baked beans and SpaghettiOs, Mom baking homemade Toll House cookies or Jiffy blueberry muffins from scratch, the wonderful cooking smells in the warm house after being out in the cold, breathing the crisp, windy, cold dry air, watching TV until you ate until you were very full (no PB&J today), playing with the Cookie Monster Counting Game and listening to my brother's Miss Nelson is Back cassette on our Fisher Price Tape Recorder.

He played it to annoy my Grandma Lee mainly who lived with us; he thought he was being cute and funny. She had some choice words for him which she meant to be funny, "If he wants a swift kick, she'll give it to him"(in the behind, LOL) or a "lick'n." That's how they spoke in her generation. I remember, because he was recording at times, too, old school recording, Fisher Price, she was a sweetheart and led a hard life, but I was her favorite. "You'll never know how much I love you," she would say. I didn't, I was too young to really understand. She lost her Dad at age 12 and cried her eyes out until she needed eyeglasses.

There was a hopeful feeling, maybe it's so bad out, sometimes it was two feet, once three feet in 1995 or 1996, if anyone remembers the New York Blizzard of 1996? Then the bad feeling in the pit of your stomach when it's getting late—oh, no! School tomorrow and did you do your homework, did you call your friend to make sure there's school tomorrow? Two-and-a-half-hour days were the worst; you still had to get up at the same time, maybe you got to sleep an hour later, but not me. Basically it was watching the news channels and looking for your school to see if your delay turned into a closing. The time was also spent listening on the radio for school closings and Dad shoveling snow in the driveway. Who could sleep? You had more time to eat and watch TV, maybe brush your hair. It was slippery and terrible outside, the bus was usually late, then once you got there, all cold, bundled up, snowing, messy, slushy, it was about 11 am.

This was when I was in 4th grade in Catholic School, Our Lady of Good Counsel Academy. The teacher just waited for everyone to arrive, many were late, icy roads, it was cold and flu season in school, many kids bringing Kleenex & yummy Luden's cherry cough drops that every kid wanted if they were coughing or not. In those days, unless you had a high fever, you went to school, you didn't get sent home unless you had a temperature over 101.

Catholic school never sends you home, don't even bother going to the nurse, except for the one time a girl in my class asked to go to the bathroom and the way she said it so sweetly, me at age 10 just instinctively or psychically knew she was going to throw up. I still wonder how I knew; she didn't say anything like that. She came back, told the teacher, and she got sent home. I went to the nurse once with pains on the right lower side of my stomach. She didn't send me home, and no, it didn't turn out to be my appendix.

Then they sent you to lunch. You prayed first then had to go outside to walk to the cafeteria. It was good food, though, and cheap, like $2. They had junk food machines too, 4th grader. On the way back I did slip on an ice patch, but just got up and kept walking. I had to wear a plaid skirt, no pants, just floral girls underpants, no tights, just knee socks, school uniform, and loafers.

No recess on snow days, so no slide, swings, or monkey bars. You went back to class, talked to the other kids, then maybe read out loud from the history book when they went around the class and it was your turn. Then you prayed again, copied down the homework from the blackboard, bundled up and packed your backpack, and waited for your bus to come and take you home. I had mittens clipped to my winter coat hoping I didn't lose them and a Fisher Price coin jammers wrist band my Mom put my lunch money in so I didn't lose it. Before then I either put it in the side of my sock or on the inside or bottom of my shoe.

The whole day was a waste, nothing was accomplished, everyone was cold with a runny nose. I mean, with a two-and-a-half hour delay you never accomplish anything. By the time you get there, you eat lunch, and then get ready to leave. It might have been only three inches of snow, but dangerous, icy roads. At least at home with your parents you'd be well, safe, and make lifelong lasting memories, having hot chocolate with Mom, playing in the snow until you were somewhat white and blue, watching cartoons, and just soaking up a legal hooky day, even if you were just sleeping and making up on your sleep debt from all the nights you stayed up late finishing homework and waking up early for school. There should be no two-and-a-half hour delays. It's unsafe, a waste of the bus driver's time, everyone's time, and no one learns anything, they just feel bad and think what did I go to school today for, we did nothing, learned nothing, now I just feel sick and want to go home and get in my warm bed under the covers, then have my Mom's warm, home-cooked dinner and not do homework, have my temperature taken to see if I could miss school tomorrow (I should after all I went through today), running after my own tail, so to speak, and go to sleep.

What a day.

MIRROR OF MY WORLD

Christian Karen Berman

OUR FIRST NIGHT AT THE NEVELE

It's our first night at the Nevele. It was a hectic morning leaving early on the 2½-hour trip to the Catskills. We stopped off at Ho-Jo's for Brunch. Larry and I had the Children's menu—one egg, bacon, fries, ketchup and chocolate milk. A rare treat, the chocolate milk. My parents and Grandma Lee had the adult version with OJ and coffee. As soon as we arrive we get into our swimsuits and go swimming. We usually wait until the next day; how fun that we can go right now and live it up.

That night my Dad puts me in the junior dining room for the Day Camp. I'm one of the oldest in the Day Camp. It goes to age 10. Daddy say's I'm 10, they probably can't tell, but I turned 12 the month before. I'm not sure if there is a teenage camp, but I'm fit in much better with the six- to ten-year-olds. There were actually a few girls taller than me, too. I'm 4'8" and 81 pounds.

In the children's dining room, many young kids start with buttered rye toast and chicken noodle soup. Picky eater me doesn't eat much. I enjoyed the breaded veal cutlet last year when I was there, but it wasn't on the menu this year. I picked the veal chop, with a glass of grape juice. I didn't care for it much; maybe it wasn't cooked enough. I probably had a Cherry Twin Pop for dessert. My parents never let me have Popsicles, or a Swirl Pudding Pop or ice cream. After dinner we meet our parents in the lobby by the water fountain. I wasn't feeling good. My stomach felt weird and I was nauseous. I'm not sure I told my parents first, but I threw up while I was sitting in the lobby with them. I got some on my "Don't Worry, Be Happy" dress. Then my Mom took me in the Women's Room if I had to throw up more and to clean up my cotton dress, a size 10 girl's.

Then my Dad sees and finds out and he needs to take me back to our hotel room and he said, "You're sick? How did you get sick?", touching my forehead. He carefully planned this trip in mid-July, carefully checking the weather to make sure it would be warm and sunny, no rain, and that no one was sick. When I was eight or nine years old, we had to cancel a trip because I had a fever and was sick with the flu. My Mom wasn't happy about that at all, but my Dad said it wouldn't be fair to me, that I wouldn't be able to enjoy the trip.

We walk back to our room, 612, my parent's old honeymoon room; my Grandma Lee had the adjoining room next door. You need to go outside after the lobby and it's about a six-minute walk back to our room. There was a water fountain with the most refreshing, cold spring water, the best I ever tasted. Then up four stairs to our room. There my Dad took my temperature, the baby way, in the tush. It was 100. He was worried now. We're on a six-day vacation and I'm far from home and sick. My Mom, brother and Grandma had followed along and now come in to join us. My Mom tells me to go get in my nightgown and get ready for bed. My Dad tells me I'm sick and can't go to the nightclub with them. That's where you dance, get a Cherry Coke on ice, listen to jokes that are too old for you, so you don't understand them. This is not for kids, the nightclub, but we always went anyway. Then there is really nice singing. It goes on until after midnight. I need to go to my Grandma's room so she can watch me and I sleep in the twin bed next to her with my pretend sister, Jen. I got her pajamas on, too, so she could go to sleep with me.

Grandma would probably have come with us, but I couldn't go because I was sick. I felt better after I threw up, except for my fever. My Dad is about to leave for the nightclub with my Mom and Larry. They dance there. My Mom is yapping about everything with my Grandma, da-dat, dat-dat-dah. About everything and anything a mile a minute, like she always does. So, that's me giving my Dad that "I know" look. He just wanted to get going and not miss all the fun.

I couldn't sleep in that room, maybe we talked or watched TV, I can't remember that part. My parents didn't stay long at the club, they were worried about me. I don't know if they brought Children's Tylenol, but they must of if they brought a thermometer. Maybe they got a good deal on some at the convenient gift shop for double the price. Well, I didn't have medicine, my fever went down on its own. I slept in the next room with my parents. My brother and I shared a twin bed, no one touched each other, and woke up feeling so much better.

   I went to breakfast with them that day, so they could watch me and make sure I was okay, like I didn't throw up or anything. The waitress Tony said, "I didn't know you had a daughter." Later or the next day I was all better and back at the day camp for fun and to be with kids my own age. It was boring hanging around my parents. They mostly stayed by the pool. Larry was almost eight, but not in the camp, not sure why, but my parents kept him with them. Maybe so they wouldn't be lonely or because it was too active for him with hiking, mountain climbing, and horseback riding. They liked to keep me busy. I got bored easily as a child.

MIRROR OF MY WORLD

Christian Karen Berman

GRANDMA LEE BABYSITS

My parents never went on vacation alone once after they had kids or rarely went out at night, just a few times like for my dad's late night parent-teacher meetings at my Dad's school or Karaoke Night at our Temple or a Dinner Dance night at the Temple. They loved us and our company so much, they always wanted us to come out for dinner with them and didn't want to leave us home alone, even though they wouldn't be gone longer than an hour and a half. When I was older, even at age 12, 13, 14, sometimes I chose to stay home and relax and watch TV and they would bring me a Cheeseburger Deluxe platter. That meant onion rings and french fries.

One night my Dad took my Mom into the city for parent-teacher meetings at 8 pm. That meant they had to leave at 7 pm and our 80-year-old Grandma that would hardly walk, but lived with us, had to babysit an active 7 and 11-year-old. How fun for her. I used to try to guess her age, but she would never tell me her real age. My guess was 64. I think she agreed, she must have been flattered. Then I said to her she was still young. I kinda thought to myself she might be older and was surprised she wasn't that old. She lived with us anyway, but we were little so she had to watch us; my parents wouldn't be home until after 11pm. Grandma had not been able to walk up the stairs since I was age six and I'm not sure she even had a phone number to reach my parents if she had to, so us little kids were pretty much on our own.

I don't remember that much of the earlier part of the night. Maybe we made mayo and mustard Kraft Cheese toast and talked. I remember setting out my Disney sleeping blanket on the bedroom floor, then Larry and me going into his bed, but I slept at the end where his feet were hoping they wouldn't touch me. We were having a sleepover. I usually slept in my parents' big bed with them, so I was afraid to sleep alone. Larry slept alone. I dunno if I fell asleep, but I woke up around 10:30 pm. and turned on the lamp light. I thought I heard my parents' come home, then Larry woke up and I think they went to peek in on us and thought it was sweet that we fell asleep in the same bed. Then I wanted to sleep with them.

Christian Karen Berman

MeMORieS aNd THOUGHTS OF MY PReTeND SiSTeR JeN

I'm age 11-3/4's here with my Kid Sister doll, Jen. They didn't have many big realistic dolls in the 1990s, no Reborn Babies then, so I played with her for years. She was part of my family, even had her own wardrobe. I shampooed her hair with Baby Johnson's shampoo. I gave her a shorter haircut at age 12 to make her look more like a real two or three-year-old. I would give her

MIRROR OF MY WORLD

different hairstyles every few days. My Mom would take her in the car to pick me up from the 7th grade. I would sometimes feed her white bread and ketchup. We would watch *Full House* together and I made her a bed by folding an old comforter in front of the night table. She was like my real sister. We went to McDonald's together and on vacation in hotels together.

I stopped playing with her a little after age 16, when I was old enough to sadly realize she would never turn real like Pinocchio or return all my love. I grew up then and life got sadder and lonelier. I wanted to believe it might happen, if I gave her enough love. I wanted a little sister so much. No one loved a doll like I loved her. We couldn't afford much, so she was my best doll, my pretend sister Jennifer Lauren Berman.

Kids today haven't too much imagination and need to be entertained by devices or in group activities. They have not much creativity to play on their own and by age 10 are pretty much mature and grown up these days. I find that sad. Even the clothes for kids today aren't so cute. They're like little adults after age 12, they don't even want toys or ask for them. They want new clothes, new devices, and maybe art supplies.

[Christian Karen Berman](#)

Sweet Sixteen Party in Manhattan

I was age 11. I remember a few days before the party, I had a play date with my best friend Andrea Bulla from Catholic school. We were both in the 5th grade together at Good Counsel Academy. My Mom was telling her Mom, Regina, about the dress she had just bought me. I think she even showed it to her; maybe it was in the car in a bag and we'd just come from Sears department store. It was a beautiful, light blue chiffon dress, puffy short sleeves and a drop low waist, flowing white lace bottom. My Mom might have even gotten me a slip to wear underneath and white tights. My Mom also bought a matching headband, light-blue-and-white lace bow, with my shoulder-length dark brown hair and bangs I kind of looked like a young Snow White or Alice in Wonderland. It was April.

The party was for my Mom's old friend Marlene's 16-year-old daughter, Wendy. She also had an older daughter named Stacy. It was late and dark out. I remember going over the big bridge. It was dark with so many different colored bright lights. This was exciting, being out so late at such a young age and going into NYC. It must have taken an hour to get there. I enjoyed the ride and the cool music playing on the car radio.

The party was at night, in a fancy, big hotel called The Water Club. We got there about 7 pm. We went to greet the host's family and the live music was playing too loud and was hurting my Dad's ears; he used to talk on the ham radio as a teenager and it had made him have very sensitive hearing. He asked if they could make it a little softer. They couldn't.

The party didn't start yet and my parents, Larry, and me were getting hungry. For lunch I probably had the chicken McNugget Happy Meal, with BBQ and hot mustard dipping sauce, but that was probably around 1 pm, so we walked around the big hotel and found a bar. We all walked in, even though I was 11½ and Larry was age seven, they still let us in. We sat at a table and ordered drinks. Two Cherry Cokes with ice and candied cherries in them, and two extra glasses and ice water and there was a big bowl of mixed nuts we were all munching on, so much so the waitress gave us another bowl, no charge. I remember a bartender there had an unopened Kit Kat Bar and started singing "Break, break, gimme a break, and break me off a piece of that Kit Kat Bar." All the waiters were laughing and enjoying themselves. We were, too. We were the only ones in the bar at the time. We had the place all to ourselves.

Finally, they started serving hors d'oeuvres, then we kinda went our own way for a while, my Mom talking to her friend and us looking at the large assortment of finger foods. There were a few girls there a little older than me—13, 14—that I started to talk to and tag along with. I remember the servers slicing pastrami for me and they put it on a little rye/pumpernickel bread with a nice sharp mustard. After I got a few interesting foods, like a baby knish, kasha varnishkes, pigs in a blanket. I went to sit by the tables with the other girls and ate a little, tried a few things. Then went back and found my parents and sat with them. It was a big spread. They had assorted fruit, bagels, lox, different cheeses, little baked appetizers, maybe even ribs and fried egg and spring rolls and you could go back as much as you wanted. It was all you can eat, a lot of people there too, teenagers, but mostly adults. I must have drank an orange soda.

The hotel was by the water, hence the name The Water Club. You could see boats and water outside, flowers and little trees inside. It was getting pretty late, almost 9 pm, and they didn't even serve the main course yet. It was weird to me, because by 10 pm I was usually finishing my homework with my Dad helping me, then getting ready for bed. We never had dinner this late, usually 6 pm.

It was now after 9 pm and we finally were in the main dining room. We were choosing what to eat on the menu and my parents ordered Prime Rib for everybody. I never had that before. We also had Shirley Temples with cherries in them. My parents had white wine and a Coke. It was taking a while, so I wandered off with my Dad and brother because the music was still loudly playing and hurting my Dad's ears. Then we came back and started talking to the other guests at the big round table, the whole giant room had big round tables full of the host's friends and family.

The lighting in there was very dim and they had many balloons—pink, purple, white. There was a stage in the back of the room. I told the older lady at the table I was never out so late. It was exciting. I was eating dinner when I should have been getting ready for bed. Luckily, it was a Saturday night and I could sleep in tomorrow. I'm sure my Dad, being a teacher, he felt the same way.

Finally at 10 pm, the food came. I was not impressed. I'm only a 5th grader, remember. The prime rib was thick, chewy and fatty, greasy, too. It came with mashed potatoes and asparagus, or some kind of veggie, maybe green beans. I didn't like it. I just had a few bites. Luckily, I had the nuts and pastrami earlier or I would have starved or fainted. I would have rather had kid food—Micky D's, Cheese Doodles. Real food. I tried to pull the thick, white fat off the side of the meat. Yuck! I think the rest of my family and others enjoyed it. Maybe they also had fish or chicken on the menu, but my parents ordered for me. Too fancy for my blood. I like the school cafeteria food—Sloppy Joe's, meatball wedge, and tacos. That's good stuff, yummy.

We finished dinner, except I only picked at it and only had a few bites. We were waiting for dessert to come. It was almost 12 pm. I told the old lady at our table excitedly; I was never up this late.

My parents asked when they would be serving dessert, a big white cake I assume. The music was still loud and dessert wouldn't be served for another hour. My Dad was getting tired and the music bothered his ears so much. It was loud, but I have kid ears, I didn't care too much. Finally, my parents said goodbye to their friends and sadly we had to leave before dessert. I was getting tired, too, but excited to be out partying so late. Maybe they had goodie bags too, if we waited. I don't really remember seeing the sweet sixteen girl, or her older sister. (The family and girls had once come to our house to play by our pool, the plastic kind that gets to be 6' by 2' when you add water from the old green hose. I was three then. I

MIRROR OF MY WORLD

saw once a photo of them. I remember eating a half a saltine and drinking apple juice after coming in from the back porch.)

Then we all left and went down big stairs with a big banister, sad to leave early. I remember my Dad driving home in the dark with bright colored lights all over in the background and going over the big bridge to return back home. it was so interesting and I wondered if we would ever be back again. My Dad drove both ways. Nice music was playing on the radio. We finally arrived home. Everyone was tired. It was almost 3 am. We woke up my Grandma Lee and she was like, where were you so late? The party started late. I was so tired, never up this late in my whole life.

We all quickly went upstairs not to disturb my Grandma and our land turtle Lucky Alexis in the tank. Larry went into our bedroom and I took off my fancy light blue dress, my Dad unzipped the back. I just slept in my underwear at the end of my parents' bed, too tired to even put on my pajamas, and went right to sleep. (I might've been a little hungry, my Dad, too; he went downstairs with my Mom and made himself white toast with PB&J and OJ before he went to bed; maybe my Mom had a snack too.) My parents slept at the other part of the bed. I couldn't sleep in my own bed yet. Off and on I had, but I slept here best. Besides, sleeping in my parents' bed, I was a pretty normal 11-year-old-girl. That was one of the best nights of my life and I woke up hungry. I think we had McDonald's Happy Meals again; they were the best.

Christian Karen Berman

BRONCHITIS

I was age 11 and had bronchitis, the croup, and strep throat with that. I was in the 5th grade at Catholic school. It was early May. I remember clearly going to see Dr. Rothman and having him give me a penicillin shot in my tush. I can't remember coming down with it, I was sick so often as a child. I know I was happy I would be missing a few days of school, though. That sick, but loved feeling, knowing you can sleep and will be fussed over and spoiled a bit, by overprotective, concerned, loving parents.

That night I was having trouble breathing, lots of congestion and phlegm. My Dad was making me a hot cup of Lipton tea to sip to help open my breathing passages. My brother Larry wasn't sick. He was driving my Grandma Lee crazy downstairs playing *Ms. Nelson is Back* on his Fisher Price tape recorder.

This part I know verbatim, because Larry recorded it. I listened to the cassette not that long ago, so I remember it.

Grandma (in the background): "You want a swift kick, I'll give it to you."

Dad (asking Mom): "Is her tea ready yet?"

I'm wearing a light blue short-sleeve mesh boy's shirt with a collar in a size 10/12, sipping tea and spitting up a little. My fever was about 103. My Dad gave me a teaspoon of Ventolin, a yummy, sour green apple syrup that helps you breathe. He called the pediatrician around 11 pm. He said to take me outside to see if I could breathe better and if that didn't work take me down to the E.R. He and my Mom were also giving me cherry-flavored Children's Tylenol liquid, plus a teaspoon of Amoxicillin pink bubblegum flavor throughout the day, one: to lower my fever, two: to fight infection. I slept, didn't eat much, can't even remember what I ate. My parents always gave us Peppermint Pattie's when we were sick.

Well, after I was outside I started to feel nauseous like I was going to throw up, so I'm like, "I'm going to die, I'm going to the hospital. No, I don't feel better." My parents both walked into the house and told my Grandma Lee to watch Larry, who was age seven. Dad said, "We're going to the hospital," which surprised my Grandma. The last time I was there I was age three and unconscious, had a serve reaction to the 3-in-1 vaccine, so we rarely ever went to the E.R. unless it was a real emergency.

I told my parents to wait and ran upstairs. I didn't like to leave the house empty-handed. I grabbed my stuffed dog, Brandon (my parents must have been so poor, my brother and I use to fight over who gets to keep this dog, we both wanted him; why didn't they just buy another stuffed dog? It didn't cost that much, maybe $10-$20.)

We drove into the E.R. parking lot. Luckily, it's only a few minutes away. When we walked in, they saw us right away and brought us into a room. It was 11:30 pm. They thought me and my dog were cute. It was empty, too. In those days (early 90s) you only went to the E.R. if it was a real emergency.

We were waiting for a pediatrician from my group to come see me. They took my temperature the baby way, in the tush again. They acted like it was no big deal to pull down your pants. I was sick and just listened. 101 fever by butt, I thought it went down a bit. I can't remember them taking my blood pressure. They didn't have a pulse ox. (oximeter) until early 2000, so when I said I couldn't breathe, how did they know the O2 in my blood?

They gave me an O2 mask to put on. I couldn't breathe in it. It was blowing cold air on me. I was supposed to swallow it. I tried to keep it on. They didn't do vitals or take my blood.

The doctor arrived, new to the pediatric group. Dr. Speilsinger. I told him I felt like I would throw up and asked what I should do. He said, "I'd probably feel better if I did throw up." I did not like that answer. He told my parents to give me a Coke or Pepsi, that might help me feel better and ordered me to have an injection, to help me breathe better. Again, pull down your pants, in your tushie, all day. I nervously asked the nurse if it was a fresh needle. She kind of thought I was cute and smart for asking that and smiled and looked at my Mom, then gave me the shot. It hurt, as usual. They said I could stay and be on O2 until I felt better. I tried to throw up there, but I couldn't do it and I didn't like wearing the O2 mask.

I was ready for this adventure to be over and to go home and try to breathe and maybe sip Pepsi and go to sleep. It didn't look like I'd be going to school anytime soon. I really didn't like feeling so sick, though. I don't think they even gave me a children's hospital gown to wear, maybe they didn't have one. (Dr. Speilsinger is still practicing and we still keep in touch every now and then. He knew my parents and brother well. I was with the group until age 22.)

My Mom made hot dogs and baked beans the night before I would return to school. Partly I didn't want to go back, partly I couldn't eat it. Still trouble swallowing, swollen tonsils, loud barking cough. She told my Grandma and Dad I can't send her back to school if she can't eat dinner. I still had congestion. The next day my Mom got me a toy to play with from Big Top. I asked for it—Bouncin' Babies. I needed something fun to do besides watch TV.

My best friend Andrea called me after school. She said she could hardly understand me. It was hard to talk and make out my voice, so raspy. It was bad, white pus buds on my big red tonsils, one of the sickest I ever was. I was out from school for two weeks. We didn't talk long. She knew I was sick, my throat hurt to talk. I had thick, dark yellow phlegm now and then with blood sometimes.

My Mom was out taking my Grandma to Dr. Biers; he was my late Grandpa's doctor too. She didn't catch it, she had other problems, like walking and diabetes. Then, maybe picking up all my homework. It was the end of the year. I don't think the school cared if I did the homework, they just wanted me to get better. It was my first time being home alone. It was for over an hour; my Dad and brother were at school.

I looked out the window and saw a raccoon. I yelled to try to scare it off, because my Mom and Grandma would be home soon and I was worried it might attack them. I was scared for them. I was in my parent's bed; they came home and scared the raccoon off.

The other problem before I returned to the 5th grade—I was so sick, I didn't have the strength to brush my hair for a week or two, I'm not sure how long, but using my child hairbrush to try my best

MIRROR OF MY WORLD

to get all the knots and tangles out of my short shoulder-length hair, I wasn't used to. I used water, too. It took what seemed like a half-hour or more to get my hair untangled. I was worried I'd never get the knots out and have to go to school with matted hair in the back or get a shorter haircut, when I was trying to grow it long. I was finally over the Tomboy stage and finally decided to be a girl again. Having it cut short would have been the worst thing for my already gender confusion. I was happy I decided to copy my young role model Punky Brewster and be a girl again and not a Timmy Martin or a Beaver, or Dennis The Menace. I copied from my favorite TV shows at the time, very scientific, lol. Well, I got well a few days after and returned back to school, finally.

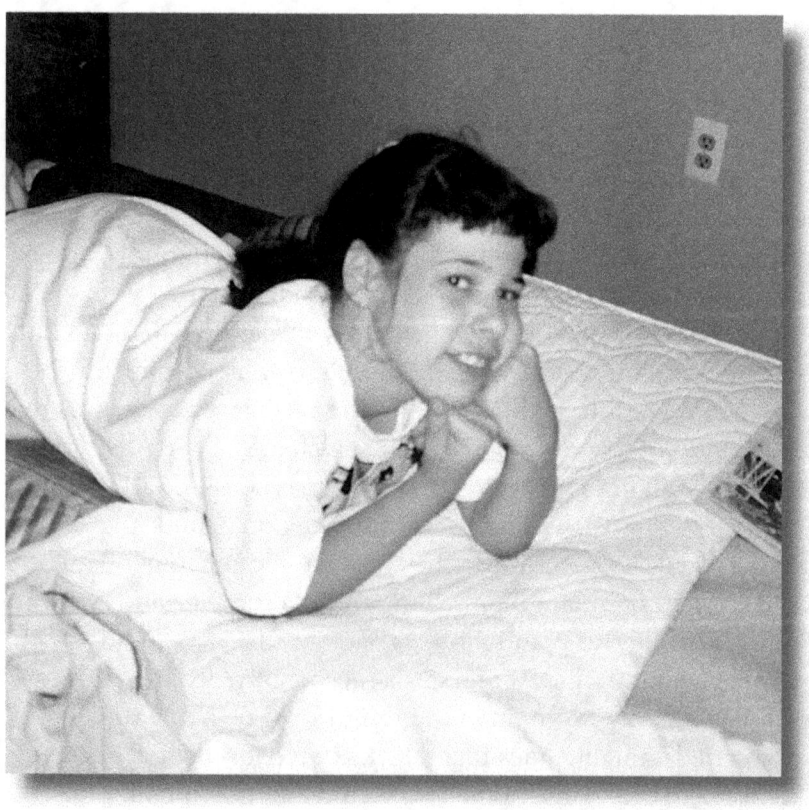

[Christian Karen Berman](#)

GOING TO MY CLASSMATE'S 1950S BIRTHDAY PARTY IN THE 5TH GRADE

It was a sunny Sunday afternoon. I can't even tell you what month it was for sure, but I'm thinking February or March. I can't even tell you for sure whose birthday it was, but a girl in my class. I will tell you what I do remember—this was a 1950s style diner. The girls put on a song from the *Dirty Dancing* soundtrack that I didn't like, but it did remind me of home and my Daddy, because he's the one who likes that movie best (my Dad did show us kids a lot of grown-up type movies when we were young more than kid's movies, because he liked those movies— *Dirty Dancing, The Sure Thing, Pretty Woman, Awakenings, Regarding Henry*, but we also saw *Cinderella*, too.) Then everyone in my class ordered cheeseburgers and french fries. Many ordered root beers with their burgers. I was never taught to drink root beer. I don't think my parents liked it; they never drank it. I did come to like it at age 18, when I was more into drinking diet soda. So, I ordered a Coke. I didn't think the food was that great. My friend Andrea was enjoying her root beer and I was wondering how she could have liked that. I don't remember much else about the birthday party; I'm not even sure if there was cake and ice cream. I'm sure the girls brought her presents. I can't remember if I even got a goody bag. I wish I did, maybe.

Skip ahead to that night. I must have gotten home from the party around 3-4 pm. It's now 7-8 pm. I'm in the bathroom getting ready for bed. I have a slight tummy ache. I can just tell for sure I'm not feeling well. That hot and cold, queasy, woozy feeling. I could tell almost for sure I was running a fever. I felt so happy and elated about this. That relaxed feeling you get when you know you can just go to sleep and not worry about the stress of getting up for school early the next morning. That warm and fuzzy feeling that your parents will worry and fuss over you for the next few days. I didn't even mind seeing my pediatrician. I liked them both, but I'd rather just sleep and rest in bed, watching TV the next day, and getting waited on by my Mom. Ironically, since Larry and I both didn't like going to school much, Sunday nights we usually did take our temperature and asked our parents for that old-fashioned glass and mercury thermometer to take the baby way in your tush. I think that's all they had back then in the late 80s, honestly. We'd hope it was close to or over 100 degrees so we would get to skip school. So, even though I feel pretty sick, I'm not worried about that at all, that's a good thing, it means no school, a day off from school. I'm just incredibly happy, almost on a high and sure of myself I will have a fever, just wait until my Dad finds out. I know something he doesn't know. Happy feeling. Did I get sick at the party from the little of the burger I ate and my soda? It was a big burger for an 11-year-old girl. I only had about half, and half a Coke.

So I walked out of the bathroom into my parents room and yeah, I mostly did still sleep with my parents back then, not all the time, but most of the time, because I slept better and felt safe and sound, even though I had my own room that I shared with my little brother and my own bed. I told my Dad who was on his side of the bed and grading papers for his students to be handed back tomorrow. He was a high school mathematics teacher. I told him I didn't feel well and I think I had a fever and he said well, let's go and take your temp. He might have touched my forehead and cheek. Then my Dad shakes down the thermometer and washes it in the bathroom sink.

I lie down in the next twin bed, under the covers, and he hands me the thermometer and I put it in my tush. Then he says to wait 5 minutes and looks at the old fashioned alarm clock and times it. It's the kind with the second hand going around, maybe 3 minutes, 5 just to be on the safe side. After one minute I ask if I can take it out now. I ask every minute. It didn't hurt, just impatient. He asks how I got sick. I think my Mom walks in around then and

asks what's wrong. My Dad tells her he's taking my temperature and that I'm not feeling well. Then my Dad says I can take it out now. I try to read the thin red line on the old thermometer, but my Dad grabs it from my hands before I have a chance to read it. He says something like, "Oh my God, she's got something." A fever. We got a sickie.

Not knowing worries me more the way he says it. Makes me scared and not want to know. He makes it sound bad—is it 105, 104? Am I going to die? Do we need to call the doctor and go to the hospital emergency room? I think all this softly in my head. "What is it, what is it," I say, worried, "tell me."

"It looks like 101," he says. A big letdown. Oh, is that all it is, I think to myself. I take the thermometer out of his hands and look for myself. Then my Mom says, "What am I going to tell Regina?"—my best friend's Mom. She was just well and at the party. "Andrea is going to wonder why you're not in school tomorrow. Is that where you got sick? How could you have gotten sick that fast? I better call her and tell her."

MIRROR OF MY WORLD

My Mom walks downstairs to tell my Grandma Lee, "She's sick and running a fever, she's not going to school tomorrow."

"What's wrong," Grandma Lee says.

"She must have gotten sick from another girl at the party. I'm going to go call Andrea's Mom and tell her, she's not going to school tomorrow."

I hear something like that from listening from the upstairs hall. Then my Dad says, "It looks like you're not going to school tomorrow."

Then Larry walks in from the next room and says he doesn't feel well, either, and he wants to take his temperature. Always copying me. Larry is age seven and goes to my Dad's school, the lower division, Horace Mann Elementary School, and he's in the second grade. So my Dad says, "Okay, let's take your temperature, too, and see what you got." Then my Dad yells downstairs, "Bev, do we have any Children's Tylenol for her?"

"Do I get to stay home from school?" I ask, just liking to hear it again for myself.

Dad says, "No, you're not going to school tomorrow. You're sick. Did you have any homework due?"

Then my Mom comes up. "How is she? I told Regina she is running a fever and came home sick from the party and she won't be going to school tomorrow. She hopes Andrea didn't catch anything, too."

I do remember it being cold, like the winter months, but I had a warm, happy feeling inside and under the covers was warm, too. Dad says, "Bev, does she need any medicine for her fever? Do we have any still good? Check the date."

My Mom walks over to me with the chills under the covers, comforter, warm and cozy, but still hot and cold, kinda achy, headachy. "I'll go look," she says. Should we call the doctor on call? By now it's probably after 9 pm. Mom goes downstairs to look for the Children's Tylenol.

My Dad says, "Okay, Larry, you can take it out now. Let's see what it is. Looks like you have a little fever, too. It's about 100. We better keep an eye on it. We will see what it is in the morning."

My Mom walks back up with two Children's Tylenol boxes or bottles. When you have young kids, especially back in the late 80s, early 90s and not many 24-hour pharmacies and kids waking up sick in the middle of the night, you know to keep some medicine on hand, because it will happen, you just never know when. Can you read the date? Is it still good? A whole fun night of attention on me and fussing, just because I have a little fever. Now the worst of it all—I have to take the medicine. Well, it all goes with being sick and the experience and very much worth the sick day.

My Dad says, "Okay, you got to go take your medicine now. Do you want to come in the bathroom?" Mostly, so I can drink water from the tap and in case I spit it out it will get in the sink and not all over the sheets and covers. Then he asks what flavor do I want, cherry or grape. Well, of course cherry. Grape is the worst, it'll make me throw up. It had in later years. Then not sure if he uses the measuring cup, which might have been lost, or the silver teaspoon. "Come on, come here, come in the bathroom." I sickly pull my body out from the warm bed and instantly feel achy and chilled, like I was getting worse and my fever was going up.

My Mom says maybe we should call the doctor. I'm having trouble standing and sit on the toilet seat cover waiting. My Dad's looking at the dosage. Eleven years old, he asks my weight, I'm maybe 76 pounds, my weight was thin to average weight for my height and age. I need three teaspoons. He carefully pours it on the spoon and says, "Come on." I slowly take it. Of course, some gets spilled on my shirt and I quickly drink water to wash it down. A bit bitter. The water helps a lot, not as bad as I thought.

My Mother peeks in and says, "If you take your medicine, we'll get you a present." That makes me feel good inside, too, and I take the rest a little better, with a yucky expression on my face.

My Dad says, "Come on, just one more." I do it, drink water, and then wash my sticky hands and mouth. Then I use the bathroom and rush back to my spot on the bed and quickly go lay down under the covers. My parents like taking care of me as much as I liked being cared for and fussed over.

MIRROR OF MY WORLD

Then my Dad says, "Let's get you to bed," and turns off the lights and takes all his papers downstairs as he starts getting ready for bed himself. He loudly announces that he thinks we all should go to bed early tonight, meaning before 10 or 11 pm. I think my Dad would sometimes stay up to watch *CBS 11 O'Clock News*. I just laid in bed and relaxed. The medicine started to kick in and put me to sleep. My parents soon get into bed with me. I think I'm in the middle of two twin beds and sometimes fall in-between the middle of the mattresses and have my own cozy little hard space there, or I lay my head on my Mom's chest. She has a warm flannel, floral-printed long night gown. My Dad is wearing a light blue men's shirt like pajamas in plain cotton. Sometimes I go over to his side at night. I can't remember what I'm wearing; maybe a winter night gown or just a shirt and underpants. The sheets are sometimes light blue or a floral print on cotton. There are many comforters and blankets. A nice floral puffy comforter, a red and blue floral printed cotton comforter, an off-white chenille stringy blanket. My Dad would often be cold and liked lots of covers and blankets. (Now, looking back in retrospect, my Dad did have mild autism symptoms, like very sensitive ears for any noise that most people couldn't even hear, but he said that went back to his old ham radio days—it hurt his ears. In his yearbook, his friend wrote if brains were dynamite, he'd blow up the world. He was one of the smartest in his school and college growing up and my Grandpa Joe was Valedictorian of Columbia University and got a degree in Pharmaceutics and owned his own pharmacy, called Berman's Drugs Pharmacy.)

My Dad had a red plaid flannel bathrobe and brown leather slippers. My Mommy had pink fluffy, furry slippers. When I was younger Larry and I had the cutest "Bert and Ernie" slippers from *Sesame Street*. I think they were the biggest size 2-3, but would they stretch more as our feet grew. We got many fond years with them. I think we could have got a couple more years in, but dunno what happened to them, thought they'd stretch as much as we needed them to forever. Our parents did sometimes throw out toys and stuff when we were at school or not looking. Yeah, that hurts bad when they do. I saw those in the *Mr. Mom* movie, too. The bathroom had pale blue towels hanging on the outside rail of the glass shower door and light blue matching toilet paper. Inside hanging on the back rail of the shower I always remember a My Buddy rainbow-striped shirt and red overalls hanging, like my Mom had washed them and they were drying. I wonder what My Buddy was wearing then? Was he naked? I guess some baby boy clothes my brother had outgrown. On top of the shower, my Mom would hang our clothes to dry. We didn't have a dryer, just a washer. Our house was built in 1954 and never updated—no dishwasher either, besides my parents. We had a royal furry blue carpet on the bathroom tile floor so our feet wouldn't get too cold in the winter months, one in the middle and one by the toilet. Even the toilet was light blue.

The next morning, everyone had went to school—my Dad and Larry. My Mom had called me in sick to the main office. I had slept late and my Mom was taking my temperature. It was maybe in the low hundreds, but I did NOT want medicine, yuck. I went downstairs to say good morning to my Grandma Lee and my turtle Lucky Alexis, a box turtle. I usually never ate breakfast on a school day. The bus came too early and my stomach was honestly still asleep or my Mom did drive me sometimes and I had to leave by 7:45 am, so there was no time, just enough time to put on my maroon plaid school uniform and rush out the cold door with cold dew on all the plants outside and rush to school. I can't remember if my Mom called the doctor, wanted to make me tea and toast, or if the doctor wanted to see me or rest it out a day or two. I didn't throw up or have diarrhea, just feeling woozy, maybe an upset stomach and just not well—hot, cold headachy. Maybe I slept that off. I watched TV for sure, and played with some toys quietly if I did see the doctor. Mom hated to take me to the supermarket after, in fear other adults and parents might see me out when I should be in school and think I'm playing hooky. I doubt they would call the police or a truant officer, though. She didn't want

MIRROR OF MY WORLD

them to think she was doing anything wrong, like letting me stay home and have fun on a school day.

I think Mom gave me a Hi-C juice box and I went back in bed to rest and watch TV. Later the cure-all came, a Peppermint Patty, a dark chocolate circular candy with strong mint powers inside. I'd get this almost every time I was sick if I wanted it or not, our secret home remedy. I guess it was a treat. I ate it, maybe it worked. Also Mott's apple juice. By lunch, if I wasn't too sick, I'd be getting a slice of pizza with an Orange Slice soda or Sunkist orange soda. I watched whatever I could find on TV that a kid would like, kid shows, Nickelodeon, *Eureeka's Castle,* The Disney Channel, *Family Ties.* By the end of the afternoon it was always "Heathcliff, Heathcliff, no one should, terrorize their neighborhood, but Heathcliff just won't be undone, playing pranks on everyone...!" *Dennis the Menace* cartoons, too. My parents did not lock the cable box with **HBO** and **SHO**, but grown-up stuff did not interest me, only looking for kid shows, no need to. But if Larry and I ever saw naked men and women we laughed and thought it was funny on TV.

After my Dad came home, he'd come upstairs to see how I am, take my temperature, which my mom had trouble getting me to take—well, I was already home from school, no real need to, now. My Dad or Mom would often get me a little girl's brush, comb, and mirror set at the local pharmacy to bribe me to take my medicine and get a Get Well gift. He'd see how I'm feeling and if I needed to take my medicine. If I was well enough to eat my Mom's dinner and no fever, probably school tomorrow. If my appetite was poor or my throat hurt and I still felt sick and tired, one more day home and maybe an early morning trip to my doctor. I sometimes got a Barbie doll from my Mom, too, or my Mom had to go to my school and pick up my school work if I was home sick for more than two days. After three days, if I wasn't too sick, I usually felt very guilty like a criminal and felt I was out enough. I'd better go back to school, this is wrong, unless I was very sick. It was a nice few, calm, worry-free relaxing days catching up with my favorite TV shows, too.

Christian Karen Berman

LYME DISEASE TESTING

At age 11, I needed to get tested for Lyme disease. We lived in a very woodsy, countrified area and I played in the backyard all the time with my brother. The pediatrician usually just had the nurse give my thumb a prick for blood work, which was traumatic for me. My Mom would have to sit next to me and I'd bury my head in her lap. Once I think she said I bit her, it hurt so much. They would suck up the blood in two extra thin plastic vials.

This time the blood sample would have to be taken from the vein, a major procedure 11½-year-old me had never had. My pediatrician, who's still practicing and I talk to from time to time, would take the blood.

I was so scared before they did that, I wandered off and was literally going into other rooms looking for a closet or place to hide, behind the examination table, maybe behind a desk, or in other unused rooms. But they found me and brought me into a room.

They told me to lie down on the table and had three nurses hold 11-year-old me down. I did try to move. It was scary and hurt. My Mom was in the room, too. They finally got the blood. I probably screamed and cried and said it hurts. After, I felt nauseous. We were just about to leave and I ran to the bathroom feeling like I was going to throw up. Now, I'm a pro and barely flinch, but then it was torture.

They gave healthy kids magazines out there and sugar free lollipops, yuck. My Mom used to say to the receptionist, she's here so often she should work here. My Mom used to be a nurse to a cardiologist. Honestly, with the allergy shots, getting sent home from school when I was actually sick and my Mom drove me straight there, we were there about three times a month or more. They did give us Ronald McDonald plastic hand puppets with ice for our allergy shots in 1989. We always loved McDonald's, too; got the Happy Meal every weekend.

MIRROR OF MY WORLD

Christian Karen Berman

MEMORIES OF MY MOM

When I was going to my 14th birthday party, with two close friends and their younger sister, my Mom wanted me to wear my first training bra from L.A. Gear. It was two pastel triangles, just a flat cotton bra. She got one in pink and one in blue. I chose blue. It had a plastic clap in the front. It was very uncomfortable. It fit, just never wore a bra before. I wore it under my blue floral sundress. The flat bra looked cool, but served no purpose but to be uncomfortable, didn't really need one then, but I forgot about it once the party started. Didn't wear that one again.

I was age 11, getting over a bad case of bronchitis and croup, was out of school for two weeks, and had strep throat, too. On a lot of liquid meds. I had been in the E.R. one night and could barely talk on the phone to my friend. My Mom got me a doll pack of Bouncin' Babies at Big Top. I had asked for it. It was nice she got it for me. I couldn't even leave the house except to go to the pediatrician. I had a fever, but I felt loved. I wish I was allowed popsicles back then. We had a no popsicle rule and no Rainbow cereal rule, candy bars and Fruit Roll-Ups were okay, though. Go figure.

When I was around age 12-14, I was sick and my Mom got me Polly Pocket. It was a light purple heart compact that opened up to a pastel yellow little house or cafe. She use to watch *The Young and The Restless* and when I was out sick, I'd watch with her, because there was nothing much else on TV at lunchtime in the 1990s. I'd take out all my Barbie dolls and Skippers and pretend they were Nikki, Jill and all the other characters on the show and made up a story to play. The girliest I've ever been. I was 12 or 13 and had about 20 Barbies, maybe a few Skippers or Staceys and a Todd. No Kens. For lunch I'd ask for a pumpernickel bagel or a pepperoni slice of pizza and an orange soda. I didn't eat much. I was small.

My Mom always never forgot my birthday and in my 20s, I didn't even want to celebrate my birthday. I was depressed and felt

MIRROR OF MY WORLD

old. She got me a little rag doll with my initial K and blond yarn hair and a card. She used to want to get me a birthday card in my 30s and we didn't have much money then, so I said I'd rather her put the money into a gift for me and don't waste money on the card. Last night I was thinking and sad and wished I had a card to me from her in her writing and maybe there's one somewhere, I don't know where. I cared about the toy, doll, or stuffed animal more than a card. Maybe she wanted me to have a bunch of cards to remember her after she died, with her sweet words and sayings. In my 20s and 30s, the farthest thing from my mind was that she wouldn't be here for much longer and I needed a card to remember her by. This makes me so sad. I really miss my Mommy.

My Dad wrote cards to my Mom and has teaching packets with his writing everywhere. My Mom didn't write much. Not sure I have anything in her writing. Maybe a few cards to my Dad, but it's not the same and I'd havta look for them. I do remember her telling me, "Don't put yourself down," and the Nursery Rhyme when I was a toddler, "Oh how I love to go up on the swing, up in the air so high."

In the eighth grade, I looked forward to Fridays all week. My Mom would go to Big Top, a local toy store and for a dollar or two get me a little bag with a plastic baby in them and a small blanket. I would get one once a week. They were all different, very cheap, but I didn't ask for something better. I just didn't think we could afford more. If we could and I was more spoiled I would have asked for a nice real baby doll. Then she would go to Gristedes supermarket while I was at school and get a box of Entenmann's blueberry muffins or Freihofer's vanilla and chocolate cupcakes. When I was really young they had lemon frosting.

Then after school some days we would stop at Micky D's for a McNuggets Happy Meal and a little toy, of course. Once at home, I would watch cartoons, draw a picture or two for my Daddy, and wait for him to get home between 4:30 and 5 pm. Then my Mom made Shabbat dinner, lit candles, and made stuff I didn't care for much. I think it was noodle pudding, potato kugel, potted chicken paprika with onions and peppers, and challah egg bread. I'd try to eat it with ketchup. I rarely got to go to the supermarket, so whatever Mom picked out I ate. I had Grandma Lee and turtle Lucky Alexis in the house.

When Dad came home, I yelled, "Daddy's home!" and maybe jumped into his arms for him to pick me up and showed him my drawings. I missed him all day. Then we ate dinner. I ate upstairs in my bedroom on the floor in front of my TV. I can't remember what I watched then, maybe *Full House* reruns. I played with my brother, Larry, and my doll, Jen. She was sick and we were using the Fisher Price phone to call the pediatrician. We talked to Elsie the receptionist, telling her what was wrong with her. A few times I recorded it on the tape recorder. I loved going to my pediatrician so that's what we usually played.

Then it was time to open my little baby doll, like two inches, and see which one I got and have a cup cake and milk and watch ABC, TGI Friday. The lineup was like *Baby Talk, Family Matters, Step by Step*. After that, I would go downstairs. My Dad would be having a peanut butter on toast snack or grading papers. Maybe I'd sit on his lap or he'd make me one with sliced bananas and raisins, sometimes maple syrup. Sometimes we'd stay up with my Dad to watch the news, then bed.

The next morning my dad would usually already be up eating oatmeal and peanut butter toast. I would wait by the stairs and my

MIRROR OF MY WORLD

Daddy would come over and I would jump from the third stair into his arms for him to catch me. He always did and carried me into the kitchen, put me on a chair, and would cook me Quaker oatmeal in a pot. I actually ate it. He did a good job, added creamer at the end.

Then I would quickly check for what's on TV, but be getting ready to go to Sears. Getting dressed, I wore a sweatshirt with a picture, denim overalls, size fourteen. I was 5'1" and 86 pounds, very skinny. My Grandma stayed home, but we would all go to Sears. They had a Micky D's there. We would all get lunch there, the usual.

Then we would go to the shoe department just to sit and relax. My mom would look with me at the girl's clothes and we would buy a few items I wanted or needed. A nice shirt, nightgown. I would then look with Larry and maybe my Dad in the baby section to buy Jen a new baby outfit, or a baby toy, something on sale. They had free American Baby magazines to take that I would read, loved that. They use to have a toy department, but can't remember when I was older if they did. That's why the baby department was next best. I'd try to fit in the child car seats, just look at everything. Then my Dad let me get a few items. We stayed there about two or three hours, then went home, looked at the stuff we got, then got ready to go out to the diner for dinner. I usually ate the chicken fingers with French fries and BBQ sauce on the kid's menu, or cheeseburger, or tuna plate. We only ate out once a week. They had mints at the end, sometimes sucking candies or sprinkle cookies, depending which diner; we ate at two different ones. When we got home, we'd watch some TV and get ready to go to bed.

I always hated Sundays, I don't remember what we did, but it was homework day. That's why I hated it. Hours of homework, my Dad helping me with it. Why do they ruin a weekend with homework? My dad didn't believe in homework; kids worked hard enough all day in school. I was dreading school tomorrow, a full week's worth. The younger grades were more fun, less homework, but the weekends wouldn't have been appreciated if I was home all week. I'm glad I wasn't home schooled, boring.

Christian Karen Berman

Happy Halloween

A sweet old woman neighbor in her 80s, who knew me and my Grandpa Jules since I was a toddler, took this photo while my brother Larry and I were trick or treating. My Mom looks overwhelmed. I was 11, Larry age seven. I had just watched *Double Dare* on Nickelodeon and my family shared a pizza pie, with soggy, oily tomato sauce and canned mushrooms and fresh onions, my parents pick, what a combo, but us kids accepted it, but it was kinda gross.

Mom always took us and we never were out that long. Maybe we started out around 7:20 pm and by 8:30 we were home, sometimes only out a half hour and filled a plastic pumpkin. We used to have the Halloween Happy Meal at Mickey D's a lot. Why does it always rain on Halloween?

When I got to be older, like a teenager, my brother & I would go out ourselves, start around 6:30 pm, finish close to 9:30 pm, until the neighbors stopped answering the door. When I was older and out by myself, they always told me to be careful. One time they gave me like seven karate coupons to share with my friends. I loved the people who gave goodie bags, pencils, mini chip bags, moon pies, and left a big bowl out front. Now I feel too old to enjoy Halloween.

MIRROR OF MY WORLD

Christian Karen Berman

Happy Halloween Memories

Halloween, I remember as a 12 year old walking out the front door with my Mom to drive me to school, the front door had a Halloween decoration on it as well as the porch door. I enjoyed looking at them as I came and went from school, working up my excitement level for the actual Halloween night. They were the thin cardboard kind—one was a scarecrow, one a pumpkin with a happy face. Also on our front window were two more Halloween cardboards, maybe a ghost, witch or another pumpkin, taped with Scotch tape to the glass window inside, plus 2 hard plastic pumpkins on the windowsill. That gave me such pleasure and joy in mid-October to just look at the pretty decorations, knowing Halloween was near. When I was a teenager she would get a few little real pumpkins to put outside. I never had the heart to cut them up. I felt they were real and it would hurt them. I loved the cute baby pumpkins. The weather was cool and crisp, autumn leaves on the trees. Trick-or-treating was near.

    The TV had Halloween movies on. I remember The Worst Witch, an oldie but a goodie, they would rerun every October. My Mom would buy those Halloween Entenmann's orange cupcakes with candy corn on top; they still make it, but it's sweeter than I remember. I used to look to pick out the ones with the most frosting and candy corn. When I was 14, she would buy the crumbly, orange sugared pumpkin-shaped cookies that I would have with the cupcake. To balance out all that sugar, my Dad would make me rye toast with Skippy creamy peanut butter on top.

At 14 I remember I was 5'1" & 86.5 pounds. We didn't have junk food in the house back in the early to mid 1990s. The sweets were dessert, but no chips. My snack my Dad would make for me was the P.B. toast with banana slices, cherry jelly, and red grapes. Or my favorite cereal, Triples (why did they stop making this? I loved it) with his half and half coffee creamer. Today's kids Costco haul is all junk food, chips, candy, sugared cereal, cookies.

MIRROR OF MY WORLD

My first real Halloween I was four or five. I wish my Dad had taken photos. I know I had a Halloween party at school at age six, but can't for sure remember if I was a Care Bear or what. I remember seven or eight better. I made my own costume. I was Adora before she turned into She-Ra, and even had a little She-Ra action figure. I was trying to be creative and save Mom some money. I wore my own clothes, and the neighborhood kids and parents traveled in a small group with a flashlight around the block. No one knew who I was. I had an orange plastic pumpkin to carry the candy. We went to more houses than usual because of the group. I was happy about that, but didn't get as much candy back then as I did as a teenager. Then they gave handfuls and goody bags.

At nine, I got a black plastic spider at the school Halloween party, probably candy and pretzels, too. On Halloween I wore one of my Mom's old 1970s dresses and made a crown out of cardboard and tin foil. I was a princess. Our neighbors, Dell & Fred, gave Larry and me a full-size candy bar, but Mom didn't trust her, so she took the candy bars away. She didn't like how she was so interested in our lives. My Mom was just being a protective Mama bear; I liked talking to Dell. Once when I was real sick with something, I was sleeping in my parents' bed with a high fever, dehydrated, about seven or eight years old and the Dr. said to give me a soda. We did not have soda in the house back then, only orange Tropicana & Mott's apple juice. My Dad wouldn't go shopping late at night just for a can of soda, Now we go to CVS twenty-four hours. Dad went next door and asked them if they had a Coke or a can of soda He said I was very sick. She gave us a can of Mountain Dew, but my Dad came to my room to wake me and come downstairs, Dell wanted to see me. I didn't want to go, I felt terrible, in PJs, messy hair, half asleep and came to the stairs to groggily say hi to them. She smiled and said "hi" and "I hope you feel better." Before I went back to sleep, my Dad opened the soda and I took one or two small sips and went back to sleep. It was a bit odd to wake up a sick child from a deep sleep just because my Dad asked for a can of soda for me, but I was so cute, she just probably wanted to remember what having a young daughter sick looked like. She was in her late 60s.

Christian Karen Berman

MY TOYS

They all got lost or thrown out over the years and just mysteriously disappeared like many stuffed animals and dolls I loved. Once I actually came home from school about age 11 or 12 and found some in a white trash bag. My beloved Wuzzle Hippopotamus was in there, but my Mom saw me taking my old toys out and yelled at me not to and I sadly stopped, regretting it until this day. I suppose she was spring cleaning my room and getting rid of some old toys. Since then I pictured my blue Wuzzle hippo, behind the end of a rainbow in the water at the end of the earth, just waiting for me sadly. A primitive idea, but that was my first thought all these years later when I thought of my Wuzzle stuffed animal. It hurt a lot. I had replaced him a few decades later with an eBay one, but now he accidentally got thrown out, too. Most of the toys I asked for, over my years of kiddom, weren't much, but from commercials, of course.

My parents rarely took us into toy stores. They were big, and Mom and Dad were afraid Larry and I would want to buy the store out, I guess, and have a fit if we didn't get a little something, which wasn't true. They had taken us to Big Top, a small, more expensive toy store with less stuff, and Sears toy store every Saturday and we could sometimes pick out an inexpensive toy after lunch, which made it so hard for me to eat lunch—not really hungry, way too excited to go look at the toy aisle, and I couldn't get there fast enough. Like really happy, excited, like it was the best thing in the whole world. That's why it was great to be a kid in the 80s, when a $5 toy would bring you so much joy for weeks at a time. That was a Mini Glo-Worm; I had a regular Glo-Worm, a My Little Pony, Fairy Tails Bird, and a My Child doll with yellow blonde hair that took me a good 15-20 minutes to pick out after giving a twice-over to all the cute and beautiful new arrivals in the store, and I proudly with love named her Dana and took her on vacation with us one summer. Even did her pigtails perfect for the occasion. A Heart-

MIRROR OF MY WORLD

to-Heart Bear, Rainbow Brite, My Friend Jenny, yellow Funshine Bear (I wanted the pink Cheer Bear, my Mom picked this one out for me), the Wuzzle, Need-A-Littles, Chatty Patty, Kid Sister, My Buddy, Cookie Monster Counter, Fisher Price Kids Sunglasses, Coin Jammers, Time Jammers, Fisher Price Barn Garage school, Main Street, Little Mart, Kosh ball, Strawberry Shortcake doll... we didn't have many stuffed animals so Larry and I would argue and have discussion about who would keep Brandon, a $10 stuffed golden retriever that looked like the dog Punky Brewster had. Our parents couldn't afford much. These toys were bought over 10 years in my childhood.

Child's World was a rare treat. We'd go there on my birthday to get a new bike or pick out Susie Scribbles. It was only 10 minutes away and next to Pizza and Brew, where we went often, but we'd only go in Child's World maybe a few times a year. Sometimes just to look and not buy and get anything, maybe a new cassette tape for my Susie Scribbles or to try out bikes. I loved to look at almost every aisle—the doll aisle, the Fisher Price aisle. It closed when I was age 14, so I don't remember it as well as I wish. My parents did not let us stay long.

Caldor had a toy aisle, too. We got little things like a pail and inflatable tube, wings/swim fins and ball for the swimming pool. McDonald's Happy Meals also gave us our weekend toy fix. As a kid, you just need toys often, that's what you do. A book seemed like punishment or homework to me. There was that Scholastic thing they'd hand out in the 3rd and 4th grade. We couldn't afford much. I got a puppy and cat poster once, maybe a book of jokes. It was a real treat that your parents felt, "Well, since it's school, we'd better get you something; we want to look like good parents." Sure all the parents felt that way. It wasn't often, once in a blue moon. Also the book fair, my Mom got me a book I loved, a baby book, *Karen and Her Kitten*, because my Mom bought it for me as a surprise when I was sick and also it had a soft grey little kitten finger puppet inside the book you can put your finger in. Not sure about other books, but I had *Ramona Quimby, Age 8*, by Beverly Cleary, *Romana the Pest*, *Ramona and Her Father*, and *Tales of a Fourth Grade Nothing* by Judy Blume. Other toys were Slinky,

Lego's, Tinkertoys, wooden blocks, Bristle Blocks, Etch-a-Sketch, Speak and Read, and the Little Professor, the Magic Pad, and a Magnet Ball Drawing Board, He-Man action figure, a small Teela and She-Ra, My First Barbie, Peaches and Cream Barbie, The Heart Family, Bedtime Barbie, Skipper, Stacy, Todd, Polly Pocket, Bouncin' Babies, and that's about the main ones off the top of my head. There was also Silly Putty, a painting book, watercolors and a plastic water snake, too.

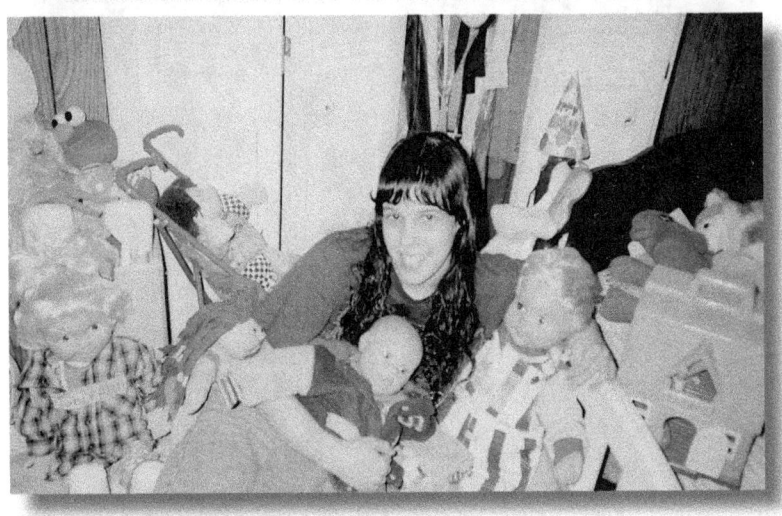

MIRROR OF MY WORLD

Christian Karen Berman

GOING TO MOUNT KISCO

My parents bought me Minnie Mouse roller skates for my 12th birthday. The white, blue and pink Velcro ones in a girls size 5. I loved them, I used them until I outgrew them. I got many athletic presents on my 11th birthday. A pogo ball, a Skip It, a hula hoop—you know, stuff you can play with outside. My Dad liked badminton. We had that, too. I also played wiffle ball, like baseball with a plastic bat and ball. We had an outdoor large hard plastic swimming pool with green turtles on it. It was like 5' or 6' long and 2' deep with a built-in slide, but I think I was age 12 then. We had those plastic inflatable balls and swimming rings. It was the best being a kid in the summer. I was so happy.

We went to McDonalds in Mount Kisco, almost an hour drive, and we always got me and Larry the Happy Meal, then we went to Carvel for a soft serve vanilla and chocolate ice cream cone, then after we looked at Caldor's and picked out an inexpensive toy. When we got home I'd go on my tire swing or ride bikes with my brother, or walk over to my younger neighbor's Emily's house to see what she was up to. After that, we'd go out to the local diner Flagship and get dinner. They made homemade popovers there. My Dad liked to walk around the block after dinner. Then we'd sit outside until it got dark, watching the fireflies and having a Disney Banana Pudding pop or Mickey ice cream head. After, we come in to watch reruns of *Bewitched* on Nick at Nite and I'd have a cup of ginger ale with fresh blueberries in it, my own creation, like a kid's version of a martini with green olives in it. When I was older I'd have club soda with olives in it.

My family would go on day trips! I would wake up, hear my family on a July summer's day outside enjoying the day. It was noon, I was 12, I'd go outside and meet them. Somedays my brother and I would ride our bikes in the street. In the early 1990s I didn't think you needed to wear a helmet. I didn't have one; I remember it being cool accessories, and that was an expensive option we couldn't afford. I have always been very coordinated, only fell once off my skateboard, never off my bike. Other days Daddy would set up the big swimming pool for kids with the water hose and fill it high. It was two-and-a-half feet deep and about six feet long. He might have even heated a pot or two of hot water to make the water less freezing cold. Not exactly the Y, but for a kid, fun, with an inflatable beach ball and water ring. I loved going to Mount Kisco. It was a long scenic ride that seemed like 45 minutes. I'd bring my pretend sister Jen, who was my little sister and a My Kid Sister doll. As a 12 year old girl, what I wanted most in the world at that time was a little sister. A lot of my friends had younger siblings and sisters, and necessity is the mother of invention. I fixed her hair with barrettes and ponytail holders and even shampooed and cut her hair and changed her baby clothes from age 11½ - 16.

In Mt. Kisco, we'd get Friendly's chicken fingers and french fries, bbq sauce, Happy Face Sundae on the kids menu, McDonalds Chicken McNugget Happy Meal, Carvel swirl cone for dessert, and look at the strip mall there or Caldor's. McDonalds used to have a yummy cheese Danish and mini chocolate chip cookies. When we got home after the long ride, I was bored and tired.

I'd look to find some younger neighbor friends to say hi to, like half my age, age six. I always seemed younger than my real age. Larry wasn't really like having a younger brother. By the time I was 11, he was two pounds heavier than me! I was 72 pounds, he was 74 pounds. We were almost like the same age; he's four years younger, though.

Christian Karen Berman

SNACKS

When I was about 12, my Mom would get me Handy Snacks. It was club crackers in a rectangle plastic container with cheese spread and a red plastic stick to spread it on with, a real treat for a kid. Also my Mom would make potted paprika chicken with onions and green peppers in a big pot with water and tomato sauce from a can. She cut one breast in half for Larry and me to share with a small red potato, margarine, and string beans (as she called them). I think we shared a chicken breast until I was 15 or 16. I'm not sure if it was because we were so poor or she wanted to keep the portions small because I didn't eat much. Larry ate well and asked for more string beans and he had two hot lunches in school sometimes.

When I was little we rarely had any dessert, three Chips Ahoy cookies and milk if I asked, nothing special. I never liked those much, but my Mom kept buying them. Once when I was seven, I was having Chips Ahoy cookies and milk and I told myself, "I'm going to dunk it and leave the cookie in the milk until it turns white like the whole milk, it always came up clear. I left it in maybe 40 seconds or more and I was astonished it actually came up white, so much so I showed my Dad and was suspicious something was wrong with the milk. I looked at it, maybe tasted the cookie. It was sour, spoiled milk. I didn't eat it after that.

I had a recipe I made at age seven. I put a lot of Creamy Skippy in between two Chips Ahoy cookies and made a cookie sandwich. The salty PB and cookies with milk were so good. I tried making Rice Krispie balls, PB in the middle. Not good, but hey, when you're seven, you work with whatcha got.

My Mom didn't get much groceries or interesting ones. I got to pick a mini box of chocolate chip cookies or cereal once in a while, but not often. I wasn't a spoiled kid and didn't have much of a say in what I got to eat—Swanson TV dinners like Turkey and

MIRROR OF MY WORLD

Stuffing and Fried Chicken—it was a treat my Mom would get me often, because my dad had trouble getting me to eat my Mom's dinners. He even told me the story of Karen Carpenter when I was six or seven in my bedroom because I didn't eat my dinner. He scared me a bit, too. He said something like she died from not eating. He made me think by skipping dinner I might die. At seven I knew nothing of losing weight or eating disorders. I knew who she was, too—I played my Dad's record on my Fisher Price tape recorder. I'm not sure if I wasn't hungry or just hated the food. I hated my PB&J for lunch, too, with Wise Plain potato chips and Chips Ahoy cookies and a Hi-C fruit punch juice box. I kind of miss it now. I did love my Mom's tuna salad. She probably added the two hard-boiled eggs in it to make the two cans of Tuna to go farther for 5 people. My Grandma lived with us. When I was 11 or 12, my Dad would make me Kraft Mac and Cheese that I ate the whole box of. I liked that. They got wiser—feed me what I like and I will eat it. I wanted the frozen kind, though. When I was older in my early 20s and knew about coupons, I cut them out of the Sunday flyers, but Mom was too proud to use any. She didn't want people to think she needed to use coupons, but it would have saved money.

Christian Karen Berman

CHRISTMAS, AGE 12 – EARLY 1990S

Christmas at age 12. I'm in the 6th grade at public school. (This photo was taken around this time in the 6th grade, I can't help but think I look so young, like age 9).

This is a week before Christmas and it's after my friend Marion who has long brown hair (I loved how long her hair was, I wanted to grow mine that long) and bangs like me, is by our lockers outside the classroom, asking for a candy cane, because she says she was chewing on the back of her pen and it broke and she swallowed ink and she wants to get the bad taste and blue ink off her tongue. I look in my locker to see if I have any sucking charms in my coat pocket from our local diner. I don't. Then she is telling me about Secret Santa and since I pulled her name in class to buy her a gift, she says that makes me her secret Santa. At lunch we are talking about what we want for Christmas and I say a Talking

MIRROR OF MY WORLD

Cabbage Patch Kid. She says "I don't mean to burst your bubble (what an old fashioned phrase for an 11-year-old to say), but they don't make those anymore." They made them a few years before in the late 1980s, but I never got one and still wanted one. I didn't go to toy stores often, I didn't know (I got one of those Talking C.P.K. dolls a few years ago mint-in-box on eBay).

There are a lot of kids, mostly girls, but boys too from my class sitting at the lunch table and some girl with a pen and clipboard is asking kids to sign a petition and kids were just signing it. Then the girl asks me and my parents' voice comes out, "I'm not signing anything. My parents told me to never sign anything, I don't sign anything without my lawyer." Then, she says, "It's to show a video of a real woman giving birth to a real baby in health class," and then I'm like, "Oh, I'll sign that," and I do. I'm not sure what I was eating for lunch, a slice of pizza, cheeseburger or chicken nuggets and BBQ sauce, it came with canned pears, corn, and chocolate milk.

After school my Mom takes me to the local pharmacy about two minutes away from the school by car to get me some candy. She does that every day after school. I see which I feel like today. I remember liking a BarNone bar, not sure if they still make those. I was allowed to choose two. I might have chosen Gummy Bears, Twix, a dark Hershey bar and almonds, a Whatchamacallit bar, I can't remember, but I told her my friend Marion wanted a candy cane, because I picked her in the class raffle. She bought her one for 15 cents. The prices were good back in early 1990. The next morning in class Mrs. Rita takes the attendance and then reads the lunch menu to us, and if we are buying lunch we raise our hands so the lunch ladies have an idea how much hot lunch to make, then one kid takes all of this to the attendance office. Then we all stand and say the Pledge of Allegiance and put our hand on our chest. It's on the loudspeaker, too (do schools still do this?). Then Mrs. Rita says, "there has been talk about Secret Santa. There is no Secret Santa this year. That was last year. We are not doing that this year." I had given Marian the candy cane in the hall before class started. She thanked me. Now she looks at me and smiles. Well, she's a nice girl and my friend and it was only 15 cents. She's about two inches taller than me, too. Mrs. Rita says that for our Christmas party, we are having a pizza party, in class, so there will be no hot lunch that day and to bring in $1 for one pizza, $2 for two pizzas and $3 for three pizzas and say if you want plain or pepperoni.

At recess I was saying, "Let's do what they do on Double Dare and go across the monkey bars and run through the tires and do an obstacle course, just for fun." The girls said they pay you to do that on that show, we'll do it, if you pay us. I said it would be fun. I guess that was the end of that discussion. My neighbor Jen and sorta friend said, "Does your dad have a bald spot on the top of his head? I think I saw, he does." I wasn't sure. I didn't know. How could she see the top of his head? My Dad's six feet tall and she's only five feet tall. Our dads were friends at Horace Mann School and they lived on the next block from us. My Dad would sometimes commute to work in her dad's car, on the days when the weather was bad. We were both in the 6th grade at this middle school, but not in the same class. I told my dad what Jennifer had said that night and he said, "Her dad is all bald on top." My dad just had a little thinning hair on top; you could hardly tell it was thinning (last I heard about Jen was 10 years ago from my dad; Jen was married and in the Military, she went to West Point).

Last day of the 6th grade before Christmas vacation, our English teacher, who was a man in his 50s, showed us a Disney movie in class on VHS. *The Little Mermaid*. I felt too old to be watching such a baby movie in school, because my Dad showed Larry and me his favorite VHS movie, *The Sure Thing*, with John Cusack.

At recess days before the party, my friends were all saying how we wanted pepperoni pizza. I got one small slice of plain pizza. Some kids were big and got three slices. It came with a small paper cup of Coke. It wasn't enough, I was still hungry after. I was about 90 pounds then and 4'11 inches. We all exchanged gifts. I gave Marion the gift my Mother had bought for her, a very nice pink embroidered stationery, lined notepaper book. It had pink balloons or a ballet girl with hearts on the side of the paper. She loved it. I wouldn't have liked that. I wasn't so mature, I wanted a doll, of course. I received this nice gift from a poor girl, she was Spanish, an inch or two taller than me, thin, with shoulder-length dark brown hair, bangs, and a pale complexion. Her name was Erica; she gets free hot lunch, so I know she's poor. The gift was a cool red, blue, and yellow fanny pack. I loved it, too. The teacher gave out candy canes and we had no homework. It might have been a half day that day, I can't remember.

When my Mom came and brought me home, my dad and Larry were already home. They bought a real pine 5' Christmas tree. My Dad put a few books under the Christmas tree stand to make it look taller. It upset me the way he did it and made the tree look weird. I didn't know what he did at the time, but I didn't like it. I ran to my bedroom upset to cry and mope for a few minutes. Then I came back down and calmed down and took the books underneath it out and started to decorate it and make it look nicer. Then I went back up to my bedroom to not miss the Christmas episode of *Punky Brewster* on reruns.

Afterwards, we went to our older neighbor's house across the street, Mary and Danny, to get yummy homemade white-powdered Italian Christmas cookies and look at their big beautiful Christmas tree. Danny was a retired tailor like my Grandpa had been. I liked Mary's big crocheted Santa that she made out of yarn and her little antique glass and quartz elephants in different sizes and shapes around the mantel and on top of their bookcases. Also, this little plastic toy Christmas soldier I looked at. She said she'd give it to me one day (she did, she kept her word, I had forgotten about that; the year before she got sick and went into a nursing home, I was age 19 or 20 then. They were such nice old people, like real Grandparents almost, in their mid-70s around that time. I wish I could have visited them more or helped them more, but kids and teenagers don't really think like that. I wish I had).

After that, we came home to Grandma Lee with love and happiness in our hearts and couldn't wait to eat the yummy-smelling yearly cookies she baked just for my family. My Grandma Lee sadly didn't come with us; she couldn't walk the stairs, she was afraid to slip and fall. My Mom made potted chopped meat with onions and peppers in a red sauce, little red potatoes, and latkes with ketchup and apple sauce. We drank orange juice or a Hi-C fruit punch juice box. Dessert was boiled chestnuts and Christmas Entenmann's cookies, Mary's cookies and maybe pumpkin pie. We drank ice cold Milk or eggnog. We watched Christmas shows like *Frosty The Snowman* and *One Magic Christmas*. Back then, you didn't get off school until December 22nd or 23rd. I liked school anyway.

This was one of my best Christmases ever. I wasn't sick and got everything I asked for. I asked for more than usual, but my parents bought it all for me at the Big Top Toy Store. All together, all my toys probably only cost only seventy bucks back then. I got a Barbie doll, Little Miss MakeUp, a Christmas Teddy bear, or stuffed puppy, a little dog and you could brush his hair, maybe a new Etch A Sketch, a Tinker Bell princess hair brush, and Labyrinth wooden marble game my Grandma Lee bought me. I didn't know what to play with first. I put it upstairs after my Dad took some Christmas photos, later around 4 pm. My family went out to the diner for Christmas dinner. We all shared two plates of turkey, chestnut stuffing, creamed spinach, mashed potatoes with popovers and butter, with a Cherry Coke and two 7-layer chocolate cake slices for dessert.

MIRROR OF MY WORLD

Christian Karen Berman

WHEN BICYCLE TIRES MEET WET GREEN GRASS

My parents had to go to my Dad's math party during one afternoon. It was around April. I was age 12½, my brother 8½. It was a rainy Saturday. My Grandma Lee who lived with us was babysitting. By that meaning, keep us out of trouble and from getting hurt. She was in her early 80s. She had trouble walking, she couldn't do much. No TV in the living room back then, but two TV's upstairs. We were both bored. What did bored little kids do in the mid-1990s before You Tube and the internet? I looked around the house bored, found my Mom's *Parents Magazine*, saw it was about kids, they had cut-out Valentine's day cards and nice pictures in it. There I discovered many old issues of *Parents* and my love for that magazine developed. I usually would go exploring in the basement, climb on furniture. I was pretty good that day. I just read my Mom's magazines, maybe drew a picture.

My brother was bored. We didn't live in a cave, we had The Disney Channel, Nickelodeon, Game Boy, maybe Sega Genesis handheld game. It was his, I was never into video games much. I played with dolls and Barbies back then. Larry wanted to go out on a grim, dark, rainy afternoon and ride his 20-inch bike. We both said no. I think our parents said we could not leave the house and maybe not to go into the basement. I told Larry, "You're not allowed, you will get in trouble." So I think he said he would do it in the backyard, so he would not be riding his bike alone on the streets. I'm not sure Grandma gave her okay to this; I don't think so. No iPhone's back then, not sure there was even an emergency phone number they gave of the restaurant. They had been gone for many hours, like three, they were at least an hour or more away with traffic, not sure where, maybe New Jersey. (My Grandma had babysat me before when my parents had to go to a Sweet

MIRROR OF MY WORLD

16. I had bronchitis, strep throat, and was very sick with a 104 fever. They had to go into NYC. They were gone four hours. I was age eleven. My parents just put me on my brother's old Winnie the Pooh comforter, crib size, to rest and sleep. It was literally just to watch that I was okay. I had to be downstairs. My Grandma Lee couldn't walk upstairs for many years now. They might have given a phone number then; she couldn't drive, either, so it was risky leaving a sick 5th grader alone. I think they gave me my medicines before they left and took my temperature, so she would just ask if I'm okay. I don't think they even left my pediatrician's number. I was okay then, but I did end up a few days or a week later in the E.R.) Larry went outside to ride his bike with us telling him not to. She gave up; she couldn't chase after him. I went back to what I was doing. I was watching Larry ride in circles in the backyard, the grass was wet, not sure if I saw or heard him fall. Larry came in whining his foot hurt, that the grass was wet, and he fell off his bike and hurt his ankle. I think I was like, "I told you not to go and so did grandma, you didn't listen." He was whining, moping, complaining, not sure if she took him seriously and called my parents, or just waited.

My parents came home. I think the house was messy. I was bored and looking for things to do, cut-out cards, magazines, markers, crayons, paper. Larry told them, then we all told my Dad. My Dad didn't take his complaints seriously—he only fell off his bike and on the grass, not the cement. Then my Dad walked over to a neighbor and asked what to do, It did look a bit swollen. They said if he is still crying and complaining it hurts, take him, you have nothing to lose, get it checked out. (We rarely went to the E.R., it had to be a real emergency; we once went when I was very sick at age three from a vaccine, then age eleven, once when Larry was three and was having convulsions from a fever; he had to stay over in the hospital then.)

My parents, brother, and me all went to the Emergency Room, as it was called back then in the 90s. My grandma had to be all alone again, not thrilled about that. I had to go, couldn't miss this excitement. They left at lunch, came back about 5 pm. Boy, was there a wait in the E.R. I was starting to get bored and wished I stayed home, just sitting and waiting, doing nothing, not sure if there was a TV back then. It wasn't as exciting as I pictured. I was always bored, loved excitement, hated to miss anything or be left out. Daddy spoke to me. I was the good one who listened. Finally, Larry was seen. His foot was red, swollen, they did an x-ray, and put on a big cast for his whole leg. He was right, it was broken. They told him not to do that again and said why didn't you listen? We had no helmets back then, they had them, but we didn't. Luckily, he didn't ride in the street; it could have been worse. I did try to say no and stop him, but we were both about the same size. Then we went home, had dinner, maybe in the diner, can't remember what I even ate for lunch. It was an adventure, but kinda boring at the same time.

MIRROR OF MY WORLD

Christian Karen Berman

CRiMe iN THe LOCaL LiBRaRY

It was in early summer, just as school had let out. Somehow my parents and brother ended up in the library, I can't remember why. Summer reading list. We'll, maybe my Dad had to look up something. This was in the early 90s before we owned a computer. We were all sitting at a light brown, big wooden library table, very modern for that time. Larry and I were looking at some kid magazines I'm thinking *Highlights*, *Sesame Street* and *Parents Magazine*. I'm not sure if my mom came or stayed home with my grandma. I saw the subscription pull-out card from *Highlights* or one of the magazines and asked Larry if it would be okay to pull it out, because I wanted to subscribe. A Down syndrome man in his teens or early 20s noticed what I did and without my knowledge went to tell his boss at the library. Larry and I were talking and my Dad was reading something as a man approached us and sternly asked or said that your kids or your daughter has been ripping pages out of a book or magazine. My Dad didn't know what he was talking about and looked concerned and asked us kids if we did that. He said his worker had seen us do that and where is it, acting much like we're in trouble and he was going to make us pay or do something. I said all we did was tear out the subscription card to subscribe to the magazine, innocently, but intimidated, scared, and showed him. He looked down, confused and back at the young man and apologized to our Dad a bit embarrassed and said sorry that the worker was mistaken and for bothering us. Especially since I had just turned age 12 or 13 and Larry was only seven-and-a-half or eight-and-a-half, we weren't quite ready to go to juvy yet.

He walked away and we soon finished up quickly and left to take our Mom to Mt. Kisco McDonalds. I think my Dad was embarrassed, too, and we all felt awkward. I didn't think I was doing anything wrong and probably wasn't, but I never did that again.

MIRROR OF MY WORLD

I think it was the biggest crime in the library besides unreturned and overdue books. I felt weird about it, but lesson learned—do not subscribe to a magazine if you're in a library. It's not worth any possible trouble it may cause. My excuse, I was only 12 or 13 years old and didn't know better.

Christian Karen Berman

Bad Attitude

I'm age 12 or 13. I did something to upset and frustrate my Dad. I can't remember what, so it probably wasn't too bad. I remember hearing on some old home videos my parents talking about I was picking up a bad attitude from the other middle schoolers, that I wasn't like that before, with me in earshot, too. So, we're in the upstairs hallway, my Dad picks me up and carries me downstairs and tries to throw me on the couch. I held on to him and didn't let go so he couldn't. When he finally put me on the couch, I say, "Can you do that again?" with a smile. I think I won that battle.

It was around this time that my Dad started calling me Kay Joy, after a radio station he listened to, KJOY 98.3 in Long Island. He also called me Kay-Kay, Mickey-boo (because my middle name is Michelle), Punky (after one of my favorite TV shows, *Punky Brewster*), and silly ones like Coo-Coo and Gigigagagoo.

MIRROR OF MY WORLD

Christian Karen Berman

BACK TO SCHOOL, 7TH GRADE

In the beginning of August, my Dad would say how many days we all had left to enjoy each day of summer before school started, because he had to go back to school as well, but as a high school A.P. Statistics and Geometry teacher. I remember we savored each summer day and made the most out of it. I got up around 12 pm. I would hear my family outside, waiting for me to wake up. I would put my hair in a ponytail and go outside to meet them. We usually went on a ride to Mount Kisco, a 45-minute scenic trip, to McDonald's, Carvel and Caldor. Sometimes I took my kid sister doll, who I pretended was my real three-year-old baby sister.

Then on those long summer nights, we would sit in our backyard. Larry and I would have these Disney character banana Pudding Pops. We would talk to my Dad and I'd look for fireflies. My Mom inside with my Grandma and turtle, Lucky Alexis. At night I loved reruns of *Bewitched*, so I created my own dry martini (they were always having drinks), a kid-friendly Diet Ginger Ale, with blueberries on top; we didn't have olives in the house.

It's the mid-1990s. It's Saturday, a week before school. My family went to Sears. My Mom and I are looking in the Girl's department for back-to-school clothes. I'm entering the 7th grade this year. My Mom is making me try on blue jeans. They're big. They're a 12½ Pretty Plus, but she doesn't know that; we find that out much later. Another younger girl in the dressing room says, "Don't worry, you'll grow into them." (I finally did; they still fit me at age 17½—I got my money's worth.) We always went to Sears on the weekends, to Micky D's for a Happy Meal first, Chicken McNuggets and whatever toy came in the box. I can't remember what else my Mom bought me, but we usually picked up some extra clothes when we went, even though I luckily was small and could wear my clothes for two years. I was a 10/12 girl's size.

MIRROR OF MY WORLD

The night before school my Dad would write my full name across my backpack in large letters with a black Sharpie so everyone would know it's mine, maybe label a few other things like my binder. In those days the school did not give you lists, all you bought was the basics—loose-leaf paper, folders, pencil bag, pencils, sharpener, a pen and your own combination lock. In the 6th grade we still used cubbys. I liked that better. Everything was nice and new, a fresh start to have everything neat and perfect.

Morning came quick. This year I start school before my brother. My Dad has faculty meetings. That nervous butterfly feeling in the pit of your stomach every year, is it because I'm nervous and it's empty? I'm wearing a light blue denim jumper and a pink and purple tie-dye shirt, with white Keds, very popular in the 90s. I remember sitting at a big, empty lunch table alone (once I got to know everyone, all my classmates sat with me), eating my delicious giant square pizza, vinaigrette salad, canned pears and drinking chocolate milk, just thinking about and looking forward to seeing my Mom and brother in just a few more hours. I really missed my Mom and couldn't wait to tell her all about my day. In gym they got your height and weight. I weighed a few pounds more than I thought. Then my Mom and brother came to pick me up, the moment I was waiting for the whole day. I remember later in the school year when my English class was finishing reading the book *Our Town*, thinking of my happy life in the present, tears came to my eyes because I didn't want anything to change.

I didn't want to grow up and be sad.

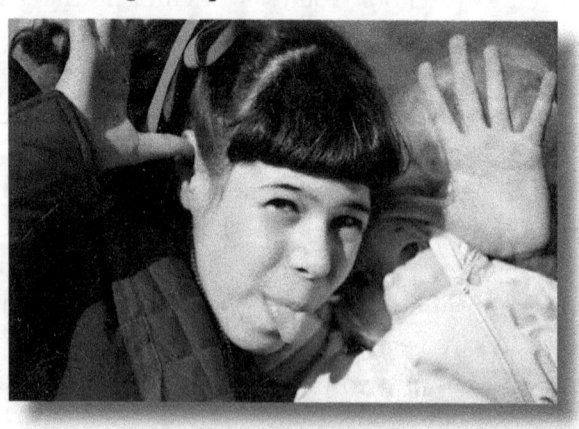

Christian Karen Berman

END OF A GOOD DAY

I'm in the 7th grade. I already missed school a few times from that common cold you get in the beginning of the year that makes you feel lousy. It's winter, maybe January, February. I'm in school, it's around 10:30 am. It's either between periods or I ask to go to the nurse. My stomach is really bothering me and I'm not feeling good at all. In 7th grade the nurse trusts your judgement and doesn't say you're not sick enough, you can't go home. So she calls my Mom and I wait, kinda holding my tummy. I think I'm carrying my backpack, so I don't need to go back to my locker. First time I ever been to this nurse, not sure how I even found her. No fever. My Mom walks in to pick me up and I'm happy to see her and ready to go home. I can't remember if we stop on the way home to pick up a few items at the A&P.

MIRROR OF MY WORLD

We finally get home. There is snow on the ground and it's a cold, windy, frigid day. I'm waiting on the porch for my Mom or Grandma to open the front door and I fall or trip backwards and fall on the light blue metal shovel, it slices my light blue leggings in half by my tush. It's very embarrassing that I lost my balance. Mom sees, then I run upstairs to see the damage and see there is even a long semicircle red scratch line on my butt. Is it just one of those days? The good part, my stomach is feeling better and I go downstairs to sit in the kitchen with my Mom and Grandma Lee. They are sitting at the table and me on the floor by the bottom cabinet, hungrily munching on Better Cheddars. I didn't have lunch yet. These are really good.

My day just got better.

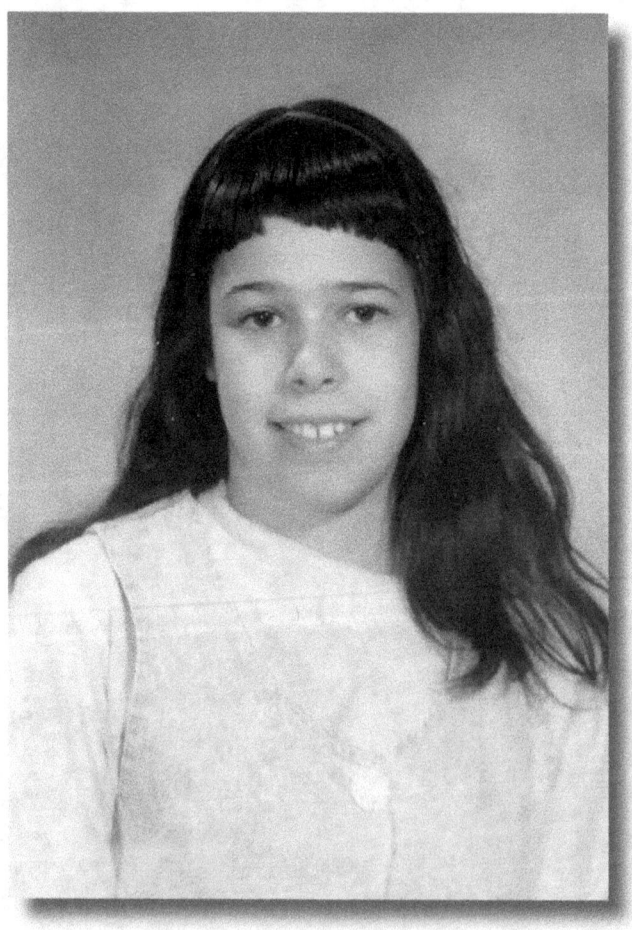

Christian Karen Berman

Bullied

In the 7th grade, in Mr. Burch's science class, there had been a girl who was bullying/picking on me for a while. I had told my parents, who had told my guidance counselor and she had said there was nothing she could do without proof. I actually kinda liked the girl and wish we could have been friends, but she didn't like me. So it was sort of a boring class today, we shared one big table. I had the countertop to myself. My bully was at the table right across from me. I wrote a note (yes, passing notes in class before texting was invented, how clever was I, LOL).

I wrote on a half-piece of loose-leaf paper, from my big blue binder, something like, "Why do you always have to be mean and pick on me and make me feel bad? I wish we could be friends. Can you please stop picking on me?" I wrote it to her name and signed my name too for evidence and then passed it to her and she wrote something back to me. It was like, "Nothing personal, I just don't want to be friends and maybe you're so easy to pick on and I enjoy it," or "I'm sorry they pick on you." I honestly can't remember, but she incriminated herself nonetheless. I think we passed notes a few times. I asked if there was anything I could do to get her and her friends to stop or be friends with them. She said she couldn't control what her friends do. I was nervous about her figuring out what I was doing. She was a much bigger girl than me, too. I didn't want to get beat up or something. I was happy I got to keep the paper and my plan worked. I showed it to my parents or guidance counselor and she didn't bother me again. If it was in today's world, you just wouldn't dare to be so brave, you might be hurt badly for doing something like this, by the bullies. This was in the mid-1990s.

MIRROR OF MY WORLD

<u>Christian Karen Berman</u>

SUMMER

I remember my Mom driving down with me to Big Top Toy Store, after we dropped Larry off at the Y Day Camp. It smelled like the beginning of summer. School had just ended. It ended late, too, the end of June. Today's kids only have to go until the end of May. It was so exciting. It was really early in the morning, 8 or 9 am. The guy that owns the shop had to tie the six-foot across, two-foot-deep pool, onto our trunk or the roof of our car. It was 50 bucks in the 1990s. The best my Dad could do at the time towards having our own pool, much better than the soft plastic collapsible ones. This was strong hard plastic and sturdy. Summer had just started and so much to look forward to. I was age 14 and Larry age nine-and-a-half. I was in Day Camp, too, the same summer, too, but my camp started later than Larry's. It was a girl's arts program, with arts and crafts, ballet and Jazz dance, acting class and swimming. It was at the same Y, just a different part of the building.

The camp also had the tie-dyeing white shirts rainbow colors outside, ceramics class, dress up like it's the 1970s day, pajama day, too much make up day, and dressing in a costume day (I wore my black Halloween witch costume hat and all, counselors putting make-up on campers). It was from age 7-16. I had just turned age 14. My eye got red and puffy from the make-up or eyeliner and my Dad was concerned at pick-up time and talked to one of the counselors about my eye. It was an all-girls camp, only me and a few girls were the oldest. Many girls were age seven to nine. They were in higher level ballet classes, too. I was in the beginner group with the younger girls, even though I took six months of ballet and tap dance after school when I was nine years old. I liked ceramics and swimming best.

You had to bring your own lunch, though. That part I didn't like, reminded me of school. Sometimes they would give us chocolate donut holes or a small slice of Carvel ice cream cake at the end of the day. It was a long day, 9 am - 4:00 pm. I loved the vending machines.

After camp, my Mom would get Larry and me a Sunkist diet soda and Dipsy Doodles. Dinner at home was good then—meatloaf, ketchup and onions and flavored rice cakes and something else like health salad and pea and corn salad with a dill sauce and a baked potato.

I one time had a fainting spell outside, when we were playing baseball. I felt weak, dizzy, blurry vision. The counselor told the director and she asked what I had for breakfast. It was late so I only had time to have a chocolate Chips Ahoy cookie my Mom gave me on the way out the door. Then she asked what juice I wanted. I said fruit punch. She gave me orange juice and called my parents to take me home for the day and rest. I had been lying on the couch in the lobby where she brought me, couldn't see straight and felt weak. When my parents came, I jumped in my Dad's arms. He didn't like that, but I liked to do it. I was only 86 pounds back then.

After that fainting spell, I wasn't allowed outside in the sun and we had to have a morning snack because of me, so no one else would get low blood sugar. Mom always gave me a sour plum for my mid-morning snack. I had a fainting spell in the 6th grade and got sent home, too. I'm not sure if I skipped breakfast or Mom gave me an oatmeal cookie in the car. I was always running late. School starts early. Sometimes I'd get up, get dressed and go. Sometimes I'd put my hair up nice if I had the time. School was around 8:15 am.

Christian Karen Berman

MIRROR OF MY WORLD

Christian Karen Berman

ELEVATORS AND DAY CAMP

Larry and me playing in the Fallsview swimming pool. We both are very happy. The Nevele day camp I liked better, so I didn't go to this day camp, you had to go on an elevator to the playroom down in the basement. I went for one night and then didn't want to. I was afraid of elevators even then, that was the main reason I didn't want to continue. I was the oldest of the children in the dining room, but no one seemed to mind. I walked with my Dad a lot down to The Nevele, next door. We tried out a few Catskills hotels. My parents played a lot of tennis, they had to walk off all the food. I didn't like walking and tennis. I think I should have gone to the day camp. I was age 14.

I think he chose three meals a day, they had two meals, too. What a spread all the hotels had. Breakfast, Danishes, muffins, rolls. The leftovers we feed the ducks in the lake. I had Frosted Flakes and pancakes and OJ for breakfast. Daddy had oatmeal and the egg and bacon and home fries. I was worried about cholesterol even then. I didn't want to have eggs every day. I even gained weight there and I was active the whole time—swimming, tennis, walking, there was so much walking. I was about 87 or 90 pounds and 5' 1" and was 93½ pounds when we got home. We also had egg creams in the coffee shop. My Dad thought I was skinny and kinda wanted me to gain weight.

He wrote out a star chart that summer. I went to an arts camp, with dance, acting, ballet and swimming and lost a few pounds. Daddy did take the scale to weigh us all. At night all the old couples in their 70s and 80s were heavily smoking in the lobby, thick, white clouds of smoke, donut holes, I remember, many were fat, too. This was in the mid-1990s, before the nonsmoking rule. When we got back to the room, my Daddy said my hair smelt like smoke and cigarettes like that was a good thing.

MIRROR OF MY WORLD

Christian Karen Berman

FIRST DAY OF 8TH GRADE

It was the first day of the eighth grade. I wore a long, soft denim skirt that flowed, matched it with a white short-sleeve shirt size girls 14. Keds white slip-on sneakers size 7½ women's. I also had a dark green backpack with a pink, yellow, and blue zipper. My Dad wrote my name across it in big letters with a black Sharpie marker the night before school as he usually did. I had shoulder-length brown hair and bangs. I made my own breakfast, instant blueberries and cream oatmeal, you added hot water, but I never made this before and didn't know how much water to add. It was good but dry, thick and salty. I might have had OJ, not sure. I was nervous and still hungry, too, since I barely added water.

My Dad and brother were getting ready to go to Horace Mann School. Larry was going into 4th grade. It must have been 7:15 am. My Mom had to drive me to school, I was out of district. I was getting bullied in seventh grade, so my guidance counselor thought it was best I find another school. Yes, again, it was Hommock's Mamaroneck Middle School. It took 25 minutes to get there with no traffic so we had to leave early to get there by 8 am.

I got there on time. I saw this cute blonde girl, straight hair three inches past her shoulders and thin bangs, and her twin sister. Margie and Katie. Margie turned out to be in my class. It looks like it will be a fun year.

In gym class we had to stand by the wall and get our heights. My head went to 5'1", and then they weighed you. Mine said 90 lbs., but I told the lady that at home it was 87.5 lbs. this morning, so she changed it to 87 pounds. I was self-conscious about my weight even then.

One day I was late to Mrs. Dato's math class. I was wearing blue denim overalls and a blue jogging coat with a zipper and hood, size girls 14. She made a joke about my Mom must be driving crazy and raced to get here on time (1st period) and then said,

MIRROR OF MY WORLD

"I'm sorry, I'm sure your Mom drives very carefully. I was only kidding." The thing is, it was true what she said—my Mom does drive like that sometimes.

During the holidays they had Cabbage Patch Kid Mini Dolls in the Micky D's Happy Meal. I had been wishing they would get good toys like this in the Happy Meal and they finally did. My parents would take me after school often for a Chicken McNuggets Happy Meal. I didn't eat much of my lunch; Mom always made a PB&J on Home Pride white bread, potato chips, two or three Milano cookies, grapefruit or cranberry juice box. I use to get Hi-C Fruit Punch, but I was watching my calories. I was in acting class my parents signed me up for in school. I drew the cover of the play my group was working on, called *Frosty Returns*, and I made up my character Danny Olsen and a classmate interviewed me for the play, with me saying I went to an art and dancing camp last summer. Took my photo, too.

One day I really didn't want to go to school, but I got in the car anyway with my Mom. She drove almost a half hour. The parking lot was empty when I got there. We must have been late. I waited, opened the door, but I wouldn't get out of the car. I didn't really want to go. Why? I wasn't even sick or tired, I don't know why, I'd miss Mom. I didn't feel like going through a whole day of many classes. I didn't mind going, my parents even worked it out that I didn't have a 1st period class and could get there later. Well, my Mom was surprised and reluctantly drove me back home and walked in with me and said to Grandma Lee, "We're back, we're both back." She was shocked. During the years I heard my Mom tell this story to my Dad many, MANY times—if I didn't want to go, why didn't I tell her?

I was trying to look good and not bad. My Grandma was surprised to see me back, too. My Dad would say throughout my childhood, Grandma would pay you $5 to go to school and you just wouldn't go. I went most of the time. Maybe that was showing something was wrong. I needed more home time than others. I was happy to be home. Just that warm, relaxing, safe home feeing.

In Gym once we had to run around the school. I did and was the head or close to the front of the line from beginning to end.

I did amazing but needed a long drink of water from the water fountain after. Another time in gym, on a cool, wet crisp morning, I had to kick the soccer ball. I ran and kicked it hard and my Keds sneaker went flying up in the air with the ball. I think the whole class laughed at that one. Maybe I needed a size 7 instead. I had to hop and get my sneaker back, that was a good one.

In Mr. Rabbico's English class the first day, he asked for our parent's phone number. I opened my small notepad and showed him my Dad's work number and he copied it down and thanked me. We had Vocabulary bees in his class. It was fun. He made us read *To Kill a Mockingbird*, and *Lord of the Flies*, too. Before Christmas vacation he showed us the classic movie *A Christmas Story*. Some kids were sucking their rainbow candy cane Ms. Dato gave us. Mr. Rabbico called my parents in to school for a meeting. He said I was too thin and he was worried about my weight and asked if anything was wrong. My weight was 86.5 pounds, just fine for me, but my parents appreciated his concern.

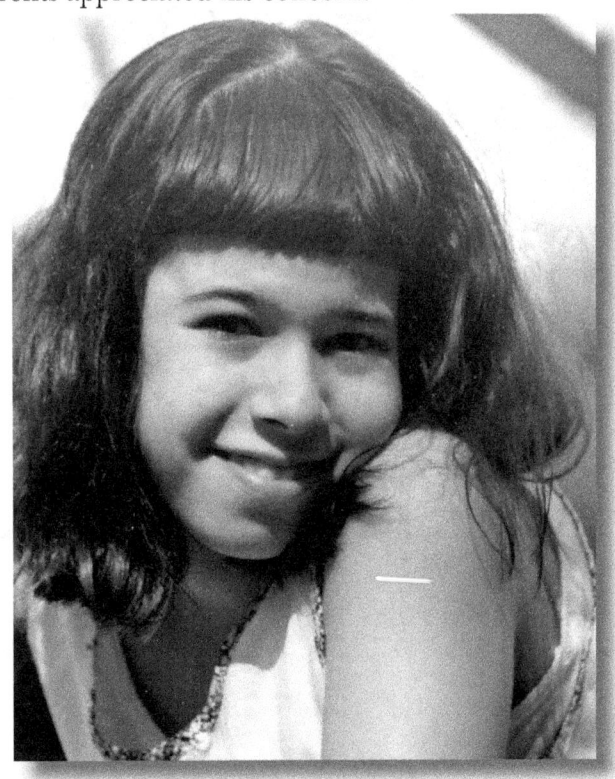

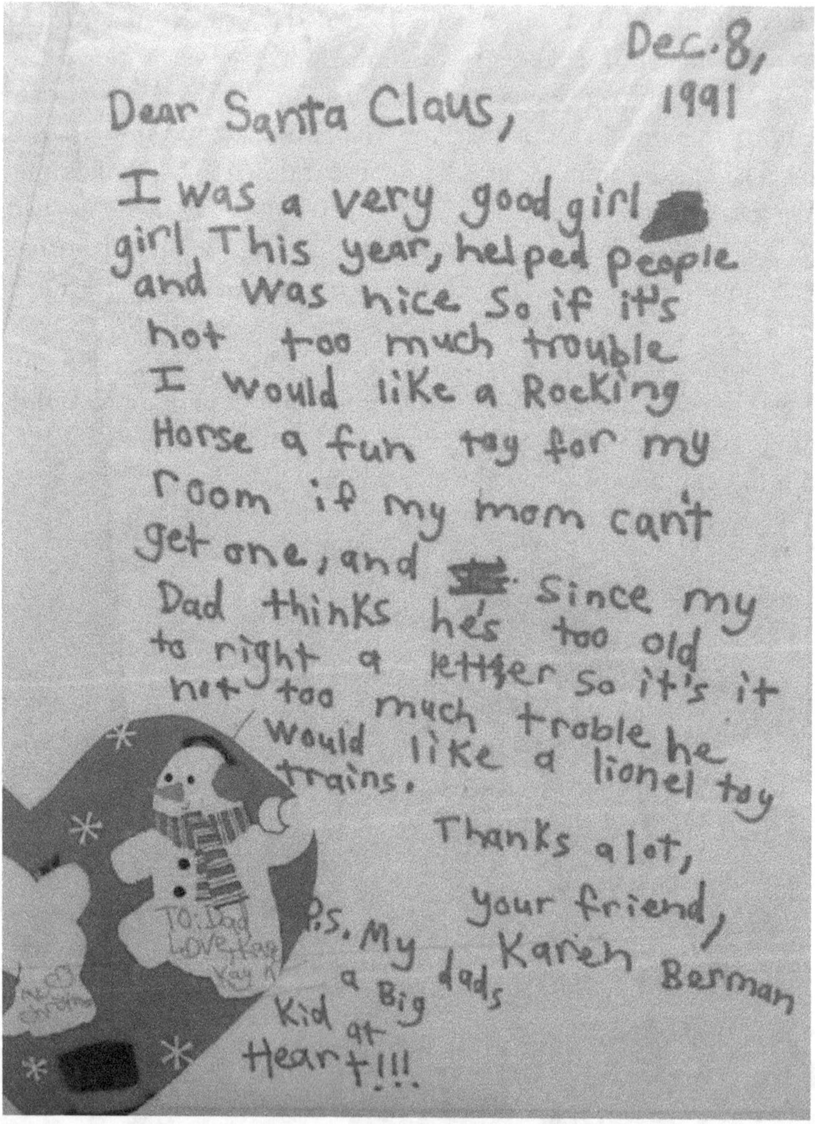

MIRROR OF MY WORLD

Dec. 8, 1991

Dear Santa Claus,

I was a very good girl girl This year, helped people and was nice. So if it's not too much trouble I would like a Rocking Horse a fun toy for my room if my mom can't get one, and Since my Dad thinks he's too old to right a letter so it's it not too much troble he would like a lionel toy trains.

Thanks a lot,

your friend,
Karen Berman

P.S. My dads a Big Kid at Heart!!!

Christian Karen Berman

THE LAST DAY OF THE 8TH GRADE BEFORE CHRISTMAS VACATION

My Mom and I were probably running late for her to drive me to school. It was 25 minutes away and always a rush to get to my first period class. It was hard going from my warm and cozy bed, quickly getting dressed, to 30 degrees freezing cold outside. You could see my breath as white clouds. We went into the car and Mom was trying to turn the heat up quickly to warm us up. I could write on the car window with the dew using my index finger. It was just my finger, I wasn't wearing any gloves. I drew a heart, a star, and maybe a cloud, a free MagnaDoodle. I was wearing my long purple winter coat and possibly my MC Kid winter hat; they got a lot of years of use, my clothes. I had a big dark green backpack with three rainbow zippers, pink, purple and yellow. My Dad wrote my name big with a black sharpie neatly across my backpack.

I had Mrs. Dato for math. She was nice, funny, in her early 50s and about 5'3". She had a short bowl cut with black curly hair and big glasses, wore a ruffly blouse, and long skirt. I remember that the school worked my schedule so I had my frees early and didn't have to be at school until 10 am, which made it easier for me to be able to sleep a little later and be more energized and focused for the rest of the day and miss much less school. But I still didn't have time to eat or drink for breakfast.

In the 8th grade my usual outfits were a big purple sweater with a girl on it and yarn hair. I must have worn that until age 19. They made things well back in the mid-1990s, to last wash after wash. I wore that with soft, elastic waist blue jeans. I also loved these blue denim overalls in a girls size 14, that I begged my Mom to buy from the Sears catalog. I think it was $28, which was a lot of money back then. I didn't have many overalls in my childhood and thought they were the best thing in the world, so cute. I must have worn a white turtle neck with printed, multi-color little stars on it underneath. I wore a blue zip-up hoodie over it. My hair was a few inches past my shoulders, rather straight, bangs, and I was 5'1" and a skinny 86 pounds. I still had a Grandma Lee that lived with us, waiting for me when I got home from school, and a Chinese Box land turtle named Lucky Alexis Berman.

In Ms. Dato's Class today, we were doing Geometry, but with these fun math puzzles. They were colorful little blocks shaped like triangles and squares. We'd break up into groups and try to be the first group to build the puzzle correctly and do the math with it on paper. I sometimes would pretend I was still in elementary school when days were fun like this. She handed out Rainbow Tutti Fruity candy canes to everyone in the class. There were about 20 students. I was having a great day.

The next class was Mr. Robbico. He was early 50s, with tan skin, a long, curly brown mullet hair style and wore a blue denim shirt and blue jeans with a brown braided leather belt. It was Language Arts class, English, another fun class. We used to have vocabulary bees. I was pretty good in vocabulary, never won, but came close. I was one of the smallest in the class. Today was a fun day. We went down to the library to watch *A Christmas Story*, the movie our teacher had recorded on **VHS** and was showing us on the **TV** with a built-in **VCR**, just to enjoy the day before school was out for the next two weeks. It was one of his favorite movies. Many kids sucked on their rainbow candy cane during the movie, but I wanted to save mine for later. The library was dark and he tried to make it special for us. After the movie, he told us he had bought this library book that was his favorite book, that he kept taking out to reread and shaved off the library's name with a razor, because he was now the proud owner of this book he loved. He valued books and seemed to love them.

The next period was lunch. I brought my lunch in a brown paper bag and usually just sat alone at the lunch table and ate, or picked at my food, and only had a few bites. What did my Mom give me? Mostly what I didn't like—PB&J, sometimes a turkey sandwich and as a rare treat chicken salad on rye, left over from her dinner at the diner, her other half of a sandwich. That was thoughtful of my Mom. With a juice box of grapefruit juice from Ocean Spray, it has less calories than fruit punch, I thought. I was watching my weight. Cape Cod potato chips wrapped in tin foil and 3 Milano cookies.

There was no playground in the middle school. The boys played sports outside in front of the building and the girls walked around and talked. I didn't really have any close friends, but I was well-liked, not bullied.

The next period was acting class, Theater Arts. Mrs. Dena Calavado was my teacher. She was early 30s, had tan skin, long, dark brown curlyish hair and about 5' 3'.' This was the fun class, too, I liked her. We were working on the play for class *Frosty the Snowman*. I played one of the children I made up, Brian Olsen. Katie Jones was the Snowman. She had shoulder-length yellow blonde hair and a few bangs. Cat had blonde, mid-length curlyish hair. She was a friend. It was a nice class. The teacher gave out to the class of about 15, mostly girls, four mini crispy chocolate Palmer candies wrapped in foil. One girl said she didn't want any and was fat and on a diet. She didn't look heavy at all. She was tall and thin. She had childhood arthritis. I saved my chocolates for later, too. I put them in my lower backpack outer pocket. I always liked to save things for later to look forward to them.

In between classes, when I was walking down the hall with a girl classmate, she asked me the Christmas song they played in *Home Alone*, she couldn't remember it. I finally guessed it right, "Have Yourself a Merry Little Christmas." She also said I was so skinny, she could pick me up. I took that as a compliment.

I won't go into Social Studies. It was boring, the teacher couldn't teach and barely knew I was there. I dunno her name. She was 30s, medium weight, mid-length brown hair. It was the last class of the day, I probably tuned it all out. Books, worksheets. I just know I didn't like what could have been a fun subject, really bad teacher, I was looking at the clock, just waiting for it to say 2:35 pm. so I could grab my dark green backpack that my Dad wrote with my full real name in the back so no one would take it, with a black sharpie, Karen Berman, and leave. I carried it with me all day, not sure if I had a locker, never used it, this was easier. I waited in the school library and my Mom picked me up there. She and my Dad didn't want me waiting outside in the cold to get sick. I was so glad to see my Mom when she finally picked me up. That was always the best part of my day, that I looked forward to.

My Dad and Larry got out early from school. They were in the car waiting. We were all out for Christmas vacation. My Mom and I walked to the parking lot, not sure if she carried my backpack or me. She probably did, it was heavy. Daddy was so happy to see me and I was happy to see him. Now we're going to Micky D's for a Happy Meal. Larry and I got Chicken McNuggets. My Dad took me there because he thought I was too skinny and wanted me to eat more. I think he just got a sundae and hot apple pie. They gave mini ice cream cones with rainbow sprinkles to the kids who asked for free, they were really good, too. I got the Cabbage Patch doll Happy Meal, Larry got the Hot Wheels Cars. Boy, did I love those little dolls and tried to collect them all. We went there at least one or twice a week. I wished for the longest time that they would have little dolls like that and now they did. A wish came true.

Once at home, I ate my mini chocolate and opened my mini Cabbage Patch Kid, then told my dad about my day, gave him some test papers and a book report on Peter Pan I got back, A+. I got 80's and 90's in the 8th Grade. I was a really good student back then. I rarely missed school, only a few days, some I was sick, a few I just didn't feel up to going. Afterwards, I went to watch *Full House* and *Charles in Charge* reruns on TV, and then my Mom was making dinner—potted paprika chicken with peppers and onions and red skinned potatoes, or turkey cold cuts, with a sweet potato, latkes, apple sauce, and Russian dressing. I drank a box of cranberry juice or apple juice. For dessert, a large sugar cookie, a Christmas cupcake, and Skippy Creamy Peanut Butter on warm rye toast, with a cranberry juice box or milk. I watched *The Muppets Christmas Special* on Nick at Nite. It was a really good day, no school tomorrow, sleep late and Daddy's homemade oatmeal.

Christian Karen Berman

MY SaiNT PaTTY'S DaY aT AGe 14

I got home from the eighth grade. Some days we stopped for a Happy Meal on the way home. I don't remember if we did that, but my Dad got me a new Cabbage Patch Kid birthday doll. I usually didn't get presents on this day, but this year I did. I watched two episodes of *Full House* which my doll watched with me. Then we went out to the Flagship Diner. My Dad ordered two plates of corned beef, cabbage and potato, to share. I was about five foot one and eighty-six pounds. I didn't eat much. It was the first time I was trying this and not liking it. Then Dad said it was an Irish delicacy. I tried to like it, but now I like it more. Then we got home and had dessert while I watched TV reruns on Nick at Nite. I had a cupcake, Skippy creamy P.B. on rye toast, and my Mom got me a big green sugared shortbread cookie. That was my kinda food, it was more my taste as a kid. When I was younger my Mom always had trouble finding me a green shirt. I don't really remember celebrating St. Patty's day at school, but was just wearing a green shirt to school.

MIRROR OF MY WORLD

I loved going on summer vacation to the Nevele especially! Everything was so exciting, even calling for reservations! We all as a family, including Grandma Lee who came with us, looked forward to this trip each year! I always was enrolled in the day camp from since I was age seven. Never Larry, just me. Why? Daddy wanted Larry to hang out with them or they treated him young then or Daddy said I got bored easily and needed a lot of activities, something like that. Then my Mom would start washing and packing everyone's clothes a week before. We usually took two suitcases and one carry-on bag, a diaper bag for medicines, sunblock, camera case, etc. My problem was choosing which toys to take. At age 10 I took a blond My Child Doll Dana and a Lassie dog stuffed animal.

We had to get up early and leave by 9:30-10:30 am! Daddy would clean old junk out of the car and park in the back by our garage so our neighbors wouldn't know we wouldn't be home. He told the next door neighbor to keep an eye on our house and take in our newspaper. We cancelled milk delivery for the week (we haven't got milk or the newspaper in many years). I always wondered why they never got chocolate milk! Daddy would load up the car in the early morning. So much stuff, plus Grandma and our toys. Daddy was trying to force me to eat a few chocolate chip cookies for breakfast. Grandma said not to. I was too excited to eat, not hungry, happy!

So we all got in to the car full of stuff. by the time they got a few blocks most every summer even if we left by 9:30 am, they'd turn around and go back home! My parents wanted to check if they left the stove on, lights on, fridge open. We were going to be gone five days, four nights. We couldn't afford more!

I adapted very well as a child. I'd have been happy staying over a month. I looked forward to this all year. Fun, excitement, yay! Okay, back home, everything was usually turned off. I think my mom packed fresh plums and Archway chocolate chip cookies, juice boxes, ginger ale. Then maybe everyone made sure they went to the bathroom; it was a long trip with traffic. Okay, by now it was like 10:20 am. The radio was on, "Valerie" by Steve Winwood was playing, then "One Good Woman" by Peter Cetera. We were on the highway! Larry and I played the car game—we used to collect

Matchbox cars, so we'd name different types of cars. Yeah, we were squeezed in the back tight. It was hot and sunny, we were getting bored! We sang "Down By the Bay" and other kid songs out loud. Daddy was recording us with our kid's Fisher Price tape recorder.

We had a camcorder but he was afraid to take it. It would break, lots of work recording us, too, but it would have been awesome to have the memories I see in my head on video! He took a camera one year, a cheap Kodak, the next year Minolta 7000i. He was very into *Photography Magazine* and cameras then and I was the main subject. He said I never took a bad photo and how photogenic I was. We stopped off at Howard Johnson's for lunch. We all got eggs, bacon, buttered toast, french fries and had that with ketchup. It wasn't a choice he picked, but the kids got chocolate milk and it was in the kid's menu. The three grown-ups got O.J. and coffee. After, Daddy got wintergreen lifesavers! I miss those days. It was like Heaven, such happiness!

Then whoever had to use the bathroom went and we left to hit the road. More music, very hot car. We were getting tired. Nice scenery—farms, horses, cows, music playing.

We finally arrived two-and-a-half hours later from when we left home. Us kids screaming and cheering, yay, we're finally here! We usually requested room 612, I think. It was their honeymoon room. We unpacked and changed into our swim suits and went to the big pool. Then came back, showered, and daddy took me to the night camp to have dinner with other kids age 6-11. I was nervous and I think I'd of rather been with them. I always had a cherry Twin Pop for dessert. Daddy never let me have those because he said I'd get a sore throat. He was very strict on the rules he had. That was the main rule, and no ice cream in the winter, no rainbow cereals. Daddy used the lowest #6 Coppertone sunscreen. I usually got bad sunburns that were really red and hurt. The day camp didn't give anyone sunscreen, either.

Then after, we'd go to the nightclub. They had mints when you left the main dining room for the grown-ups. Larry and I would dance and be the center of attention. Everyone else there was in their 80s and smoked cigarettes. Then someone on stage told dirty jokes I didn't understand and I got tired.

MIRROR OF MY WORLD

The next morning was fun. I had to wear my swimsuit under my clothes, too. My parents dropped me off in the children's dining room, my usual Pops cereal and pancakes and syrup and the counselor would cut it up for the kids and put butter in the middle. Then they'd take whoever had to use the bathroom to the main lobby before we left. One day hiking and mountain climbing, the next horseback riding, swimming, arts and crafts, lunch (my very favorite then: mac and cheese; I drank grape juice and had a Swirl Pudding Pop for dessert). The kid's pool had a big slide, but I'd just learned to swim and stayed around three feet. I was small. I was brave enough to take the inner tube to six feet and back, but it was hard to swim there and back—it was a big pool! In Arts and Crafts, we did lanyard necklaces, bracelets, and a Popsicle ashtray. They had good rainbow sprinkle cookies with milk. They had an arcade. They had a wishing water fountain you threw pennies into, and a gift shop, too. I got a metal Slinky once and played with that around the hotel. Their water fountains tasted great, like fresh filtered spring water. It was fun!

I miss those days, some of the best in my whole life. I miss my childhood. Even elementary school wasn't that bad. I miss my toys from my childhood. I was very happy then. I don't think I ever felt sadness or depression. I loved my pediatricians. I got bored sometimes, but I had Nickelodeon and the Disney channel since I was seven. I didn't have the $100 talking dolls, bunkbeds, swing set, but everything was great then. I would have liked another sister and brother to play with, though. I had baby dolls and stuffed animals, but mostly I had a lot of love. I was very loved.

Even when I was well and didn't want to go to school every now and then, I was given a great day, not punished. I felt guilty though, but remember the hokey days. As young as age six, I pretended to have a red sore throat in the 1st grade to go home. I missed my home, my TV and my Mom, and I was bored copying stuff off the blackboard and just would rather be home. They sent me home. After a while they got wise, the school nurse, and never sent me home. I faked headaches and being nauseous a few times. Other times they were real. I was only seven. Another time, age seven, my Mom told the principal I didn't want to go to school again. She said to send the truant officers over to force me to go. I don't think they had those, but I was ready to hide! My mom picked up my homework, they sent me many bear stickers that had clothes you stick on them and said to get well. Then my mom got me a plastic grey sword and *Garbage Pail Kids* cards with gum. It was an awesome fun day!

My Mom always doted on me and bought me toys as a child. Daddy, then, I remember yelling at me to eat my dinner, take my medicine when I was sick, go to the doctor, go to school. But he was nice. I slept with them. I think Larry slept on the floor by their room and when he was older in his own bed. I slept with them on and off until I was a teenager. I was always like the younger child.

MIRROR OF MY WORLD

Christian Karen Berman

Taking Medicine as a Teenager

Well, when you're older, they try to give you a chewable or large pills to swallow to show you're not a child anymore. I was probably age 15. I was sick with tonsillitis. My Dad came up to his bed where I was sleeping, crushed up one or two large pills in Welch's Grape Jelly and tried to feed it to me on a big tablespoon. Uhh! It tasted dreadful, kind of sweet and salty in a bitterly, yucky way. I boycotted and couldn't eat Welsh's Grape Jelly for the next 15 years (my Dad had bought it; I had a PB&J for old time's sake). I could not get that horrible taste memory out of my mind. Terrible, yeah, made you really shudder good. As a child that's how my Mom always made my PB&J's, with Skippy Creamy Peanut Butter on Wonder Bread or Home Pride. The chewables were bearable, but uhhh. Then when I had a sore throat in my 20s my Dad had to open these caplets, I think it didn't come in liquid syrup for this drug. What did we have on hand to mix the little capsule in? Hunts Lemon Meringue Pie pudding cups, or IHOP Maple Syrup? We tried it in both. Terrible in both. I could barely get any down. Sadly, to this day I haven't had any Hunts Pudding or IHOP syrup in the little prepackaged cup. The homemade ones, yes, but still can't eat these to this day remembering the bitter, icky taste.

I also still took Children's Liquid Tylenol in my teens, 20s, and early 30s. The child-size dose, too. The bottle said it was recommended for children 11 and over or 95/96 pounds and over. At those ages, I was only only 10 pounds more. I remember hating the grape flavor and still can't drink any grape juice (only Donald Duck Grape Juice). I've tried many other brands since then. They all taste like Children's Grape Tylenol to me. Cherry and bubble gum taste slightly better, this is back when then made them with dyes in the 1990s and early 2000s, so at least it looked like what it was supposed to taste like. Today it tastes worse. I've had it, like

MIRROR OF MY WORLD

sugar granules, too sweet, but maybe not real sugar and clear, no colors. It would put me in a deep sleep for a long time, but I was sick and needed the sleep. A few times it made me dizzy and the room spin, that was really scary. I have improved from my childhood. If I need to take my medicine, I don't spit it out. I know better now. It cost money and it can't get me well if I don't take it.

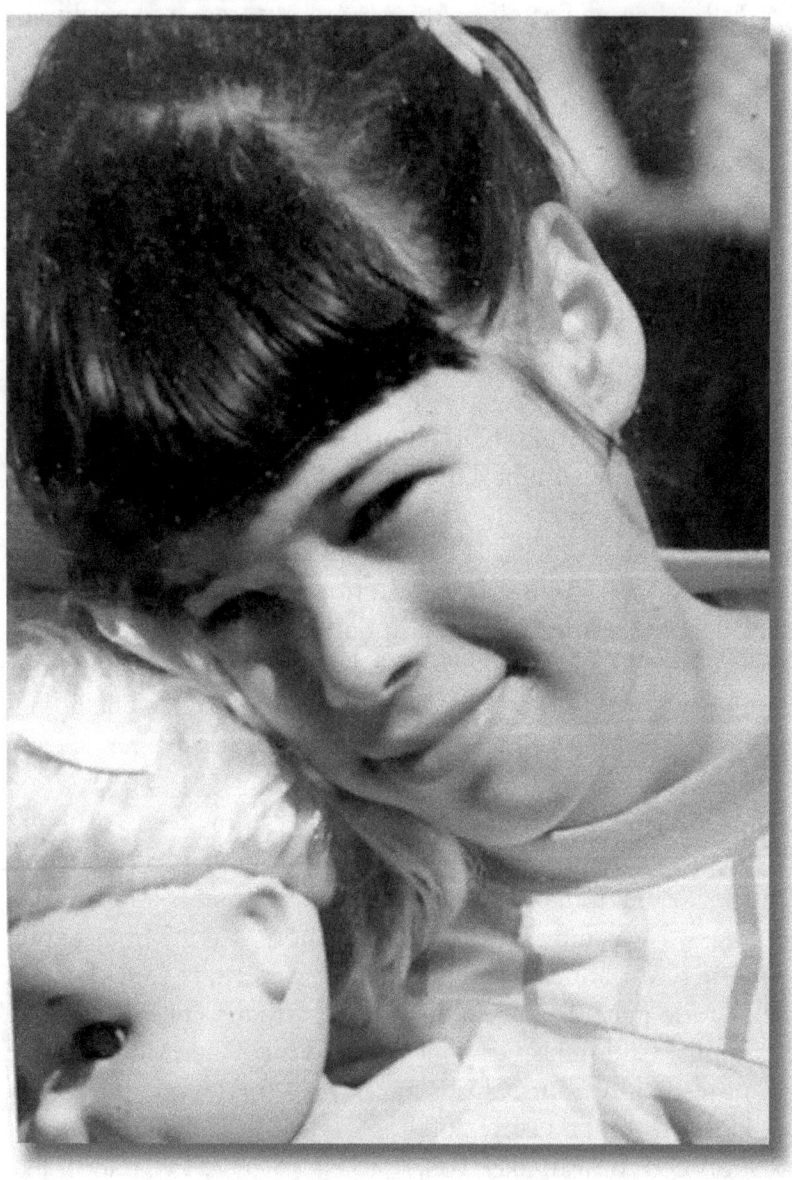

Christian Karen Berman

THE NEVER-TOLD STORY OF MY GRANDMA LEE

Her given name was Lily and my Grandpa called her that, but she told us to call her Grandma Lee. When I had just graduated from the 8th grade and middle school, my Grandma Lee lived with us, and wasn't doing so well. I remember one time I went to Dr. Martin Biers with her and my Mom. She fell exiting the stairs in the old house-type building and my Mom went in to tell the doctor and he went out to check on her and help her up. He was probably in his late 60s then. He became my doctor much later on, but always playfully threatened to send me back upstairs to my pediatrician. He was a wonderful doctor. He was still working until his late 80s and sadly died of brain cancer some years ago.

One beautiful summer's morning in late June, where you could smell the sweet fragrance of all the purple and pink pansies and red roses. It was just after school had been let out. My Grandma had so much trouble walking. She could barely make it into her old orange, rust-colored, velvety soft easy chair. My Dad said we had to hurry up and get ready to go to the hospital pharmacy and rent a wheelchair for her. I was having a cup of Shredded Wheat cereal in a bowl of milk, no spoon, just dunking them. I was wearing a one-piece cotton sun outfit. I was really worried about her. My whole family went in and talked to the pharmacist and he gave us the best wheelchair. It took about a half hour to get it back home to her. It was something we never done before, even with my Grandpa Jules and she was a proud, strong, tough woman, but sweet and funny at times. My Dad helped her get into the wheelchair once at home. My Grandma had this infection on her foot; it was a scratch that had got worse and infected. Being a diabetic, foot infections came easy and were hard to treat and cure, plus she had bad circulation. She was 84½ years old and about 5' and 116 pounds. I had just turned 15 a few weeks before; I was 5'1" and 86 pounds. I was skinny.

My Grandma had asked me to give her a haircut. She was too old and couldn't do it anymore and couldn't get to the hair salon, plus didn't want to pay their high prices. I was honored, flattered, but nervous. She had cut my hair and bangs until I was 10 years old. We only had home haircuts then, probably to save money. I carefully and skillfully worked on her hair. It had been a little longer than shoulder length. She liked it short. She used to dye it dark brown. It was mostly grey now, but not thin, as you would expect. She looked pretty good for her age. She liked it shorter in front, longer in the back. She would only trust me with this, not my Dad who also cut his own hair, or her daughter, just me. I myself had been trimming my bangs since age 10, not my hair. It took about an hour, but it was even, perfect, as good as any hair salon could do and free. She always would tell me, "I love you more than you will ever know." As a young 15-year-old, I didn't really understand, but smiled back at her.

My Dad was discussing with me and Larry how we would get my Grandma to the doctor. Her infection was getting worse. It was greenish, yellow, pus-filled and had a really bad smell. It had gotten worse fast, plus my Dad and us kids in school couldn't of had the time to take her to the doctor on a school day. My Mom couldn't have done it herself with the wheelchair. Back then in the mid-1990s, calling an ambulance was for emergencies; we never did that. My Mom looked up my Grandma's symptoms in an old medical book. We thought, no, she couldn't have gangrene. My Dad practiced carrying me out of the house in the wheelchair with Larry carrying the other side of the wheelchair to see if they would be able to carry my Grandma's weight out (my Dad would pick me up often anyway, at my request, or I would still run and jump happily into his arms). They were worried she would be too heavy for them to lift or drop her. We didn't do my brother, because at age 10½, he was already 5' and 120 pounds. I was the lightest and safest to practice on. I thought it was fun. They had no problem. My Mom was 5'6½" and 145 pounds. My Dad was 6' and 190 pounds.

That night we packed for the trip to the podiatrist. Juice boxes and a Hershey bar in an insulated baby bottle bag, just in case my Grandma got low blood sugar. She used to ask my Dad to go to the local market and pick up a Hershey bar for her when her blood sugar got low so she wouldn't faint. When she started getting sicker, my Dad had to begin testing her blood sugar. The testing kit we got came with a VHS video to watch, no YouTube instructional videos way back then. He was scared to take her blood, something only nurses did. He wasn't diabetic back then and had never done this before. He did it for her. I got used to having my blood sugar taken. It sometimes hurts a little (I'm not diabetic but tend to have low blood sugar sometimes). When we got to Dr. Kagan's office he was alarmed by the red and swollen, pus-filled foot he saw and told my Dad to take her right down to the hospital to admittance. She needed to be admitted to the hospital as soon as possible, there was nothing he could do. My parents did not realize how serious this was. They got her back in the car and we drove straight to the local hospital.

When we got there about 15 minutes later, we walked in the sliding glass doors and my Dad decided we would probably be there a long while, so we all went to the cafe there and ordered a nice lunch. My Dad had a boiled hamburger, he loved the ones my Grandma use to make him when he was courting her daughter. He said these were almost as good. Larry had grilled cheese and French fries, my Mom and I shared a tuna salad sandwich on white toast. We all had Diet Cokes in a glass with ice. I think my Grandma had a tuna sandwich, as well. All the food was pretty good for a hospital.

I overheard some man sitting at the counter, excitedly telling everyone that his wife just gave birth to a healthy baby girl. I was happy for him. I wish my Mom would give me a baby sister, too. Then we went to look in the gift shop next door to the cafe. They had candy, cookies, Life Savers, gum, baby toys and big stuffed animals, and jewelry. My Mom found this beautiful, light blue, thin nightgown she wanted to buy her Mother to wear in the hos-

MIRROR OF MY WORLD

pital. I was looking at the "I'm a Big Brother", "I'm a Big Sister" T-shirts. Also a soft baby ball. An old saleslady came over to talk to me and I asked the price of the ball, said I wanted to get it for my Grandma. The saleslady thought I was being silly, then I told her because she could squeeze the ball when she had pain. It cost $4.

Then we were waiting in admittance a long time and finally got transported upstairs. We started on our long journey of a day at 9 am, now it was close to 5 pm. We looked at her hospital room. She wanted my help in the bathroom. The nurse came in later to get her more settled and asked us if she could drink water through a straw. It was getting late and we were getting tired. We told her we were going to leave and go home and have dinner and come back around 7 or 8 pm. Visiting hours were until 9 pm.

We finally got back home. I was glad to be home. My Dad made homemade Egg McMuffins with cheese and ketchup for everyone, maybe a few potato chips on the side with a cup of Tropicana orange juice. I just had one sandwich, nothing else. I was so skinny, my Dad would usually make me eat more or encourage eating a big meal. I was happy he didn't.

Then we all hurried up to go back to the hospital and visit my Grandma. We were all very close and had never really been apart and left her anywhere alone before. It was getting dark and late when we got there, we were all getting tired from the big day, but happy she was getting the care she needed to get better. She had an I.V. in her. My Mom did buy her that beautiful, light blue, thin nightgown, not sure if she was wearing it, but it was fancy with little satin bows and expensive for back then around $30-$65, but she was worth it. She had a roommate the first day. The roommate was by the window, my Grandma by the bathroom. We promised her we would be back early the next morning. It was hard to leave her and strange going home to an empty house, just the four of us and our box turtle Lucky Alexis. Now my parents would have a chance to be the real adults and parents now that the matriarch was really sick and alone in the hospital on the 4th floor. I was scared of elevators like my Dad, we would take the stairs. We didn't mind the extra exercise.

Christian Karen Berman

HOSPITAL STAY

The next morning in late June around 8:30 pm, we all get up early and get ready to go to back to the hospital. We miss Grandma and want to see how she is doing. She needs us. I just turned 15. Larry is 10½. It's kind of hard for me to leave the bathroom, because my Dad kind of implied that I shouldn't use the hospital bathroom because of germs and possibly AIDS.

It's a beautiful, warm, sunny day, but we are heading to the hospital. Visiting hours start at 9 am. We didn't even eat breakfast yet, just get up and go.

When we arrive, Grandma has a new hospital room all to herself. She is doing okay, glad to see us, and in good spirits. I feel kinda sick and woozy. I get like that sometimes when I don't eat. With all the stress and running around with my Grandma being sick, I haven't been eating well. My Dad's been too stressed and preoccupied to try to get me to eat more food, plus no time, lots of running around. I might have told him I feel funny or don't feel good or asked when we were having breakfast. I don't think I knew the word faint then. He himself was hungry and wanted to go down to the hospital cafeteria. My Mom wanted to stay more with her mother, but Daddy said we'd be right back, so we all went to go forage for breakfast.

We went to the employee cafeteria. The cafe wasn't open so early and the staff said the prices weren't expensive here. There were eggs, fried potatoes, pancakes, bacon, sausage, hot oatmeal, cold assorted cereals. I can barely remember what picky me ate, maybe eggs and ketchup. I know my Dad ate oatmeal and cream (his favorite) and a little of everything. I might have drank chocolate milk or OJ, or maybe my Dad got a big plate and gave me a sample of his to taste and I had Cheerios or Frosted Mini Wheats. I wasn't the best eater. Then Larry and me looked at all the fun snacks in the vending machine and soda machine that I liked and would eat. 75 cents for a can of soda in the mid-90s and snacks about 85 cents.

Then we walked up the four flights of stairs to visit with my Grandma. The doctors came in to look at her and talk to my parents about what was going on. I looked out the big hospital window. The doctors started talking to us about amputation or just operating on the one leg to open up her veins. The IV meds weren't getting down to her severely infected foot. One of her feet was red, swollen, lots of pus, and she had to wear slippers that were cut open because regular loafers or shoes were too narrow for her very puffy foot. The doctor's name was Cohen, like my Grandma, and she said "Yes, maybe somewhere down the line we're related." That was a good, interesting sign. He also said if he operated on her foot and the operation wasn't successful, she would be too weak to survive the amputation.

There was a nice place near us called Burke Rehab, the same one featured in the award-winning movie *Regarding Henry*. They said they would give her a prosthesis and she could learn to walk again on a new leg. My Dad told my Grandma, "Don't you want to live to see your grandchildren graduate high school?" Then she started to cry.

I was picturing her getting a new plastic leg and learning how to walk again with no leg. It was overwhelming for me. Looking back, I'm surprised the doctors talked like this to a 4th and 8th grader. The thought of them cutting off one leg over the knee to make sure the infection didn't spread and they got it all, was such a surreal and scary thought. To see such a thing in my Grandma…what a long journey she had ahead of her to overcome and recover.

It was close to lunch time. My Dad hated to miss a meal. I wasn't hungry and wanted to stay upstairs and spend quality time with my Grandma. My parents let me and went to the cafe for lunch. Dad and Larry probably had the burger and fries with a Diet Coke, Mom tuna on toast. My Grandma and I were alone. We went over her food menu for the week. I was sitting next to her; she was on the bed. I would read it to her. It was on thin card-

board and she would say which meals she liked best and I would circle it with a pen. I remember they never gave her what I circled anyway, just what they wanted. They thought 116 pounds was thin, so she could eat anything she wanted, but on a low sugar diet because of her diabetes, Type 2.

I remember one meal was Swedish meatballs and Brussels sprouts. It smelt good to me, but she said "Feh" whenever she didn't like something. Then I was thinking I'd better ask her something important to me, I just should, I don't know how much longer she would be here in the back of my mind, I guess. I couldn't remember the names of all her dogs she had growing up, so I asked her that. She said, "The Spitz was Whitey, there was Brownie and Nellie." I think they were mixed breads. She had so many dogs and cats growing up and they all got along together. I can't remember anymore, there must have been eight. I don't know if she lived on a farm, or where in New York. I should have asked more about her parents and what they did for a living and what they were like. Why her Dad died when she was 12 and what of. All I know was she cried her eyes out and then needed eyeglasses and became very attached to her Mama, then my Grandpa and Mom.

What happened to her brother Louis, why did he die young? My young, little mind did not think so deeply and advanced. I wish it did. I think her dad Benji Precker died in the War, but I'm not sure. She graduated high school at 14 and was a child prodigy, loved to read books. They could never understand why I hated to read so much. In my generation in the 1990s, if you didn't like to read, just rent the movie and write the book report.

After lunch my parents had to take a break from the stress, so we all went home and said we would be back after dinner. At home my Dad was talking about how he needed a vacation this summer and he couldn't do another year of school without one. The only thing is we had to visit Grandma every day, two or three times a day, and we couldn't be far from her. So, no Catskills Resort this year, no Kutcher's, Nevele or Fallsview. That was 2½ hours away. So my Dad called around checking out our local hotels within 15-20 minutes away, not much fun or much of a trip, kinda depressing for all of us, but necessary. He called the Marriott, Arrowhead, we finally agreed on the Rye Town Hilton. We would only swim and sleep there, the rest of the time we would be at the hospital with Grandma. She was sick, missed us and her home, and we were her only family she had. She lived with us since I was age six and my Grandpa died.

On the way back to the hospital, it was getting dark. In our light blue, four-door car, 1990 Oldsmobile Cutlass Ciara, the most meaningful songs were playing on the radio—"These Dreams" by Heart and "Hold on My Heart" by Genesis. Even as a child, I thought it was so touching, momentous, that what I was going through in real life right now was being played in real time in the car on the radio, on the way to visit my sick Grandma in the hospital. I understood what the lyrics meant, too. I doubt anyone else noticed. I always remembered this.

At the hospital, we went to the employee cafeteria. The cafe closed about 5 pm; it was close to 7. The food was delicious and I don't like most foods. My Dad got two big plates for him and my Mom and gave us half, homemade mac and cheese, stuffing, maybe turkey, meatloaf, or meatballs and some veggie, like cooked carrots or mashed potatoes. It wasn't healthy food. I even brought my new, big baby bib. It was white quality plastic with red trim and some kinda little prints in the middle. I was regressing a little back then and reading American Baby magazine. It was free. I wanted to still be a baby, maybe because of what my Grandma was going through and I'd be in the 9th grade, in high school starting in September.

Then for dessert I was looking around. I wanted the big bowl of vanilla pudding the staff lady had put on the cart and covered in plastic. I told my Dad. He asked her. She told me I could have all I want for free. Boy, did that make me happy! I got a plastic bowl, filled it to the top and ate more than half of it. It was cool and creamy and yummy. Yellow vanilla custard color. Then Larry and me went to look at the vending machines in the cafeteria. I can't remember getting anything then; we probably had a Diet 7-Up or something with our meal or apple juice. Then we walked off our big dinner up the four or five flights of stairs and down the long hallways to visit our Grandma. I remember she wanted me to take her small container of skim milk home with two packs of Graham Cracker snacks for me to eat and enjoy. Grandmas always like to give their grandkids gifts when they visit. I went home, put them in the fridge, and saved it for later. I had enough dinner today. I was full.

MIRROR OF MY WORLD

Christian Karen Berman

THE RYE TOWN HILTON

That July summer, there wasn't much time for fun, riding bikes, fun trips, going shopping at Sears and Caldor. It was going to the hospital three times a day to spend quality time and check on my Grandma. The day we were checking in at the Hilton, my parents and I quickly packed our clothes in our suitcases, a few days before, not weeks before like we use to, but it really didn't matter—we were only 20 minutes from home if we needed to stop by the house and pick up more clothes or anything. It hardly seemed like a real vacation if we were checking on our own house, instead of asking the neighbors. I think my parents canceled our milk delivery. I'm not sure about the newspaper delivery. My Dad might have just got the *USA Today* paper in the hotel. He loved reading the morning paper.

We had to leave our Chinese box land turtle Lucky Alexis with our elderly neighbor (in her early 80s). She lived alone. I'm sure she loved that. She had no pets. Her name was Mrs. Newman. She used to babysit our goldfish Dodger for a week when we went on vacation in the summer, and he lived two years. Lucky Alexis was in a large heavy glass tank, no water, but drank water from a little saucer dish. She would have to feed him two or three times a day. He wasn't more than a pound. A slice of banana, a sliced strawberry.

What Lucky Alexis really liked was leftover scallops from my Mom's dinner at the diner. That's what he really went for and gobbled up. We once paid $15 a day for six days, to have him stay at the pet store we got him from when I was 10 years old. When we came back to pick him up, he was severely dehydrated. He was so dry and white, like E.T. when E.T. got sick from missing home. He even looked like E.T. He was in the back with other pets in tanks that were ignored, no one fed him or gave the poor little guy water. He nearly died. We came back a week later to get him home just in time. When he was sick once, I had to give him pink Amoxicillin that the vet prescribed in an eye dropper. He lived eight years with us until he sadly died.

We were going to try to make the best of this rather sad vacation and try to enjoy ourselves the best we could. Kids need a little fun and happiness in life. At check-in they gave our Mom two Rye Town Hilton water bottles and fanny packs to give us kids. After the bellhop brought our luggage to our room on the cart, we got settled and looked around for all of ten minutes. Then we went to the restaurant. They happily welcomed us and gave us a complimentary homemade chocolate chip cookie platter to take to our room and enjoy. We saw a lady who my Dad knew and who used to work in my Dad's cafeteria at his school. The cookies were the best ever, melt-in-your-mouth yummy.

Back at the hospital there was a new problem, not with our Grandma, but they were saying no more than two visitors at a time per room, then no one under 12 can go up. That they forgot to tell us before, because my Grandma was so sick. This was not okay. At first we waited in the lobby and obeyed the stupid rule, then I came up with an idea. My parents got the hospital passes and went up first. Then I told the front desk that I wanted a pass to the medical library to look up my Grandma's illness. They let me and Larry have a pass to get past security for that. I think I actually stopped in there a second and took a quick look, then we both sneaked upstairs to meet my parents. How unsafe to split up a family and let two kids wander around a big hospital alone. We ran in, me smiling. I outsmarted the system. I think they left me with Larry, but it coulda been my Mom or Dad, I honestly forget.

Upstairs Grandma had IVs, a nitroglycerin patch on her chest for chest pains, and a urine pouch attached by a tube, which I found scary. They found a lump on her lung, too. She wasn't getting better, she was getting worse. One late night when we were all there, she was begging the staff and my Mom to go home, very adamant to leave. Security was even called, two guards, that's how upset she was. The nurse or guards were making my family leave because it was after hours. My Grandma was so homesick and had enough of the hospital, but couldn't come home. She wasn't

discharged, because it was medically unsafe for her, she needed the IV meds and operation. I asked the nurse if my Mom could stay a little longer to calm her down. She said no, it wouldn't help, and we all sadly walked out, upset ourselves to go back to our nice hotel to have our vacation. Some vacation. This is a lot for a young, sensitive 15-year-old girl to go through.

   I couldn't sleep the first night at the hotel. My Dad put some Classical music on the radio to help me. If I got a few hours of sleep that night it was a lot. The next night he wouldn't let me have Pepsi or Coke. He told the waitress apple juice for me. I liked it better than soda, anyway.

   The next day they transferred my Grandma to the Coronary Care Unit. She wasn't doing well. Now there were rules for kids to go to the C.C.U. The only problem was I wasn't sure of the rules. If you're under 12 you can go with your parents, but if you're over 12 only two adults can go. Larry was age ten and I could pass for 11-13. I had been eating off the kid's menu at the hotel to help save money and I ate like a kid, anyway. They thought I was a little kid. I told the young woman at the front desk I was 13, then she gave me a pass. My whole family went. Then once up there, an older woman asked my age, so I said 13. She said I had to leave. Larry, too, she told my parents. I didn't even see Grandma, just the white curtain she was behind. This hospital was not being nice. So was I too old or too young? You can't ask the rules when you're trying to trick them and break them. No way I looked over 16 or 18, so maybe no one under 18 allowed, so why'd she ask Larry and me our age? We sadly went back to the hotel for lunch. We didn't get to visit with our Grandma. I think she was there for a heart attack or trouble breathing, but I'm not sure.

At lunch at the hotel, I was drawing on the kiddie menu. So was Larry. My favorite meal was fried chicken with mustard coleslaw and crispy French fries, but I'd usually have that for dinner. Maybe grilled cheese, tuna fish. I had been having trouble breathing myself at night. My Dad wanted us to go swimming after lunch. He said, "Don't worry, you'll feel better after you go swimming." I did.

Visiting Grandma a few times a day was fun, and running back and forth, too, it was a lot and not really a vacation. We'd get up and go straight to the hospital or sometimes have the big breakfast buffet. What a yummy spread. The kid's was cheaper and they gave us chocolate milk instead of coffee, or you could get hot cocoa. Early in the morning, 8 am, we'd go down to have breakfast. They had Danishes, muffins, croissants, jams, sliced cake loafs. Then the hot bar—eggs, fried potatoes, bacon, sausage, apple crepes, eggs Benedict. Then the cereal bar—Dannon yogurt, fresh fruit, granola, cottage cheese, assorted dry cereals, hot oatmeal with cinnamon or nuts to add. It put the hospital breakfast to shame. Adults were $20 and kids $10. In our minibar in the room a soda was $2.50 for one can. Even today you can get a twelve-pack of soda on sale for that price. We drank Diet Pepsi once as a treat and shared it. Insane prices for the 1990s. There was this trick at the hospital soda vending—you keep your hand on the Diet 7-Up button a long time and you get two for 75 cents. I always did that and we brought it back to the hotel to drink later.

In the hotel, they only had tennis and in and outdoor swimming, baby pool, and shuffle ball. I had a swimming tube to go to the deep end and it fit me. I brought my pretend sister Jen with us and my bear Wuzzly to sleep with. I loved them so, still have them.

I changed her baby clothes. There was a hotel camp. They did nothing extra but color by the pool on paper and watch a movie at night. That was boring and didn't interest me. By the pool, they sold Haagen Dazs chocolate almond bars. One was $4.50. That was so expensive, but people bought them, not us, the supermarket was much cheaper. They had a big dinner buffet at the hotel one night, Tour of Italy, all kinds of homemade pastas, pizzas and cakes. My Dad couldn't afford it, but kids were half price. It was $40 for adults, I think. Only I got it. I got samples of everything, but just picked at it, but for dessert my Dad said get one of each cake, then the manager saw and came around to our table and said you can't share, is all this for her? My Dad said yes and he walked away. There was chocolate cake, cheesecake, fruit tart.

MIRROR OF MY WORLD

Self-portrait, drawn when I was 14 and in the 8th grade.

Christian Karen Berman

LOSING GRANDMA LEE

We're home from the Hilton. Daddy is sitting on Grandma's tan, plaid-ish couch in the living room. It's early in the morning, around 9-10 am. I go sit on the floor to talk with him Indian style. He tells me they found her unconscious and not breathing and did CPR on her and saved her life by reviving her. That kinda was scary and shook me up. Real life to a 15-year-old in the mid-1990s. My world of 'nothing bad can happen' and 'doctors can fix everything' is confusing me, not good. We get ready to go and visit her.

At the hospital, they are going to operate on Grandma and the doctor is talking my parents out of the bypass on her infected foot. My Mom says it's my fault for telling the doctors my Grandma's real age, that I just found out myself. I thought she was 62. She's 84½. Thinking back, the doctors probably see her true age on her file. Later that day, before I leave, I'm not much of a hugger, but realize the severity of the tragic situation. I lean over her and give her a big, tight long hug. I remember my hand touching her plump, kinda sticky hand and her tubes touching me. My Mom and Larry are with me, my Dad's at home.

The next thing I remember is my Mom on our kitchen phone with the long curly white wires and I take the phone from her. I rarely ever spoke on the phone at that age, maybe a few years ago. It was my Grandma. I told her I hoped she would be okay, and she would. She hoped she would be okay, too.

The next thing I know my Dad takes us back for another vacation to The Rye Town Hilton. We pack a quick suitcase and go after visiting Grandma and talking to Dr. Finley, the one who would do the operation on her. In the back of my mind, I thought it was a mistake, the amputation, and the doctor should just do the bypass. It's too much work for him to do both if the first one didn't work.

MIRROR OF MY WORLD

We were walking in to have dinner there. I felt worried, like we made the wrong choice, but as a child, I didn't have any say. Maybe I should have strongly pressed the issue, but I couldn't be sure which was the right answer. It was bothering me a lot. We had dinner, Daddy a cheeseburger or grilled Ruben sandwich, me fried chicken, crispy fries and mustard slaw on the kid's menu, for dessert vanilla ice cream, wafer, cherry and whipped cream. I had been saving the stems of the cherries. I liked to bring something back with me. I did bring the kiddie menu and crayons back.

That night in the hotel, we talked to Grandma again on the phone. The doctor was going to do the amputation early in the morning. I was so nervous for her, I felt it myself. You would have thought I was being operated on in the early morning. I didn't want to sleep with Larry in the twin bed, I wanted to sleep next to my Daddy, so he let me and my Mom slept with Larry.

I was so worried for her, kept thinking of her. She didn't even eat dinner and she's diabetic. I woke up having trouble breathing, a lot of trouble breathing, I didn't know why. I told my Dad I can't breathe. I thought for sure he would rush me down to the E.R. and then I would be with my Grandma and be able to see her. I think we went to bed around 11:30 pm and it was now about 4:30 am. I wasn't faking, for sure. I never had this before and felt fine when I went to bed. I'm not sure why; too much chlorine from the swimming pool? He didn't even call my pediatrician, my Dad—he gave me my crayons for my kid's menu and a pad from the hotel or the back of the kid's menu and told me to draw a picture. He told me to draw on Larry's bed and had one night light on and my Mom went back to sleep with him. 4 am. I can't breathe and he wants me to color. I listened to him like I always do, and did, then a half hour later it went away and I was getting sleepy, so I finished my picture and went back to bed with my Daddy.

The next morning, I felt fine. It was probably hyperventilation due to extreme anxiety due to my worrying over my Grandma. No one told me that, though. Also, my Grandma was still waiting to have her operation. She couldn't eat so they have her on a saline drip. I felt such worry and pain in her. My Mom did, too. Oh, what worry for someone so young! I had such fear for what she was about to go through and barely comprehended it. Just the mere thought of it was agonizing. She couldn't even eat or drink for two days because of the horrible wait. I wonder what her blood sugar was? She must have been hungry.

The operation was completed. We went to visit her that night. She was in I.C.U. They let us go in two at a time. I went with my Dad and then again with Larry. I looked down where her leg should be. Horrible. It wasn't there and cut high above her knee. She had tubes all over her and even in her mouth. What a scary sight for her two loving young grandchildren to see. I was much more affected and sensitive to this.

I saw she also had a big diaper on. She told me to tell the nurse at the nurse station that she had to use the bathroom. I went over and told the nurse and she said, "She has a diaper on." I went back and told my Grandma this. I'm sure it broke her spirit and she couldn't really talk on the ventilator, but was mouthing the word, "Beverly," my Mom. She wanted to see her daughter. So my Dad and me did the right thing. I took one more last look at her, maybe said "I love you" and touched her hand, and walked back out to the waiting room with Daddy and told my Mom she was asking for her.

That early morning, at 5:30 am, Dr. Biers calls us and said to my Dad that if we wanna come and see her again, we'd better go soon. They were doing CPR on her and trying to save her. We were at home again by then and I was sleeping in the bed with my parents, but the phone woke me up. Overhearing what I thought I heard, shy, quiet me, was adamant that Dad give me the phone, he told the doctor I wanted to talk to him. I grabbed the phone and said, "Don't stop CPR, do whatever you can to save her, keep working on her. I don't want her to die. Please save her. Don't stop." I was loud. Strong. Determined.

I was wide awake now and didn't know if we could see her. Daddy didn't say. I wanted to. We anxiously waited for the doctor to call back with any news of how my Grandma was doing. Maybe it's best the phone didn't ring right away. I didn't want to know, rather not know. Why didn't Daddy rush us all down to see her, so she knew we needed her? She might have lived. Maybe because she couldn't use the bathroom, she lost all will to live and missed Grandpa and her parents too much. Her time on Earth was up. I waited downstairs, paced. No one talked. I went by Lucky Alexis's tank (our turtle).

The phone rang. Dr. Biers told us the bad news. No one talked. I went to Lucky Alexis's tank again trying hard to cry, because you're supposed to cry. I could barely force myself to cry, not sure why. I couldn't cry on command. It started to be a rainy, gloomy day. When people you love so much die, it always rains and thunders hard. What a sad day. Now it was just my immediate family. My parents were the real adults, and at least I had my parents. Now it was just the four of us, a closer-knit family, but empty and broken, different. Mom kept saying life was fragile to everyone, even to the gas station guy fixing our car.

I was sick, constantly touching my heart to make sure it was still beating, having trouble breathing evenly all the time. The Rabbi came over to give her condolences. Dad made everyone eggs, ketchup with potato chips, I barely ate. It was like that for days after. I wasn't even taken to my pediatrician.

I went to sleep in my parents' bed and woke up the same way on her funeral day. I don't know how I was able to put on my floral aqua sun dress and make it to the funeral. My Dad's mother came. I only saw her a few times, barely knew her. She was in the living room telling me about Brown, Daddy's imaginary friend at age four.

At the funeral, I tried not to cry and hold it in or let anyone see me crying and the tears. It affected me the most. Though after the funeral when she was buried, I felt a sigh of relief, like she was okay now, or it was over. My Dad told the Rabi and he said that was normal and common. My heart and breathing got better soon after. The stress was over and gone. Days later a praying mantis came right up to us at the end of my Dad's car. Never happened before. That was Grandma Lee saying goodbye and letting us know she was okay now. I would hear shushing noises in the kitchen a few times; that was her as well. Years later the downstairs TV set would turn on every day at 11 am and once a scary part of a TV show went off at exactly that part I was watching it to see. That was my Grandma looking out for my well-being. She's with my parents, her parents, and husband now.

You left a big, sad, gaping empty hole when you left our family. We missed you more than you'll ever know and more than we thought we would. We became a lonelier, sadder, isolated family and wished we had many more years with you. Even though you were 84½, you were sharp as a tack. I loved you. We all loved you. I know our lives would have been different, happier, and more fulfilled if you had stayed with us longer. Larry and I would have gone further in our education. Maybe my parents might have been healthier and lived longer. It's not fair to put the blame on you; you wanted to live. It's just that you fulfilled our lives more and there is a sad emptiness without your presence. Every person is important and when someone goes, you really notice how much they really meant to you and how they added to everyone's life. I hope you're with your husband, your parents, and my parents, and all the dogs we loved.

I loved the stories you would tell me, bribing me with five bucks to go to the second grade and I still played hooky and turned it down. I made the right choice, too. Watching all my favorite TV programs, exploring the basement, playing with all my toys and getting to spend a full day with my Mom & Grandma Lee was priceless, more than $1,000 wouldn't have meant as much as to have one whole day for me to relax and have the time to really live in the moment and enjoy my childhood.

I loved all my childhood days, especially the ones where I could just miss school and be myself, even if I was sick. It's nice just being at home sick and doing what you want and being loved, cared about, and fussed over. The days I was playing hooky were better, though. I could eat lunch, play with my toys and Larry, and even go outside, but I had to be careful that no one noticed. A kid outside playing at home or going out on a school day back in the mid-1980s was a real no-no. You had to be a little sneaky about it. I was sick and wanted to play on the porch at age seven. Grandma reluctantly let me but said if anyone came and tried to grab me and kidnap me to yell for her. Luckily no one ever did.

    I would always give her waist a big hug in the morning after she would say to me, "Good morning, Mary Sunshine." She really understood kids, but not why I did not like to go to school. Sometimes bribing me with a new Cabbage Patch Kid doll or a big stuffed musical Hello Kitty doll worked, more than five bucks did, anyway. I was something else and a piece of work, in a good way.

    When I was seven, you taught me how to play cat's cradle and how to braid my hair. You never got a chance to teach me how to knit and crochet, though. I wish you had more time to share more of your stories with me. You said you were never in the newspaper, so at age ten I wrote my own newspaper and mentioned you in one of the articles on white paper and red Flair pen. The other article was about the attack of the Allens, not Aliens, the Allens. My Dad said I spelled it wrong. I was a funny, adventurous, sweet and kind, generous, caring little kid. I hope I made you and Grandpa Jules proud of me.

    Grandpa Jules… I remember on Fridays you would bring me assorted green and pink leaf and pretzel-shaped bakery cookies and Grandma Lee would bring me nonpareil chocolates. I didn't like when you left to go home. I wish some days you could have stayed longer. I didn't like when you made me give some of my toys and stuffed animals to donate to the Salvation Army. I didn't like when you wanted me to sleep in my own bed and not with my Mommy and Daddy who were wonderful loving parents, I mean who wouldn't want to sleep with them? I didn't like when you wanted me to go to school, or when you came over to visit and then told my Mommy to give me and Larry baths early, because I wanted to spend quality time with you and Grandma Lee and play outside.

    I see now you wanted me to do all the good things I could learn. Honestly, I'm still trying to learn some of these things and it's still hard. I liked having hours in the afternoon with you to play heads-and-tails by flipping quarters, to make you dinner on my little Fisher Price stove with fresh grass, green weeds and dandelions. I remember I wanted this beautiful yellow rare rose growing in the middle of the woods in our backyard. You could see it. How it got there all alone is still a mystery to me, maybe just so I could share this story with everybody. The wind probably blew a magical seed there and it's a miracle it actually bloomed. You, all dressed up nice after work at the tailor shop, Hamilton Tailors, went to risk your life with the weeds of the jungle and thorns to walk to it and pull it off just because little me saw it, loved it, and wanted it, and you grabbed it, twisted it off, and bravely found your way back to me and gave it to "your little princess." It made me feel very special and important and happy, but my Mom was sad. "Now will no more roses grow back? Did you leave the root?" I thought only of the "now" and so did you, and Mom thought of the tomorrows. It was a thoughtful, selfless act on your part, just to try to make every day happy for little me.

I liked sitting on your lap. I remember you trimming my fingernails. I wondered why my parents couldn't, but you enjoyed trimming my little baby fingernails at five years old. I remember all these little, but important, details. Daddy did say you wondered why I didn't like to sit still on your lap and listen to you read. Early onset ADHD, perhaps.

We took long walks, but my legs were littler than yours and it was hard to keep up. You looked forward to time with me. You only had a short time left, but I don't think you knew that, so we had to make our time together on earth count.

I wonder what would have happened, how things would have been different, if you had only lived a few more decades. Would I have been brighter, tried harder, and went further in school, or would I still have rebelled a bit, and still liked to be a little slacker? As my Mommy would sing to me sometimes as a toddler and a few times in the later years, "Que sera sera, whatever will be will be, for our future's not ours to see, Que sera, Que sera." I guess we choose part of our future and the rest is just plain luck.

MIRROR OF MY WORLD

    I like to think I would have tried harder to make you proud growing up. It's sad you never got to see me as more than a six-year-old little girl, but sometimes growing up as a seven or eight-year-old, whether it was my imagination or not, I felt someone was watching me sometimes when no one was there. Maybe I pretended it or wished it was you, or as a natural actress I liked the imaginary, invisible audience to be a bit of a show-off. Maybe you and a few older relatives in heaven were watching how well I was turning out, by just by being plain old, adorable, charming, little me. I wish I had a home video of me at that time to look back on myself, but my Dad couldn't afford a camcorder until the late 1980s and even back then they were very expensive for a teacher's salary. I never forgot about you, Grandpa Jules, and I hope you watched over me and watched me grow up, too, and maybe helped me somewhere along the way.

    I love you and miss you, Grandma Lee and Grandpa Jules and Daddy and Mom.

A picture is worth 1,000 words. I'm age 15. My family is staying at the Rye Town Hilton. I'm with my favorite bear, Wuzzly. I slept with him until my early 20s. I still have this bear. My Mom bought it from Sears on December 12th 1990; it was the first day of Chanukah. She used to put him in the washing machine to keep him clean. You can see the happy look I'm giving to my Dad, who's taking the photo. Larry is relaxing on the carpet watching reruns of *Who's the Boss*. My hair is wet because I just came out of the swimming pool, then took a shower. My Grandma Lee is at the hospital, been there a month. We visited two or three times a day. It's about 25 minutes from the hotel. She's not going to make it more than another month, but I don't know that yet. The doctor's plan, after her leg amputation, is she's going to Burke Rehab to learn to walk with a prosthetic leg. She will have to stay there another month. She wants to go home, though, like right now. Misses home. She gives me Graham Crackers and milk from the hospital when I visit. I don't think they had a pantry back then. She has diabetes and is 84, so she's prone to bad infections. The I.V. meds didn't work. She has bad circulation. After she dies my life won't ever be the same, not carefree and happy—sickly, lonely, sad, troubled. She lived with us since I was age six and helped raised me after my Grandpa died. We all won't be happy anymore.

My Mom's probably taking a shower. It looks like we're going to dinner soon. Sometimes we ate dinner in the hospital cafeteria. It was pretty good for a hospital. Tonight, we're eating here. I'm going to eat my favorite on the kid's menu, fried crispy chicken, French fries, mustard coleslaw, with apple juice, dessert French vanilla ice cream and wafer triangle. Also, a kid's menu and crayons. They think I'm age 11. I'm not going to correct them. In the morning for the kid's buffet, since Larry and I don't drink coffee, the waitress makes us chocolate milk. My Dad knows her from his school cafeteria. She used to work there, remembers my Dad fondly. They talk about old times. When we first arrived we got a complimentary plate of homemade chocolate chip cookies when we went to the Cafe. Also at the front desk, kids' water bottle and fanny pack for Larry and me. My Dad took a large, insulated mint green diaper bag with little bears, my idea, to keep all of his medicines and lotions from getting too hot. This photo tells a whole story.

MIRROR OF MY WORLD

Christian Karen Berman

A HAPPY THANKSGIVING

I wanna share a Happy Thanksgiving I remember with everyone. I was age 15. I had been a very sickly, skinny 15-year-old, about 5'2" and 93 pounds. I couldn't even go trick-or-treating that year; it was raining and I sadly wasn't well. My brother had to ask for extra candy for me, then we split the candy. He was only age 11. I wasn't able to sleep and was up early. I had a cold and sore throat. I was in my room watching Q.V.C., the Home Shopping Network that was big in the mid-1990s. Everyone was talking about their turkey. Daddy came in my room to check on me around 5:30 am. I was stuffy, congested, and thirsty, so he put some ginger ale in my baby cup to sip and went back to sleep! I'm not sure if he checked my temperature.

Then it was the morning. I lined up all my very favorite stuffed animals in my parents' bedroom in front of the TV to watch the Macy's Thanksgiving Day Parade. Things seemed like a big deal back them, like everything was happy and mattered. We didn't have a TV in the living room back then, just in the two bedrooms. I got bored watching the parade. My favorite character back them was the Big Bird balloon.

Then I went downstairs. Daddy made me fresh hot oatmeal with half-and-half cream and maybe banana slices on top. I actually liked it and finished it. I rarely ate breakfast or oatmeal. Daddy ate it every day. Not the kiddie kind which I did it sometimes (yeah, they had those back in the 1990s). Daddy made it in the pot. I was getting bored. I think he put some Christmas music on the radio and took some photos outside. I think we even had Thanksgiving pictures on our living room windows, like a scarecrow and pumpkin. I know we use to put Halloween ones on our door and living room windows.

MIRROR OF MY WORLD

As a kid, each holiday was a big deal. I had a box turtle named Lucky Alexis then. This was the first Thanksgiving without my Grandma Lee. She died in August of a leg amputation from gangrene; she had diabetes.

We got ready to go out to a diner and eat dinner. My parents ordered two plates and split it with me and my brother. We had no family then, either, and no one could cook. We couldn't afford much, and I didn't eat much anyway. Turkey plate with all the fixings. It was good, and chocolate cake for dessert. It was about a 20-minute ride to the diner, so we listened to beautiful Christmas music on the way and back.

Then at home I watched TV and had a candy cane, roasted mixed nuts, Christmas cookies and ate Triples cereal. I loved that cereal. I miss it, it was really good. I wish that they still made it. I only had one real meal that day so maybe I was hungry.

The only memory I have with an actual family on Thanksgiving Day is when I was five years old. Grandpa woke me up. I was napping on the couch and tired. My Grandma and Mom cooked an actual real turkey and dinner in the oven. I remember I didn't like it and was very tired and would have rather kept sleeping. I did hate when my Grandpa had to leave and go back home. I wish he could have stayed longer. He had diabetes and had to take his insulin, I guess. He died two months after I turned six, a heart attack from an accidental insulin overdose. My Grandma died when I was 15. There really wasn't any family but them.

My Grandpa came over every day after school and played with me. He brought ice cream, chocolate nonpareils and assorted bakery cookies. He probably shouldn't have, but that's what Grandparents do and I was a skinny five-year-old, too! He also took me and my Mom to McDonald's once when I was four. I had a plain hamburger, that's all.

[Christian Karen Berman](#)

THE LAST DAY OF SCHOOL BEFORE CHRISTMAS VACATION, 10TH GRADE

That day before school lets out for Christmas vacation is the best day to go. It's filled with excitement. What a relief—this would be the last day for a while! It's usually a fun day with free candy canes and Christmas movies, plus I liked school sometimes. It was fun hanging out in my school library looking up stuff, talking to the librarians, three ladies with white and grey short hair in their late 60s, one taller and heavyset, having them teach me to use the microfilm machine and Xerox things I liked and wanted to save, to look up old stuff and take some interesting things home to read.

The year before I had read every issue of *Parents Magazine* the school library owned, cover to cover. They had from the years 1988 to the early 1990s. Just for fun, during my free periods over the year, a hobby of mine I enjoyed looking at older car seat models and learning about child development and enjoying looking at the photos in the magazine, too, always wishing my parents had given me a real baby sister. That's why I carried my Kid Sister doll Jen all the time, from age 11 3/4's to age 16. All my parents' friends had one more kid. I would have been so happy, I was too young to express it in words that I wanted a baby sister, but my actions spoke louder than words—necessity is the mother of invention. Also back then *Parents Magazine* went up to age 18. I was reading about child-rearing and learning about psychology and how to be a good mother, but to me, it was just fun and I was enjoying reading it. I was only age 15 at the time, always looking forward to the end of the day when my Mom would pick me up from school and I could see her, then she drove me home and started making dinner and soon my Daddy and brother would be home from school.

MIRROR OF MY WORLD

History Class was early in the morning, maybe my second period class. The teacher was really nice, too, and bought us all a cinnamon and sugar twisted donut stick from a donut shop in two big boxes to make this day even more special for us. Money out of his own pocket. Most ate them in class, but I wrapped mine up and put it in my backpack to save it for after school. I hoped it would be okay next to my books, and last.

I remember walking to my next class, it was around 10 am. I knew the lady math teacher had a meeting with my parents the day before because she and another teacher were worried I lost some weight and wanted me to gain some weight back over Christmas break. I was not happy about that. My parents told me about this. It was nice they all cared, but it felt awkward, though. I had gained weight, I was 110 pounds. I lost weight on purpose. I was just a little too heavy. I lost weight by eating an apple before dinner and more veggies with my diner. Not like I didn't know why I was losing weight; I wanted to be skinnier again and there was so much walking in school, down all the long hallways and up and down many flights of stairs—it was a really big school, you know.

I guess I might have walked the halls a little extra on my frees for more exercise and to visit my friend the nurse just to talk. She was in her late 60s and enjoyed my company and she said I should be more independent and walk a few blocks after school for exercise. I didn't do that then, until the spring. It was cold and I was still young to walk the streets alone after school. Even my guidance counselor had said I should get more exercise and walking the halls in school didn't count. I even thought it was a lot of walking. I think my weight went to 97 pounds. I was about 5'3" then. I'm 5'4" now, my weight fluctuates from 104-108 now, I guess that's my standing resting body weight, as my Dad taught me.

Next was lunch. I never ate lunch in high school, so that's when I went to the school library to talk to my librarian friends and have fun, maybe read a *Parents Magazine* or look up my favorite actors in the big red book of *Who's Who in America*, not knowing my own father would be in those book in the future for being one of the best teachers in the world and *Who's Who in the World*.

After was Sculpture, Mr. Dabney. I had asked special permission once again. The first was a tribute bust of Ted Knight from *The Mary Tyler Moore Show*. I was a fan of the show and of Ted. This time it was a Christmas present for my Mom and Dad, a big ceramic heart and written on it was "Merry Christmas Mommy and Daddy, Love, Kay-Kay." Half of the heart was painted green, the other half red and I pushed my hand down on both, for them to have my hand forever. You could even see the lines in my palm and finger prints too, embedded in the ceramic, plus I had also dipped my hand in red paint to make it stand out even more, it came out great, better than expected. I got that idea from watching *To Grandmother's House We Go*, where Mary-Kate and Ashley Olsen, a/k/a "Sarah and Julie," leave their Mom a clay ceramic handprint that they made in kindergarten as her Christmas present before they run away to their Great Grandmother's house to give their Mom a vacation from them.

MIRROR OF MY WORLD

    Then in English class, there was a Christmas Party. Some students brought Edy's or Dreyers ice cream, three big tubs of ice cream. I didn't eat any, I can't remember why exactly. but I think they had soda, chips, and cheese puffs and two classes watched a movie, maybe *The Grinch that Stole Christmas.* That part is fuzzy in my memory, but what I do remember was before class ended they asked if anyone wanted to take home the leftover ice cream. I happily raised my hand and volunteered to take the chocolate chip flavor and vanilla bean. I guess the other kids had ice cream at home or their Mom would buy them ice cream. This was a "'no no" in my house at that time and a forbidden treat, not weight related but because my parents thought for sure it would give me a sore throat to have anything ice cold like ice cream and popsicles. It wasn't until I was 16, 17, they loosened up this rule. Me taking home ice cream helped pave the way, I believe. The teacher said it would be in the freezer in the teacher's lounge and to pick it up at the end of school day. Yay, I get yummy ice cream for free, two big containers of it, too.

    The long day was wearing on me. I was starting to feel sick, like really sick, not faking. School was almost over and I would be getting free ice cream—why would I want to leave early. I felt icky, hot and cold, chills, headachy clammy, kinda achy. I was a little tired. Did I eat breakfast that day? My Dad used to make breakfast some days before he left before his school, homemade pizza bagel with ketchup, Heinz baked beans and mustard or brown shredded wheat and banana slices with milk or cream cheese on a toasted bagel with ketchup and potato chips. I can't remember if I ate breakfast that day or I was just running late, slept late, and just ran out. Either way, I knew I was sick. Not getting sick, but already sick. I had all the symptoms I felt when I was sick and what a time for it to come on all of a sudden, right out of the blue. Maybe it was from sitting in a room full of kids snacking and watching a movie gave it to me. I guess I caught a germ from another kid that works fast, one minute fine and dandy and the next minute sick as a dog. I had no time to go to anyone but the closest nurse. Our school had two nurses. The other nurse was stricter, never sent me home, never thought I was sick enough, just had me lie down in the other room and rest. Once when I was having an allergy to another classmate's very strong perfume and started to feel short of breath and have trouble breathing, she didn't even really believe me or want to send me home. Well, anyway, after lying down and being bored for twenty minutes, the allergy slowly went away and she sent me back on my way to my next period class. She didn't even let me use her phone and call my Mom to come pick me up from school.

Well, I was supposed to walk to health class, but instead I took a quick detour to the "mean," "cold" nurse's office. She was closer by and I was starting to feel worse. It was an emergency. I walked in, the time was about 1:30 pm nearing the end of a long day, and I said, "I don't feel well," and sat down. She's the one that said "You carry your whole life in your backpack." Yes, I felt that way, too. It was true, full of books, my binder, notebooks, and Xeroxes. Easier than having to constantly go to your locker, just one less thing to worry about. I liked having all my stuff with me at all times. She said something like, "School is over in an hour and it's the last day before Christmas vacation, couldn't you tough it out?" and took my temperature with one of those newfangled, pre-wrapped plastic disposable thermometer strips. I put the cool hard plastic, very thin, long strip under my tongue as far as it would go and nervously waited. Would it show a fever to validate how sick I really felt? It couldn't just be in my head. The nurse was waiting and thinking, I bet she doesn't even have a fever, school's almost over—why is she playing sick now? I honestly didn't feel well. It just came on all of a sudden. I rarely ever run a fever, especially at school, when you want to. She took it out and looked at it. It was 101.7. I was very sick. I did have a fever. Well, what do ya know? I'm sure she was very surprised, too. She was about 5"6, a light brown and grey short men's haircut and average weight, blouse, long tan shirt, and eyeglasses.

"Are you going to call my Mom and send me home?" I said. She just asked me to tough it out until the end of the day. I reluctantly agreed, but was surprised she wouldn't send me home The one time I actually go to the school nurse and I'm really sick and even have a fever—how often does a miracle like that happen? Not often at all, a few times in your life as a student, maybe. She doesn't send me home. I actually had forgotten about the free ice cream at this point, because I was feeling so sick, so luckily I stayed another hour. School ended at 2:35 pm. I told her I was late for health class and if she would please write me a hall pass and a late note, which she did and said feel better and maybe wished me a Merry Christmas.

I arrived at health class and handed my lady teacher the note. She did look similar to my school nurse. I was having trouble passing this class and a few months later my Dad had to call her from his school and beg her to pass me with a 65, same for my Spanish class teacher. I told my teacher I had 101½ temperature and the nurse wouldn't send me home and I feel sick. She told me to just rest my head on the desk. I did and held my forehead and looked at her like, you know I'm sick, send me home. I think I was having a sick headache, too. She said class will be over soon. It seemed long, but soon ended and I could leave. I walked back to the English Department and asked where they put the containers of ice cream. A teacher thankfully showed me, walked me there and gave them to me and then I was free for a while, free to go, my day was over, now to find my Mom, tell her I'm sick and go home and bring my ice cream to our freezer before it melted. She was surprised I was carrying 2 big containers of ice cream and that I was really sick and had to go to the school nurse and I was so glad to see her and finally be going home. All in all, a very good, memorable day, except for the parts I forgot.

I wrapped up their present with Christmas wrap and surprised them with it on Christmas morning. They liked it and were happily surprised. I do remember being pretty sick, fever, not able to eat much, watching a lot of Christmas shows and movies. The first night I was feeling a little better, I begged for my ice cream and dug into it, eating a lot from each container, and it was so good, cool and creamy. It was a rare treat and helped me feel better sooner. Lowered my fever and soothed my sore throat. I was probably watching *The Muppets Christmas Carol* or a special. I can't remember much of anything besides getting to eat lots of ice cream at home while I was recovering from a bad case of the flu.

Christian Karen Berman

A Baby Sister!

On April 1, 1996, we adopted my baby sister, Mary! It was a cold, raw, rainy day in New York. It was one of the happiest days in my life, because I always wanted a baby sister and a red golden retriever since I was a little girl. We already had a Shih Tzu puppy named Ritchie Patrick who was nine months old and I was so happy my Daddy added a very welcome second puppy as a new member of our family. She was very sweet, smart, affectionate and very loved by both my parents and me and my brother Larry. I taught her how to use a baby busy box and she understood English and listened to us in the first few days. We treated her as a baby and child, she didn't really know she was a puppy or a dog. She was born January 20th, 1996. Very sadly she didn't stay with us as long as I wanted. She died just shy of her 13th birthday, January 2nd, 2009.

I have missed her very, very much since and she was the best sister you could ever have. We useta have a secret handshake where I'd say SISTERS FOREVER, and she'd give me both her paws, a double high-five! When it was cold in the winter, we'd snuggle together to keep warm. When Daddy came home from work, I'd say, "Daddy's home!", and she'd get off the couch and run to the front door wagging her tail and then go to the kitchen excited and lying on the floor waiting for us to give her the leftovers of our take-out dinner. She was one of the family, loved to kiss and hug with both her paws and sat on the couch like us, understood almost everything, and very much like a human child.

It was the worst day ever when she left us, but the happiest times was in the summer when she'd run faster than me to the backyard and race me to see Daddy. I used to say, "Race ya!", and boy could she run fast! She loved to run, eat, give high-five's, chase Ritchie around the house and fall down and roll over and play with him,

MIRROR OF MY WORLD

when she got him. They were a close brother and sister and loved each other, too.

Some of my nicknames for her were Pumpkin, Stups, Mom. When I came downstairs in the morning, I'd say, "How's my little Poophead?" and I'd rub the top of her head and she'd look up at me and wag her tail. When we first brought her home, I couldn't decide on a name. She went though many names—Ashley, Emily, Brighten, Margie, Samantha, Mary-Kate, Mallory. The vet got very confused. Mary-no-name probably did, too, even though she was only eight weeks old! So, for a week we didn't call her anything until I finally decided on a simple sweet Catholic sister saint's name, MARY THERESA! My Dad musta bought me books for baby names, too, and then I go pick a simple pure name like Mary! It fit really well, too. She was a real sweetheart. A very well-behaved, loving, caring and nurturing daughter and sister and Mother.

MIRROR OF MY WORLD

Christian Karen Berman

CONNECTICUT

My Dad took us on vacation to Meriden, Connecticut in 1996. The boarding school was called Choate Rosemary Hall in Wallingford. He had to go to a private school over there to study up about a new course he had to take in A.P. Statistics and he had to take us all with him. I had to leave my seven-month-old puppy Mary at the vets to stay over. I remember I cried a lot after I gave her to them. It was the first time we had ever been apart, and I loved her very much. I felt I was giving her away and my Dad bought me her. That was sad; I just burst into tears crying. I was crying uncontrollably. I couldn't help it.

The next day, we left. We stopped at Friendly's Restaurant in Mount Kisco on the way. The little guy came with us—Ritchie Patrick. I got a mint chocolate chip ice cream sugar cone and I didn't like the chocolate chip part, so I gave that to Ritchie. I was just a teenager then and didn't know dogs weren't allowed to have chocolate, especially small 20-pound dogs that were only a year old. Looking back, I feel bad about that, but it wasn't all that much and he was fine.

Then we all were tired when we finally got there. There were two rooms, one with one big bed for my parents and another room for me and my brother with two twin beds. I couldn't sleep in a strange room in a strange state with my brother, so I went to go sleep with my Daddy. I think we all ended up in that bedroom, my brother maybe on the floor in a blanket with a pillow! Daddy had to get up very early and drive to the school, like at 6:30 am. They all went to have the breakfast buffet, everyone but me. I was asleep on the bed and they left me alone with a one-year-old Shih-Tzu.

We were staying at the Ramada Inn, not exactly 5 stars, but it was okay. I woke up to a loud, barking Ritchie jumping on me and giving me little dog bites and nips on my back to get up, literally biting my back or wherever he could, my arms, he would not let me sleep! I didn't want to get up. I didn't even know what to do, he was being the boss of me! I had to wake up, put my sneakers on and take him for a walk in a strange place alone with no permission of my parents. They didn't know where I was or would be going alone, but I did. Ritchie didn't give me a choice; he wouldn't leave me alone!

He was a very smart puppy. I thought he had to pee. I took him outside, I think we were on the 3rd or 4th floor. I took the stairs. Then I went inside to find my Mom and Dad. I think they wouldn't let a dog in the restaurant, but my Mom saw me, and Larry took Ritchie, and I went to go see Daddy. They saved a couple of packaged granola berry bars for me. They were good but Daddy had real food—eggs, bacon, fried potatoes, toast and butter, ketchup, oatmeal, coffee and orange juice. Then he had to go to work and leave me alone all day.

There was no lifeguard for the swimming pool. It said, "swim at your own risk" and you needed parental supervision if you were under 18. My Mom didn't want me to go swimming. She couldn't swim and I'm not the best swimmer; I can't go in the deep end, so that was disappointing and very sad. I was getting very bored.

Mom bought me a Diet Lemon Snapple. The ice machine and the vending machines were the highlights of the hotel, sadly. Then I brushed my hair, washed my jeans in the washing machine (my Mom helped me with that, I didn't know how!). Then we went downstairs.

Another highlight from the trip—free Hostess Mini white powdered sugar donuts, as many as you can eat. They were in a big glass bowl with red Kool-Aid in another big glass bowl. I'm thinking we didn't have much money; that was my breakfast and lunch. I had five mini-donuts and maybe two cups of red punch. My snack was a low-fat, light Milky Way from the vending machine.

We took a ride in a van to Ames. It's like a small Kmart store. They give you a free ride. My Mom could drive but Daddy took the car to his seminar at the private boarding school. We looked around for an hour. That's as much time as they give you. Honestly, it wasn't a fun trip. Boring, dullsville, but an adventure.

Then nap time in the room till 4ish, then Daddy came home. Then he and my family went to Friendly's to eat. I had to babysit Ritchie in the car. The restaurant didn't allow dogs, lucky me! I don't think I was allowed to have the engine and radio on. It wouldn't be safe; I could get kidnapped! The window was open. It was hot, July or August.

They took out for me a chicken parm sandwich with fried onions. I ate that in the hotel room. Another night, Daddy gave me half of his turkey bacon club sandwich with Russian dressing with French fries and ketchup. Another day, we went to McDonald's. I remember loving the vanilla ice cream cone. We went back again the next day just to get me another one.

I did go swimming once with Larry. I brought Wuzzly, my favorite teddy bear I had since age 12. I always slept with him. We all slept in one room. They also gave you free toothbrushes at the front desk. I think it was the only vacation I was happy to come home from. This photo was taken in the hotel lobby by the front desk.

MIRROR OF MY WORLD

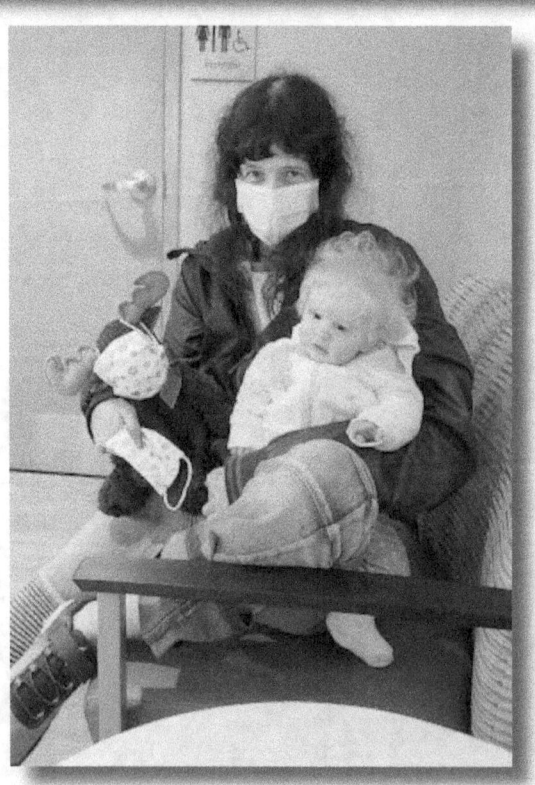

Christian Karen Berman

EVERYBODY'S SICK (IT'S ABOUT EVERYONE BEING SICK)

As a teen and young adult this was one of the most depressing times in my life, one of the worst times in my life up until then (oh, if I only knew the worst was to come).

When we all were sick together.

I remember one time, I was 17 to 23, not sure which time it was because it's kind of a blur and there were many times we all got sick together. It was not fun seeing my Dad, my protector and caregiver, sick. My Mom and Dad would be lying in their big bed with the light on in the middle of the day. No one eating much or eating real food. No one doing much but sleeping and throwing up and taking their temperature. I was lying on the floor next to my Dad in the bed. On the floor, feeling sick, too, but who was sicker? The game we would play—it's Time for the Temp. We would all take our temps the baby way back then and the one with the highest fever wins. Does everyone play that game or just us?

My Dad would talk about what to do for dinner or call his doctor for medicine. My Dad would pick up his medicine at an old-time pharmacy and not a CVS. As for dinner, my Dad would usually want SpaghettiOs and toast and margarine. My Mom wouldn't let him, or approve of it. Well, one time when I was sick at age eight and after I barfed and wanted Beef Ravioli in the can and said I was hungry and told my Mom that I wouldn't throw it up, because I was hungry and wanted it, she finally gave in and guess what, who lost? I was wrong. I threw it right back up, but thought I could handle it. He'd end up having margarine, cream cheese and jelly, sometimes even add Skippy Peanut Butter on white Home Pride toast and dunk it in hot Lipton tea or coffee or make hot Quaker Instant Oatmeal, put in and half-and-half and the pink packets of Sweet'N Low, of course. Yuck! There was Campbell's Chicken

MIRROR OF MY WORLD

Noodle soup or Vegetable soup, Tropicana Orange Juice, Canada Dry Ginger Ale, saltines. Yucky stuff no one wants to eat, even if they are sick. I can't remember what I ate sick, but once Daddy brought me a 10-calorie, sugar free, Starburst Pop, then a second one of a different flavor. Those were so good! Wish they didn't discontinue it like they did the Pudding Pops in early 2000. I was sleeping in my pink and purple Oshkosh winter coat, in my early 20s. It was so nylonily silky inside and comfortable, a girl's 14, and I would say it's the color of grape Children's Tylenol and Pink Amoxicillin, because it truly was. I loved it.

I remember one time at age 17, I woke up feeling not good. Weird. Sick. Went into my parents' room and told them my throat feels funny. Then a few minutes later, I went to the bathroom, threw up, felt better, but stayed there and maybe threw up a few more times and feel asleep on the cold tile bathroom floor. I was so weak and tired, afraid to leave the bathroom, too. I needed to be by there. I woke up feeling so thirsty, I think my Mom called my pediatrician and they said I could only have a few tablespoons of apple juice an hour or I'd throw up again. I did. I'm not sure if my Dad went to work or stayed home. Maybe it was the weekend, think only I was sick then. It wasn't fun, but I felt loved and cared about more than before.

Another time Larry had gotten me this baby doll in a yellow box dressed up like a bumble bee with two little baby teeth at CVS, either the before-Christmas sale or after. I think it was before. Larry later was throwing up in the downstairs bathroom. I felt bad for him, but it was gross. I did feel happy I got the small doll, then worried about the germs, but it was okay, still factory sealed in the box. Another time after I threw up, we were all having the stomach flu. Daddy, or my Mom and Larry, went to Italian Village Pizzeria and got many Italian ices all around—lemon, rainbow, chocolate. He told them we were all sick. I'm sure the pizza place just loved to hear that and loved to hear we picked them to go to and share all of our germies with them. They were handheld sizes and about six of them. I was sick, but so weak and so thirsty I took rainbow and was licking it. My big red dog Mary sitting next to me sick, seemingly concerned about me. She wasn't more than a puppy then, maybe only a year or two years old. She was sweet. I was sitting down licking it. She didn't even make a grab for it. Then later, sitting next to me when I was sitting on the floor, by the door frame of the bathroom door, she was next to me watching me and rested her head on top of my legs. I just felt I better stay by the bathroom a while, just in case. She cared about me. I barely knew her then; she was just a baby.

Another sweet memory when I was older and sick, I think age 19 or a few years older, I was lying in my parents' bed on my Mom's side by the door. She actually made me homemade chicken noodle soup, by scratch or possibly using Mother's Chicken Matzo Ball soup and adding real chicken drum sticks in it. I'm not sure how she did it, but she made a real effort, not just opening a can of Campbell's Chicken Noodle soup. She didn't have a table or tray so she went into my room and used my Lego kid's table, you know it had little circle bumps so the Lego's would stick in; it was green, red, blue, and yellow, four squares. Yeah, they had that in the late 1990s. I'm not that old, as you might think. She put my soup in a bowl on the table next to my bed. My Dad carried the Lego table in and Ginger ale or orange juice.

Once when I was seven or eight and lying in my brother's bed, my Dad was there and could tell I was going to be sick. He picked me up and tried to rush me to the bathroom, but he didn't make it far or fast enough. He had to clean it up by the heating vent by the bedroom door. That's one of the worst jobs of being a parent, but I guess if you love your kid enough, you love everything about them or accept it. No one else wants to do it. Who do you call? No one. You just suck it up and do it yourself.

Now when I'm sick I'm never as sick as when I was a little child. Larry and I get yummier sick foods, Sugar-Free Jell-O, green or red sugar-free Popsicles, assorted sugar-free juices and Gatorade. I like Campbell's Chicken Noodle soup now. It reminds me of my childhood and not as bad as you think, plus it really does help you feel better right away.

We're honestly still big kids, love Trix yogurt so much. So glad they finally brought it back. It was always my favorite. All the kids 80s and 90s foods we still love. Fruit snacks. I think my parents

MIRROR OF MY WORLD

must be looking down and thinking we're kids in a candy store. Cheese hot dogs, hot Cheeto's, Smores, Lucky Charms. I still have my kid tastes and sometimes enjoy those cheap, inexpensive foods best. I used to eat every Lunchable they would make, Pancake and Nachos were my favorite. I even miss Kid Cuisine, thinking of trying that again. I eat healthy when I feel like it, but then get bored and want to eat something good.

Christian Karen Berman

MY LaTe TeeNS

I haven't written much about my late teens, 20s and early 30s. It's because it doesn't seem like that long ago, like my early years do, those I miss the most. I remember I watched so much TV back then. *Thunder Alley* with Edward Asner and Haley Joel Osment, I would watch while I was in high school. It was on at night. I'd eat a stuffed pizza slice and Rice Krispies Treats cereal after. I loved that TV series. It wasn't on long though, 1994-1995. I watched *Grace Under Fire* reruns, *Brotherly Love* reruns, *The Suite Life of Zack and Cody, Cake TV*, and movies like *How to Eat Fried Worms*.

On the weekends my Dad would take us to Kids-R-Us. They would send us flyers with 20% off and had the coolest clothes, great sales. I would buy these black jeans with a chain on them in the back pocket, rocking cool. I also bought this dark pink and purple Oshkosh coat with snow overalls, it fit well, kept me warm and comfortable. I could fit in a 14 and 16 size. I loved it so much, I would sleep in it when I was sick. I watched the movie *Stepmom* and the old movie *The Little Prince*. I would write a lot of scripts and pretend I was a real TV writer. I watched Nancy Grace in my 30s. We would also go to Toys-R-Us and the Playground.

I had the freedom to eat what I liked as a young adult and didn't have to eat my Mom's cooking. She was a sweet mom, but I didn't like her cooking or my Dad's going to the deli. I didn't like most of the food they tried to feed me or Chinese. I ate potato chips and a can of baked beans or chili baked beans, Trix cereal, Oreo's and milk, and Lunchables, the nacho and cheese and the pancake one. In my early 20s, I still liked kids' food and junk food. I ate Pizza Hut sometimes, half meat lovers, half veggie, the child spaghetti and meat sauce. Papa John's, Little Caesar's Pizza, Taco Bell, K.F.C., Charlie Brown's, Outback Steakhouse. I miss the late 1980s foods so much. Nabisco Giggles cookies where the best.

MIRROR OF MY WORLD

1994 Triples cereal. I also loved Betty Crocker Fruit Snacks in my early 30s, My Little Pony, they stopped making them. Yummy. I tried many fruit snacks. They changed the recipe, they are so terrible. Larry couldn't even eat them and we had to throw them out. Fruit Roll-ups too.

I wish they would bring back some of the good old snacks from the late 80s and 90s. My Mom got me Whistle Pops, you suck them and when you would blow on them, it would whistle. I was like 10. Keebler had these Crispy Sour Cream & Onion Potato Crisp, light and airy, or crackers. Fruit and oatmeal Swirlers cereal. The snacks aren't as good as they used to be. I haven't seen sherbet pops in a year, the rainbow push up frozen sticks. I miss the Starburst Sherbet Pops, only 20 calories, they were so yummy. Trix Yogurt they brought back, but not all the flavors. I love those.

I wish it was the late 1980s now. I wish I could walk into my house and it'd be the good old days. I now understand the saying, "You can never go home again." Even though it's the same house and I'm home, it's not the same, my home.

In all the years I lived here, my Mom changed lightings, got rid of the shutters I loved, got new furniture, carpets, it's much older too, but mostly it has no parents, Grandma Lee or turtle Lucky Alexix and goldfish Dodger. I remember in the movie *Artificial Intelligence*, when David finally came home, it wasn't the same. It was so sad. I cried the few times I watched that part, with the tall skinny robots. I can't watch anything that makes me cry like that. *The Lovely Bones* made me cry. I ran into my parents' room sobbing to my Dad and jumped in his bed crying hysterically. I think I woke him up. He was worried and didn't know why I was crying. When I was finally able to stop crying, I told him. It was the part where the girl was looking in her parents' house, wishing she could go home and be back with them, but someone hurt her, so she couldn't. I only saw it once. I didn't like crying so hard, so I never saw it again, but that's what it means—you can never go home again.

Christian Karen Berman

ONE OF MY GOOD DEEDS

I was age 19. It was in February, late at night, about 11:30 pm. I was probably in my bedroom at the time, working on a new script by hand. I wanted to be a TV writer and was dedicated to writing TV dramadies. I was pretending I was a real TV writer and my wish was to be at the Emmy's one day with my people where I belonged. *Promised Land* and *Chicago Hope* were some of the shows I loved at the time.

My Dad and brother had eaten a BLT or a grilled cheese with greasy, undercooked bacon and fries and coleslaw at one of the diners we would go to often and were very sick with food poisoning, sick enough that they had to go to the E.R. this late at night. I think the doctor on call told them to, or it was just THAT BAD and they were THAT SICK. I won't go into detail, but it's what you think, both.

I can't remember what I ate. Maybe a cheeseburger or turkey club, maybe a kid's chicken fingers plate. Knowing me, I probably didn't eat anything, maybe just a bag of potato chips and organic Jewish canned bean chili at home. I'm not sure what my Mom ate, but she didn't get sick; maybe scallops and shrimp and pasta and broccoli with a baked potato. She liked that stuff.

Why did I even go? I wasn't sick. Surely they didn't need me tagging along. I loved adventures at age 19 and we rarely ever went to the E.R back then, especially anywhere after 7 pm. I couldn't miss this. Yes, to me it was the most exciting adventure, like I was Nathanial on the TV series *Promised Land*. I knew they were sick, but nothing really bad ever happened back then and everything always turned out okay in the end, just like in the happily-ever-after fairy tales.

It was about 12:30 pm. I was in the waiting room alone. I think they wouldn't let me go in, too. I was bummed about that, didn't want to miss any excitement. There were many empty chairs.

MIRROR OF MY WORLD

Then three teenagers came in. Two boys were in a real gang knife fight and got stabbed and they were bleeding enough for even me to see. Their shirts were ripped with some scratches on them and a black eye, aged 17 and 18. It was kinda cool and scary at the same time, like this was almost TV. A 16-year-old girlfriend was with them and started talking to me and asking me my age. I said guess. She was saying I can't be older than her.

Then a nice black lady with a toddler girl came through the entrance doors. The 16-year-old girl started talking to the baby who was a little sick, but while we were waiting, we were so bored and talking to each other. No iPhones to distract you or play with, no texting, talking or taking photos. Everyone asking why everyone else was there and actually talking and getting to know each other. There was a TV on, maybe it was a news channel, but no one was interested. There was one payphone at the end of the waiting room, but it was hard to work and there were people using it. Besides, my family was all here and accounted for, the only ones I could call was our puppies asleep in their crates. We wouldn't trust them alone yet. They roughhoused a lot. We wouldn't want them to gang fight and hurt each other, too. Nah, but just to be on the safe side, I had a 16-pound, 16-month-old Shih-Tzu and an 86-pound, one-year-old red Retriever. They played. The little guy usually always won, too.

Then the nurses took everybody in the back to the E.R. to be seen and I was alone, except for an older Spanish couple in their early 50s. They were closely sitting next to each other. I walked over to make conversation, being a bored teenager and getting used to talking to strangers during the long wait. My parents and brother were in the E.R, not the waiting room. The woman was heavyset, with long black hair in a back ponytail, both still wearing their winter coats. The lady was crying, to my surprise. So I asked her what was wrong. I'm not sure she understood English, nor could her husband, and I couldn't understand much Spanish. I got a 65 in it in high school.

She was holding her heart in pain and the loving, supportive thin husband was very upset too and was trying to tell me something. I had seen him go to the front desk before in vain a few times and try to explain, but was shooed away rudely and told to wait and it's not his turn yet. Maybe he didn't have insurance, I don't know. This upset me so much and made me worry for her crying in pain. There was someone in the security office that was supposed to be watching us from a small surveillance room to make sure there was no problems. He was sound asleep at his desk. So I went to the front desk. No one there. The whole place was empty now, so I yelled to them from where I was. They were in a hall and then a different room. I said loudly "Nurse, Nurse, Doctor. This Lady needs to be seen now, she is very sick and I think she is having a heart attack." (I was worried her husband would be able to understand me and worry more.) "Can you please take her to the back? Is there a doctor here? Can you help her? Does anyone hear me? Is anyone there?" No one came out or heard me.

This was before people were super vigilant, before 9/11 "see something, say something." It was 1998. The couple looked at me desperately and helplessly, pleading for help. So, I went to the other front of the E.R and tapped first, then knocked hard and loudly on the glass window and woke the black security guard and said it seriously and urgently. "This woman needs a doctor, she is having a heart attack. I tried to tell the nurse, but no one is there and no one can hear me." He woke up by his computer and unlocked the door and walked out of the office and walked over to the couple and the husband smiled and nodded at me and said thank you. The guard finally took me seriously and quickly escorted them out the door to where the E.R. was. When the guard came back he acknowledged me, too, with a nod and I smiled back.

I was so pleased and proud of myself for speaking out for a sweet couple who couldn't speak for themselves and defending their rights. I was usually shy. This was out of character for me, but she was very sick and needed help and no one was listening to her husband or understanding him. I felt urged to do this. It was a strong gut feeling that took over me. Also, chatting with the teenagers made me feel more like talking to strangers in the E.R, like it was more acceptable.

I was the only one in the E.R. left and by now it was close to 2 am. It was a long wait and a long night. I was watching TV now. I was so proud and looking forward to telling my Dad when he got out. I think my Mom came out once or twice to quickly check on me. I didn't tell her, though.

Also, coming to the E.R. was also research in my mind for a new script for me to write about, so I know more what the E.R. was firsthand. Last time I went Larry had a broken leg and I was 14. The time before that I was age 11 and had bad bronchitis at 11:30 pm as well. So it was rare we ever went to the E.R. What if I stayed home that night and just watched TV and went to sleep, would the lady have been seen in time to help save her?

I finally got to go visit my Dad and Larry when my Mom came out for about ten minutes. 'Only one visitor' rule, I guess, or they thought I was too young. They were hooked up to I.V. fluids in different curtained cubicles, but the curtain between them was a bit opened. There was an emesis tray there, too, and maybe a big bucket. There wasn't much to do or see and I think my Dad didn't want me to catch anything and get sick, too, so I went back out to the waiting room.

I'm not sure if I told him now what I had done or waited until we got home. I might have told him, but both had a 102 fever and were tired, not sure if he understood me then. I got bored and went back to the waiting room and my Mom went back to them both.

It was so nice to have a real family; this is what a true, real family is, that sticks together in sickness and in health. I never thought I would be like the orphans I use to write about, some got fostered and adopted. I never thought this would happen to me and I'd be without a family for real.

Soon the teens were discharged and so was the lady with the two-year-old girl. We all reunited, the 16-year-old with sandy blonde hair picked up the black chubby cute girl and gave her a big hug in her arms, then I copied her and did the same thing. I never did anything like that before, but it felt good, like I made friends and belonged. People were nice and helpful, and I did a good deed and saved a life at age 19. It actually turned out to be a good night. As my dear friend Bruce Gold always says, "turning lemons into lemonade." Find the good in everything, because it's there and life is what you make it. Choose your day, choose happiness.

I remember more. My Mom did have grilled cheese, too, but she didn't like bacon. Maybe she just had a tomato in it like they did. When I visited my Dad in the E.R. I saw the man whose wife I helped and looked at them or waved. He thanked me and smiled at me. I then proudly told my Dad what happened and after I left the E.R. I think the man told my Dad how I helped his wife. He knew I was my Dad's daughter and wanted him to know what a good thing I did for her. Man, I miss everything about the good old days.

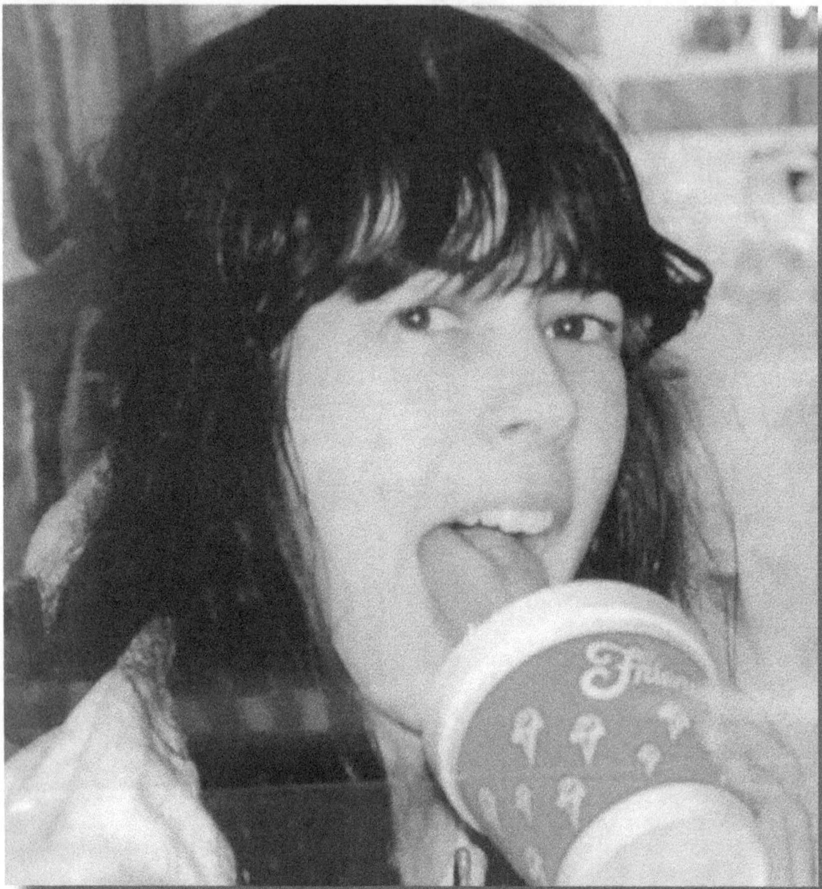

MIRROR OF MY WORLD

Christian Karen Berman

DOG BITE

I got snapped at by our Shih-Tzu in my early 20s, twice, and needed to go to the E.R. for stitches, like nine stitches on my bottom lip. It was hanging off and bleeding but didn't hurt. Some lady let me go first, it looked so bad. When it first happened, I ran upstairs to my Dad and said hospital and my brother and I quickly got into the car. My Dad drove. My Dad called my Mom at Temple to meet us there. I needed an I.V. medicine drip. It was my lip and it was bad.

They got me a kitten stuffed animal at the hospital gift shop. I was Eskimo kissing our dog Ritchie, our noses rubbing together. Daddy was taking photos before and using the flash and he snapped at me and bit my lip hard. He had two sets of teeth. His baby teeth never fell out, oddly enough. He was a biter and bit Larry and my Dad, too, at different times. He was also a barker and all of 16 pounds back then, maybe 20 pounds when he got older.

Mary was my Dog. She never bit me, just kissed me. She loved me. I loved her so much and still miss her. When there was a storm and we were alone she would go to me and she was my best buddy.

MIRROR OF MY WORLD

Christian Karen Berman

THE LITTLE FUGITIVE

Age 22. It was a Sunday morning, not only wasn't I feeling well, I was in a bad mood. One of my back teeth had been achy, too. I was worried my parents were going to force me to see a psychiatrist or even put me in a mental hospital. I told my Dad in the living room to make an appointment with my pediatrician. I had just started seeing my parents' primary care doctor, but he's not in on Sundays. Dr. Biers keeps telling me he's going to send me back upstairs to my pediatrician anyway, like when I don't hold still or act like the child I still am (lovingly, like a great uncle, he was my grandparents' doctor, too, the old family doc). Plus, I had been seeing my pediatricians off and on when I can't get an appointment with Dr. Biers.

I decide to run away. Last time I ran away I got very thirsty. I didn't take any supplies. This was my rebellious period I now regret, but it does make for an interesting story to look back on and it's true.

I pack my kid's backpack, I put in a can or two of Diet Coke, two mini watermelon-flavored applesauce cups, a little black toy gun that looks real for protection, toy metal handcuffs, maybe an extra shirt. Still in my tomboy stage, I put on these black dress shoes for boys, brand new, plus not so comfortable for running away from home. I push my way out the door and run before they can stop me, to the best of my memory.

I run up the street to the top of the hill by the middle school and start to slow down and have second thoughts. I want to turn around and go home, then I see a police car and get scared, like I'm in big trouble. Now I know I can't go home and have to run away from the police. (I didn't know at the time, the police were coming to help a sick elderly neighbor; it had nothing to do with me.) I cut through the yard of the school. They were having a football game and BBQ. I wanted to use the phone in the school to call a homeless shelter or Covenant House, a young people's

MIRROR OF MY WORLD

shelter in NYC. I read a book about it once; it seemed nice and loving. I had quite the imagination if you could tell.

They would only let you in to use the bathroom, so I walked on down the blocks, thinking if I needed to, I could knock on the door and ask them to call my parents or an ambulance for me. I heard a helicopter; thought they were looking for me. They might have been. I hid behind a tree, a real outlaw and rebel without a cause. I stopped in a parking lot where they had a doctor's office, asked to use the phone. They wouldn't let me; I had to be a patient. I kept walking, about two miles by now, surprised I was in such good shape, wearing hard boy's dress shoes now, mind you.

I finally saw my pediatrician's office. It was before 2 pm and still open. I could even see the hospital if I walked another mile. I couldn't. I happily went up the stairs to a much-loved and missed safe place. Dr. Speilsinger, one of my doctors, was on call there. I asked the nurse if I could please use the phone. She let me. I called the Covenant House hotline. Then she went to go get my doctor and he walked over and asked what I was doing there. I told him I ran away from home. He wasn't at all happy to be burdened with this on a half-day working Sunday just before closing time. (I wanted to show independence and/or get attention.) The person on the phone rudely asked if I was in the hospital and she was no help at all. My doctor said I'm going to have to call your Dad. He asked me my number. I was being a punk and wouldn't give it to him. So he asked the nurse to look it up on the computer. I was still in the computer system. He called my Dad. I was scared. My Dad said happily, "You found my daughter!" The doctor said she came to me, she ran away here. I actually just ended up there, accidentally on purpose, but it wasn't planned. He asked if my Dad could come pick me up. They both were not happy with me.

I was still talking on the phone. I was thinking what to do, maybe lock myself in the bathroom and hide. Then a few minutes later, I saw the police come up the stairs. Just like in the movie *It Takes Two*, I duck and hide under the desk, scrunched up knees to chest, still half-talking softly on the phone, so they can't find me. I see the cop's feet. I'm wearing the same shoes as them.

I slowly stand up and hang up the phone. My gig is up, I YI YI. My Dad had gone to the police who showed up to help Mrs. Newman. He said he couldn't find his daughter. He didn't have a photo of me, but gave them my height and weight—5'4", 107 lbs. I was actually only 104 to be technical. He had to call them and tell them that he found me, so they would stop searching and know I'm okay. I started crying because I was scared and knew I was in big trouble.

They started talking to me outside. A Dad and young daughter looked scared there was cops in front of the pediatrician's office. Then they put me in the back of the police car, crying. I kinda wanted to be handcuffed, but I wasn't. Thought it would be cool to see how real cuffs fit and if my small wrists could slide out. They just said to stop crying, it wouldn't look good for me at my hospital evaluation. They actually were helpful, nice and on my side.

In the hospital, the cops asked if there was a need to search my backpack, like there's nothing you could hurt yourself with in there. I said just a can of Coke. They said, "Well, you can't hurt yourself with that." I thought to myself, if you pour out the soda and rip it open you could. I had a small, black toy gun and mental handcuffs. Both looked real, might have got myself in real trouble.

I was there a while getting blood work to see if I had drugs in my system. Nope. They let me go home after all the blood work was normal and watched me for a few hours. A psych doctor spoke with me and said I was okay to go home. They gave me a copy of my blood work and the name of a doctor.

My Dad forgave me. Thankfully, he wasn't mad at me anymore. I was happy, relieved to finally be going home and not to a mental hospital. I had enough of an adventure for a while. I made my favorite for dinner I'd been looking forward to. I made myself, with a little help, boxed homemade Mac and Cheese with crunches. I was hungry and thirsty. Didn't eat or drink all day. I'm sorry I made my parents worry about me. I don't know why I thought they were against me. I was watching too many crazy movies like Gloria and the remake or something. This was the last time I ran away. It was actually a hard day, not fun. I don't know why I did this, but the brain isn't fully developed until age 25. Maybe impulse control.

MIRROR OF MY WORLD

Christian Karen Berman

September 11, 2001

I went to sleep around 7 or 8 in the morning, like many young adults do after they finish high school and college and are just trying to figure out their new life as a young adult. I was probably up all night, writing scripts and watching TV, *Grace Under Fire* reruns maybe. I'm not sure if I said goodbye to my Dad that day before he left for school/work that morning. I don't really remember that, but I got Taco Bell that night, not sure if I asked for it or not, that part is a bit fuzzy.

After the disaster he was brave. Rough to stop at Taco Bell in the Bronx, Yonkers, New York. I remember vaguely asking my Mom to go to Sears and buy my kid sister doll a cute baby dress in a size 12 months. I wanted to play with her and dress her up.

I went to sleep in my parents' bed, because I'd been sleeping there my whole life and wouldn't sleep alone. A few years before, my Dad and Mom took my bedroom so we could all get better sleep. Yes, as a teenager I would sometimes go to sleep with them in the middle of the night or wake them up and want to talk, so this worked better for my Dad. I'm sure most teenage girls do this, but many do not admit to it.

I remember at age 17-19, I woke up sleeping next to my Mom with my arm around her. She had a light pink flannel nightgown on. Nice memory. A lot of times I was up all night and would go on my Mom's side to cuddle and sleep with her or to tell my Dad a problem I was upset about or even sleep in the middle between them. It would ruin their sleep, so we switched rooms. It worked better for everyone. I still couldn't sleep well in my own room. I'd slept with them since I was a baby and they got me in my own room from age seven and up, but never consistently.

I remember waking up on that day around 12 pm. I heard my Mom upstairs in the hall or next bedroom frantically going on about something and talking about something she heard on the car radio. Her voice was fast-paced and nervous. I was half asleep and I asked

MIRROR OF MY WORLD

her if she bought Jen the baby dress at Sears and was it the best one. She said there was an emergency on the radio and she had to turn around and go home and the traffic was terrible and everyone was crazy and she never made it to Sears, maybe major traffic, too, and panic in the streets. I was a little annoyed with her for that and thought she was exaggerating and making a big deal over something silly. I think she might have said we were being attacked, but not sure, I went back to sleep. I had no idea we were living in the scary movie *Independence Day*. She might have mentioned she should call my Dad and ask him to come home. I thought it was nothing with nothing, you know how some Moms get excited over little things they might misinterpret. I was more chill and went back to sleep.

The next thing I remember is waking up late, maybe 9:30 pm. My Dad got me Taco Bell, a bean burrito, chalupa, nachos, refried beans, taco pizza, cinnamon curls and chocolate taco. I liked that routine. I would sometimes sit in the kitchen and nurse on an Arizona Apple Berry Iced Tea, 16 oz. bottle, with 15 calories. We would get two different kinds at CVS (I don't think they even make them anymore) and I would talk to my Dad about his day, about my problems, anything I wanted. Our special time together, like at 5-6 in the morning was before he went to work. He would come up to my bedroom if I caught him in time before he snuck out early to work, an hour commute. We would talk and watch Breakfast with Bear on the Disney channel. I loved that kids show at 6 am.

I heard something about what my Mom was telling me in the morning, now that I was fully awake and it was coming from my Dad. We didn't have time to talk.

Larry heated up some of my Taco Bell in the toaster on Reynolds Wrap and brought it upstairs to my bedroom as I turned on my TV and was trying to figure out for myself what was going on. I was eating and watching this horrible disaster unfold before me. I felt terrible for all those poor innocent people and wanted to go into the city myself and help find them and dig them out of the rubble. People jumping off the top of the buildings to their death, they had no choice or to be burned alive in pain.

This hit close to home. I didn't think I said goodbye to my Daddy in the morning and he was only 40 minutes away from the Twin

Towers that the two terrorist planes crashed into and most of my Dad's students' parents and students at Horace Mann School upper division worked in the Twin Towers. In fact, some faculty and many students stayed until late at night or overnight until their Mom or Dad could be found to take them home. I'm lucky my Dad came home relatively early and at all. He knew of a guy that would have been in the Twin Towers, but he had to take his little five-year-old son to Horace Mann Elementary School Kindergarten to enroll on his first day. Boy, that guy is lucky and dodged a bullet. My Dad didn't have school the next day.

I was glued to the TV and would have it on constantly the next three days and kept watching, hoping they found more survivors alive, and thinking of all the pain and suffering everyone in New York was going through.

Also, about the other plan—the failed attack at the White House, how scary. I even asked my Dad if I could go help look for more survivors. He said no. I did find myself happy that I was still alive and to enjoy life more.

There was supposed to be no planes in the air, and we heard loud planes flying close to our roof like never before, maybe security planes to watch and make sure our air was safe from another terrorist attack. I would run downstairs and duck as the loud planes roared over, thinking they would crash into my house for real. I had nightmares when I fell sleep to one of the news channels that planes were crashing into our house. It was so real to me and so scary, we were thinking there was another attack. We live about an hour away, so this was real to us, living so close to Ground Zero, as it's now called.

Daddy and Larry got Boston Market for dinner for everyone. It was a nice dinner. I still watched the news, would be asleep trying to stay awake to hear what happened, waking up and going to sleep a few hours on and off. I was glad my Dad didn't have school the next day. I was now going to be worried and scared for him to leave home and maybe he wouldn't come back like some other parents never came back to their kids. But everyone in my Dad's school was lucky. Their parents didn't die and made it out of the building alive.

MIRROR OF MY WORLD

My worst fear back then for the longest time was my Dad would go to school and never come home. I honestly cared and worried more about him than myself, be it a car accident, which sadly and ironically he had on a blizzard day he had to go to school, New York City schools never close, you know. After my Dad called in to the headmaster's office about how he skidded into a telephone pole, then the school did decide to finally close and sent everybody home. He did hurt his knee and legs in the car crash and went to the E.R. My Mom and brother came to pick him up. I think he couldn't drive and the car was not drivable and needed AAA to come and be towed. I think I tried to stop him. I always hated when he left the house and went to school, especially in a bad blizzard. Another time a pebble smashed into his car windshield. I worried about school shootings and now this 9/11.

I remember it was comforting when David Letterman spoke very eloquently on his Late Show about the terrible losses and how nice everyone was being, why can't people help and be nice all the time? I remember I was glad to be alive and wanted to be happy, so I looked through all my *Parents Magazines* and *Healthy Kid* magazines and pulled out happy kid advertisements and photos of happy kids and toddlers and hung them on my walls to try to look at them and be happy, loved, and secure with them surrounding me. Maybe Dave had said to surround yourself with happy things you love. I took that to heart.

I also asked my parents to please buy me the hot pink Lands' End Kids girl's hook and loop closure Capri pants I had been wanting. It taught me to do and buy things that will make me happy and live in the now, because you never know. Live each day like it was your last and to the fullest. That feeling was strong inside me after 72 hours of watching the grief and then the happiness when they found a live person in the rubble, buried alive. Like watching a real-life horror movie. Nothing ever like this, to live in the real *Twilight Zone*. Everyone in the world was kinder for a few months, more appreciative of their dear friends and how fragile life was.

I was a fireman that Halloween. Daddy helped me put white tape on Larry's old Lands' End Navy Blue Raincoat and he even stopped at the Halloween store on the way home from work to buy a fireman's hat for me. Maybe he should have gone to the real firehouse. I was so touched by that gesture. I still have the red fireman hat I wore 10/31/01, though it's old and got crushed by accident in my baby dolls' basement with some other dolls. My Dad wrote Ladder 7 on the old raincoat with a black sharpie. Then that night, I said to my Daddy, is it right, is it safe, should I really be going Trick-or-Treating? (Forget I was early 20s and about 10 years too old anyway, people were thinking something really bad and sinister might happen on this night and everyone should stay home this Halloween to be safe.) My smart and wise Daddy strongly insisted that I go Trick-or-Treating with Larry, otherwise we're letting the terrorists win, that's just want they wanted. He told me to go and have fun and don't let the bad guys win and take our freedom away.

It was a great and happy night, and a safe night. One person asked if I knew someone at Ladder Number 7. I said I was just supporting them (and standing up for what I believed in, and Democracy; I didn't say those words, but wish I did). No one noticed my age. In fact, everyone was out having the best Halloween. More parents and kids came out to show everyone the bad guys did not scare us and we will not live in fear. My Dad supported that motto first.

I got a lot of cool pencils and goodie bags, too. It was a great Halloween to live free. I shared all my candy and chocolates with my family and we had our two dogs that would go crazy, barking anytime a Trick-or-Treater would knock at the door. I guess my parents had a fun night, too. Turning lemons into lemonade again and choosing your day, life can be the best or the worst, it really is what you make it. John Ritter, a very good man, and my Mom also died on this date some years later. 9/11 is really like the saddest, worst day ever. I hate my Mom had to share this day with so many. I wanted her to have her own special death day, if she had to die. And some have asked was she in the Twin Towers. It was 15 years later and sepsis, colon cancer. Life is hard and sad. Be nice and helpful to everybody, they will remember you so kindly years later and brownie points in Heaven for all your good deeds.

MIRROR OF MY WORLD

<u>Christian Karen Berman</u>

MY DADDY

I'd like to share a few stories about my Daddy.
When I dream about him at night, he's not dead but still sick in the hospital. I kind of forget he really died at night and I think I'm begging his doctor to get him better and save him. Even my mom's alive and well in my dreams. I wonder why?

A few years ago our furnace broke during the worst cold front. Cold winds blowing in. It was wintertime, I forget the month. Daddy, my Mom, and Larry would go into the car to warm up on Daddy's insistence. He was the boss of the house and life of the house. He had the most energy, boisterous spirt; the house never seemed lonely with him! He was loud, talking on Echo Link, watching TV... He was also very sharp and extremely bright and in with the times, politics.

Well, it was freezing that day and I was under a few covers fully dressed and in a winter coat, too. The window was open only two inches for air and blowing in. They came home for me wherever they went. Daddy told Larry I should come down, he wanted to check on me. The house was like 46 degrees, and I didn't feel well or sleep well—tired, cold, achy, and short of breath. He put me on his lap to warm me up and held me. Since the air was dry and the windows shut, I felt I couldn't breathe good. Larry brought down my pulse ox monitor. I put it on my finger. It surprisingly said 98 %, then I felt better! I liked being on his lap and being held. When I was at the hospital with him and they were setting up his room and the nurse wanted me to wait in a waiting room—Daddy was on a gurney—he said no, he wants me with him.

He was always afraid of losing me, that I would get lost or taken. During Halloween the last time I Trick-or-Treated I was 25, best Halloween ever, lots of candy and goody bags! I was a skeleton that year. I had the black ribs shirt, black chain jeans, very cool, painted grayish face and a black cape from Kids-R-Us. We use to shop there on weekends. They had great deals; it must be why all the stores closed. Well, Larry was following me with the car, he couldn't really keep up with me. This was before I had fear, like when I watched Nancy Grace, it made me afraid of being kidnapped and stuff I didn't know about. Larry told Daddy he lost me. My Mom even came out looking for me and I was running to houses and I was like just one more house, then just one more house again. I kinda knew it was probably my last Trick-or-Treating. They thought I was a teenager but the oldest I saw was 13!

When I got back, Mom said "I found her." Daddy yelled how he was worried, he didn't know where I was, something could have happened to me, I don't know what's out there, why did I run away from Larry? He thought he might have to call the police to find me! I was with Larry filling up three bags with candy leaving them in the car. It was just within a mile radius from our house around the neighborhood. I didn't know most of them, but they were nice. One told me to be careful; she saw I was alone. Another old lady said, "You're a bit old, but you made an effort," meaning good costume! Another old lady said Snickers was her husband's favorite snack. I told another lady she had a nice selection, assorted chips! One had Moon Pies. Another lady said, "Take all the candy, I want to get rid of it so my kids don't eat it." I walked up lots of stairs and hills. I really knew how to work the hood. I loved the goody bags and the people who left big giant bowls of candy! I had four full bags of diabetes treats when I finished.

Daddy was worried, but he hugged me and looked at all the candy and had some. We had enough till Easter. He kept it in the trunk of the car. I think I washed the face paint off and had fish and garlic Yukon gold mashed potatoes and a salad bar from Charlie Brown's Restaurant for dinner that Daddy picked up on the way home from school. The next day I was achy when I walked from running around the hood from 6:30-9 pm. It's sad after 9-ish—they usually turn off their lights and not answer the door anymore. It was so much fun!

I used to call the switchboard operator sometimes to talk or find my Daddy, especially if I felt sick. No matter how long I wait, he won't be coming home from Heaven; no time off for good behavior. My Dad is watching me, sad he can't seem to help me much from Heaven and there is no one that cares about what happens to me to help me. I even went to his school with him a few times. It was too hard to go often; what a hard long day. I woke up at 5 am to eat breakfast, got ready at 6 am, by 6:30 am we had to leave to commute into the city and beat the morning traffic. Bronx River Parkway. It was about a 50-minute drive.

We got there, he got his coffee, and showed me off to everybody he saw. He knew everybody working there half his life. We walked to his classroom. He starting setting it up. Everyone said, "Hi, Dr. Berman!" At first it was fun and exciting, nervous, then it got boring and long, the day. Then I started to feel sick. I tuned out his teaching, not on purpose—I didn't understand it. I usually drew a picture. I watched him for a while teach.

Dr. Stephen Berman
Math

MIRROR OF MY WORLD

Then he went to the office, got supplies, proudly introduced me. "Did you ever meet my daughter; this is my daughter." Then he was setting up his handwritten slides for the projector. I was drawing on the blackboard or green board with chalk. Then I said hi to the switchboard ladies, Mary and Olive, then they said they remember when I was little and I got so big.

Then lunch, a long walk through the campus to get to the Cafeteria. I got black coffee; I was getting tired. The lunch ladies wrapped up a plate for me for later with an Oreo pie. Then Daddy maybe called home with me, then he was setting up a movie for his next class—A.P. Statistics and Social Science—and he turned off the lights and showed *Love Story* and the movie made a pretty girl cry. Not a romance fan at all, he once made me read the whole book, too, in the summer. I think I was 17. It was an old 1970s book in good shape, original. His, I guess. Then some girls said it's so cool I'm his daughter and smiled a lot. They were in awe of me. Even a 14-year-old boy copied that I rolled up my sleeves. Daddy was the Big Man on Campus there. He said you can't wear your baseball cap on backwards and no caps, (this was when that was popular), there was a dress code. I was dressed nice, a new outfit from Kids-R-Us.

The last time I went I think I was 25. I got some smell-and-sniff markers to draw from the math office. They keep you awake. I cut out red paper napkins in his own office making snowflakes. It was near Thanksgiving or Christmas time. He had a desk, phone, file cabinets. He was in administration, head of clubs. His boss walked in when I was cutting red paper napkins into snowflakes; they complettely covered his desk. I was caught red-handed. Daddy said I wasn't feeling well and tired and that he couldn't stay late for the Math Department faculty meeting. His boss said, "Well, you gotta do what you gotta do."

I copied my hand and medical bracelet. I was photocopying my hand—yes, only I would do stuff like this! I have personality. I was even wearing a cool thin braid on the side of my hair, very cool! I had hypoglycemia that came out a lot, fainting spells sometimes that put me in the E.R. often until I learned to watch my sugars and carbs. My lowest blood sugar recorded at a physical was 47 and I didn't black out or have blurry vision. It musta been lower when that happened; I just felt yucky and woozy at 47 (70-120 is normal blood sugar). I needed to wear a medical alert I.D. bracelet then and it said I had hypoglycemia and heart problems and my home number and doctor's number. It was big on me. I should have got the child-size one. My grandpa had a medical necklace. He was diabetic and took insulin. Well, I colored in my hand from the Xerox with markers. He put it in his file cabinet.

Finally we were getting ready to leave and say goodbye. He got me a bottled water. I felt faint. He stopped at a children's clothing store in Yonkers on the way home. We just looked, but I even tried on some clothes. Then he stopped at Pizza Hut for dinner and I probably got half veggie, half meat lovers. What a stressful day. I was overtired. I ate and watched the *Gimme a Break* episodes I had recorded with Joey and Matthew Lawrence, my favorite then. They were in reruns. It was around 2006, I think. I was glad to have some alone time and go to sleep. It was a super, great, happy day spending time with my Daddy and having him all to myself, just us two having a fun day together at the Horace Mann High School, showing me off and knowing what an important person he is there and how much he's valued and needed by everyone.

MIRROR OF MY WORLD

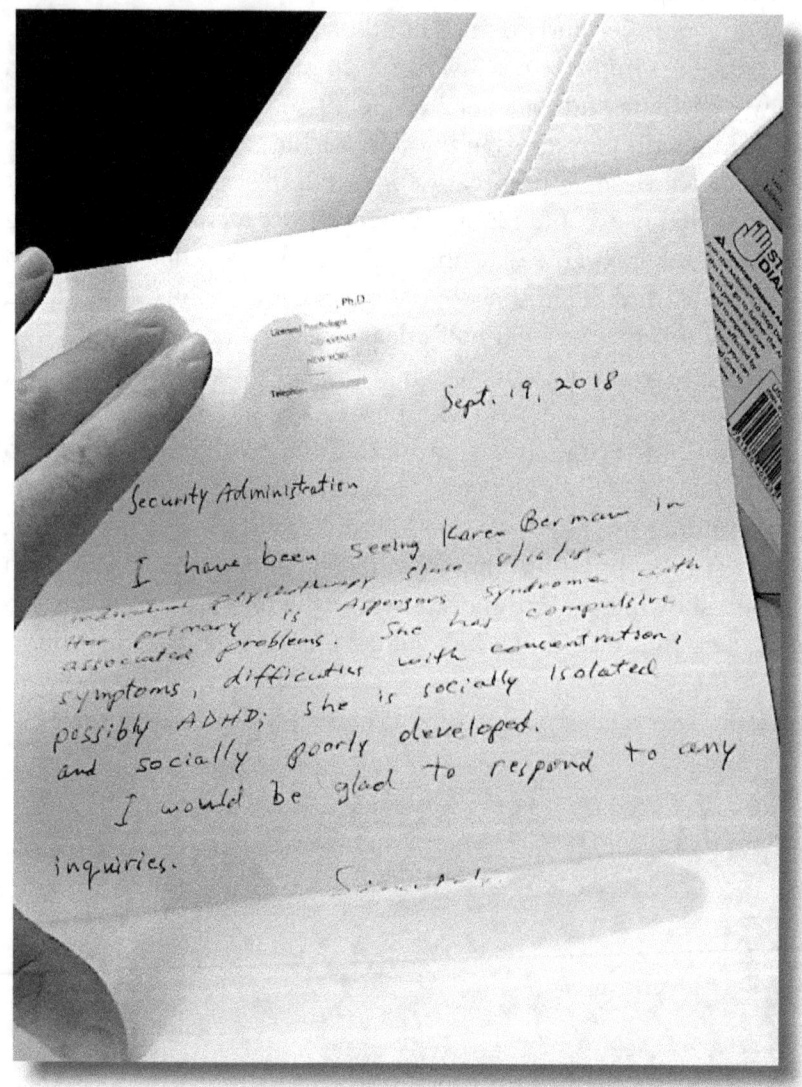

A letter from my therapist confirming my official diagnosis of Asperger's Syndrome.

<u>Christian Karen Berman</u>

NOVEMBER 27, 2009
MY LATE GRANDMA LEE'S BIRTHDAY

I was having a painful, swollen left elbow. I am a writer and had been over-writing, binge writing scripts on my bed. I also had been over-showering and my elbow skin was dry and cracked. I also was wearing a Lands' End Kids light blue knitted sweater that was a bit coarse on the skin after leaning on it for many hours a day while I was handwriting scripts on my bed, with the TV on in the background.

My Dad said my red elbow was hot to the touch. The plan — he was going to come home from school early to take me to the Emergency Room with my Mom and brother.

At the E.R. the doctor put a large needle inside my red, swollen, left elbow to try to drain liquid and take it as a sample. The Indian doctor wore two pairs of plastic blue gloves, just in case. I tried to hold still, but it hurt so much I cried out loud like a baby and moved. It was kinda spreading down my arm, the red swollen infection. First it was bursitis, then cellulitis.

A nurse found out my real age and asked if I was lying. She thought I was a child or teenager. I said I look young because I have Asperger's Syndrome and I don't get out much. She didn't really believe me—I could tell by her voice and look—but accepted my answer. But I did look young.

The doctor gave me an oral liquid medicine, Cleocin, and told my family to come back to the E.R. tomorrow afternoon. He was going to look at it and if it didn't look any better, I would have to be admitted into the hospital. That's kinda scary, but it was an emergency; I guess I didn't have a choice. I didn't want to get worse and sicker.

Afterward, we went to a restaurant in Mamaroneck, N.Y., about a half-hour away from the hospital, and took out some food to go. I got spicy beef and bean chili and a cheeseburger. Then we picked up the medicine the doctor called in for me at CVS pharmacy and went home to eat our dinner.

I ate in front of the TV in my bed, as usual. I remember my Mom and Larry got me a stuffed Snoopy from CVS after finishing my dinner, and my Dad giving me my medicine, two syringes of green apple flavor, my favorite.

I went to sleep with my Snoopy. I remember being nervous, but comfy and relaxed with my new friend and maybe a new pillow and blanket. I remember being cozy and Snoopy helped me sleep. Some stuffed animals I was allergic too, gave me trouble breathing, but not him. I loved him.

The next day I was still nervous. My stomach was upset, too. My Mom had gone to Gap Kids to get me a lightweight beautiful winter coat and a cute sweatshirt. Mom loved the Gap for me and her. I was weak and tired, but thought I'd better brush my hair or I won't look good for the hospital. It took a lot of energy I didn't have with my wet hairbrush to get the knots out, but I did a good job.

I was so sick I was even running a low-grade fever, maybe 100.6. My arm did not look any better, worse if anything. I just knew they were going to admit me and I needed to be there to get better. My Dad came home. He left early, told his boss he had to take his daughter to the hospital. His boss/friend Lionel usually said, "Well, you gotta do what you gotta do." So nervous to leave my bathroom, knowing I wouldn't be coming home for a long time. I'd have to sleep in another bed. I left, looking out the car window in the backseat on the five-minute ride to the E.R., just nervous, knowing I wouldn't be going back home to my house with my family.

In the E.R., they saw me right away and the doctor drew a big purple circle with magic marker around my lower left arm to where it was spreading, hot, red, swollen and filling with fluid. The Indian doctor said he never saw anything like this before. He had the nurse give me I.V. meds, because the medicine he gave me was ineffective to my strain of bacteria, strep or something. Not sure what I had, but it was serious and the doctor gave me vancomycin.

I had to take two I.V.'s in the bathroom with me, another was just I.V. of saline fluids. Then I saw my face was all red. It seems I was allergic and having a reaction. I worriedly told the nurse. She said it's normal, your body has to get used to it. I had no other allergic symptoms and my vitals were normal, just nervous, and the nurse said they are finding a room for me upstairs to be admitted soon. I had to sign some paperwork, too.

It was kind of exciting my first time being admitted, just like in all the TV shows I had watched growing up, like *Diff'rent Strokes* when Arnold has his appendix out and his friend Alice had her tonsils out, when Sam had his tonsils out. I wasn't wanting to try to go home or freak out, I know this is where I needed to be because I was a very sick girl.

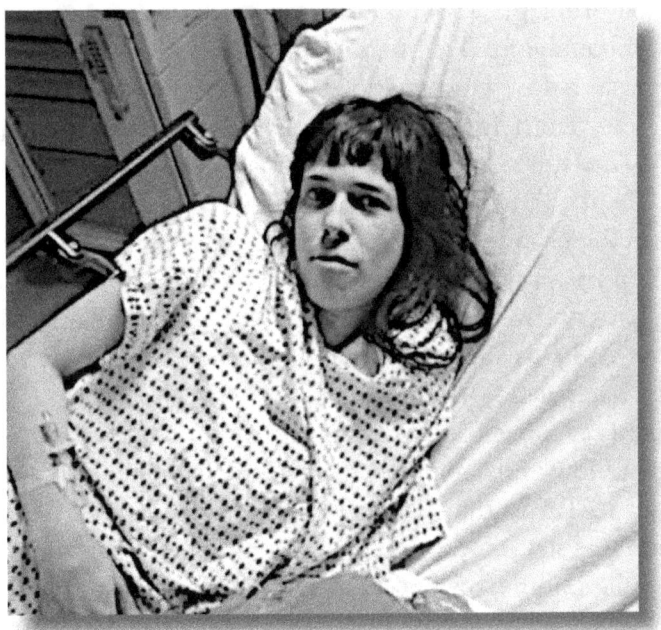

My parents were worried. The doctor explained I needed to be admitted and watched and on I.V. meds until the infection in my arm was cleared up. Right now, it was spreading all the way down to my hand. I was scared. Something bad was happening to me. I sadly said goodbye to my parents and brother. I wouldn't be going home for a long while and I just had to accept it and hope the meds work and I get better soon.

MIRROR OF MY WORLD

They wheeled me upstairs in a hospital gurney, still having both I.V.'s on my arms, with a purple circle drawn around the red swollen arm, no pus inside, though. It was late, around 8 pm by now. We had gotten there around 4:30 pm. I didn't even eat today. I ate last night, woke up early afternoon and got ready to go to the E.R., no time, and who wanted to eat? I felt kinda sick. I didn't drink, just got the I.V. fluids. They showed me I had my own phone in the room, and to dial 9 first and I can call my parents. I had the bed next to the window, a TV (that didn't work well and had an unclear picture, I would find out later; they never did fix it for me like they said they would). I didn't like sunlight. I wanted the shades down, not the sun coming up on me waking me up and in my eyes. There was an older lady in the next bed, 80s, she had stomach problems, I found out from her later. The nurse just said nothing contagious like pneumonia or bronchitis.

The year before I lost my dog, Mary, a couple days after the New Year. The year before that, no one was home and I had tachycardia. My heart was racing. I had too many Diet Cokes or Mountain Dews. I called my Mom and brother Larry panicking that I need to go to the hospital. They were on the way to my Dad's school to pick him up and didn't believe I was that sick to turn around and come back and take me to the hospital. I had to call an ambulance for myself. I was sure I was dying of a heart attack. It was scary. Always in the cold, winter months.

I asked my nurse if my parents or brother could come and bring me my pillow and Snoopy dog to sleep with, said I couldn't sleep without it. Partly that was true and I missed them already and scared I was sick, alone, and in a hospital unit. Thankfully she said yes. I called home, or the nurse did. My parents were too tired to come back, but Larry said he would and I was so happy to be able to see him again before I had to go to sleep.

The nurse stopped the saline. It was making me go to the bathroom too much. I finished the vancomycin for now, because my face was beet red, kinda red patches on my cheeks and forehead. I waited anxious and happily for Larry pacing, then calling my parents again and Larry was in the car on his way. When I saw him come in with my Snoopy Dog, I felt so happy I wanted to hug him, not sure if I did though. He stayed a while, but it was after 9 or 10 pm by then and past visiting hours, so the nurse said he could only stay a few minutes. I was happy she broke the rules a little, for already homesick me.

I talked with him about if my parents were worried or what they said, showed him my bed and my room and he almost wanted to stay a while in a chair, but I wasn't a baby. I said I'd be ok, but sadly he had to go home and leave me all alone in the hospital that night and for I don't know how long. I just wanted my arm to get better and the red swelling to go down. It looked pretty bad even to the doctors and me.

I had called my family around 11:30 pm to say goodnight and how much I miss them. In the middle of the night my old lady roommate is very hungry around 2 am, eating Keebler Club Crackers and drinking hot Lipton tea from the pantry, telling her night nurse how hungry she is. She had just had an enema the other day from what I gathered and has been on a liquid diet for her stomach issues. Then she went back to sleep and it was quiet. I went to sleep looking at my red and puffy arm knowing I had no choice and need to be here.

I wake up in the hospital bed about four hours later, early morning around 6:30 am. First thing, I look at my arm and relieved to see the redness and swelling has gone down. The medicine is working, and I only had a half dose. Oh, good. I look around, look at my roommate, go to the bathroom, look for the nurse. I tell her my blood sugar feels low and ask if she could take my blood sugar. I was hungry last night and didn't eat all day. She said she would take my vitals and breakfast should be here in a half hour or so.

I tried to relax and go back to sleep, but I couldn't. I wasn't feeling great, probably low blood sugar and thirsty. I called home, hoping to talk to my Daddy. He was going out the door and couldn't talk right now, but said my Mom and brother would come by and visit me after they dropped him off at school in the Bronx, so that will be an hour or two from now.

The nurse finally comes to take my blood pressure and oxygen. It's in the normal range. I tell her again my blood sugar feels low, but she just says my breakfast will be here soon. So I lie down trying to go back to sleep until my breakfast comes. Then I go find her and ask what's for breakfast. She tells me it's usually cream of wheat or oatmeal with eggs and pancakes. I asked if I could please have a Dannon plain yogurt, too, so she calls that in to the order.

My breakfast is finally here a good half hour later. I got eggs, potatoes, and oatmeal. The oatmeal is great with milk, not liking much else. I have a large plastic bottle of Lipton iced tea my parents brought last night and a bottle of Aquafina. I drink a bit of orange juice. They had forgot my yogurt, so I told my nurse and she called them again and a nice lady brought it to me from the cafeteria. As I was eating around 8 am, my Mom and brother walk in, keeping me company. Then an old man hospital visitor walks in. He says it looks like I'm doing better, I'm eating. I ask Larry to get some large oak tags, the sunlight coming in from the big windows are bothering me and the shade doesn't close right. The infectious disease doctor walks in, looks at my arm, says it looks better, talks to my Mom, and then leaves.

Things really get busy in the early morning. Then a Sister comes in to pray for me and gives me a thin wafer and we say the Father's prayer together. That was nice. Then the food service lady comes by and asks what I want for lunch. She said a few choices and I asked for an egg and tuna salad sandwich and chocolate pudding and ice cream for dessert. They sure feed you a lot here. Then Larry helps me with the TV remote and the TV is fuzzy, not working great, so we try to tell the tech or nurse and they said someone will come later to look at it. I then get up and look around, walk in the hall with Bev and Larry. Then they had enough and wanted to go, said they'd be back later with my Dad and oak tag.

I'm looking for something on TV to watch, then my lunch tray comes and they set it up for me. It's a tuna and egg salad sandwich with potato leek soup. Soup is gross and so is the tuna. I like and eat the egg salad sandwich and chocolate and vanilla ice cream and blueberry muffin while watching *Dr. Phil*. After lunch I wasn't feeling too good, upset stomach and short of breath. Thought I was allergic to something. I asked the nurse for my vitals. She reluctantly took them and said I was okay. I'm getting lonely and bored. I call my Mom and she and Larry will be over soon. Larry comes in with the oak tag and tries his best to put it up by the big windows. He brings me a big stuffed dog he got at CVS as a surprise. He had also got me a soft and fuzzy little rocking horse before I went into the hospital at CVS. it's still in the living room. Then they have to leave to pick up my Dad from school. He has bad knees and can't drive.

They were too tired to come back that day. I was sad. Everyone was ignoring me. The dinner I didn't even want wasn't coming. I had called my parents again and telling them everyone here was ignoring me. Then my nurse noticed how sad I was and called the cafeteria to try and get me a late dinner of beef stew and talked with me a little. I felt much better and happier. I watched a Christmas special on TV, *Rudolph the Red-Nosed Reindeer,* and picked at my dinner. It was soup, beef stew veggies, chocolate chip cookie, slice of cake. Then after, time for me to have my vitals and my I.V. of vancomycin infusion, the real reason I was here. She set it up and put it on a slow drip so it wouldn't burn my veins, she said. It hurt when she put it in. There was an old line set up from yesterday, but I felt the needle pinching in my arm. I think she put a new line in. I called my parents, then watched some TV. After, I just watched reruns on TV so I wouldn't feel so sad and lonely being here and not in my own bed in my own home with my family. I watched *Late Night with David Letterman, Malcom in the Middle* (I loved that show), and maybe *Everybody Loves Raymond* and *Everyone Hates Chris.* The TV still wasn't very clear, kinda fuzzy, and then I went to sleep.

The next morning, I'm looking for stuff to watch on TV. My arm's a bit better. The doctor comes by to look at it. I'm already asking when can I go home? The doctor said I needed at least a few more days and more medicine and they needed to take more blood work. The Sister comes by to pray with me again. I'm walking around the halls in the hospital, in my hospital gown, to get some exercise and go exploring. I'm bored. The nurse said I had to stay within my unit and I couldn't just wander around the hospital. I told her I had some chest pain when I walked and needed an ultrasound. She said she would make a note for the doctor.

Then around 6:30 pm my parents come to visit me. I'm so happy to see my Dad, but not eating my pizza I ordered for dinner, not liking it, not too hungry. It was kinda boring, looked like Pizza Hut. I gave it to my family. They ate some and Daddy asked for hot coffee. I did eat a bit of dessert, cheesecake and chocolate pudding. I wasn't on a restricted diet, they let me order anything they had. My height and weight was 5'4" and 109 pounds. Daddy said he was tired and had to go now and I was sad about that and wanted him to stay longer. I walked him to the elevator. He was in a wheelchair for his bad knees and before he left I sat in his lap and gave him a big hug. A nurse saw and smiled.

After they left, I asked the young tech for something to do. Another nurse told her no books or magazines because of germs. So she printed out some crossword puzzles and games for me and gave me a new pen to use. I was in good spirits today, just looked at them, then called my parents to talk again. I found a new movie I never saw before on TV called *Elf*, with Ed Asner, my favorite actor. I'd heard of this movie, now I had to time to enjoy it as I wait for my I.V. medicine to be ready for me before bed.

I woke up a few times in the middle of the night after dozing off, having trouble breathing. I told the night nurse. She asked if I ever had this problem before when I slept away from home. I hadn't slept away from home since a few years ago when I was 25 and slept over a few nights at the Rye Town Hilton with my parents. She asked if I ever had Ativan before. I said no, I don't think so. Then I realized the big stuffed dog Larry brought me I was allergic to and was causing me trouble breathing. I told the nurse, moved it aside or put in on the chair, and calmly went back to sleep with my stuffed Snoopy dog, my faithful, loyal friend.

I hadn't been sleeping or eating well. I had been asking and begging the doctor when I can go home. He and the nurses knew I wasn't happy here, lonely, bored. My arm was looking better, but not totally cleared up yet. I asked about doing the rest of the I.V. treatments outpatient, so I can eat and sleep at home. He would think about it and let me know. I was here already three or four days. The TV still wasn't fixed. My Mom was there the night before telling my Dad that I shouldn't stay here anymore. She felt bad leaving me here. She said they should take me home with them. She thought my new roommate was weird, scary. She had brain damage or some problems. She was smoking a plastic spoon backwards and making funny loud noises. She had a pad to wet the bed. I'm not sure what was wrong with her. She didn't talk, you couldn't communicate with her. I remember her name was Joy. I was happy my Mom missed me and wanted me to come home.

I wanted to go home, too.

It was December 4th, 2009. Day 4. I asked the Nurse when the hospital would start decorating for Christmas and would be getting a tree in the lobby. I was tired, but in a good mood, excited about Christmas. Watching *Elf* helped get me into the spirit. The doctor came in to see me and all I could talk about is when am I going home, can I please go home so I can eat and sleep better? I asked about outpatient, and he would talk to some of the other doctors and let me know later.

For breakfast, the nurse brought my tray. I had Keebler Club Crackers, with plain yogurt and Cream of Wheat and I didn't like it, so I asked for oatmeal. There might have been French toast, or pancakes, but I didn't like it. Nothing much on TV. I would go through all the channels and there was even a hospital channel saying to wash your hands well. I called Larry and asked for my hairbrush. I hadn't brushed my hair since I'd been here and it was a mess. I still had the purple circle on my arm. I thought of bringing My Loving Family minivan with the people to play with, but thought it would get all germs here and ruin it.

That night I knew would be my last night I would be here. I couldn't take another day of this. Nothing on the TV that barely worked, being bored and tired in bed all day. When you do fall asleep, they wake you up to take your blood pressure. I didn't like and couldn't eat much food, heavy, tasteless, yucky. That night, even though I wasn't hungry and just tired, the nurse made me order dinner. I can't remember what it was, but I had a little Yankee bean soup. It was red, watery, beans were hard. I had opened my window a crack. It was getting stuffy, but it was so cold outside. A nurse and old black man tech came to tuck me in that night after my medicine and vitals. I had called back and said I was cold. I closed the window more and he brought me two warmed blankets and an extra pillow and said goodnight to me.

MIRROR OF MY WORLD

I slept so good and sound that night, but it was still cold and drafty. I got up early to close the window and go to the bathroom. My poor roommate looked cold, too. I called my Dad early, 5:45 am, before he left for work. It would be impossible to reach him all day in class. I think he had a cell phone, not sure. He wouldn't have it on during the day while he taught. I probably said I want to come home and asked if he would visit me. My family had skipped the day before. Even the nurse noticed no one came to visit me that day. She seemed sad for me, but they were tired and knew I was being taken care of.

The next afternoon the nurse came in and helped me change into a fresh hospital gown and said they wanted to do an echo cardiogram on my heart in a half hour and I was happy to hear that. I asked if I was leaving today. She didn't know yet. A volunteer from the hospital named Mary Elizabeth came to wheel me in a wheelchair for the ultrasound of my heart. I got there and the older technician recognized me. I had a heart test from her before and she asked why I was here. She rubbed cold jelly on my chest. At least it was a field trip break from being in my room all week. My nurse would not let me go exploring in the hospital, just down the aisles peeking in different rooms. After the tech gave me a fresh large gown, they would call someone to wheelchair me back to my room.

Back at my Room, I remember not wanting to order lunch and they said is that because you want to go home? Well, yes. I even told the nurse so much food, they feed you all day long. At home I got one or two meals a day. Here, so much food and none of it too edible.

The nurse came back in with great news—after this I.V. I can go home tonight. I was here five days and finally getting out, my hair brushed nicely. I had to have four more days of outpatient treatment, but I didn't care. I was going home, kinda like getting out of prison. I probably started to pack my things up, my crossword puzzles, my Snoopy dog, some crackers and PB&J snacks. The nurse started my I.V. early today so I could be discharged by 7 pm. She even put in a new PICC line, but it hurt and my hand where it was in seemed to be red and puffy. I had buzzed the nurse to tell her twice, she was ignoring me. Then I noticed Joy, my neighbor, was falling off her bed and holding on tight to the rails. I buzzed quick to tell them "Joy is falling off the bed." Then two or three nurses ran in here fast to help get her back on the bed, she even cut her hand on the bed. She was in her mid-50s or 60s and sadly had brain damage. The nurses thanked me for helping my roommate. Then I asked since she's already here if she could please look at my hand and she did and fixed the PICC line.

I was so tired during my I.V. treatment I had fallen asleep by accident in my bed. The lady who prays with me woke me and asked to pray for me, so we did. I even asked the nurse if they gave me a sedative to put me to sleep. She said no. I was so tired from not sleeping for more than four or five hours a night.

Larry called and said he was on the way to pick me up, yay. I ordered my hospital dinner wrapped up to go. It was salmon with jasmine rice and veggie soup. I had to take off my comfortable big hospital gown, not sure if I put my old clothes back on or Larry brought me new clothes. I wistfully took my last look around at everything, including the bathroom. Almost sad this experience was about to end. Still, happy to be going home from this ordeal and back to my own bed to recuperate.

Larry and I left, got in the car, radio playing, and then we were home. Oh, how good to be home again. I say hi to my parents, go upstairs. My bed has new bedding and a comforter Larry had bought me at Bed and Bath Kids, a pink patchwork design with satin pillows. So nice to come home to beautiful new bedding. Also a wooden bed tray a foot high, so I wouldn't have to lean on my elbow and hurt it again. It was still a little red, tender, and swollen. Larry also got me real food shepherd's pie. It was so good to be relaxed, near my parents, and eat a good meal in my comfortable bed. Then I went right to sleep, a sound, deep sleep.

I woke up and few times and was sure I was back in the hospital room, even the surroundings looked the same half asleep. That happens when you stay somewhere else for nearly a week. I went to sleep at 10 pm, then around 4:30 pm my Dad woke me up from a deep, sound sleep to go back to the hospital to get my I.V. treatment. I was still tired but knew that was the deal and I needed to finish taking care of this so the infection was gone for good and it wouldn't come back.

I put on a fresh navy and grey cuffed sleeve polo shirt from Gap Kids, size 14-16, and went to the hospital. Larry took me. There was finally a Christmas tree in the lobby. It's beginning to look a lot like Christmas. Once there I had to get my sticker name pass, sign in, fill out a form, write my height, 5'4", and weight, 110. Then we walked four flights up the stairs for my I.V. treatment.

The nurse took my vitals. Found a show I liked on TV. She found the movie *Elf* again, that was on TV a lot in December 2009. She put in my I.V. and asked me if I wanted dinner. It was seasoned, roasted chicken with mixed veggies and rice and lentil soup, with yellow Jell-O and chocolate chip cookies. It sounds good. I would be there about an hour-and-a-half. She ordered me dinner. I said the I.V. upsets my stomach and if she could please wrap it up I could take it to go.

I saw it was starting to snow out. I asked her to close the bathroom door so I could watch the beautiful snow flurries in the dark grey, blurry sky. Larry just dropped me off. I was watching my movie and called him. He was at a supermarket, Baldacci's, and taking out some butternut squash soup and homemade chili with all the fixings to go with my yummy hospital meal. I was feeling better, so happy the holidays were near. My elbow just had a little red bump now and I was getting my appetite back and had a nice movie and good dinner to look forward to, and it was snowing so beautifully.

After my dinner was all wrapped up, the nurse took my oxygen before I left and it was 100%. She did say if I didn't feel good later I should go to the E.R. I was concerned about having a reaction to the vancomycin. Only a few more I.V.'s and I would be as good as new, life was good.

About my poor little Snoopy dog... because of contagious germs by my sleeping with him and having a badly infected arm, he had to be put in my clear comforter plastic bag and be put in the basement, because I couldn't throw my good friend out. Just like what happened with the Velveteen Rabbit.

Christian Karen Berman

LOSING ALL MY BEST FRIENDS IN THE WORLD

January 2nd, 2009. I remember that day very clearly. That was the day my best friend and little sister, our dog Mary, died. She was having trouble breathing, so my brother Larry rushed her down to the animal hospital two days before. She had an operation. My Dad paid $4,000 to try to save her life without even thinking about it! Mary was part of our family, very loving, as we were to her.

The operation didn't go well. She had internal bleeding from it. They didn't explain what killed her. Maybe because they thought I was younger than I was and didn't want to upset me even more. Maybe a heart attack. Clogged arteries.

She was about 10-15 pounds overweight at 100 pounds, but she was a big girl and liked to eat. If she got hungry enough, she'd grab a challah off the table and gobble it down before you even knew she swiped it! She ate my Rainbow Sour Belts, too, kids sour chewy candy. I hid that from her. She found it and ate that, too. But she wouldn't even eat the chicken noodle soup we bought her fresh from the Jewish deli that early morning.

She hadn't been eating, just very thirsty and drinking a lot of water. I was very worried about her and a little hysterical to one of our vets. They didn't believe me, two of them didn't, when I said how she was gasping for breath and couldn't breathe. I told Daddy when we were watching her at the hospital to tell her she would be okay. He didn't do that, but gave me a scared, guilty look, like, "Uh-oh, what am I going to do with you? How are you going to handle this?" I was crying hysterically and having trouble breathing myself. I called her Pumpkin and Mom; she had a few nicknames.

The vet wanted my permission to put her to sleep. I couldn't do that. I loved her. We slept downstairs the night before. I was on my *Winnie the Pooh* fold-open couch. We had a very big day. I was at the

MIRROR OF MY WORLD

vet with her that day for at least an hour, after I cleaned the house that morning. I was scootering around the house in my purple Bratz scooter, which tells you how young I was. I was too tired to make it upstairs that evening and went right to sleep on my kiddie couch on the living room floor. I never did that before. Mary slept by my feet but woke up having trouble breathing. Then she was better. I told her to comeback and keep me warm. She did.

She understood English impeccably! No training or tricks, you could just talk to her and she understood and listened, was potty-trained, went out and came back by herself, except the last year. She couldn't hardly walk. She was overweight and had arthritis, it was very hard for her. I always worried about her. She was like my weight. I was about 109 pounds.

After she died, I was crying too much and too upset and sick to eat for almost a week. My Dad was worried about me. I was 104 a week later. I always shared my leftovers with her I was very upset she couldn't eat, so I didn't want to eat either. My very young logic. I had three dreams a night about her. We were sisters and very close. We use to cuddle to keep each other warm. My wish for her is that she was such a good girl in this life, she should be reborn a real human baby girl. What the Buddhists believe.

I had the lady vet doctor read out loud her dog tag after she died. I wrote it after my Dad bought her at two months old from Shake a Paw for $500. "Hello, my name is Mary. I'm lost, take me home. I miss my Family! Reward!" I still remember it. Daddy sent in for her tag.

That night on the news, after I thoroughly finished washing and sterilizing my hands from hugging her, thinking it's contagious, I turned on the news and just heard that Jett Travolta also died that day from a seizure. John Travolta's teenage son! I was in shock. That's the first thing I heard when I turned the TV on, the 11:00 *CBS News*. My thoughts, Jett just got a new friend in Heaven; now they are there together, maybe waiting together. Not comforting to me, but it surprised me, I'm not the only one who lost my best friend that day.

I couldn't replace our dog then. I kept picturing her watching me sadly from Heaven giving her love to another dog. My dog waited all day for Daddy to get home from work to take us to visit her at the hospital. She waited loyally all day to see us just one more time to say goodbye. I could tell she had gone blind. I thought she was better. I wasn't ready for her to die and leave me. I was crying so much it upset her. She died maybe 10 minutes later. She collapsed on the metal table after seeing our other dog, a Shih-Tzu. Mary sensed our other dog, Ritchie, was there and put her head up to see or sniff him, excited to see her friend. Only seven months apart in age, they grew up together. They used to chase each other around the house, but she was younger, even though much bigger than 16-pound him, and let Ritchie win and would fall down and let him catch her, conceded to him and let him be the leader, because he was older and here first. Ritchie Patrick died December 12th, 2014, at 19½ years old, almost a world record. Mary was 18 days shy of her 13th birthday when she died.

Watching her die traumatized me. I felt everyone would die and leave me.

MIRROR OF MY WORLD

BRONCHITIS, PART 2

I was sick a lot even in my 20s and early 30s. My Daddy always took me very seriously, my Mom said I just need to relax. When your heart's fast and you have trouble breathing that is no time to relax. Once I was home alone, sick with a fever, sweating, and shaking, too sick to wake up much and take my temperature, which I was too afraid to take; I knew it would say 105.6. I felt that terrible. I was on something, Tempur-Pedic, Pedia-Care or Children's Tylenol, but I was due for another dose. It knocked me out, a child's dose! My Daddy was at school teaching, my Mom and brother probably out shopping or getting dinner. I wasn't even near a phone. I was in my room asleep on my bed.

Another time I had 102.5 fever, Daddy wanted me to go to the E.R. I was too sick to move or get out of bed. I slept that one off. Another time I had trouble breathing, Daddy made me come downstairs to the kitchen to use the vaporizer to help open up my breathing passages. It worked. Boy, was he smart! Then a few years ago I had terrible bronchitis. I saw my doctor that day, Dr. Biers. He asked Daddy if he heard me cough, to make sure he told me to hold still and stop wiggling. He was in his late 80s and my grandparents' doctor; he was super kind like a great Uncle. He took X-rays. I had 102 fever and only had green diet Jell-O that morning. It made it hard to breathe. I was hot, cold, tired, and just feeling yucky!

I got worse that night. This was before Thanksgiving, November 19th, 2010. I woke up and was hungry and thirsty and had eggnog ice cream. It made my congestion and breathing worse. It was 3 am and I was in my Dad's arms, having trouble breathing. He told Larry to take me right down to the E.R.

They gave me a strep throat test and took my temp which was normal then, around 100! They sent me home an hour later. We

MIRROR OF MY WORLD

went to CVS to get popsicles and drinks. I could barely talk or swallow, my throat was terrible! It was fun looking around there at 4 am. I got home and had another asthma attack, so Daddy sent Larry back to CVS for Robitussin DM. It helped for a while, but if you can't breathe and lie down you can't sleep. I watched *All in the Family*, the ones with Stephie. It was a very hard night.

Daddy was OD'ing me on Robitussin so I could breathe for a while, then early he made an appointment with my pulmonologist. I had been there in the past and not did so well on the breathing tests and the bike riding test, but I had another attack there and the male nurse called Dr. Lerhman and said you better come fast, she's really short of breath. He came quick, took my oxygen, it was 91% out of 100%; that's terrible. Anything under 95% is bad! He gave me a breathing treatment, where you breathe in steam and medicine to open up your lungs. I had more Robitussin. It was keeping me awake to breathe. I had lots of gross light green thick spit, yellow and clear spit. He gave me steroids, Cleocin, and an inhaler and said lots of steam. He didn't think I'd like being away from my family in the Medical Center Hospital. I came close to getting admitted for bronchitis.

Then we had to go to Mamaroneck CVS to pick up all my prescriptions, it was a fun day—three doctors, no sleep! Then they wanted to stop for Chinese on the way home. Long day. I got home, watched more All in the Family, and went to sleep! The next day I still had lots of spit and could barely talk. Very raspy, sore voice. The E.R. called to check on me and said I sounded terrible. Now they cared and believe me, they did nothing. I was living on green apple flavored Cleocin and Robitussin and cherry, orange, and grape ice pops. That's all I could eat for four days. I almost died. I was never that sick!

I watched *Room For One More* on TCM. It's an old movie about orphans getting adopted, being accepted for their own self, even though they had emotional and psychical problems, being loved and wanted. Daddy made me better by forcing me to take all my meds. He gave them to me. I was like 109 lbs. when I first got sick, I went to 104 lbs. in four days. I couldn't be left home alone because I had asthma attacks from bronchitis. I had hyperactive reactive airway disease. I didn't want to use the inhaler and become dependent on one. My first real meal was mac and cheese and Maui onion potato chips, for dinner chicken and pignuts and baked beans, sticky toffee ice cream for dessert. I was better now. My family loved me and got me all better.

When I was sad, Daddy made silly faces to cheer me up. He'd smile funny and make his eyes big and be like, "Now don't laugh," and he'd try to make me laugh. Sometimes I did because he was funny, other times I laughed because I felt bad that he wanted me to so much. When I was sick, first I got from Daddy, "Come here, let me see." He'd touch my cheek then tummy. Then he'd say, "Oh, yeah, you got something, go take your temperature." I hated that, I didn't like the plastic strip in my mouth. He had to ask me a few times, "Did you take your temperature yet? Go take it now, tell me what it is. What's your temperature?" I finally took it three times to get the median, then I'd have him guess. He was a good guesser, he usually got it right.

We did stuff like this for fun. Guess my weight, he usually guessed right, it was usually 102 pounds, same as my blood sugar. My blood pressure was usually like 102/67. He'd say "Larry, go take her vitals," something Larry had to do every day with my Dad because he was diabetic and on blood pressure meds. I was more voluntary. If I felt sick or was up that early in the morning when he took Daddy's vitals and I didn't eat yet, he'd take mine, too, every few days or once a week. Daddy used to take my vitals before he got too sick to take them anymore. Diabetes runs in my family. My maternal grandparents had it, as well as my Daddy and brother, so he wanted to keep a close eye on me to make sure I didn't start getting high blood sugar, too.

He liked me on a low carb diet, lots of protein and veggies. It also was good for my ADHD. Actually, when it came to taking my temp, I liked it as a child. A fever got me out of going to school. I wouldn't mind taking it as much as it took to get a high reading. But now a fever would either get me in bed, or just doing nothing like watching You Tube or on Facebook. Worst case, which I

MIRROR OF MY WORLD

sometimes liked, was going to the Emergency Room if I was sick enough. I usually was there four times a year, once with a 103 fever, food poisoning, etc. Then I got, "Larry, take her to the Emergency Room!" It seemed often. It was usually kind of serious, but sometimes I'd rather not go, but sometimes my parents both came with me and it was fun, the attention.

Daddy thought I had strep throat once. My parents came with me. I felt cared about and loved, even though I was feeling tired, throat hurt, 100.6 fever. What wasn't fun was stomach pains and having to get dressed at 3 am because the doctor on call said I had to go to the E.R. right now. They thought it was my appendix, but it was food poisoning. It had hurt all day, my tummy, and didn't go away at night. Uhh! I kept waking up and feeling my stomach still hurt and wondering why it didn't go away yet.

I came downstairs. Daddy was still awake and talking to my Mom. He made me take my temperature. It was 101 fever! (My Mom didn't understand, she was having a little dementia problem, then Daddy said, I remember, "I have a child that is sick!" Then she apologized and said she was sorry that your child is sick. It was very hard. She forgot things, even sometimes that they were married!) Then I think he yelled for me to go get ready and dressed for Larry to give me a new shirt and take me to the hospital. I have been a sickly child most of my life. That's also why my Daddy was so over-protective of me, I was his baby.

It's very sad my Mom sometimes forgot things like us, but still remembered her Mommy and Daddy and wanted to go home. They died when I was young. We all loved them very much, too. Grandma lived with us after Grandpa died when I was six and helped raise me until she died when I was 15.

With the five-hour tests and treatment at the hospital, I was glad to be getting discharged and not having to stay over and be admitted. They gave me two I.V. bags of fluid for dehydration. My tummy hurt too much to drink. I needed a CAT scan with dye and Benadryl I.V. It was very scary, but I came home to a very loving Mommy and Daddy. My Daddy was very protective of me. He even called the E.R. the next morning to find out what I should eat. I didn't want toast, chicken noodle soup, and tea. I think I was hungry by then and wanted my regular good food diet. He took excellent care of me, even just a few days before he died, he was still my advocate. I'm not close and bonded or connected to anyone now. I have no one to talk to who cares and loves me. My brother takes my vitals and takes good care of me, but emotionally we're not close like that. It was just my Daddy and me who were best buddies. This is why I am so sad—I have no one to fill the empty void, no one even wants to try, honestly. He'd even call if he was in the hospital if I wasn't feeling well and wait on the phone till Larry took my vitals to make sure I was okay and so were my numbers.

Our red retriever Mary Theresa had a real love for my Daddy. I think she liked him better than me sometimes! She knew I was more of a sister and he was a daddy. When we were by ourselves waiting for Daddy, Mom, and Larry to come home from school, usually in the living room on the couch, when he came home, I'd yell, "Daddy's home." She got off the couch, ran to the door, and her tail would be wagging hard and fast. She was very excited. He'd come in tired and she'd be wanting to jump on him, kiss him, and wagging her tail! He'd be like, "Okay, I know, I love you, too. I'm glad to see you, too, okay, enough!" (smiling) She loved him so much, then she'd wait patiently for him to finish his supper and help him with the leftovers. She liked his spaghetti and meat sauce at California Pizza Kitchen. She didn't cost much to feed even though she was a very big girl, as a two-year-old maybe 86 pounds, when she was older closer to 100 pounds. She ate our leftovers. She didn't like dog food. She ate it as a puppy, but as a puppy she was also in a big cage and needed to be watched outside or tied up to the basketball pole or tree with a rope so she could play in the yard without running off.

In the summer after we went outside and were walking down the green grassy trail to our backyard, I'd say, "Race ya," just like in the dog food commercial, Purina Puppy Chow at that time in 1997. She'd run faster than I could to the back yard to see Daddy in a lawn chair by the woods and run to kiss him excitedly and wag her tail. She loved him so much. She was a Daddy's girl, too. I was

MIRROR OF MY WORLD

wondering when my Daddy got to Heaven if she was there to do the same thing, run to him with love and kisses. My Mom took her out to go potty, but eventually just kinda left her out and taught her to go by herself.

With me, Mary protected me when people came to the door. Barked. I was home alone with her a lot. Once someone wouldn't go away and was banging on our door, a man in blue work coveralls, with a black pick-up truck, looking around our property. A burglar. I was 24 years old, scared, and called my Dad's office. He didn't pick up. I called the neighbors; the line was busy. I waited it out. He left. She must have been barking at least 45 minutes! I was too afraid to call anyone else, he'd have been mad and come back to get me, the bad guy! It was very scary. She protected me.

We usually cuddled. She gave me her paws, very bright girl. She didn't like butterscotch pudding.

We had another dog, but he was more Larry's dog, Ritchie. He was kind to me in one way—he knew I hated going out in the car. We weren't that close, but strangely, he must've known I was nervous and afraid to go out. He sat on my lap. He was 20 pounds. It even surprised my family. We used to be closer, but Larry kinda took him from me when I got Mary and was possessive of Ritchie. He didn't like when I braided his hair, put it in a ponytail or pigtails and dressed him in baby clothes.

There was a home video Daddy played once where I was diapering a six-month-old Ritchie. Larry got very upset and didn't even want Daddy to show anymore of the tape. I was only 18 years old. I'd love to find that tape. I was so cute, I looked 14, and Mary was in it, too. My room was full of toys. Mary was teething on my Barbie doll! Then I sang Annie songs, "It's a Hard Knock Life" and "Maybe." I was good. Mary put both paws on me and was licking my whole face. It's such an adorable home video.

Christian Karen Berman

MIRROR OF MY WORLD

Christian Karen Berman

HURRICANE SANDY

I was looking forward to this exciting event. My Dad had been watching all the news stories on all different channels, CNN, ABC, NBC, CBS, *Channel 12 News*, and it was coming our way, due to hit anytime now. It was also just before Halloween. Two exciting events coming together. I was drawing another picture of my favorite person at the time, Judith Eva Barsi. I thought this one looked just like her, close to perfect, even had the date on it: Oct. 29th, 2012.

I didn't think the hurricane would be much. Sure, we watched evacuated people on the news huddled in shelters, asking for donations, but stuff like that never happens here. It would be like a big thunderstorm for a few hours, plus I'd get supermarket goodies to snack on. That's always fun. I believe the supermarket people went crazy. No bottled water left, or much of anything. I remember I didn't go, but my Mom and Larry were supposed to get nonperishables. They got me yellowfin tuna cups, some frozen Mexican Lean Cuisine.

That night it was coming in. On the news my family heard the Governor of New Jersey, Chris Christie, yell, "GET THE HELL OFF THE BEACH." I, at this point, thought it was still funny. Then you heard the wind and rain pound the house and it start to come down. I hope we got enough supplies. We all went to bed. You could hear the trees pounding and banging on the gutters of the house. I thought it would be over soon.

The next day, it was dark, raining. The driveway was flooding and the basement, too. If you didn't get the supplies you needed, it was too late now, you were trapped. We watched the news. That's all you could do. You had to keep the windows open so they wouldn't break from the pressure. We had our flashlights ready, our supplies handy. Gotten some fresh coffee for me and Daddy to keep in the fridge. All the stores by now where closed, not sure about CVS.

MIRROR OF MY WORLD

    The lights and power just went out. It was scary now. My Dad was calling the power company to let them know there was an outage, hoping we didn't lose phone power. He was saying he's old, sickly and will catch pneumonia in this cold. After waiting, they said there was power outages all over due to the storm and they will let the power company know. My Dad turned on the radio, the flashlights on, the temperature in the house was dropping fast.

    This is serious now. I'm nervous, scared. Why isn't the heat and lights going back on? No TV, either. It must have been hard in the Dark Ages, hence the saying "Dark Ages." This is why they went to bed early then. The temp dropped from 76 to about 69, which wasn't terrible yet. I wasn't happy, though. Couldn't even make a frozen dinner. Microwave didn't work. I had a can of tuna and a can of Diet Lemon Nestea. Everyone put their coats on and my Dad said we should all get in the car to warm up a little before bed. He was cold.

Drawing of Anissa Jones (*Family Affair* actress)

I drew a drawing of Anissa Jones in the back seat of our car, while my Mom, Dad, and Larry warmed up and listened to the radio. I came in to have to use a flashlight to go to the bathroom, in my winter coat, no less. It was disorienting and weird. Then I finished my drawing in the living room, by flashlight. I don't think we each had our own flashlight, either.

The next day, it was still dark, rainy, depressing. It was cold, about 50 degrees inside by now. Nothing to wake up for. Slept in my coat. Nothing you can do in the cold darkness. Sure, a little sunlight came in, barely enough to see. Dim, darkness was all, plus freezing. I don't think we had space heaters back then, either. My Dad mighta got two mini-heaters, but I can't remember if it was for this storm, I think years after.

It was so miserable in the dark, cold house. We all piled up, dressed in our winter coats, to find a supermarket or restaurant open to get some more food. The fridge wasn't working and all the fresh food we spent money on had sadly spoiled.

The storm we weren't prepared for. Some people had generators, we didn't. There was a hurricane in 1985. All the schools were closed, but it was nothing like this. Streets, driveways, and basements flooded. So this pizza place we went to sometimes had lights. My Dad ordered four angel hair pasta plates with extra sauce and meatballs. Next door at Shop and Stop my Mom and brother got me Smoked BBQ Wheat Thins to go with it. The weather was bad. We were about 10 minutes away from home, but just wanted to get home before the weather got worse.

I ate in my bed, in my winter coat, under the covers, where I would usually watch TV. No TV today. How sad to eat with no TV, in the dark. It was the worst thing I ever went through up until that point. My Dad called the power company again. Thankfully the phone still worked. My Dad told them he was freezing and getting sick and he has a heart condition and there's a lot of sick elderly people on our block and we need power. The temperature was in the low 40s in the house. We all warmed up in the car, then listened to some radio.

MIRROR OF MY WORLD

The next day the same, but my family had some take-out from the local market and I just drank two cups of hot coffee to warm up my insides.

The next day, my Dad had court filing for bankruptcy, with his lawyer friend helping him. They all went. I didn't need to go; I was lucky to sleep through it and be able to hibernate. They were gone at least seven hours. We had no working phone by then. If I woke up and needed help or was sick, I wouldn't have been able to call them or anyone, or an ambulance. It was a scary nightmare.

Better to sleep as much as possible until life returns to normalcy. I hadn't slept well until today, hard bundled up in a winter coat, freezing. Thought how much longer can this go on? Can I survive, barely any place to get food, too cold and dark to even brush out my hair, can't do anything. Daddy and my family got home later. I went downstairs so happy to see him and give him a hug. It was comforting. It was nice he was out in real society, wearing a blazer and dressed all nice. He hugged me back and said everything went well. He called Con-Ed again, to try to get some heat and lights back on.

We had been without power for four days. I couldn't take much more. I couldn't function like this, feeling sick, depressed, confused. Finally, the power was back, the lights all went on, the heat was starting to come up. It's a miracle. We were saved.

Daddy thought the phone calls helped them make us a priority first. I couldn't have lasted much longer, suffering like this. We had a flooded basement, as did our neighbors. All the food we needed to take photos of to be reimbursed by FEMA. And we sent them. We were. We dumped out all the food, then Larry went to the deli to take out burgers for all of us to celebrate. We had power and finished the bankruptcy case. The food wasn't very good, but I was so happy to have electricity and be back to normal and survive and tell my story.

It was one of the worst things I ever went through, a five-day ordeal, the biggest nightmare to date, but many had it worse and lost their homes.

Christian Karen Berman

MY DAD'S FAVORITE MOVIES

My Dad's favorite movies, to the best of my knowledge:

The Prime of Ms. Jean Brodie
Brigadoon
The Graduate
Peter Pan
Blazing Saddles
The Paper Chase
Kramer vs. Kramer
Back the Future
The Baby M Case
The Sure Thing
Biloxi Blues
Awakenings

Some Kind of Wonderful
Pretty in Pink
Chances Are
Lean on Me
Stand and Deliver
Goodbye, Columbus
The Sound of Music
Baby Boom
The Ernest Green Story (TV Movie)
Summer School
Big
Love, Actually

The TV shows he liked:

Live from Lincoln Center
Room 222
Welcome Back, Kotter
Let's Make a Deal
The Price is Right
Wheel of Fortune
CNN Live

Anne of Green Gables (mini-series)
Hogan's Heroes
Love Sidney
All in the Family
The Mary Tyler Moore Show
CBS News

MIRROR OF MY WORLD

Christian Karen Berman

MY MOM'S FAVORITE MOVIES

My Mom's favorite movie:

Falling in Love

She liked TV shows:

The Waltons
The Young and the Restless
Our House

And she loved all the Hallmark specials about Christmas and Romance.
So did my Daddy.

MIRROR OF MY WORLD

Christian Karen Berman

THE NIGHT OUR CAR GOT STOLEN

A true story. This happened about ten years ago. My Dad and my brother were talking about the car payment was due. They didn't have enough money and they needed to pay before midnight or they would lose their car insurance. It was a lot of money to borrow from someone, so my Dad called his old friend. She was nice enough to loan us the money. I vaguely remember them asking her about PayPal or Western Union. She and her husband were not sure how it worked, so it was taking a while for them to figure it out, even with my Dad and Larry explaining it to them. The last week or two, we usually ran outta money if we didn't watch it carefully or if we had extra expenses. We received the money from his friend and Larry paid before midnight, maybe 8-10 pm.

Daddy was up late, as usual. My Mom was sleeping. I was not feeling good at all. I had a really bad sore throat. It hurt and bothered me, so much so I couldn't sleep. So I walked into my parents' bedroom and told my Dad. This was around March. Daddy came into my bedroom to sit with me and poured me a paper cup of Diet Cranberry Ginger Ale. Larry just got a new bottle and I was thirsty, too. I was sitting in my bed, under my covers sipping it. It helped a little. I dunno if we had any, but popsicles would have helped more. My Dad asked me to take my temperature. I can't remember, it might have been in the normal to low range. I'm not even sure we had a blood pressure or pulse ox monitor back then to check my vitals, like we did a few years later. Well, I was still feeling kinda sick. I was hearing a loud noise outside my window. I asked my Dad if he heard it. He wasn't sure. I insisted I heard some loud noises outside and to come by my drapes and listen. It was around 2:30 am. He said they were probably just letting the water out of the fire hydrants, they did that sometimes in the middle of the night. It turns your water in the bathroom brown when they do. I tried to look outside the best I could, but my curtains were so long and thick and it was so dark outside I couldn't see

MIRROR OF MY WORLD

what was going on. I heard loud screeching or something. My Dad heard it, too. We both wondered why they were working on the streets so late at night, but it was late, even for us, and we both had to get back to bed. I was afraid to go outside and look. I didn't like to go outside much as it was, even during the day most of the time. Daddy didn't tell Larry. We didn't really think anything much of it and we were tired and we both just went back to sleep.

I think I actually went to sleep, too. The next morning around 9 or 10 am, that time was vital for everyone. Blood sugar, blood pressure, 02 and temp, just like they do in the hospital. It also was the time when my Dad would call around about lunch with me to find out what the local places and the hospital were serving that day to see where we wanted Larry to take out from that sounded the best. The hospital food back then was really good. My Dad wasn't that well, so he was in and out of the hospital, but nothing that serious back then. Larry and my Mom went outside and couldn't find the car. It wasn't there. He was confused and told my Dad. My Dad asked if he parked it on the street. Larry insisted it wasn't there. Then my Dad called his friend and asked what to do, that our car was stolen. Stolen!

I was up and said, "I told you I heard something last night. You didn't believe me, they were stealing our car." Well, we both were tired, it's a safe, family-friendly neighborhood, it's the last thing my Dad would ever expect. Nothing ever happens here. I mean, we get blizzards, dogs barking, hurricanes, wildlife, flooded basements. The biggest crime we have on our block is when a package gets misdelivered, then my Dad hadda call our neighbors and ask if they got my package and Larry sometimes hadda go door to door. It happened with my baby doll from eBay and an Oshkosh clothing order. It happens often, actually. They always return it eventually. People are good and honest around here, when you can find them. Mostly nobody's ever home. So who would steal our car from our driveway in the middle of the night? Why our car? It was rather nice and new and only a few years old, so much so that we still had payments on it.

My Dad's friend said to call the police, so he had to call the police. He was so nervous to call them. I don't think he ever had to call the police before and to report a stolen car, no less. I think when I was a child about nine years old, some 20-something-year-old neighbors down the block were having a loud party with loud music all night long, so he had to call and complain about the noise, no one could get any sleep. I wasn't sure if the music ever stopped. I still heard it in my head. I slept next to my Mom in the big bed then. Well, my Daddy musters up the courage to talk to the police and tells them his car was stolen in his driveway last night while we slept, and what was their response? It wasn't stolen, it was repossessed. Noooooo......! My Dad argued we paid it. It must have got there too late, the money, so they took our new car back.

We were all kinda in shock and disbelief. We didn't even know what to do now. Nothing like this has ever happened to us before and we did pay hours before midnight. My Family was all upset and kinda yelling and frantic and didn't know what to do and who to call and my Dad called his friend again to tell him what happened and ask what to do, then he called the car place and the bank, a lot of phone calls, a lot, it was getting near 12 pm now and my throat did not hurt anymore and I was getting hungry and wanted my Dad to call around and find me the best meal for lunch. This was taking longer than I thought, too long, there was nothing I could do to help, but yell with them at people on the phone and make a lot of angry commotion, so I went upstairs to brush, wet, and detangle my long hair for over an hour. It needed to be done anyway, I might as well get it over with. I was waiting and hoping the issue would soon be resolved and Larry would be able to pick up his car. Luckily we had another car, too, at the time. I finished my hair and my blood sugar was really starting to feel low. I can't remember if Larry or my Dad took it or not, but it was usually in the low 70s to mid-80s.

Finally, around 1:30 pm, the misunderstanding and mistake was fixed. Larry went to the local market and took out some nice lunch. It was something good we all liked and Larry didn't feel like going further anyway after all of this unnecessary aggravation. It was a hard, memorable time, but the good part was, we were all in it together.

MIRROR OF MY WORLD

Christian Karen Berman

FOOD POISONING

I really miss my Daddy so much all the time. He was the only one who loved and accepted me for my true, authentic, own self. I remember one time he was in the hospital, I got food poisoning from a deli we took out from. I shared a half a cheeseburger, fries, smoked salmon and a bagel. I felt sick and nauseous after and had a fever of 102. That's very high for me. I rarely get that sick and run high fevers. My heart was fast and I just felt yucky, hot and cold, clammy, sweaty hands.

I was talking to Daddy on the phone who was in the hospital for something, probably cellulitis. He said Larry should take me right down to the E.R. I think I had a low oxygen, it was 94-95%. My Mother did not want to come with us and started putting up a big fuss. She couldn't be left alone. She used to wander out of the house looking for her parent's house. She had early onset dementia.

I had gone to bed feeling sick and short of breath. I was sleeping with the handset phone, Daddy on the other end in the hospital for comfort. I felt so bad, my oxygen was 93-94%. Well, I woke up early with a racing heart, very hot and high blood pressure. Larry had to take me now. It was a real emergency! My Mom was sleeping. It was around 7:30 am. He pretty much just dropped me off in the E.R. and went straight home to take care of my Mother.

The E.R. took blood work and an EKG to take care of me. I said my Dad was in the hospital, too. I think I called him on the phone in the E.R. They felt sorry that I had to take care of my sick Mom and my Daddy was sick, too. Basically, the treatment was a shot cup of purple yucky grape Children's Tylenol and a cup of ice water I was forced to take because I had a fever of 101. Then I was discharged and felt too sick and tired to even visit my Dad and went straight home to bed and woke up 14 hours later to go about my normal, miserable cleaning-the-house life. I called

MIRROR OF MY WORLD

Daddy early that morning. He waited on the phone and made me take my temperature again. He was the only one in my whole life that ever cared about me, but my Mom and brother Larry cared about me second best.

Daddy used to try to get me to eat my Mom's meals by making them more special. I was 15 then. He'd cut up her chicken, put it on toast, heat up a can of baked beans, put onion powder on top and pour it over my food. He'd make me toast with peanut butter and cherry jelly or banana slices for snack. He tried to be a cook best he could. I spent a lot of time in the pediatrician's office growing up, like at least a few times a month for something. Our second home. They gave out *Healthy Kids* magazines and sugar free lollipops. I liked it there. They always remembered me; they were very nice.

I felt very loved and happy as a child. I loved everything!

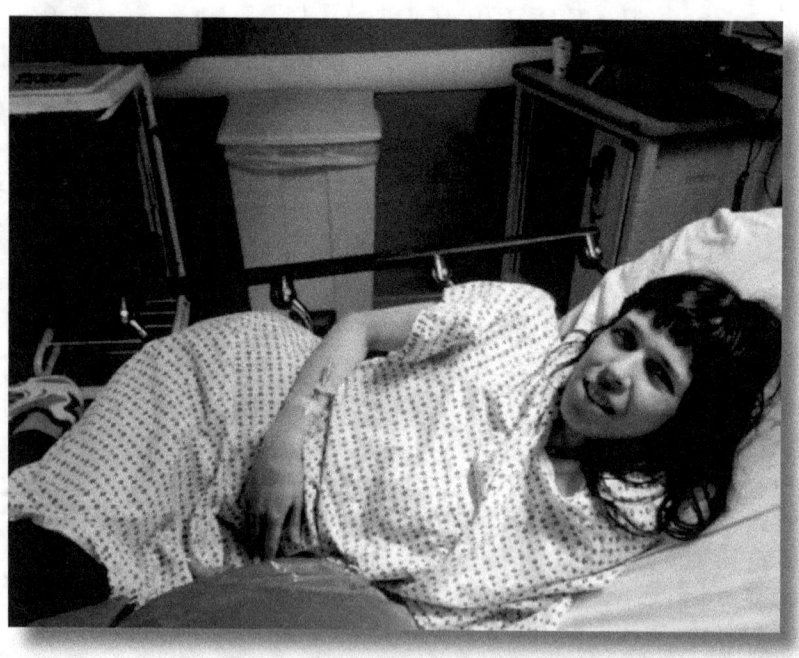

Christian Karen Berman

BREAKING DADDY OUT OF GREENWICH WOODS

The hospital thought that this place would help my Dad walk better. He was there only a day or so. I had visited him there once, lied in bed next to him because I missed him so. It was hard to go home to a sad, lonely, empty house. A nurse kept coming in and looking at me lying in bed next to my Dad. I was dressed as my Dad, just tired and wanted rest, sleep and get in a few cuddles and snuggles.

The next day my Dad is complaining he doesn't feel good to the nurses, that he's hot and cold and his legs are red and swollen and he has cellulitis again, but they are not giving him medicine. The doctor is not doing anything, and they won't take him back to the hospital for treatment. He is very upset by this and has had enough. He wants Larry to come get him and take him back to the E.R. to be admitted to the hospital again.

I talk to my Dad by phone early that morning. I just got up and haven't eaten in a day, but this sounds exciting. This is going to be a fun day; I wouldn't miss it for anything in the world. My brother had picked up dinner for me at the hospital where we use to take out from. He was heating it up for my breakfast. One container had beef teriyaki, another meal was turkey tetrazzini and green curry Indian Mulligatawny soup. Larry opened a can of 3 bean salad to add to it as my vegetable. I was hungry, it was good. I might have had microwavable Jolly Time Popcorn, too.

So, I got ready and we were driving to the rehab through Connecticut. This place was recommended highly for my Dad. He didn't like Sarah Newman Nursing Home. Or the place in Portchester—he couldn't take it there at all.

Before my Dad went home, they wanted him to get rehab first. When we got there, it almost looked like a hotel. I saw a talking parrot I said "hi" to. They had nice green floral carpeting. I saw my Daddy; he was packed up getting ready to leave. The staff wasn't happy, but he was feeling really sick and wanted to go to the E.R. I looked around for what I thought was the last time I would be there, in the nice bathroom, too. Then we packed up the rest of my Dad's belongings and hightailed it out of there. I looked at the place to make memories and with my Dad in the wheelchair, we got him into the car and started our new adventure, going back to the same E.R.

It took 15 minutes to get to the E.R. It was quite a boring wait in a small room. I was getting tired. They blood-tested my Daddy, took all his vitals, gave him a nice hot lunch. We must have been there five hours. I was bored and wanted him just to be discharged so we could go home already. Many doctors and nurses had come in and were nice. I can't remember if my Mom was in the same hospital this time and we visited her, too, maybe the time before. The hospitalist said he was fine and could go back to Greenwich Woods. To all of our surprise, they called an ambulance to take him safely back there. Larry and I would follow by car. An hour later the EMT's finally arrived to get my Daddy in the ambulance.

We followed and were back. By now it's almost 7 pm, dark out. We're all tired. They gave him a nice room right away, but we have to go on these old scary elevators down to his new room. It's one of the only rooms that they have left in the place. This part of the place isn't nice. It's a locked part for some of the more mental people who might want to escape. We had to take two old elevators to get there and a man is escorting us.

In the room it's stuffy and cold. The bed's not comfortable and seemed old and has a funny smell. My Dad is in an empty part of the home, not being as much attended to. He just wanted to go home and I wanted him to go home, too. We sat on the bed together and all made a decision against doctors' orders to leave and we told the nurse. She asked why. Mostly he didn't like being put in the basement in an old room at the end of the hospital, locked in.

We wheeled him out, only problem we had to go on these elevators again. I'm claustrophobic. We were so happy once we got him outside and his stuff packed up in the car and we were outta there.

Christian Karen Berman

At home I had a diet cranberry, raspberry Snapple drink. I was thirsty. Larry went to CVS to get us some snacks. It must have been 9 pm and we were hungry. Daddy got Ritz and Laughing Cow Cheese. I got Great Grains Date cereal. I went right to bed, though.

In the morning, I'm eating some cereal and snacks with my Daddy, watching *Highway to Heaven* on TV—the one with Dick Van Dyke, I believe. Then Meals on Wheels comes to deliver my Daddy a nice, healthy whitefish lunch. Then the social worker calls. Daddy picks up. He always had all the phones and remote controls by him. She tells him she has to come check on us now, because we broke Daddy out of the home without permission. She knows us and knows he's okay, but it's protocol. She'll be here within the hour. What a fun adventure.

The last movie I watched with both of them and Larry: *The Parent Trap 2*.

The last movie I watched just with my Mom and brother: *Little Monsters*.

The last movies I watched with my Dad and Brother: *On the Second Day of Christmas* and *The Christmas Bunny*.

The last TV shows I watched with my Daddy: *Father Knows Best*, "The Christmas Cabin," (the first Christmas episode), and *Lassie*, "The Christmas Story"—during Christmas, Timmy finds a struggling single dad caring for a young sister and brother. They are afraid they're going to get taken away from their dad because he is poor, out of work, and he can't afford to feed his kids. My Dad really enjoyed this episode before he had to go into the hospital on January 19th, 2018.

MIRROR OF MY WORLD

Christian Karen Berman

STORIES OF MY DADDY

My Dad's first job, he was a Professor at Pace University in N.Y.C. They gave the newcomer the worst job. This was in the late 1960s. The teens were out of control, opening and closing the big windows and doors in the middle of winter. It was like a bad scene out of the movie *Summer School,* he got all the juvenile delinquents. My Dad told one young man who was acting up that he had to go to the bathroom. The kid insisted he didn't haveta go, but my Dad said he did. Well, that's how he got one boy to cool off from acting bad. He also sent half the class down to the principal's office. A few minutes later, the principal came back and she wasn't very happy, saying matter-of-factly, but in a losing patience, pleading tone, "You can't send half of the class down to the principal's office and you can't tell a student he has to go to the bathroom if he doesn't have to go." After that the whole class was cracking up.

My Dad's first grade teacher was Mrs. Carrasics. The only way I remembered her name all these years was I use to call her Mrs. Carrot sticks. Since his dad owned a pharmacy, she always used to ask my Dad to bring a box of tissues to share with the class. Oh, the perks of being in the pharmaceutical business. My Dad had another teacher that I don't think his Mom liked. When she would walk past the house, his mom, Gertrude, would go, "There goes Fat Ass Pazzini," and this was back in the late 1940s.

My Dad had a few parakeets as a teenager. One would talk on his ham radio with him and once it copied what my Dad said to another caller, "This is **K2PEJ BOY**," and the other guy asked the parakeet to repeat what he said, thinking it was another person on the radio. My Dad would give the parakeet nicknames like Keet Para. It used to fly and sit on my grandma Mama Gert's shoulder and lean over and bite her in between her nose. She would scream and run away and the bird would squawk and fly away simultaneously. You'd haveta be there, but you get the picture.

MIRROR OF MY WORLD

His parakeet would see his refection in the microphone and think it was a lady bird and he'd puff out his chest and feathers. When his bird was talking on the air, another guy came back and thought he was my Dad and asked him if he could please repeat his call sign. Another time the bird flew out his apartment window and he thought he'd never see him again, but he called him by his name Keet Para and amazingly he flew back in. He knew he was very loved and wanted by my Daddy and he loved him back.

My Grandpa Joe owned his own pharmacy in Brooklyn, New York. My Dad told me sometimes in his free time at home, he would throw pennies out the window when no one was looking, then they would look up to see where it was coming from and he would hide behind the curtain kind of snickering, thinking it was funny. It was the early 1950s, so maybe he was thinking he wanted the people to think it was actually pennies from Heaven, kind of sweet and funny at the same time. Well worth the 25 cents he might have lost throwing pennies. If only they had *Candid Camera* or a GoPro back then. There weren't many interesting things to do back in those days, so you pretty much had to get creative and entertain yourself. Being a pharmacist, if someone did get hurt, he could give them an over-the-counter remedy.

With his dad being a pharmacist, my Dad got addicted to these cough drops. They would taste good and sweet the first few minutes, then became strong and powerful. He got used to them and enjoyed them even when he wasn't sick, sort of how today's kids like Flamin' Hot Cheetos and Super Sour Patch Kids. Oh, the perks of being the son of a pharmacist. One day he decided to play a little joke on his good friend, tell him how good these tasted and asked him if he'd like to try one, too. He popped one in his mouth first to show him how yummy they were, then the boy said yes and was enjoying it, too, in the beginning, then it started to burn his mouth and he spit it out on the sidewalk and said something like, "What are you trying to do, Berman, kill me?"

Another time my Dad was five and tied his shoelaces together in kindergarten as a physical challenge and a test of faith. He asked God to untie them. When he didn't, not only was he at a loss, he told his teacher. She made my Dad hop around with his tied dress shoes all day long. She said that was a stupid thing to do and this was his punishment. When he came home that day, he told his mother and that same day she went back to that teacher and boy did she give it to her.

My Dad as a boy had a fire drill in class. There was another boy before him and when they finally turned around to go in, he said

MIRROR OF MY WORLD

"Hey, you cut in front of me, I'm telling." Obviously, he was the brains of the class.

I remember this day very clearly, I watched *Adam 12* and *Emergency* on TV and ironically very soon after, since my Dad's oxygen was very low, even on his O2 machine, my brother Larry had to call an ambulance and have them take my Daddy to the E.R. He hadn't been doing well before that, but I never thought he'd have to actually be taken by ambulance to the hospital, but he was so much worse this day. A few days before, I had given him a haircut he asked for. I had to climb over his big Lazy Boy chair and his lap many times over to get it perfect (ironically, the I.C.U. butchered his hair cut, cut it real short to put his oxygen mask over). To thank me for the haircut he sang, "You, you, you, I'm in love with, you, you you!" His cardiologist was watching him by phone. I was worried and thinking at least his hair would look good in the hospital.

There was a major flu epidemic at the time, that's why my Dad was avoiding going to the hospital. He was afraid of catching the flu (he never caught the flu the month he was there). The reason he had trouble breathing and a low oxygen level was because he had congestive heart failure and his heart didn't pump right. He needed the fluid drained from his lungs so he could breathe easier. He also had diabetes and stage 3 kidney failure which was caused by a diabetes drug he was on, so he was forced to switch to insulin and watch his diet very carefully. he was good at it for the most part, he didn't have much sugar.

I rode in the ambulance with him. I didn't really feel like going, but in the back of my mind I wondered is this going to be it, is this for real, is this the last time he'd be leaving this house? I tried not to believe it and just think what a fun adventure it was riding in an ambulance to the hospital.

A few hours before my Dad asked me to sit on his lap. He knew how much I loved sitting on his lap, this would be the very last time. He must have sensed that somehow, very sadly. On the way to the hospital Emergency Room, I asked the driver why she wasn't driving fast. She said because she wanted to get there safely and he was stable. His oxygen level was 72% and he was on an oxygen machine when the paramedics arrived. Normal oxygen is 100%, but anything less than 96% is not good. We made it there safely.

I got bored in the hospital and, upset as I was, I knew that we were going to be there a while, so I took my first selfie, in the bathroom in my Dad's E.R. room. My Daddy was my whole world and I loved him more than anyone. I never thought he could die and leave me. I loved him so much! My Daddy always smiled at me calmly and lovingly and said, "I love you more than you'll ever know!" He was my Ba-Ba and I was his Wa-Wa and his Coo-Coo, he made up all kinds of nick names for me. I sometimes called him Dr. Berman, because he really missed teaching so much and being called that. He had a Ph.D. in Education, and won a Lifetime Achievement Award, among at least 20 *Who's Who in the World* and *Who's Who in America* awards; he was a famous educator and author. In the hospital there was a sign by his bed— "Please refer to as Dr. Berman," meaning not Mr. Berman. The hospitalist called him Stevie, meant in a sweet, caring, loving way. I really miss my Ba-Ba and my Mom!

I was very worried the last two weeks, Daddy had called and said they were putting him in I.C.U. His blood pressure was very low, like 89/60-something, low like that. When I went to visit him and finally saw him it was like Christmas morning as a child, when everything was the biggest and best and you got every present you asked for and more. We both smiled and I was hugging his arm and hand. I never thought he would die, it never occurred to me, because he was all I had and I needed him so much. He didn't wanna die and leave me.

He was still concerned and talking normally when I had my alone visit with him. He said he didn't have any dreams of my Mom or Heaven, which was a very good, healthy sign. I.C.U. was full so he was in the unit they put you in after major surgery to watch you very closely and monitor you, the P.A.C.U. I tried to keep talking a lot to keep his blood pressure up. I was watching the monitor very closely. I talked to the nurse, too. The nurse wasn't coming so I told Daddy to say "Yo, Mike" very loudly and he did. I thought that was funny.

MIRROR OF MY WORLD

The last week I called as soon as I woke up at 7 am to see if my Daddy was okay every morning. I was so worried about him. He had his own private room by then and Larry said he was okay, and Daddy said a few words, too. Sometimes he was sleeping or getting a breathing treatment with the nebulizer and steam by the respiratory specialist. After, I think I went back to sleep. I didn't want him to die and leave me!

I was more concerned than Larry and wanted to talk to all of his doctors. I didn't know how sick he really was. They all knew us and hid it from me. Daddy, I think, told them not to tell me last time. The hospital specialist who knows us told me, the last time three years ago after he was rushed into I.C.U. They treated me like a kid and tried to protect me. I wish they would have been more honest the last time.

I remember the last few words my Daddy said on the phone to me. He said, "Hi, little girl," and at the end when Larry was taking the phone away, he said softly, "I love you." It was a few days before I saw him. When I did see him, he used gestures more like smiles and shrugs because he had an O2 mask on and couldn't talk well with it on. I am missing him, his worry and concern for me.

I really didn't know how sick he was. He was in his own room and he always came home from the hospital. I didn't think he could die; they always saved him so many times when he was very sick. He always got better. I called and begged his cardiologist to save him, and he did. The last time he didn't. Nobody did, or could. I called many doctors. Larry wouldn't let me talk to them when they came in the room. I had to call them at their office, even a few that barely knew my Dad. I called the hospital many times, too, to find doctors to help him or tell me how he was doing and tell them what they should do. I was his only advocate that cared and loved him best. I tried to call my old pulmonologist, but he was retired. I even called another doctor that didn't even know my Daddy to try to save his life. I was usually very shy and rarely ever made phone calls to anyone by myself, but I just pictured him suffering so, I had to. I knew he was very sick, I thought at worst they'd have to treat him or put him on life support. It didn't ever occur to me he could actually die and leave me forever!

It was very hard, out of my comfort zone, to leave the house. I called him on the phone. Larry was there watching him most of the day and night. I thought he'd be home in a few days or a week. He was better two days before he died and I missed my Daddy so much, the real Daddy that he used to be, and he was getting better and recovering. I just had to see him again. That night, it was around 7:20 pm., I woke up, called Larry, changed my clothes and when I got there he was watching *Wheel of Fortune* and eating apple sauce. I said I was tired, but I came just to see you and he smiled at me so sweetly. I hugged him on the bed and I said, "Hug me tighter!" My last real hug by him, or anyone really. I just missed him so much!

I was feeling very relieved. He's out of the woods. I don't have to worry anymore. He's okay now and will be coming home in a few days! A male nurse took Larry outside and didn't want me to hear what he was telling him. Larry was his medical proxy and I wasn't allowed to know. Larry was also trying to protect me from finding out about the very sad, honest truth, too. It was about intubating him and putting him in I.C.U. They put him on his bipap machine. His oxygen was 89%, but then it went up to 93%! I did run back in the room a few times before we left to go home, I always did, even with my Mom, just to check on him and I didn't know when I'd be able to go back in a few days and I knew I was going to miss him, but I was sure he'd be okay. He always was, and I was getting tired and sleepy and I never liked sleeping over. I was welcome to, but I had no idea he was going to die and Larry wanted to take me home and heat up my dinner. It was hospital food from the cafeteria, as usual.

I never got to say goodbye.

He left without telling me goodbye! I always pictured the last goodbye was saying everything that was never said and lots of hugging and crying on both our parts and giving me or a responsible adult some sound instructions in what to do with me when he wasn't here anymore for me, to tell me what to do with my life and future, to find someone who cared and loved me and be responsible like another parent figure! Sadly, I guess he had no close friends he trusted, and we have no family, so I had to be on my own and figure everything out for myself with no help from anybody. There was no priest, rabbi, or anyone there that terrible, early Saturday morning when he died, just a few young techs in their early 20s to comfort me. That's what happened. I did hear there were 30 people in the room when he was dying to try to help resuscitate him, the hospital staff that knew him very well for five years and loved him very much, too!

I insisted on taking his hospital bracelet home with me, so I'd leave with something of his. He always used to give me his school name tags from meetings, the nice plastic kind you pin on, so I just knew he'd want me to have that to take with me and keep forever. I got a little emotional about that, too. They had to call and ask permission about that, but they got it.

I was crying most of the time, upset and couldn't believe this was really happening.

I found out four hours after he died. Then I got to come and see him and say my goodbyes. I thought I'd have to be admitted to the E.R. I was having trouble breathing myself, lost and very devastated. I could hardly believe it was really happening. I didn't want to leave his hospital room. They wanted to bag him up. I even used my oxygen monitor on his finger to check his oxygen level, thinking he's alive and in a coma. The EKG line wiggled but had no number. I even told the nurse he looked a little blue and to please take his vitals right away. She took his blood pressure! I think he was still alive inside, but maybe couldn't talk or move.

I don't know why he had to die. I think his body failed him and the nurse accidentally OD'd him on insulin, he was diabetic. They kept drawing yellow fluid from his lungs and stomach, every few days it kept coming back. I don't know why God and everyone in Heaven took him from me, if I had nobody else and still needed him so much! I wish so very much I got to say goodbye and he told me what to do with the rest of my life and I got closure. He wouldn't even tell me or answer me that question when he was alive, or help me have a life. He was trying to protect me from the real world and keep me happy the best he could with buying me baby dolls and toys.

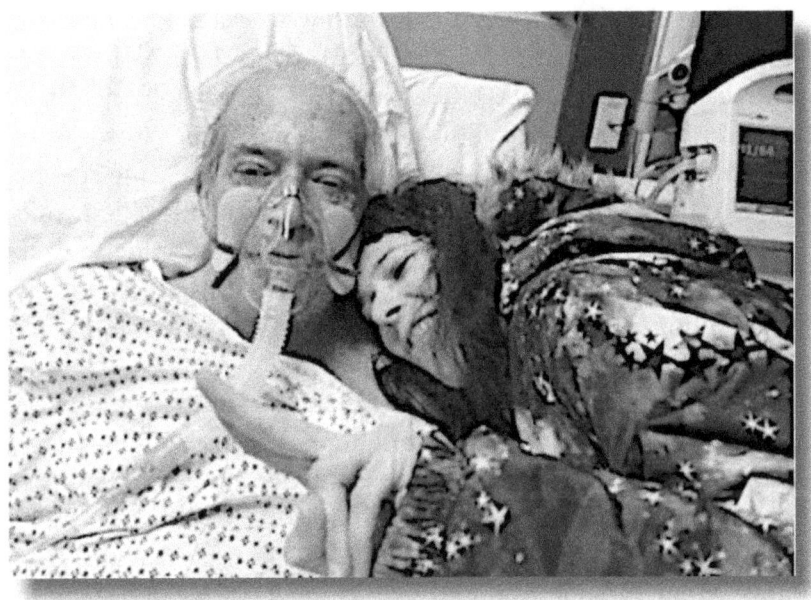

This photo was taken February 8th, 2018, at 9:30 pm at night. He died February 10th at 1:09 am. Rapid response did not work. They worked on him from 12:40 am and couldn't bring him back. I wanted to call around 12:00 am. I missed him but was afraid I'd wake Larry. I was always so considerate thinking of other people. I was working very hard that night cleaning the house for him extra good, so he'd have a very clean house to come home to and thinking then, he's at the safest place he could be in the hospital, being monitored 24/7. I didn't have to worry about him. But I was a little. I couldn't help it, I loved him! I was also thinking I should have asked for him to sign his book for me, but I wanted him to write an autobiography or the real true story of being my Father, about him raising me and interesting family stories I could save forever to remember him. I didn't understand his book or like math. I barely knew what his book was all about (it was about a diabetes research study from the 1960s with statistical data to back it up), or that he was kinda famous then. To me he was just my Daddy and I sat on his lap one last time a few hours before the E.M.T. took him to the E.R.

MIRROR OF MY WORLD

My Dad told his cardiologist this a few weeks before he died, referring to me, "I CAN'T DIE! HOW CAN I LEAVE HER? SHE NEEDS ME TOO MUCH!" His cardiologist told me that a week after he died. It was a little comforting, but truer words were never said. He never would talk about dying and leaving me, he refused to. I was upset when he was in the hospital for so long and missed him being at home with me and he was not doing so well. A few times I cried out emotionally, hysterically, and frantically over the phone, "Please don't leave me, take me with you, I want to go with you!"

I worried for the longest time when he was kinda sick and alive, after he died I'd never be able to find him again and that made me cry for him when he was still alive, like five years before he died. I'd go to his school and his classroom and he wouldn't be there or anywhere and I'd never be able to find him ever again. The Horace Mann School promised my Daddy a plaque dedicated to him in his classroom after he retired to remember he taught there for 36 long years. Even when he died, I tried very hard with many phone calls to get it there. I don't think they ever put it there, sadly. He gave his health and life for that school. He dedicated his life at the expense of his own life, my Mom's health and life, and his daughter's future and mental health.

My Daddy loved me the very best in the whole world. He always bragged about me to everyone and loved showing me off, especially at the hospital. I had the best Daddy in the whole world—Dr. Stephen L. Berman.

My Mom died of a complication of stage 3½ colon cancer, and septic shock, an internal infection. For my Mom's funeral I lovingly picked the song "My Mother," from the Chipettes. My Dad's song was "Tears in Heaven," by Eric Clapton. They were the most loving, over-protecting, giving parents in the world and I loved them more than anybody!

DR. STEPHEN L. BERMAN

My Dad had a very rich mind even as a four-year-old. He told me he had an imaginary friend he named Brown because the furniture was brown. At age six he woke up wheezing, because he had childhood asthma. His mother took him into the kitchen and made him some hot Lipton tea. It seemed to work. He said he took Benadryl for that sometimes, it was called chronic bronchitis back in the 1940s, I believe.

His mother sent my Dad away to sleep-away camp at age 10. He was terribly homesick and didn't want to do anything. He went on a train to get there; they served hot cocoa for breakfast with Cheerios! The camp counselors were very kind and tried to talk my Dad into enjoying the camp's activities, but he loved his Mom very much and just wanted to go back home. They decided since he was so unhappy to send him home on the train by himself to Brooklyn, New York.

He almost got off at the wrong stop. It was a very bad, dangerous part of NYC at the time. He said he would have got hurt, a skinny 10-year-old little boy lost in the big city. Luckily, he didn't—he got

MIRROR OF MY WORLD

off at his own stop. His mom hugged him and took him home. She made him fresh French toast and ketchup, his favorite food at the time. He also loved her mashed potatoes.

When my Dad was age 10, his dad used to make him coffee. His father Joseph also heated up Swanson TV dinners in the oven for my Dad when he was older.

When my Dad was 15 years old, his grandmother had been missing her husband terribly for the last few years, since he had died after a brain operation from a blood clot. The medical field didn't know then as much as they do now. He should have been helped to walk around and not been kept bedridden days after surgery. She was so sad without him. Her name was Annie Garfinkel, his name was Louie. She was so distraught she went to the 5th story of the apartment building and started talking very loudly, "LOUIE, LOUIE, I'M COMING, WAIT FOR ME!"—and tragically she jumped to her death!

My grandmother was too emotional and in shock, so my Dad had to go downstairs to the street and identify the body of his grandma he loved so much and he was very close to. He did that as a selfless act of deep love, empathy, and care he had for his mother. Grandma Annie use to bring him fresh rye and butter as his after-school snack. He grew up in Brooklyn, New York. I think my Dad told me it was in the Daily Newspaper, the story in 1955.

He played the piano since age eight, played stick ball, had asthma since age six, which got better as he grew up, a camp counselor in the summer for underprivileged youth, a group of 10-year-old boys, one with cerebral palsy that the kids wheeled in a red metal wagon. They served mac and cheese, ice cream bars, and the kids were all very hungry. They swam, he played basketball with them. He was also a sleepaway camp counselor from 15-20. He always loved teaching and working with children from when he was a child himself.

He was a delivery boy on his bike for Berman's Pharmacy—his father owned his own drug store. Joseph Berman, his father, graduated from Columbia University as head of his class and Valedictorian and was very smart, in the genius category, as my father was. He was also a very kind, loving and generous man like my dad was. My

Christian Karen Berman

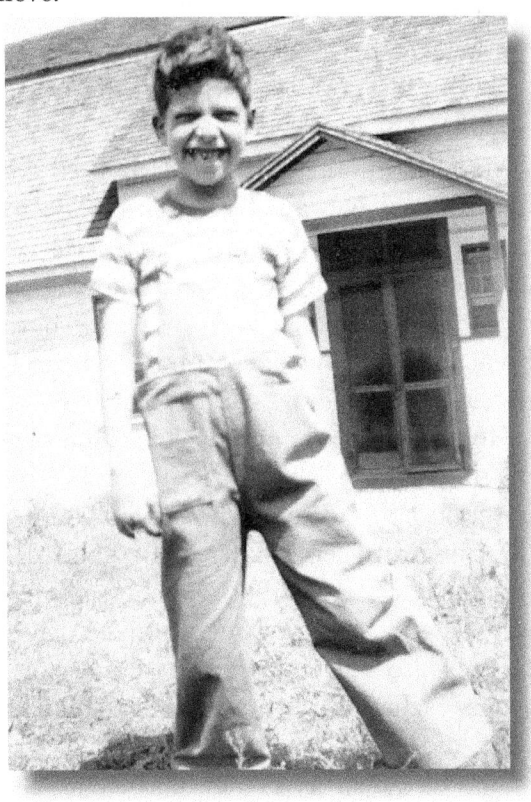

Dad taught a ham radio class at the Y at age 25. He was teaching anyone who was interested how to get their ham radio license. He had passed the Amateur Ham Radio three-hour test at age 15. He was written up in the *New York Post* for that in 1965.

When he had been a sleepaway camp counselor this 10-year-old boy woke him up crying with 104 fever. He was feeling just awful and had a 104 fever and severe stomach pains. My Dad was 18 and woke up the head counselor and told him this young boy was very sick. They found out he had a ruptured appendix. He had got to the hospital just in time to have an operation that saved his life. The boy left camp and went home after surgery. My Dad took him seriously and acted right away to save this scared and sick child!

He graduated as a B.S. cum-laude at Brooklyn College. He had a M.A. from Columbia Teachers College; he also had a Ph.D. in Education from New York University. He was a Professor at P.A.C.E. University in New York City for eight years. Then in 1974 he was hired by Inky Clark on the spot, to teach at the elite private school, The Horace Mann School, in the high school division, because they liked him so much. Dr. Berman was the first Jewish teacher to be working there. He taught selective topics, grades 9 through 12. He taught Geometry, Geometry Honors, Algebra, Algebra II, Trigonometry, A.P. Statistics, Statistical Analysis and Social Science, Probability, Student Advisor, and Director of Student Clubs. He was written up in the school newspaper many, many times. He was a favorite schoolteacher, the most popular teacher, too. Parents who have had him as a teacher in the 1970s sent their own kids back in the 1990s and they'd have the same teacher their mom or dad missed and loved so much. He met many famous people during his teaching career. He taught Walter Cronkite's grandson in his Geometry class, Tom Brokaw's kids, Nita Lowey's kids, Dr. Ruth's kids. He was friends with the people behind the popular 1988 TV movie, The Baby M Case. Mary Beth Whitehead and Joel Siegel, the real people behind the made-for-TV movie, came as famous guest speakers to my Dad's class each year to give a talk. The lawyer, Mr. Siegel, was my Dad's very good friend, who came every year for 10 years as a personal favor to my Dad, and a Dr. Berman class tradition. Mr. Siegel enjoyed talking to my Dad's students about it, too. My Dad played the movie to his class beforehand so they would understand what *the Baby M case* was really about and the big deal it was in the mid-1980s. It's about their life and fighting over a mother's birth rights versus the surrogate mother's birth rights to the one baby they both want and love so much. So interesting, controversial, and relevant even today, I believe. My father related the statistics to show his students how you can actually use math in real life and enjoy what you do. Terribly fascinating. The kids didn't want to leave the class when the bell rang, they enjoyed the talks and debating too much. He did the same with the movie *Kramer vs. Kramer*. He had the writer Avery Corman come and give a talk about the movie. One of his students was even friends with Justin Henry, "Billy Kramer" in the famous Oscar Award-winning movie. Avery Corman also wrote *Oh, God!* and *Oh, God! Book II*. Walter Cronkite came to the school and gave a talk about his life to the whole school and faculty in the auditorium. It's a very expensive school with only the best and brightest students that work hard and enjoy learning, $50,000 per student.

My Dad encouraged many kids who hated math to love and go into the field of helping people, because he had taught them they had the power to help make a positive difference in the world and change the world for the better. He had created his own course, "Statistics and Social Science," to teach his students wholesome, Golden Rule values that he truly believed in. His helping them pay it forward and them helping many other people in the course of their life, my Dad had made a positive difference in probably millions of people's lives, through the students he lovingly taught. Fair Court Trials for poor people that couldn't afford their own attorneys to keep things fair and honest.

My Dad taught about current events, the O.J. Simpson trial, the Rodney King beatings, and abuse of power by the police. *Multiple Variable Analysis of Covariance*. He loved open topics, this is 11th and 12 graders, too, basically teenagers being taught graduate level material to help change the world and make it a better place for everyone to live. He loved sitting down on top of a desk and just listening to the class's group discussions being one of them. He was a cool teacher. They wrote essays he graded relating it to the math. He tutored them and paid for many of the classroom supplies happily, out of his own pocket, if they're needed. He never cut back or cut out things to save money—only the best for his students. If true, teachers don't make enough money for all the time, love, and dedication they give, countless hours of their valuable lives just to help their students. They do it for the love and passion of teaching. He was "a shoulder to cry on" and acted as a school counselor many, many times for any students in need. Gave up extra time for anyone who needed help, because he really cared about his students.

His workday was, he left the house at 6 am, he came home at 6 pm, a very long, exhausting day, almost an endless day, but he enjoyed every minute, he told me and many others numerous times. There were many afterschool teacher meetings, conferences with parents, calling parents, grading papers… Teachers really help raise our kids, give their time and heart to them, all good teachers. My Dad won so many awards for his love of learning, teaching, education, and dedication, maybe thirty awards. He also wrote a 5-star, bestselling book about a diabetes research drug study from the 1960s about the first oral diabetes drug Orinase. They took it off the market due to a flaw in the control group study, a horrible mistake where many diabetics had to switch unnecessarily to insulin and inject themselves four times a day and check their blood sugar, which was also very hard on their system, which also led to many terrible side effects. It's an amazing find by my Dad, lots of in-depth research went in to making this award-winning book and a great read. My Dad was diabetic, as well, and on insulin. The book is called *Analysis of Covariance*, by Dr. Stephen L. Berman.

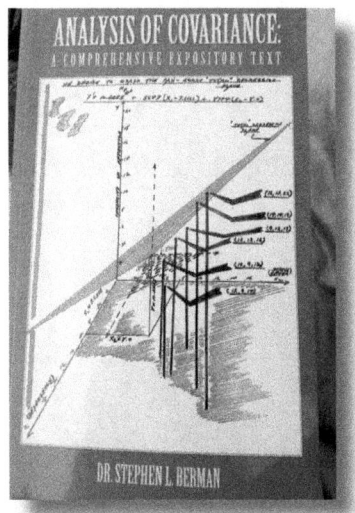

MIRROR OF MY WORLD

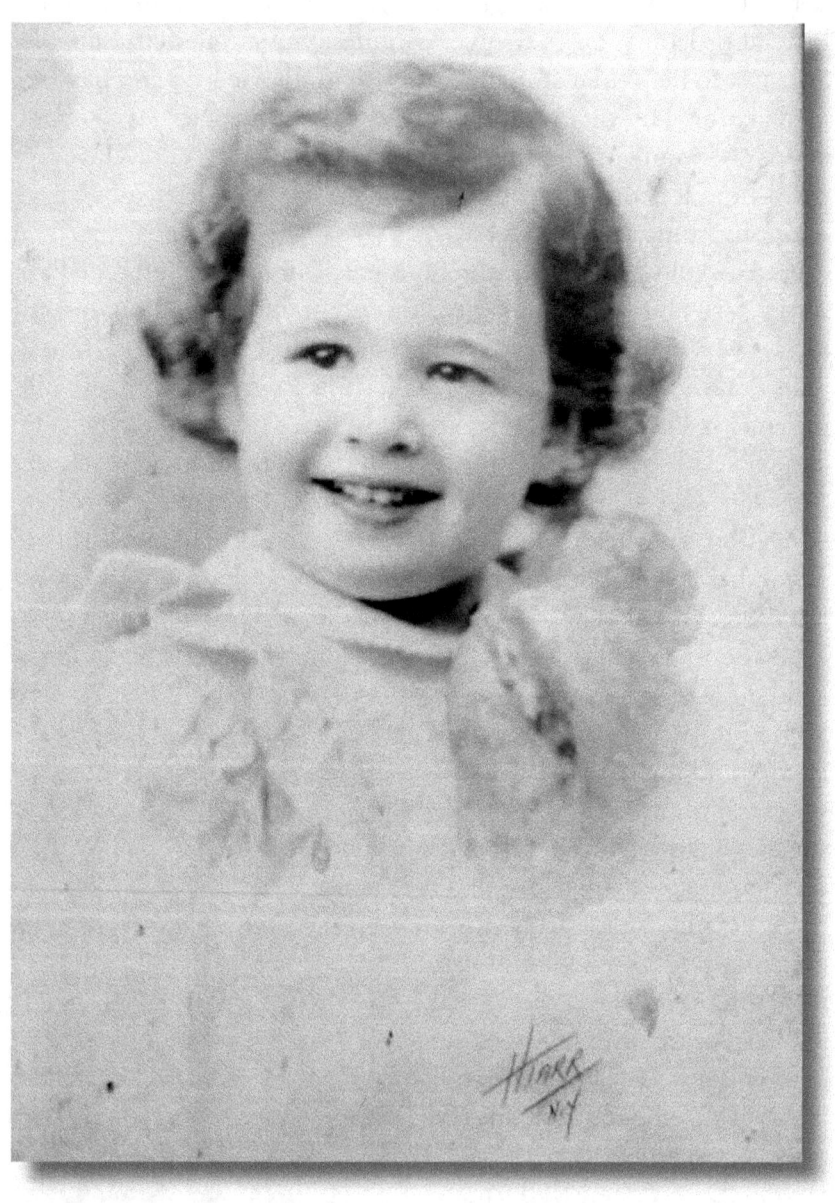

BeveRly JOaN COHeN BeRMaN

She was a very outgoing child, an only child. Her parents loved her very much. My Grandpa was a veteran and World War II hero, winning many medals including the Purple Heart. I read a letter many years ago that my Grandma Lee wrote him. The part that stuck out to me most was she called my Mother, who must have been between ages two and four at the time, a naughty Bobby! I also read a handwritten letter my Mom wrote at age eight to her Mom to get well, very sweet!

My Grandma couldn't have more kids, so she got a mixed Shepherd dog at the pound that looked like a small German Shepherd, around 35-40 pounds. She got that dog at age eight as her brother and babysitter, named Sporty. My Grandma grew up with many dogs and cats together. Whitey was a Spitz, there was Brownie, Nellie, cats. I heard the kittens and puppies grew up together. I think she lived in Brooklyn or on a farm?

Her dad's name was Benjamin Precker. He died when she was 12, I'm not sure what from, but she told me she cried her eyes out and needed eyeglasses after. Girls always miss and need a Dad so much for support, advice, love, and guidance. My Mother grew up in Brooklyn, too. I'm not sure where, the nice part in Flatbush, I think, they had a house. She had friends and birthday parties. She was a model in her teens for *Bazaar*, she had gone to a professional modeling school. I think she was in print ads, like advertisements, and in magazines. She dated in her teens and 20s. My Mom was beautiful.

She dated a soldier named Melvin and there was a Murray, too. Then she was a tennis player and my Dad saw her in 1965, asked her out on a date, she turned my Daddy down, said she was dating someone in the army. My Daddy was a strapping, handsome ladies' man. All the girls wanted to date my very successful Dad. My parents did not have autism and were very social. My Dad had been dating since he was age 15, he was winning awards since age

MIRROR OF MY WORLD

14 in the 8th grade school science awards for inventing electricity to make a record player work on wires and a raw potato. How innovative for the early 1950s! He was a born genius. That was in the school newspaper. He also had a job delivering medicine from his father's famous drug store, Berman's Pharmacy, on his bike to sick people. He interviewed the famous Sid Caesar of *Your Show of Shows* for his school paper, took photos I have, was at the top of his class, played the piano by ear. He also got his amateur ham radio license and knew fluent Morse Code at age 15 and knew how to talk in French. Very accomplished for a 9th grader.

My Mom was a medical assistant to a cardiologist when she was in her mid-20s. She read EKGs, she said, to a Dr. Strauss in Manhattan and Brooklyn. At that time my Dad went to NYU and Columbia and/or Cornell University, all A-plus's, of course. He taught a ham radio course at the Y; they wrote all about my Dad with a photo of him teaching his ham radio class up in the real newspaper in 1965.

Five years after their first meeting, my Dad was sitting home one Friday night, maybe feeling a little down and sorry for himself, a little tired from all of his schoolwork and then, he's like "Why am I staying home feeling sorry for myself? I'm going out." He went out to a dance, saw her again, the girl of his dreams, my beautiful red-haired mother who used to model.

He told me it was love at first sight. He walked over to her. She'd broken up with Melvin and Murray, her two old boyfriends. She was available. He said to her, "Can you live on a teacher's salary?" She said, "Yes." He said it was love at first sight and he just knew she was the girl he was going to marry.

He had to promise her Mother he'd always take very good care of her little girl forever. He did his very best to keep that promise his whole life, too! They married in less than a year on August 29th, 1971, at a very fancy temple. Looked like a royal wedding. It was written up in the *New York Times*, their Wedding Day. It's a beautiful true story of destiny, true love, and a second chance. It was fate, meant to be. It's a really good thing he got mad at himself for staying in and he went out that night, or where would my future be? What if they never met again, or he never found a woman he loved? I wouldn't be born or have them as parents. The lesson here is to be brave and go with your gut and see where it takes you. Don't be a talker, be a doer. That's your future.

Then my Mother encouraged him to finish up his Ph.D. He did. It took him eight years. He wrote his thesis and dissertation. It was a very thick book, I don't think I read it, but you can find it in his colleges, I believe. Dr. Stephen L. Berman!

He said Grandma Lee (Lillian Ruth Precker) was a very good cook. He put on weight from her cooking. She graduated high school at age 14, loved to read, excellent artist, very talented, gifted and ingenious! Grandpa Jules was a Taylor and owned his own very successful business/blazer suit shop after the War and worked till the day he died. He died from too much insulin and that caused a massive heart attack. He was diabetic and so was my Grandma Lee and Daddy. Daddy was a professor at P.A.C.E. University for eight years, then he got a Job at the elite private School, the Horace Mann High School in NYC. They lived in a very nice hotel-like garden apartment complex building in Brooklyn, N.Y. They loved Junior's restaurant, Carvel restaurant, and Brooklyn Pizza.

BEVERLY COHEN

Miss Cohen Will Marry

A late August wedding is planned by Miss Beverly Joan Cohen and Stephen Leonard Berman.

Mr. and Mrs. Jules D. Cohen of Brooklyn and 144 Mamaroneck Ave. have made known the engagement of their daughter to the son of Mr. and Mrs. Joseph Berman of Brooklyn.

Miss Cohen, a graduate of James Madison High School, was awarded a B.S. degree from Brooklyn College. She is presently employed as a medical assistant to Dr. Mark Straus, a cardiologist.

Her fiance, an alumnus of Lafayette High School, was graduated cum laude from Brooklyn College. Awarded an M.A. from Columbia University, he is presently a candidate for a doctorate at New York University. He is also an instructor in the Department of Mathematics at Pace College New York.

MIRROR OF MY WORLD

Christian Karen Berman

Before My Dad Got Sick, Our Last Saturdays Went Like This...

My Mommy was alive, too. It must have been in 2014 and 2015. We would all watch the show *Small Wonder* in reruns on TV. Even my Dad liked that. It was later in the afternoon. I would be on YouTube listening to music, like soft rock from the 1980s and *The Chipmunk Adventure* soundtrack and old commercials with Judith Barsi and Heather O'Rourke. Also, old Hi-C commercials and doll commercials from the late 1980s to remember my childhood. I remember seeing an old Chef-Boy-R-Dee commercial with Candice Cameron. I never saw it before, but my Dad heard it and wanted some Beef Ravioli. My Mom and brother didn't want him to have it, too much salt. It was getting close to dinner time. We had a charge at the local market and no money, so he called in some dinner before they would close at 7 pm. He asked for baloney, Jarlsberg cheese, pickle slices. He got the beef ravioli and maybe baked beans. He grew up kinda poor and liked that stuff. Besides, the local market is small and doesn't carry much. He always asked for seeded, Rockland Rye bread, just like his grandma use to bring him after school, fresh rye and butter. I'm not sure he got that this time, maybe egg salad on a bagel with bacon and pickles. We got that once. I have some recorded. My Parents and Larry bought me a mini tape recorder so I could record songs off YouTube to listen to in my room. I know, old school for 2014.

On a cold, raw, winters Sunday, my Dad was getting the local market. I wasn't hungry, only having my coffee, then I got hungry and asked for an Elvis Sandwich—peanut butter, bacon, and honey and banana, fried. They made it, I ate it. Not bad. Daddy got French toast sometimes. He ate like a kid. I was making some Jolly Time microwavable popcorn one afternoon and he said, "Whatever you're having, I want whatever smells so good." He asked so sweetly, I shared it with him and also shared a Nutty Buddy. He got to love those.

We would play this game I made up for fun. Larry got me this bag of assorted Jelly Bellies. I ate a lot, but so many were leftover, I asked my Dad if he wanted some and would play. My Daddy would close his eyes and I would take one jellybean out and put it in his mouth. He would have to guess the flavor. He guessed right more than wrong. It was so much fun for both of us. It was fun when Larry got to pick out kid-friendly foods for us all and not some boring foods my parents use to buy. We took out for the hospital a lot when he got sick. He would call around, first the local market to see what food they were serving today, then the Latino market to see if that was any better, then the hospital cafeteria to see if they had better. Larry would go down to the hospital, talk to all our friends in the dining room that worked there, and Daddy had a photo and would talk to them and see the food, too.

He knew how to use an iPhone. I still don't. He would have all the phones and remote controls with him and hoard them from us. He was a fun dude. I hated the morning shows he'd watch, *Room 222, Let's Make A Deal, The Price Is Right*. I wanted to watch Timmy and Lassie and *Father Knows Best*. We once saw a good episode of the *Mod Squad* with a missing boy, or kidnapped boy is why I liked it, cute kid.

I'd wake up in the middle of the night. A classical music concert would be blaring and I'd say softer, softer. He'd lower the volume or I'd run downstairs frantically, find him asleep and shout, "Lower the volume, turn it off, you're going to wake the neighbors," then he slowly would.

Many times I'd wake up on a cold winter's day and he'd be talking on Echo Link, to one of his many friends in different countries. Toshi, Chan, he'd talk all over the world, he loved it. He had been doing this from age 15 on and off, but it's very hard to get a ham radio license, it's a hard test to past and a long drive away. Mostly older men on it, too. He seemed so happy to talk to everyone, very good with people, people person always, so outgoing.

He liked asking them what they liked to eat. One had a farm. He talked to every country, told them about his students.

When I was downstairs, he'd put me on his lap (I wanted to sit on his lap) and put me on Echo Link to say hi, too, and introduce me. He once even talked to a boy scout leader and his troop. I remember one time before Christmas, we even had my Mom there, Ritchie lying on the child Winnie the Pooh fold-up couch asleep on his back, no less. I asked Larry to take a photo, but it was an old phone. Mary lying on the couch. I would cuddle with her to keep warm, pick her nose, play with her ears, snuggle. A Santa Toy was playing different Christmas songs. It was nice, a little boring, but my whole family was there, and Echo Link kept it from being too lonely.

I would show off many times, I was in my 20's, but everyone thought I was a child or little girl. They would call me "The Little Harmonic," or ask if I was Daddy's granddaughter. Never though the sweet, slow-paced times would suddenly end forever. Just sitting down late at night with Daddy talking, missing him if I had to go to bed.

They deserved another 10 years. They enjoyed life and living, didn't want to get sick and die. I still needed them. I wish I got closer to my Mom, spent more Mom and daughter days with her, even with my Dad. To spend time with him, I had to go to school with him. I did that many times, but I couldn't take the long, unending 12-hour days. Getting up at 5 am to eat, dress, and get ready to leave, leaving by 6, getting there by 7 am to help Daddy set up the room, four or five classes, meetings, everyone said, "Hi, Dr. Berman," and the girls in the bathroom said I was so lucky I was his daughter. I was, I just didn't realize how lucky I was. He was a really special hard-working, cool, relaxed Daddy. I would draw or Xerox my hand and he would ask the faculty in the math office, "Did you ever meet my daughter?" We would leave about 5 pm.

My Mom took me shopping at Lord and Taylor one night, got me a nice girl's shirt. I don't have enough photos or memories with my Mommy.

I didn't forget you, Bev and Daddy, I think about you all the time, I miss you, come back to your home and say hi, turn on the TV so I'll know you're still with me.

MIRROR OF MY WORLD

Christian Karen Berman

Back to School Memories

I miss going to school. It was fun wearing nice, well made, cute, back-to-school clothes. I never thought I would miss my old routine, including cartoons and a chocolate bar after school, sometimes drawing a picture to show my Dad when he came home from school. My Mom would have a milk or dark Hershey Bar waiting for me, or we'd pick out some candy on the way home from school, Gummy Bears and something else.

I remember one morning getting ready to leave for the 6th grade. My Mom drove me. I was close enough to walk, but we barely made it on time when she drove. It was about a mile away. I was thinking she gets to stay home and clean the house and be with Grandma and go food shopping and watch TV. I wish I didn't have to go to school and I could stay home. But school was much more fun than staying home. My version was playing with toys, Polly Pocket, they still have that, too. It was in the 1990s. Staying home is only fun if it's once every few weeks, not every day. That would be so boring, lonely and depressing. I so miss those days.

I remember Larry had these Rebook Air Pump sneakers with an orange basketball on the tongue of the sneaker. They were so cool. I was not that into sneakers as a child, so when I needed new sneakers, I would just pick something that fit comfortably. I got a lot of boring white Keds as a young teenager. When I was a little kid, they had Transformer boy's sneakers, red, grey and white with Velcro. I guess I wanted to be a boy and drive my Mom crazy. Why didn't I get Care Bears or My Little Pony? I can't remember the girl sneakers, but all so cute. Today kids have many sneakers. They get Nike's, so expensive, too. Many of today's kids go back to school in early August. I went back to school September 2nd. It's so wrong to send kids back to school in the heat of summer. I'm glad I got to enjoy my summer and by September when it was getting cooler, the weather, by then you're kinda more ready to

MIRROR OF MY WORLD

return to school. I remember my Dad would say, "it's August 7th, enjoy the summer now, because in less than a month you're going to have to go back to school." I remember at night my Dad and us kids would take walks or bike ride and then come home and sit in the back yard on lawn chairs watching the fireflies light up and having a Disney Banana Pudding Pop or Mickey Mouse ice cream pop. Every day was so wonderful back then, and the food was better too. My Dad and brother had to go back to school, too. It must have been lonely for my Mom. My brother went to my Dad's school and I was local, so I got home early around 3 pm and they got home closer to 4:30 pm.

Kids today are lucky in the sense that they have an iPhone and can call their parents from school. My school nurses were so strict, they rarely ever sent you home. In the second grade, in public school, I wasn't really sick, but faking to go home because I missed my Mom and my TV. I once tried a headache and even said I was nauseous and I was going to throw up, the worst you can be. She didn't send me home. I was embarrassed to ever have my Mom tell the school I threw up when she called me in sick, even if I did. To me that was the most horrible thing, I wouldn't want anyone to know, so you can tell how desperate I was to go home. (Thinking back, school wasn't that bad; I miss it. It's much worse today with all the shootings.) In fact, the teacher said I can't go to the nurse anymore. I was only seven years old. I had stomach pain in the 4th grade at recess, on the lower right side where your appendix is. She didn't send me home. That was Catholic school. Who would go to the school nurse during recess if you weren't really sick? There was a playground and friends. I never went to that school nurse again.

I almost fainted in the 6th grade from low blood sugar. I was waiting on the lunch line and felt weird, woozy, sick. I told the lunch monitor lady and she asked if I needed someone to take me to the nurse. I wasn't feeling well and knew I didn't have time for her to find me a friend to walk me. I think I knew where it was. I barely made it there. The nurse said I was white and she didn't like the way I came in. I could barely see; my vision was fuzzy and

I felt very sick. She said to put my head between my knees and she called my Mom to come pick me up. It was scary. Luckily, I just about made it into the nurse. I put my head down on the table and mumbled I don't feel well.

Lunch maybe was later that day, but I almost fainted and my Mom picked me up. I didn't eat that morning, or just had an oatmeal cookie. When I got home, I had a chocolate and vanilla cup cake, watched a rerun of *Bewitched* and took a nap and woke up when my Dad got home and told him. Why didn't I eat a decent lunch? Because I was a kid and ate what I liked. Maybe my Mom wasn't expecting me home and had nothing prepared. I had lunch money, it was a cheeseburger, corn, and fruit cup, with chocolate milk. Their Pizza was the best. I'm sure I had a good dinner, but don't remember what it was.

I liked the days I was too tired to go to school and my Mom let me stay home and sleep late. Not too often, though. We watched *Our House* reruns with Deidre Hall, on at 9 am, and I ate two or three boxes of the mini assorted cereals and milk while watching it. And my Mom loved *The Young and the Restless*. I would play Barbies before the show and pretend it was the show, Nikki, Jill, Victor. I can't remember too well, early 1990s. I'd get pizza for lunch after. *Maury* was on then at 3 pm.

In 10th grade I was sick and went to the nurse before Christmas break. I had 101.7 fever, and I had a few classes left. She wouldn't send me home and said to wait out the day. She didn't even call my Mom to tell her, and this was the mid-1990s. In the late 1980s, the nurse took your temp with a glass thermometer sitting in a yellow alcohol brine and in the mid-90s, they used a plastic strip that they would put in your mouth. It was cool though and more sanitary. I was sick a lot in my school year. If I wore a Covid mask and washed my hands more I wouldn't have gotten as sick. I did miss a lot of school being sick. The nurses never sent you home unless you needed to go to the hospital, it seems, back then.

I've watched a few back-to-school Vlogs about buying school supplies. I can't believe all the things kids need for school these days, 20 glue sticks for one 5th grader, paints, markers, pens, pencils, crayons, a camera, all different kinds of notebooks and many erasers. There had to be like 25 things on the list. In the mid-1980s in elementary school, all you needed was back-to-school clothes, a cute backpack, and a plastic character lunch box. The school provided everything else. In the 1990s, a three-ring binder, loose leaf paper, a few folders, two or three notebooks, pen and pencils. A backpack, of course, and you could really use last year's backpack if it was still in good shape. All you really used was the binder anyway. You took a few notes and wrote down the homework. They gave you worksheets and books. Back then, using a calculator was cheating. I did usually see the movie instead of reading the book. I tried, but I really wasn't much of a reader and couldn't learn or understand the book by reading. I had to reread the same page and forgot what I read. I found it boring.

I liked going to the school library to talk to the librarians, they were nice old ladies in their late 60s or early 70s. I read every issue of *Parents Magazine* they had during my frees. I loved reading those cover to cover.

I went to the school nurse to talk, too. There was two; one was nicer than the other. I guess that showed my autism. I'd rather talk to the older adults. I was afraid of the teachers. I found them not nice, and they didn't want to be bothered. The students my age didn't interest me. They didn't bully me; I just didn't want to socialize with them. They seemed more mature than me, talking about dating, driving, and the girls their eating disorders. I was more interested in my dolls, stuffed animals, toys, looking forward to my Mom picking me up from school and going home.

My Dad was very tech savvy. He always FaceTimed my brother when he went out. He loved having the newest iPhones and calculators. He knew how to go on Echo Link with his iPhone. I barely know how to work one, never having one of my own, and I didn't like the radiation it gave off. My Dad was very sharp up until the day he had to be taken by ambulance to the E.R. Whenever Larry went out and didn't call and he couldn't reach him by phone, he called Stop and Shop, CVS., Domingo's, Roosters. I told him not to, but he was worried about Larry when he couldn't reach him. I always stayed with him, happily!

Christian Karen Berman

I always had trouble spelling like for Facebook mostly. I always asked him how to spell everything. Even if he was half-asleep, he got it right because there was no red line under it, that's how I knew! I'm very happy he never lost his sharp mind. My mom wasn't so sharp at the end. She wasn't totally there, but still a little. Sadly, she had dementia.

I have this unforgettable personality if you know me, so I was the only one my Mom remembered. She said she loves me, misses me, and is proud of me. She wished she was taking me to school now. When I sat on her lap she didn't like it and even though she was half-asleep she knew my name and told me to get off. She smiled at me when I was crying and watched my very favorite episode of the 1988 TV series *Ramona* with Sarah Polley, "The Patient," episode 3. She was very sick and still watched YouTube on Larry's cell phone and enjoyed it. I told Larry to take pics of us the very last time I saw her. I really wish so badly he did! It was around 3 am, but he could of.

I really miss the old days, sorry for not being the best daughter all the time and excelling at school or being social, but the truth is, it wasn't my time to shine and become a butterfly then; it was my time to focus on me and get to know me and what I love to do.

I wish I played with Susie Scribbles more. I was afraid I would accidentally break a $100 talking and writing doll. I loved her too much to play with her alone without my Dad. I wish I knew how to make more real friends at school and had more play dates and birthday parties, but I was so close to my parents, brother, dolls, toys & TV, I felt that's all I needed and they were my whole world and I was more of an introvert back then. It doesn't seem so far away, the past, and I still really wish I could go back and treasure every day even more like the gift it truly is.

But now is my time to shine and spread my wings and come out of my shell and be that beautiful butterfly. It's never too late, it's never too late. Before she got too sick, to the nurses in the local hospital, my Mom would call me, "my daughter, the actress, the artist." As a two- and three-year-old toddler, I would say, no no no no, or na-na-noo often and got called 'the No No Girl' by my Mommy. I'm glad for all the days I played hooky as a young

MIRROR OF MY WORLD

child and kid, to get to spend more time at home in the house I love with the Mom I loved. My Mother said the song "The Masterpiece in You" reminded her of me, because I was a budding artist in the making.

> **SUPER!** Mom
>
> I love my mom because she is very nice. I love my mom. She buys me lots of toys. She is going over my Grandma's house for Thanksgiving. She is pretty. She even buys expensive toys. She lets me wear her clothes, and her fur coat. I love her.

Christian Karen Berman

WHAT I MISS MOST ABOUT MY MOMMY

#1 When she bought me baby dolls and stuffed animals.
#2 When she took me home from school.
#3 Hooky days.
#4 When she took me to Sears, Woolworth's, Macy's, and to see Santa Claus once when I was 9.
#5 When she took me to the playground.
#6 Bought me girl's clothes from the Sears catalog.
#7 When we blow bubbles together in the yard.
#8 When she took me to the pediatrician's office, the doctor, or the hospital.

MIRROR OF MY WORLD

#9 When she surprised me with the Sears Christmas Wish Book.

#10 When she surprised me with the *Good Housekeeping* magazine issue with Jon and Kate plus 8.

#11 Anytime she surprised me with a little present.

#12 When she bought me *Parents Magazine*.

#13 When she bought me children's books from the school book fair.

#14 When she made homemade cookies and muffins.

#15 Bought me these cool winter silver light blue gloves that the rainbow changed color in the snow when it got cold. I was six or seven. I loved those; they were a lot of fun!

#16 Let me stay home from school more than I should. If I was tired and didn't really want to go, she wasn't mad at me, either.

#17 She let me pick out a few good snacks from the supermarket. Yogurt drink, Giggles cookies, Rainbow Bright cereal, Crispy Critters cereal, and Honey Nut Clusters cereal.

#18 Let me pick out candy after school for a snack.

#19 Told me a few stories about Daddy, like he bought a scale for himself the same year I was born so that's why it was so special to him. And told me stories about her childhood, too.

#20 Took me Trick-or-Treating.

#21 Brought me McDonald's for lunch.

#22 Made good tuna fish salad.

#23 I was with her the first five years, because I didn't have to go to pre-K, they wouldn't accept me. I cried so much the year before, they said I didn't have to go to nursery school. They kicked me out at age three.

Christian Karen Berman

WHAT I MISS MOST ABOUT MY DADDY

#1 Running across the living room and jumping on his lap.
#2 Him catching me when I jumped in his arms.
#3 Sitting on his lap.
#4 Hugging him.
#5 Talking to him.
#6 Visiting him in the hospital.
#7 Snuggling with him in bed.
#8 Coming home to him.
#9 Waiting for him to come home from school and when he just came home! I looked forward to that event all day long. It seemed like forever. He was gone 12 hours a day most days!
#10 Being proud he was my Daddy and him showing me off at the hospital and me showing him off on Facebook!
#11 Crying to him.
#12 Him coming home from the hospital.
#13 I miss the good and the bad. I miss everything about him.
#14 His happy-go-lucky smile when he came in my room to try to cheer me up. That I miss the most and makes me the saddest! He tried so hard to make me happy. I was sad a lot.
#15 When he use to take my vitals, blood sugar, and blood pressure.
#16 Arm wrestling with him. I can't remember who won, but he was pretty strong. I'm thinking more him than me!
#17 Surprising him by visiting him at the hospital and jumping in his room and him being so happily surprised I was there and actually came. Alone time with him in the hospital.
#18 Running downstairs when he was home and seeing him smile happily at me. Just him being there was Christmas Day.
#19 Him taking care of me when I was sick and telling me old stories about him and him drawing pictures for me.
#20 Measuring our hands together, me holding onto his index finger.

MIRROR OF MY WORLD

#21 Him making silly, funny faces at me.

#22 Jumping off the living room stairs into his arms and him carrying me to the kitchen chair for breakfast.

#23 Him buying me extra clothes or toys just to make me happy.

<u>Christian Karen Berman</u>

MeMORieS OF MY MOTHeR

I called her Bev often when I was older, I wish I called her Mom, or better yet, Mommy. That word just says "I love you" so much. My parents were my whole world and the most important and loved people in my small world. When you're a child, you don't think like that and think more selfishly, like other kids have it better, more riches, famous parents. I also did like to be the center of attention most of the time and for the most part was. They still loved me so much, though; my parents were the best parents. They tried their best for me. I should be thankful for that. I was a really lucky little girl, but didn't know or appreciate how lucky I was as a kid, you never know what you have until it's gone. I need to appreciate everything and everyone I have in this world.

MIRROR OF MY WORLD

My Mom in 1976, I think. She's in her tennis outfit and is playing a game of golf at the Homowack Lodge. I wasn't even born yet; she wasn't even pregnant with me. My Mom was trying to convince my Daddy to have kids. All of her other friends were getting pregnant and having kids. I wonder if she'll convince my Dad in the next few years to have a bunch of kids? I wish we had more room in the house to have another baby brother and sister to play with.

My Mom died from cancer, stage 4, and suffered a lot through her illness. I'm very upset they didn't find out she had cancer in time to do treatments. She was failed by two medical establishments. They missed it in her physicals and said it was too late to treat when they found it. I felt helpless. No one would listen to me. It's very unfair and there's nothing I can do about it. It really hurts not to be listened to and heard. After she passed, we got a large bill from a hospice, the day before Mother's Day. Her insurance was supposed to cover everything. Sent probably on purpose just to rub it in, that our Mother is gone away and not with us anymore. On top of that, they ignored my Dad's pleas to do everything possible to keep her alive the longest they could, and neglected an infection we didn't know my poor Mom had and was suffering through that ended her life sooner than needed. Thinking about it makes me very upset, troubled and sad.

I wrote this composition for school in the third grade at age eight, when things were all happy and fun and my Mommy and Grandma were both alive and living with me, my Brother, and Daddy. I had no problems and was a cute skinny little kid and very loved. I don't have a Mom left to love me anymore or help me with stuff. I'm still young and in my 30s, not married yet and have no kids yet. I still need a Mommy. The closest thing she had to Grandkids was our two dogs, Mary and Ritchie, and our Land Chinese box turtle Lucky Alexis, and all of my baby dolls. For those of you reading this lucky enough to have a Mom alive, sick or well, be very grateful for the gift of a parent every day and hug her and tell your Mom you love her every day. Listen to them, talk to them, try not to get mad at your Mommy. Sometimes they can get on your nerves, but you'll miss their advice, annoyingness and nagging when you don't hear their words of wisdom anymore! No Mom is perfect, but they try their best to help their children and be their best friend.

MIRROR OF MY WORLD

All I needed was that horrible letter! I've been so upset, since she died before her time, hurting for her and missing her so very much. Calling for lawyers, my words fell on deaf ears, so to speak! I tried and failed! I'm so very sorry, my poor Mommy. My heart is sad and lonely for you. So sorry for what you went through, and I tried to help you, but couldn't. No one would let me. I miss you every day and really wish I had more time with you to get to know you even better. I love you very much, Mom, and miss your sweetness, kindness, and words, your funny, sarcastic, but good-meaning ones and the concerned loving ones. I still hear your nagging and miss it. I wish I got to spend more time with you, but I didn't know that you were going to die and leave me so young. The worst punishment in life is having a parent taken away from you when you're young, when she is still very much needed and wanted. Nothing in the world is worse than that!

My Mom called me "the Actress" and "the Artist" to everyone she met, and to the nurses. I know this is personal, but I'm just posting what I feel in my heart. I hope this helps others with moms that are still alive appreciate them more, spend more time with them, no matter if they live far away or have differences of opinion. You only get one irreplaceable mom as a gift from God! Be good to her, hug her a lot, love her a lot, because it will never be the same again after she's gone. All the good times are over. Enjoy every day you have with her. Go places, travel, live for today, don't put adventures and dreams off to save for a later date. There are places we never got to go together that she always wanted to travel to, which is very sad. I think about the good old days of my childhood and miss them all the time. It wasn't even that long ago, 1980s to early 2000s. But mostly the 80s and 90s when she useta drive me to school. Sorry about my tear-jerking, heartbreaking words, but I am a writer, an unknown one. Happy Mother's Day, Mom and Grandma Lee; I LOVE AND MISS YOU BOTH EVERY DAY! WISH YOU WERE BOTH STILL WITH US, SO IT COULD BE LIKE IT USETA BE!

Christian Karen Berman

THOUGHTS OF MY MOMMY AND DADDY

When Daddy was 45 minutes from home at Calvary Hospice in the Bronx, he FacedTimed the nurses and my Mom, Bev. I think the doctor spoke to him, too. I don't know how I had to get in the most horrible situation, losing both my parents so young, so fast. My Mom was only 73. That's very young today! My Daddy was the total boss of me and in charge of me, told me what to do all the time, took my blood pressure even a few days before he had to go to the hospital. Oddly, he didn't feel sick enough to take his own. I had asked him to. I think he said, "I'm alright." He use to take my blood sugar, too. When he first started taking my vitals he thought my pressure would be very high. It was like 106/70. When he first took my blood sugar the lancet was too large and boy did it gush and bleed like ketchup. The lowest I've been was 60, but in the past 47. But when he took it—85, 108, around there. He bought me baby dolls to keep me happy. He talked with me. He knew how to work YouTube on our TV and put on kid shows that was too young for him. *My Name is You* I really liked, and the "Halfway Home" song from *The Earthling*. He was a very cool Dad, never got upset. His students thought he was very cool, too. I loved seeing him at the hospital and was so relieved when he could go home.

Where is he right now?

I really miss my Mom and Dad so much all the time. I wish I thought to buy them more presents. I wanted to get my Mom a tennis bracelet and a copy of a Gucci handbag. She liked that stuff. Maybe even a nice dress and outfit, new sunglasses. I was going to get my Dad a small keyboard before he died, so I could hear him play the piano again. The big keyboard was too hard to take downstairs and set up and put back and no room. We didn't have much money and as a younger person, I just thought of myself, made my Dad a drawing and was quiet and well-behaved on his birthday. I loved them so much, didn't know how lucky I was. The good times ended too soon. They got sick too young. My Mom might have lived longer if she ate healthy and had colonoscopies. The doctors totally missed the cancer until it was too late. I wish they never found it, I would have had another year with her at home instead of hospitals and the hospice. Daddy just worked too hard for his school. He loved it, but it was a hard job that barely paid for all he helped so many students. I sometimes pretend when I wake up and think they're still downstairs.

I wish they were.

Where are my Mom and Dad?

I miss and need them. I'm lost!

I try to keep things happy, but this is how I honestly feel inside. I wake up to a nightmare without them or anybody. I speak from the heart.

To my Dad—he was a calming presence, and gave me so much love, affection, and security. He wasn't perfect and made mistakes along the way, but he tried the best he knew how with me and was always loving, protecting me, especially me, until the very end. Just my Dad going to work and being gone twelve hours a day, away from me, was a challenge for me on most days. He spoiled me as much as he could afford to do, especially in my 30s with beautiful clothes, reborn dolls and toys. He tried his best to keep me happy. I always thought he'd be with me much longer. I wish I had more time with him. He was a wonderful friend to all, husband, father, and teacher.

To my Mom—I wish I had many more years with you to get to know you better as an adult and hear more stories of when you were becoming a teenager and young woman. I wish I had more years to get closer to you. You were taken away from our family too early and put in a terrible hospice. We tried to get you out of there. You were only 71 years young at the time, and sadly died at 73. You did not deserve such a terrible ending to your life with mini-strokes, early onset dementia and, lastly, colon cancer. I'm so sorry for all the miserable pain and suffering you had to endure. I tried to help you, but the people in charge and the social workers would not listen to me, Daddy, or Larry. I wish I'd fought harder to save you from those horrible mean people. I wish I'd been older then to handle it better, but I wasn't prepared and had never been in such a horrible situation before in my life, Daddy got sick fighting, but we did try. I'm very sorry for all you went through. You were loved, very loved, even though we couldn't get you out and you didn't know it, I missed you and thought about you all the time. I was very close to you in the early years until my teenage years. I wish I could go back and live them all again with my Mommy and Daddy for I miss you both every day & think about you all the time. It's so lonely without you. You really think you have all the time in the world, when you really don't and your life and time is ticking away. I wish I went on more fun outings with you, a few more vacations and adventures. I wish you ate healthier and took better care of yourselves, so you would still be here with me & I wouldn't feel the sad, deep empty void.

Though at the same time, I think you somehow are here with me sometimes, but I can never be sure. Wishing, hoping and reality kinda pass by and you're just not sure. Things fall; is it them, or wishful thinking? I speak about them as a pair, as a set, because that's what they were and are and will be forever, I hope. I wish I could have fought for their health better, but the medical staff saw me as a child even though I was in my 30s. I wish I had more

MIRROR OF MY WORLD

mother/daughter days with you—shopping, the spa, a mini-vacation, just more fun, happy, carefree days, though I did have the best parents and the best childhood.

God Bless me and my loving parents.

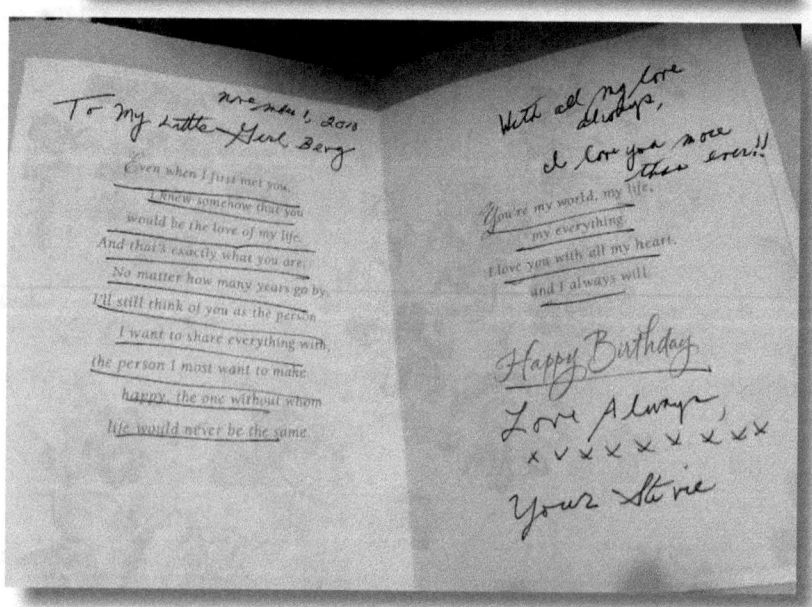

Christian Karen Berman

The Class Of 1984 Appreciates Dr. Stephen Berman

Peering into room 201, one will usually see Dr. Berman enthusiastically and briskly filling up the blackboard with statistical symbols. Dr. Berman's enthusiasm is part of what makes him so special. By conveying this enthusiasm to the students he enables them to not just learn the course material, but enjoy it simultaneously.

Dr. Berman a is best known among seniors for his course in probability and statistics. In this course, he successfully shows students how these can be used in everyday situations. His main concern is that every student understands the theories and concepts of the course.

Dr. Berman also holds the position of Director of Clubs. Each year he tries to add more clubs to the current list, seeking a wide variety in order to satisfy the student body. His bubbling personality makes it easy for everyone to talk to him on any subject and to enjoy every class that he teaches.

We appreciate Dr. Stephen Berman and hope he affects upcoming classes the way he has affected the Class of 1984.

DR. STEPHEN BERMAN

WHO'S WHO LIFETIME ACHIEVEMENT

STEPHEN LEONARD BERMAN

Title: Instructor of Mathematics, Director of Student Clubs

Company: Horace Mann School

Location: Riverdale, NY United States

Achievements:

- Inducted, Albert Nelson Marquis Lifetime Achievement (2016)
- Featured Listee, Who's Who in America, Marquis Who's Who (2009-2016)
- Featured Listee, Who's Who in American Education, Marquis Who's Who (2009-2008)
- Featured Listee, Who's Who in Science and Engineering, Marquis Who's Who (2010-2012)
- Featured Listee, Who's Who in the World, Marquis Who's Who (2009-2016)
- Named, Top One of Two, Semi-Finalist Placement (2009)
- Recipient, Excellence in Teaching, Horace Mann School (2010)
- Recipient, Citation Award (2008)
- Recipient, Highly Exemplary Instruction Citation, Dean of Horace Mann School (2006)
- Recipient, Rita and David Beller Teaching Excellence Prize for Innovative and Outstanding Instruction (2005)
- Recipient, Citation, Massachusetts Institute of Technology, Cambridge, MA (1999)

Designations: Ph.D., New York University

MIRROR OF MY WORLD

Christian Karen Berman

THE CAT IN THE MIRROR

I only recently noticed and gave much thought to the googly-eyed orange, puffy tabby cat sticker in the corner of my bathroom mirror. These stickers were very popular when I was a little girl in the 1980s. I remember my Dad came home from Big Top Toy Store early one day and surprised me with a sheet of these cool stickers. I was so touched that my Dad bought me a special present just to make me happy. I was all of age four, maybe four-and-a-half, and I didn't know what to do with them. I had just become a big sister at age four, too. I didn't want to ruin them, waste them, but keep them somewhere special, so they would last forever. My Daddy thought of me and bought them just for me.

He had an idea. He opened the plastic package and put one in each corner of the top of the bathroom mirrors, the upstairs and downstairs bathrooms. That's four stickers so far, to help decorate the house and make it more kid friendly. Then one on the top of each the bathroom doors, two more and a few on my bedroom door in a semi-circle. Through the years, they fell off, or got taken off by me. There might have been also two on the bottom half when I was little, but I can't remember. I vaguely remember pulling one off and it opened up and had yellow foam inside of it. I might have been only seven or eight or so.

Now all that remains is the one orange Tabby cat in my bathroom mirror and one in my brother's bathroom, but I haven't been in there in a long time, so I'm not sure which googly animal it is, koala bear or elephant. That old Tabby Cat Sticker lasted longer than if I put it on paper or in a sticker book that would have been long lost or thrown out by now. She is in one piece, still looking down watching over me. That sticker, oh, if she could talk, the stories she could tell. She watched me grow up from in the walls of the bathroom and is still there, even though my Mommy and Daddy aren't. It's the same mirror and the same house. The

MIRROR OF MY WORLD

bathroom has been updated a bit and changed over the years, just a little, but not the mirror with the little kitty cat.

It has watched me grow up since I was age four, watched me and even my parents get ready for the day. My first day of kindergarten. When my Mom would help me with my bath as a little girl. When I would brush my teeth. When I would brush my hair. When I would play with my Fisher Price Little People in the bathroom sink, they would go swimming in the big pool. Then when I was a little older my Mini Cabbage Patch Dolls and Barbie dolls I would play with in the sink. When my Mom bought me Freezy Freakies gloves as a child and I would run them under the ice-cold water to watch them to change color when I wasn't playing in the snow.

So many good times I remember. Getting ready for the Hanukkah party at the Temple, I would brush my teeth extra good and fix my hair pretty. Fix my hair in a half-ponytail before school in the early morning. Detangle it with spray and put it in a ponytail in the summer. Even shampoo my Kid Sister's hair in the sink with baby shampoo and I even cut her bangs in the bathroom once. Once is enough for that. Shampooing my hair in the bathroom sink. As a kid drinking from the bathroom faucet, the water was much better back then. They did not have bottled water in the mid-1980s. I had Hi-C Fruit Punch juice boxes mainly. For Halloween when I put on grey ghoulish face paint my Dad had stopped on the way home to buy me to be a skeleton. I had the skeleton shirt and chain black jeans from Kids-R-Us. The best times.

Then the not-so-good times in the bathroom when I was sick many times as a child and even fell asleep on the cold bathroom tile floor. When I woke up sick or was sent home from school sick. The time a big bee came in through the window and my brother had to suck it up in the vacuum so no one would be stung. That was scary, he saved the day. Cutting my hair as a child like a boy's and the many times I messed up my bangs cutting them myself. When I was nine and had to stand on the toilet to get a good look at me in the mirror and the seat slid to the side and I slipped off and hit my head really bad on the side of the bathroom tub. It hurt so much! I told my Dad what happened, but in those days, unless there was a deep gash and cut and blood, you didn't go to the Emergency Room. If that happened today, I would have gotten a CAT scan. (The same thing happened in *Back to the Future* to Dr. Emmett Brown, but I didn't draw the flux capacitor.) I had to stand on the side of the tub at least until I was age 11 or 12 to get a good look at me in the mirror. I was small at 4'6". When Larry and I were little and he was playing under the sink and hit his baby tooth on it and it turned darker. He was four or five years old. When I was older in my early 20s and sick and my dog Mary was sitting with me in the bathroom when I was nauseous and had a stomach bug. She was worried about me, she was watching over me. So many memories you can have in just the bathroom. So, if that sicker kitty cat could talk, I'd love to hear what she would have to say about me.

I think she cares about me and loves me.

About the Author
Christian Karen Berman

Christian Karen Berman is a passionate artist, writer, and lifelong creative. Since age 15, she has loved reading vintage *Parents Magazines* cover to cover, finding joy in nostalgia and storytelling. An avid collector of reborn baby and toddler dolls since 2015, she also expresses her artistic talents through drawing and illustration. Her artwork is available through her Facebook page, *Christian's Art World*.

Christian contributes to *The Art of Autism* newsletter and writes for Rabbi Levi Welton's blog. For two years, she wrote monthly articles for the UK newsletter, *Parenting Aspergers*. She has been skateboarding since 19 and still enjoys riding her longboard, exploring playgrounds on her scooter, and shopping. She is also a fan of family vlogs on YouTube.

Her YouTube channel, *The Adventures of the Little Harmonic*, showcases her love for storytelling—don't forget to like and subscribe! In her teens and early 30s, she wrote drama-comedy television scripts as a hobby, sharpening her writing skills.

Christian's dreams include becoming an actress, a fashion model, and a mother—continuing to embrace creativity, self-expression, and the beauty of everyday life.

Thank you for reading

Mirror of My World

Reflections on an Undiagnosed Autistic Childhood in the 1980s and 90s

Please leave a review on the website of your favorite online bookseller

MORE GREAT READS FROM HENRY GRAY!

THE LAST STAGE by Bruce Scivally
In his final days, lawman Wyatt Earp dreams of one last showdown—gold, gunmen and love with his devoted wife, Sadie.

VEIL OF SEDUCTION by Emily Dinova
In 1922, journalist Lorelei Alba infiltrates a gothic asylum for "troublesome" women—and falls into the orbit of a dark, mysterious doctor.

THE UNDERSTUDY by Charlie Peters
A kidnapping plot during a high-stakes merger quickly unravels, exposing every flaw in a "perfect crime."

THE DEVIL IN THE DIAMOND by Gregory Cioffi
First on a WWII battlefield and later on a baseball diamond, two soldiers, once enemies, find themselves bound by history, family, and the game they love.

A PRAYER FOR THE DAMNED by Joe Cornet
Bounty hunter Cole faces a deranged preacher and seeks a lost Confederate treasure in a town on the brink of violence.

THE MAN FROM BELIZE by Steven Kobrin
Dr. Kent Sterling's perfect life in paradise shatters when his past as a government hitman catches up—and the Viper comes calling.

SINS OF THE RAVEN by Steven Kobrin
Dr. Kent Stirling returns to face adversaries from his past, forcing him to confront buried secrets and fight for his life before the sins he thought forgotten consume him completely.

SHELBY'S VACATION by Nancy Beverly
Shelby runs from heartbreak into the arms of Carol, a woman carrying her own relationship scars. Together, they discover love worth risking.

TOO MUCH IN THE SON by Charlie Peters
Mistaken identity plunges Leo Malone into a twisted web of lies, gangsters, and family deception.

I CONFESS: DIARY OF AN AUSTRALIAN POPE by Melvyn Morrow
An Australian pope battles corruption, blackmail, and betrayal as he tries to reform the Vatican from within.

visit www.HenryGrayPublishing.com

THE ANTAGONIST by Emily Dinova
A mysterious note shatters Dave Collins' quiet life, unraveling his world piece by piece. Who is behind it—and why?

WHILE WE'RE HERE by T.A. Manchester
A heartfelt coming-of-age story of football, family, first love, and tragic loss. This YA debut captures the fragile beauty of youth and the heartbreak of growing up too soon.

WASTED by Sam F. Park
When a drunk with amnesia—known only as 'Wasted'—is forced into brutal labor on a powerful rancher's land, he becomes tangled in a web of violence, redemption, and truth.

POETIC ANARCHY by Gregory Cioffi
Raw, fearless, and unfiltered—Gregory Cioffi's poetry explodes with passion, humor, and rebellion. From love and loss to art and anger, every page is rallying cry for authenticity.

BILLION DOLLAR BATMAN by Bruce Scivally
From dime comics to billion-dollar blockbusters, discover the amazing story of Batman's rise from Bright Knight to Dark Knight.

REJECTED: ESSAYS ON BELONGING by Michelle Fiordaliso
Through humor and honesty, Fiordaliso explores heartbreak, rejection, and the quest for acceptance and belonging.

MIRROR OF MY WORLD: REFLECTIONS ON AN UNDIAGNOSED AUTISTIC CHILDHOOD by Christian Karen Berman
A moving memoir of growing up neurodivergent in the 80s and 90s.

HIGH: FROM CANNABIS TO CLARITY by Leonard Lee Buschel
From addiction to transformation, Buschel shares his raw, funny, and inspiring journey through decades of drugs, Hollywood, and recovery.

ABNER THE CLOWN by Jeffrey Breslauer
Young clown Abner hates his name until an expected adventure teaches him the magic of self-acceptance.

BENNETT WILL ONLY EAT BLUEBERRIES by Nicole Dillenberg (available in English & Spanish)
In this whimsical picture book, anique toy bears bring Bennett's picky-eating tale to life.

SEARCH FOR FUN WITH PAPA ROCK!

PAPA ROCK'S HORROR MOVIES WORD SEARCH by Rock Scivally & Jeffrey Breslauer
150 puzzles based on horror films from *Frankenstein* to *Godzilla* equals 150 reasons to keep the lights on all night!

PAPA ROCK'S SON OF HORROR MOVIES WORD SEARCH by Rock Scivally & Jeffrey Breslauer
Looking for more Word Search chills? In this edition, monsters from the 1960s and 70s haunt every page!

PAPA ROCK'S REVENGE OF HORROR MOVIES WORD SEARCH by Rock Scivally & Jeffrey Breslauer
Looking for more monster Word Searches? Here you'll find the classic movie monsters from the 1980s and 90s!

PAPA ROCK'S ROMANCE MOVIES WORD SEARCH by Rock Scivally & Jeffrey Breslauer
From *Casablanca* to *Titanic*, here's 150 Word Searches based on romance movies, so pick up a pen and turn on the love light!

PAPA ROCK'S WESTERN MOVIES WORD SEARCH by Rock Scivally & Jeffrey Breslauer
Hop into these 150 Word Searches and ride with John Wayne, Randolph Scott, Clint Eastwood, and cowboy favorites!

PAPA ROCK'S ANIMATED MUSICALS WORD SEARCH by Rock Scivally & Jeffrey Breslauer
You'll be humming along as you do 150 Word Searches on favorite animated musicals from *Snow White* to *Strawberry Shortcake!*

PAPA ROCK'S WAR MOVIES WORD SEARCH by Rock Scivally & Jeffrey Breslauer
Climb into your foxhole and challenge yourself with Word Searches based on classic war films from *Sergeant York* to *Saving Private Ryan*.

PAPA ROCK'S SCI-FI MOVIES WORD SEARCH by Rock Scivally & Jeffrey Breslauer
Relive science fiction's greatest hits with these Word Search puzzles covering classics from *Metropolis* to *Star Wars!*

PAPA ROCK'S DETECTIVE MOVIES WORD SEARCH by Rock Scivally & Jeffrey Breslauer
Solve 150 puzzles inspired by classic detective films, from Sherlock Holmes and Sam Spade to noir favorites.

PAPA ROCK'S MOVIE COMEDY TEAMS WORD SEARCH by Rock Scivally & Jeffrey Breslauer
From the Marx Brothers to Abbott & Costello to Martin & Lewis to Cheech & Chong, celebrate the greatest comedy teams with this laugh-out-loud puzzle collection!

Stay in touch with Henry Gray Publishing!

Follow us on Facebook

Subscribe to our YouTube channel

Sign up to our mailing list at

www.HenryGrayPublishing.com

Granada Hills, CA
"Select books for selective readers"

www.ingramcontent.com/pod-product-compliance
Lightning Source LLC
LaVergne TN
LVHW021332080526
838202LV00003B/146